P9-DTM-653

Writing Better Computer User Documentation

CAMROSE LUTHERAN COLLEGE
LIBRARY

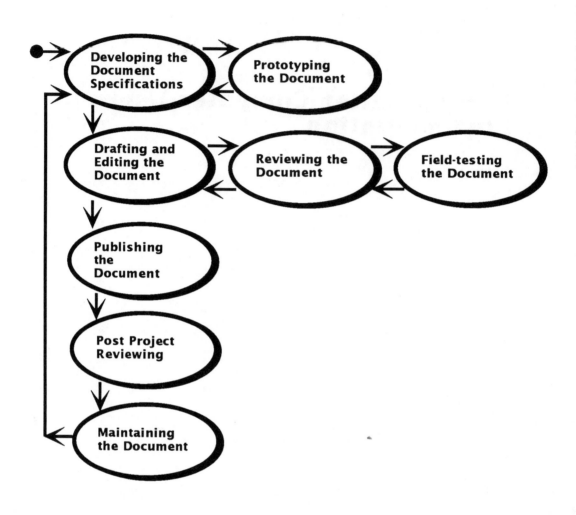

Writing Better Computer User Documentation
From Paper to Hypertext
Version 2.0

R. John Brockmann
Associate Professor
Concentration in Business and Technical Writing
Department of English
University of Delaware
Newark, Delaware

John Wiley & Sons, Inc.
New York / Chichester / Brisbane / Toronto / Singapore

Colophon

The tools used for producing this camera-ready text included:
- Apple Macintosh Plus™ and Apple Macintosh SE/30™
- Microsoft Word 4.0™ (Microsoft)
- Superpaint 2.0™ (Silicon Beach)
- Comment 2.0™ (Deneba Software)
- Word Finder™ (Microlytics)
- Illustrator '88™ (Adobe)
- Apple LaserWriter II NT™ (300 dpi)
- Varityper VT-600W™ (600 dpi) for some final graphics
- Lucida Serif and Sans Serif Fonts (Adobe)
- DeskTop Art Business 1™ (Dynamic Graphics, clickart)
- PageMaker 3.02™ (Aldus)

Designations used by companies to distinguish their products are often claimed as trademarks. In all instances where John Wiley & Sons, Inc. is aware of a claim, the product names appear in initial capital or all capital letters.

Copyright(c) 1990 by John Wiley & Sons, Inc.

All rights reserved. Published simultaneously in Canada.

Reproduction or translation of any part of this work beyond that permitted by Section 107 or 108 of the 1976 United States Copyright Act without the permission of the copyright owner is unlawful. Requests for permission or further information should be addressed to the Permissions Department, John Wiley & Sons, Inc.

Library of Congress Cataloging in Publication Data:

Brockmann, R. John.
    Writing better computer user documentation : from paper to hypertext, Version 2.0 / R. John Brockmann
      p. 384 cm.

    Includes bibliographical references, index, quick reference card.
    1. Electronic data processing documentation I. Title.

QA76.9.D6B747   1990   66519
005. 1' 5--dc20   90-12133
ISBN 0-471-62259-1   CIP
ISBN 0-471-62260-5 (pbk.)

Printed in the United States of America

10 9 8 7 6 5 4 3 2

For information about our audio products, write us at:
Newbridge Book Clubs, 3000 Cindel Drive, Delran, NJ 08370

I dedicate this book to my students around the world, but especially my students at the University of Delaware whose motto I follow:

Veni, Vidi, Scripsi.

CONTENTS

INTRODUCTION

PART ONE: THE DOCUMENTATION PROBLEM

PART TWO: THE STANDARD DOCUMENTATION PROCESS

STEP 1: DEVELOPING THE DOCUMENT SPECIFICATIONS

STEP 2: PROTOTYPING THE DOCUMENT

STEP 3: DRAFTING THE DOCUMENT

STEP 4: EDITING THE DOCUMENT

STEP 5: REVIEWING THE DOCUMENT

STEP 6: FIELD-TESTING THE DOCUMENT

STEP 7: PUBLISHING THE DOCUMENT

STEP 8: POST PROJECT REVIEWING

STEP 9: MAINTAINING THE DOCUMENT

BIBLIOGRAPHY

GLOSSARY

INDEX

QUICK REFERENCE TEAR OUT CARD

LIST OF ILLUSTRATIONS AND TABLES

ACKNOWLEDGEMENTS

I gratefully acknowledge all my colleagues who have helped with this book:

Bill Horton: mentor, guru, fount of knowledge about desktop design and Macintosh, and all-around good friend

Sandy and Sherwin Pakin: in whose school of hard knocks and sage advice I learned most of what I know about writing documentation

Pete Rosacker: who (along with his Delcastle Technical High School students) began as my student and ended up teaching me about computer graphics

Debby Andrews, Bob Day, and Nadya Davis: my University of Delaware colleagues, for their editorial comments

Joe Chapline: history's first professional computer documentation writer on the BINAC and UNIVAC I, for his historical insights and perspective

David Broughton in Sydney and all my Australian colleagues

Steve Bernhardt: for his insights into the unique processes of technical writing

Terry Girill :for all his suggestions conerning actual usage of on-line materials

Denise Brown: for her comments and examples of documentation testing and Post Project reviews

My wife, Professor Rebecca Joan McCauley: for support and guidance

St. Francis

INTRODUCTION

What's the Purpose of this Book?

Inadequate software documentation for users is a widely acknowledged problem in the computer industry. Therefore this book is designed to help you write accurate, clear computer documentation for users—documentation beyond systems and programming documentation. This book presents a systematic approach to writing paper and on-line documents, and follows the process of creating materials from the inception of the documentation project to updating after publication.

Focus on End-User Not Design or Maintenance Documentation

There are a variety of roles in most software development settings (e.g., system designers, system operators, and maintenance personnel); therefore, there are different kinds of software documentation (e.g., design documentation, maintenance documentation, and user documentation). In this range of documentation, this book does not focus on systems and maintenance documentation because:

Computer Assisted Systems (or Software) Engineering (CASE) tools are further discussed in Part 1.

- Automated systems such as CASE tools are rapidly becoming available for producing development and maintenance documentation (Arnon and Lehrhaupt, 1983; Erickson, 1983; Johnson L., 1989; QED Information Sciences, 1989 (a), (b)). Consequently, why should this book describe how to "shoe a horse" when we'll all soon be driving horseless carriages?

The Department of Defense (DOD) long ago established how it wants system specifications written by vendors. Thus the MITRE Corporation developed a system called ARDS to automate the creation of such documentation (Glenn et al., 1983).

However, there are many ideas and techniques that can be derived from user documentation to improve development and maintenance documentation (i.e., readers are readers and both programmers and users get impatient and are production oriented; both skim and scan their texts; both find that advanced organizers or overviews increase their ability to digest and understand texts; and both suffer from information overload).

To see some ways to move user documentation to the beginning of the software development process, see Horton, 1984: WE-196–9, and Step 1, Timing.

- Readers of development and maintenance documentation have a well-developed set of expectations for the sequencing, formatting, and content in such manuals. For these audiences, the emphasis in documentation should be on standardizing formats, layouts, organization, etc., so that these audiences can use their past experience with manuals to assimilate quickly the contents of new manuals. Research has shown that changing formats, layouts, organization, etc., of manuals may, in fact, handicap these readers' ability to assimilate the content of new manuals (Duffy, Curran, and Sass, 1983).

- There are already over a dozen books that deal adequately with development and maintenance documentation (ASME, 1973; Ayer and Patrinostro, 1990 (Vols. 1–6); *Guidelines*, 1976; Harper, 1981; Rubin, 1979; Van Duyn, 1972; Walsh, 1969). And, except for the impact of rapid prototyping in the last two years, the contents, purposes, and audiences of these manuals haven't changed since the first known published manual in this field, developed by Dorothy Walsh over twenty years ago. In fact, it is because of the stability of the design of these types of software development documents that automated documentation tools and the reader's well-developed set of expectations can work so effectively in this area.

Rather than development and maintenance documentation, this book focuses on users and their documentation because:

- Digital Equipment Corporation noted in their 1983 internal documentation guidelines that user documentation should be written first—not last as is traditionally done—because the user documentation is an excellent way to debug the design of a system or a program. "If a writer finds it difficult to document a system, the problem is probably the system not the writer. Holes in design, obscure constructions, and apparent contradictions become starkly visible in the documentation." So, if we are looking at user documentation from a programming and design perspective, user documentation can provide a tremendously effective design tool.

- If we are thinking of achieving the greatest good for the greatest number of people involved with computer systems, then end-user documentation audiences require primary attention because they are the largest audience for computer documentation.

At the New South Wales Department of Health (Australia), a writer translated the heading "Reference Entry" from a system point of view to an end-user's point of view in the words: "Setting Up The System."

- And user documentation is the most difficult communication situation for data processors. This is because user documentation requires communication between people with widely different backgrounds.

User documentation does not necessarily require writing that simplifies the software. User documentation is better thought of as a type of writing that *translates* the computer activities for users or readers. Computer user documentation takes data processing information and translates it into ideas that can be readily comprehended by people who are skilled in other areas or other disciplines (Hartley, 1980).

User documentation presents a situation much like that involved in translating a foreign language. When you are speaking to someone who shares a common background and language, they can fill in the gaps and make up for mistakes in your communication. However, when you are speaking to someone who has a different background and speaks a different language, they cannot make up for gaps or mistakes, and need additional explanation.

Focus on Problems Deeper than Grammar, Spelling, or Punctuation

This book is not intended to teach effective grammar, usage, spelling, and punctuation. It doesn't intend to do that because:

- Learning the rules of correct and effective grammar, usage, spelling, and punctuation requires a lifetime of attention, care, and work. There are also existing books from which to learn (Blumenthal, 1972; Department of

"Throughout this book, I use 'they,' 'their,' and 'them' for the third person singular, as it seems to me the only reasonable solution to the absence of a nonsexist third person singular pronoun. The practice is given grudging approval by the *Shorter Oxford Dictionary*: 'used instead of 'his or her' when the gender is inclusive or uncertain. (Regarded as ungrammatical.),' and supported by quotes from such eminent persons as Thackeray...and Shaw..." (Laurillard, 1987, Preface).

Treasury, 1973, 1977; Australian Government Publishing Service, 1978).

A good tip for your lifetime of learning the rules of correct and effective grammar, usage, spelling, and punctuation is to be patient with yourself. There's a lot to learn, and it cannot be done overnight. In fact, a good way to learn is to make a list of the four or five major errors you make; find their remedies, and concentrate on eradicating just these in a particular document. Then, with these problems under control, make up a new list, find their remedies, and concentrate on eradicating these problems. Continue this iterative process for a lifetime (Kelley, 1972).

- Focusing solely on surface problems of correct and effective grammar, usage, spelling, and punctuation doesn't solve the uniquely tricky problems of paper and on-line documentation. Writing documentation is like an iceberg with the largest part of it invisible beneath the waves—or the largest part invisible to the final reader of the documentation. Therefore, we will spend more time and attention on the decisions that go right or wrong before the pencil ever hits the piece of paper or the fingers ever hit the keys of the word processor. Thus, this book focuses much more on the design, testing, and drafting process of documentation than on the editing of documentation.

So, if the purpose of the book is not to examine design and maintenance documentation, and to teach correct and effective grammar, usage, spelling, and punctuation, what is its purpose?

Focus on a Standard Methodology

An example of such a software engineering methodology is the Yourdon structured programming approach.

In the 1950's, 1960's, and early 1970's, the methods used in software development were largely intuitive, created unpredictable results, and made the replication of successes by others rare. A disciplined engineering approach in software design only came about two decades after the birth of computers (Houghton-Alico, 1985).

This book's focus on methodology can be productively complemented by another Wiley text that focuses on on-line documentation style guidelines, William Horton's *Designing and Writing Online Documentation* (Wiley, 1990).

There's always room for genius programmers who 'flying by the seat of their pants' created VisiCalc, CP/M, HyperCard, etc. (see Slater, *Portraits in Silicon* (1989). But we're not all geniuses.

For more on the problems of the early "template tradition," see Part One

In the late 1970's and early 1980's, software development methods became explicit, creating predictable results and making the replication of successes by others possible. This development in systems and programming did not proceed in the direction of standard programs or application specifics, but rather in the direction of standard methodologies and processes. The standard methodologies contain similar steps and methods, and the majority of the resulting programs and systems now approximate the utility of the best earlier systems and do so much more efficiently than if the programmers and analysts had "flown by the seat of their pants" (Kraft, 1977).

In user documentation, we also need to stop flying by the seat of our pants. We too need to combine the word *engineering* with *user documentation*. However, we should not think that simple replication of document content will solve our problems. Doing so would lead us right back into the dead end of the template tradition that was not flexible enough to accommodate the varied document purposes and audiences. Rather, the replication of the best procedures used by the best documentation writers will improve the situation. The Standard Documentation Process (SDP)—the backbone of this book—offers just such a structured methodological solution (see also Pakin and Associates, 1983).

Who Are the Intended Audiences?

This book assumes no prior knowledge of either software or documentation, and is primarily for:

- Technical communicators, human factors engineers, and documentation specialists whose primary responsibilities are the development of paper and on-line end-user documentation

- Programmers who have as part of their responsibility documenting programs for end-users

- Students in technical communication programs

- Systems analysts who evaluate and generate documentation on a regular basis

- Managers of information services who are responsible for preparing documentation standards

This book also responds to the growing need of experienced documentation specialists who are looking for a research foundation for their current activities. It also covers techniques for both external documentation sold to customers and clients and internal documentation to be used solely in-house for the smooth functioning of departments and divisions.

What is Covered, and How Is It Organized?

Part One describes the problems of user documentation, what the possible consequences of inadequate documentation may be, and why these problems have occurred. This analysis of the documentation problems examines first problems with paper documentation and then problems with on-line documentation. Both sets of problems are examined first theoretically, second by investigating a specific example, and third by seeing what information surveys have to tell us. Knowing these problems will also give us an overview of the topics to be covered in Part Two.

Part Two outlines a solution to user documentation problems—the Standard Documentation Process (SDP). These chapters explain the SDP to help readers set standards in their own companies or organizations. Many of these standards and options are based on the best user documentation ideas presented in the last 25 years in books, journals, seminars, or convention talks. The ideas presented here are grounded in research from such areas as communication theory, reading theory, human factors, cognitive psychology, software psychology, and linguistics. They have also been tried and tested by data processing professionals in the United States, Canada, Australia, and Singapore.

A list of references, a glossary, and an index conclude this book. A reference card to the SDP, which you can tear out for ready use, is included on the last page.

Why a Revised Edition?

Since the first edition of this book came out in 1986, I have been on the road teaching documentation on three continents and working with and learning from programmers, analysts, documentation developers, and managers. The primary lesson I have learned is that the world of documentation has changed dramatically in just a few short years.

The words "desktop publishing" and "CASE " weren't even coined until 1986, and their very dramatic effects on the documentation process are taking years to sort out.

Thus in this new edition, you will find all the information from the first edition that has proved correct and effective as I tried it out around the world. But you'll also find new information that will enable documenters to face the 1990's and the year 2000. New information is given on:

- CASE tools and the "software factory" programming technologies that are changing the face of the workplace in which documentation takes place

"The majority of layout and design examples I've seen by such software under the guidance of nonprofessionals . . . make a freshly poured bowl of alphabet soup seem by comparison a masterpiece of clarity and design" (Sandberg-Diment, September 7, 1986).

- Research on layout, format, typography, and color that alone will make desktop publishing, electronic publishing, and the new documentation databases effective

- The effect of the new multinational audiences that documenters must face and how to design documentation for easy translation

- The effects of new techniques, technologies, and ideas such as team writing styles, document prototyping, minimalist design philosophy, hypertext, SGML, and mass storage devices such as CD-ROM and magneto-optical storage.

cf.

What's "new" with this book's layout is, in many cases, a rediscovery of the visual effectiveness of scribes' glosses in medieval manuscripts or rabbinic commentaries of the *Talmud*.

You'll also find that the new edition reflects the new professional concerns of those who write computer documentation:

- The social context in which documentation is written, tested, reviewed, and used

- The conjoining of paper and on-line documentation

Sometimes research delivers contradictory results. As much as possible, contradictory information will be visually juxtaposed so that you the reader can sort out the wheat from the chaff. These contradictory results will be signaled by the abbreviation for the Latin *conferre*—to compare:

cf.

You'll also find that this new edition exploits new dimensions of layout, format, and organization. In fact, to aid scan-zoom readers, this text exploits new dimensions of layout and organization to create a "low-tech hypertext" (See Wurman 1989; Silverstone, 1989, 31; Brockmann and Horton, 1989). You will soon observe that this book uses visualizations, advanced organizers, and tries to serve both the traditional linear reader and the "scan-zoom," nonlinear reader.

What Principles Guide this Book?

Five principles guide this book. First, the field of computer documentation is moving and changing quite rapidly as some of the keenest minds in the professions and in academia turn to it as a field of study and research. Because the field is developing so rapidly, you will find the bibliography quite extensive; sufficiently extensive to continue your own education and explore topics affecting the quality of your organization's user documentation.

Second, when the earlier edition of this book was drafted, it was intended primarily for the benefit of writers of paper user manuals. The industry, however, has quickly moved beyond paper, and so has this book. In fact, it is in moving beyond paper that today's writers of paper user manuals will be able to survive the year 2000 with manual-less software in common use. Manual-less software was the objective of the Apple Computer's Macintosh project. Although they didn't fully succeed in being manual-less, the direction in the software industry is to take much of the paper documentation and make it either superfluous because of improved interface design, or put it on-line using such new organizational devices as hypertext.

Manual-less software will become possible as contemporary culture increases its "intuitive" knowledge and sophistication concerning computers, and as the software itself better communicates its purposes and controls to the user. In fact, William Houze predicted in 1983 that with the advent of sophisticated software, 75% of current technical communication jobs will become obsolete (Houze, 1983). Gaines and Shaw concur when they point out that:

> "The use of other media [paper manuals] to support the use of computer programs may be significant initially, but ultimately it will be the computer medium itself that dominates" (Gaines and Shaw, 1984).

This book does not cover the project management aspects of documentation—for the best information on managing large projects with large groups of writers involved, see Sandra Pakin and Associates' *Journal of Documentation Project Management* and Stultz's *The Business Side of Writing* (1984).

The profession of user documentation writers needs to expand its identity and what it offers to companies or organizations. For, you see, user documentation writers are not just paper manual writers; rather they are communication specialists who have the necessary expertise to design the communication elements of the "user interface" elements of the software: the messages, the menus, the on-line tutorials, as well as the traditional paper manuals.

The third principle guiding this book is the reaffirmed awareness that the painstakingly discovered methods and techniques of communication on paper are not to be lost in the transition to a new medium but rather become more important. In many cases, the qualities of effective on-line documentation must be abstracted from the qualities of effective paper documentation. For example, the concept that effective on-line information must allow for multiple access methods of getting to information can be easily abstracted from a book's multiple access methods that range from the "keyword searches" of an index, to a "top-down hierarchical approach" of a table of contents, to a page's headings that allow access to information on a local level. The idea of "aliasing" in keywords or on-line "links" is nothing more than the application of the concept of using "See" and "See also" in paper book indexes.

Alan Kay, the inventor of WIMP (Windows, Icons, Mouses, and Pointers), noted that we often have to go away from a problem in order to really see it (1983):

> "It's like when you give someone a brick. They often think of building a wall because walls are like big bricks. But you want something one level more abstract. You don't want to build walls... Arches are not an obvious idea. Most civilizations never invented them. The Greeks didn't. They never built a structure with an arch...the arch is a nonobvious use of bricks... Essentially you have to go away from your goal to come back to it" (51).

This is the principle of effective on-line documentation that we'll see proved again and again; we have to go away from effective paper documentation, abstract from paper its tricks and technques, and then re-invent their tricks and technques in on-line documentation using different tools. (But the relation between paper and on-line documentation is, of course, a two-way street. For example, we can learn anew from on-line documentation's methods of organization that graphical overviews are needed in paper books such as the side topic menus used in this book's long chapters or steps.)

"Despite some false starts, a growing body of psychological studies has converged to show that the most effective techniques to increase the problem-solving value of technical prose work equally well in video and printed form" (Girill, Luk, and Norton, 1987, 85).

cf.

"As technical communicators we are the professionals who are responsible to see that users don't just get what they think they want, but what they need" (Edwards, 1989, 62).

The fourth principle guiding this book is that often the best solution to user documentation problems is an eclectic solution: a little from writing style A, a little from hypertext linking philosophy C, etc. Break all style and even methodological guides except one: the audience is always right. Thus we present as many sides to solutions as possible and the defects of each. This points to the need for a certain degree of humility on the part of documenters. All guidelines, standards, truisms, and experiences must be tried repeatedly in the furnace of empirical user testing.

"Gone are the days when writing was done after a product was complete and writers were given the product specification and told to 'pubs it up!' Today's information developers must work as equal partners with other product developers. The lines between hardware, software, and information are getting blurred with the advent of interactive programming, new input devices, and displayable manuals. For this reason cooperation and collaboration across disciplines will become even more important and people should start practicing it now" (Grice, 1988, 133).

Fifth, more and more documenters are breaking out of the backroom ghetto of software design organizations in which they just massaged written software design specifications. Now, documenters are tending to get information from people rather than books (Saar, 1986). They are getting information from such people as the design team of which they are a member right from the beginning, from actual users in their own environments through the application of documentation specification reviews and early prototype testing, and from fellow documenters in documentation teams and in structured documentation project reviews. Getting more information from people than from books means that negotiating, listening, and getting along with fellow documentation team members, software designers, and users will play much more of a role than ever in the past.

What's the Best Way to Read this Book?

If You Are Looking For	Turn To
Quick summaries	Reference Card in the back of the book, Tables double-ruled at top throughout the text
Detailed information and primary direction of the book	Right-hand column of text
Detailed research quotations and graphic advanced organizers	Left-hand column of text.
Ideas, comments, and research that contradict the main direction of the text	"cf." labeled material in left-hand column

PART ONE: THE DOCUMENTATION PROBLEM

Overview of Computer Documentation

This definition builds on Dobrin's definition of technical communication (1983).

Purposes of Software User Documentation

> Part 1: The Documentation Problem
>
> The Problems with Paper Documentation:
>
> Theory
> Example
> Survey Reports
>
> The Problem with On-line Documentation
>
> Theory
> Example
> Survey Reports

To write documentation in a software development environment, you must act as an intermediary between the computer system and its human users. In particular, as a writer of software documentation, you must act as an intermediary between the computer software and its users. Thus, we can define computer documentation by the following:

> Communication designed to ease interactions between computer software and the individuals who manage, audit, operate, or maintain it.

Some of the specific purposes of user documentation are to improve efficiency, to overcome users' fears of equipment or software, and to sell the product.

To Improve Efficiency

People need to understand the systems with which they are working. And they cannot afford to depend on word-of-mouth information because personnel changes are frequent in most software development environments. One estimate is that the average stay for programmers in the same job is about 18 months and that 30% of all managers have their resumes in circulation. In an environment where personnel change less often, we could rely on word-of-mouth instruction, but software design is not such a field.

To Overcome Users' Fears of Equipment or Software

When a user of new software confronts a complicated and poorly organized set of reference manuals as their introduction to a piece of software, they are apt to regret their introduction. On the other hand, if they see a simplified tutorial for the same software, they are more likely to forge ahead. In short, successful software documentation leads to successful first encounters with software and, therefore, to greater acceptance and use.

An example of a situation in which a company did not overcome users' fears is the 1983 Coleco Adam™ computer debacle as described in the *Time* magazine article below:

> "Coleco lost $35 million in the fourth quarter last year partly because people flocked to return the initial version of its Adam computer which the company offered for $600. In a statement to shareholders, Coleco blamed much of the consumer dissatisfaction on 'manuals which did not offer the first-time user adequate assistance'"(Greenwald, 1984).

To Sell the Product

An article in *Computerworld* said it best in this regard:

> "Most people agree that the quality of end-user documentation can spell success or failure for a new software product. After all, the manuals are what a customer sees first—they shape his perception of the entire package" (Desmaris, 1981).

cf.

In an AT&T marketing survey (discussed later in this Part One), only 29% said they consider the manual before purchase.

Liability Issues in Documentation

Observe the legal standardization of the labels: "Danger," "Warning," and "Caution." "Danger" implies that the action you are warning about could cause life-threatening harm to the user. "Warning" implies that the action you are warning about could cause harm but not life-threatening harm to the user. "Caution" implies that the action you are warning about could cause harm to the hardware or software. Please realize that "Note" and other such labels do NOT carry the same implications.

There were only two occurrences of "Danger," "Caution," or "Warning" in the 1919-1925 version of the Ford Model T user manual. In the 1986 Ford Escort user manual there were 113.

The documentation problems of efficiency, overcoming fears, and improved marketing may not directly affect you, the documentation writer. In fact, it may be a purely altruistic impulse that convinces you that you ought to help others avoid these problems. But writing effective documentation is also one of the best ways to avoid legal proceedings, which could affect you. Recent liability cases in the courts have shown that (Tepley, 1987; Wilson, 1987)

> anyone involved in the documentation whether in the planning, testing, or marketing can be drawn into product liability and litigation.

Most liability problems arise from failure to warn. Thus a few questions you should ask yourself when designing documentation are:

- Is the warning adequate to the circumstances of use and proportionate in intensity to the danger?

- Does the warning warn of "hidden dangers?" "Foreseeability" includes the duty to warn against all unusual or unintended uses of the product.

- Are the warnings located where they are likely to be noticed and read?

But beyond this established handling of warnings, make sure that you:

Perhaps a way to implement such prefatory material on-line without requiring the on-line reader to always read it is to have it presented to everyone the first time they read an on-line document. After the first time it can be optionally displayed somewhat like the copyright displays and initial ownership customization provided with many software application packages.

- Create a preface or other introductory material that limits your liability. Front matter should include: date, what model product is covered, what previous manuals this manual replaces, what warranties, agreements, or responsibilities are implied or not implied, and that the information is not all-inclusive but can be found in a list of "Related Documentation." Perhaps most importantly, you should include a section entitled "What This Manual Assumes" in which you detail the prior knowledge you assume the reader has in regard to knowledge about the task, the hardware, and the software.

- Be sure to include a self-addressed documentation registration card to document traceability and issuance of manuals. Perhaps an electronic mail version could work for on-line documentation, especially for internal documentation (James G., 1985).

"Implementation of alpha and beta testing may be necessary to avoid later charges of negligence in product completion" (Jones H., 1989, 452).

- Test the documentation. Prototype testing and field testing have become a necessity to uncover all the possible "foresee-able" misuses that hardware and software can be put to. Documentation writers are continually astounded by the varied interpretations that readers give to the writer's writing in comparison with the writer's intended meaning. As Bill Gates, CEO of Microsoft, said in an interview, "Testing gets you back in touch with how difficult it really is."

Types of User Documentation

First, we can classify user documentation by content—reference material and tutorial material and second, we can classify user documentation by environment—external documentation and internal documentation. Knowing these different types of documentation will allow you to make decisions on what to include in your documentation package in response to your audience and your software.

Reference and Tutorial Documentation

In a 1984 survey (Borland, 1984), the Microsoft Corporation found that everyone wanted a "phone book" that comprehensively described all the features of the product.

Reference material is technical, detailed, comprehensive, and usually organized like an encyclopedia or dictionary for quick retrieval of information. A reference manual should explain what the software can do for the user—a product capability emphasis—rather than comprehensively describing the product—a product internal construction emphasis. An emphasis on product capability in a reference manual allows the user to go beyond the necessarily constrained steps of a tutorial, and combine product features in ways never envisioned by the original product designers, e.g., I use the table construction capabilities of Microsoft Word 4.0™ to develop my page crop marks.

Tutorial material, on the other hand, selects from the comprehensive reference material and presents information in a step-by-step fashion. It is usually organized around user tasks or around a hierarchy of user needs.

In 1986 an independent market research firm found in a survey for AT&T that 69% of those they surveyed said they go to the manual's tutorial first.

What's the point of knowing there are two types of user documentation differentiated by content? Good documentation grows with users as they grow in experience and sophistication in their use of the software, and it can become a part of the product's sales appeal. The first half of the documentation of many best-selling software packages is used by the new software owner for the first month of ownership, and it is a detailed tutorial. The second half of the documentation is more like a reference manual that the owner uses after the first month.

For more on differentiating the tutorial, reference manuals, and standard operating procedures, see Major, 1989.

The results of a 15-year survey of users (Maynard, 1982) carried out by Control Data Corporation, Scientific Data Systems, and Xerox Data Systems turned up two apparently contradictory findings. Half the users accused the manuals of having too little detail, and half accused them of having too much detail. Two-part manuals with a tutorial and a reference section are the compromise suggested by these survey takers. By clearly segmenting the manual into two parts, you give readers the freedom to choose the appropriate coverage of material.

Another reason to know why there are two types of documentation is to help you match your software to the right type of documentation. When deciding what percentage of your manual ought to be tutorial or reference information, consider how open-ended or standardized the software is to the user. To the extent that the software is open-ended, can be customized by the user, and used and viewed from different directions (general database development packages for example), the material ought to be presented as a reference manual. To the extent that the software is viewed or used by the user in only one standardized way, the material can be used and viewed in only one way (a spelling correction package for example), the more the material ought to be packaged in a tutorial. This variation acknowledges the fact that tutorials' specificity of directions and examples tend to limit the readers' conceptions of the software's uses. Tutorials can, in fact, limit how users think they can use open-ended software.

External and Internal Documentation

Another way we can classify user documentation is by the environment in which it is used—external documentation or internal documentation (American Institute for Professional Education, 1981). External documentation is meant for audiences outside of the corporate or organizational environment in which the documentation is developed. Internal documentation is developed by an organization to be used by readers within that same organization.

See also the *Guidelines for Documentation of Computer Programs and Automated Data Systems* from the National Bureau of Standards for a table that discusses the relationship in time, money, and attention with the cost of the system, life expectancy of the system, and number of individuals directly involved with the system; e.g., a $100 software system to be used once for one person should only receive a minimal effort.

External documentation is usually a more expensive, professional product; it's a marketing tool, as well as an operations tool. As a result, it usually receives the necessary time, money, and attention. It is usually attractively packaged and filled with graphics.

Internal documentation, on the other hand, makes up the bulk of all documentation. However, it is often the poor cousin of external documentation—it frequently fails to receive the necessary time, money, and attention. The reason for this is simple—because it is read only inside a company or organization and is not part of a company's product. Thus, its relationship to profits may be murky at best. Also, internal documentation is not as well designed as external documentation because the writers may not receive much feedback on their work. You would let the store owner know when the product you just bought breaks, but you might not complain about a product given to you gratis by your own company. Because internal manuals are issued rather than purchased, you may not complain as loudly when they do not meet your expectations or needs.

Step 1, "Timing and Cost" for other ways to decrease documentation time and cost of documentation.

Thus knowing that internal documentation suffers because of a lack of management support in terms of time, money, and attention, and because it suffers from of a lack of audience feedback, developers and managers of internal documentation need to proceed cleverly. If the internal documentation is purchased as part of a vendor's package, be sure their documentation is carefully reviewed during the purchase decision; the better the documentation you can get from the vendor when you have the leverage of purchase negotiations, the less work you will have to do later. Internal documenters also need to carefully weigh the values of special binding and packaging that may be *de rigueur* in external packages. And, finally, to increase feedback to documenters, make it easy for your audience by developing an electronic mail method of collecting feedback.

What Choice Is There in Where to Put "System Intelligibility?"

In the world of computers, whatever *intelligibility* is put into the system is the intelligibility that the users are able to extract. Somebody, somewhere, somehow has to put intelligibility into the system. Paper and on-line documentation are only some of the many possibilities. In fact, the concept of defensive programming says that intelligibility is built right into the system and is not an after thought.

Defensive Programming

This book probably would be unnecessary if all software designers followed this guideline:

A Program must be RIGHT, and as FAIL-SAFE, CLEAR and SIMPLE as possible.
Defensive Programming can help to accomplish this.
Defensive Programming means anticipating problems in advance and coding to avoid errors before they arise.

In fact, the need and size of documentation is inversely proportional to the effectiveness of following this guideline as seen in Figure 1. Historically, the trend is definitely toward defensive programming.

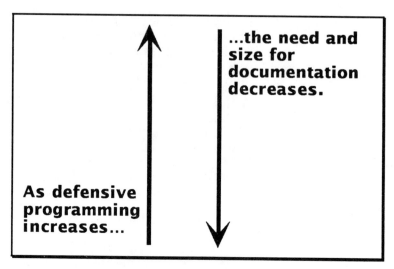

Figure 1. Relationship between defensive
programming and the need and size of
documentation.

"What I discovered on that long and interesting journey is that writing friendly software is a communications task, and to do it effectively you must apply the techniques of effective communication, techniques that are little different from those developed by writers, film makers—virtually anyone who has attempted to communicate an idea over the past decades, centuries, even in some cases millennia. It is the use—consciously or unconsciously—of these techniques that makes software successful in the market place" (Heckel, 1984, xii).

However, if intelligibility is not put into the design right from the very beginning, or into the paper or on-line documentation, why not put it into training courses? A number of companies in the late 60's and 70's made quite a profit offering training courses to users rather than put system intelligibility into the design or the documentation.

Trainers

In one company that had poor defensive programming and poor documentation, the calls by users of the company's products for training companies was so large that a dozen trainers were fully employed teaching classes. But as this same company improved their defensive programming, and as they improved their paper and on-line documentation, calls by users for training classes decreased and decreased. As the number of calls decreased the number of trainers employed by the company went from twelve to ten, then to eight, and finally reached six. At this point, the Director of Training actually said to the Director of Documentation in a last ditch effort to save their department: "Can you please leave something out? Just leave some blank pages and print on them 'For Further Information See Training.'" Needless to say, that did not happen.

Mantei and Teorey (1988) note that reducing training costs even a little can yield substantial savings .

If you want to decrease the need and cost of training courses and trainers, put more time and effort into defensive programming and improved documentation.

Phone Support

AT&T's 800 number National Systems Support Center reportedly spent $19 million in 1989 on phone support; that's about $65 a call (the average price per call in 1987 was $50).

What about giving users system intelligibility via phone calls (Bergstrom, 1986; Farkas, 1986; Ramey, 1986)? After all, it has been shown that "learners at every level of experience try to avoid reading" (Carroll and Rosson, 1987, 83). Giving users system intelligibility via phone support can and has been done, of course, but you must realize that at least the same amount—and most probably more—time, money, and effort is going to be spent on phone call support as could have been spent in a planned way in defensive programming, documentation, or training. It's just that the cost of phone support is spread out and never seen in a lump sum, so that the cost of this approach seems much cheaper. However, *Time* magazine (Elmer-DeWitt, 1986) a few years ago had some startling cost estimates of this nickle-and-dime cost of phone support:

> "Ashton-Tate, conceding that during peak hours its current staff cannot keep up with the calls, already spends 1.5 million a year on salaries, office expenses and training to provide software advice. Living Videotext in Mountain View, Calif., figures that the net cost of talking to a single user is between $30 and $40 an hour. "If I talk to them twice, says President David Winer, 'I'm starting to pay *them* to use my product""(51).

Trial and error

As market studies have long shown, "a satisfied customer tells eight people, but a dissatisfied customer tells 22 people" (Favin, 1988,118).

But if we don't want to put the time, money, and effort it takes to give intelligibility to the system ourselves, perhaps we can leave it up to the users themselves as they go through a process of trial and error. Inadequate user documentation can greatly increase human errors in computer systems. Bailey (1983) in his book on human errors in computer systems categorizes the major factors for human errors. Three categories are beyond the control of the software or computer designers and documenters. Yet they account for 50% of all human errors: environmental problems, personnel problems, and organizational accuracy factors. The other 50% of all human errors are within the control of the software or computer designers, and of these fully 60% are directly affected by the quality of the documentation efforts: training, written instructions, and the human-computer interface are all affected by the quality of the documentation. This breakdown of the human errors in computer systems and the portion that is directly affected by documentation efforts are shown in Figure 2 (Bailey, 1983).

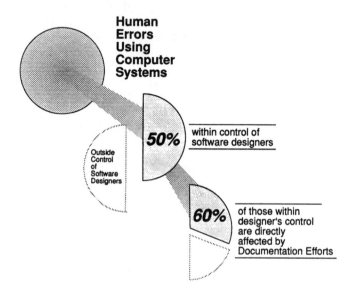

Human Errors Using Computer Systems

Outside Control of Software Designers

50% within control of software designers

60% of those within designer's control are directly affected by Documentation Efforts

Figure 2. Percentage of human errors directly affected by the documentation.

Poor user documentation wastes valuable time and effort as hopeful users search page after page and manual after manual for solutions to simple questions. Sometimes users feel compelled to use elaborate personnel or manual solutions to software problems—such as buying a typewriter because addressing envelopes on the word processor is impossible to figure out, or using a hand calculator to make calculations that seem impossible with "easy-to-learn" accounting packages.

What's the Historical Trend?

"Mickey Mousing" a system (See Lundstrom, *A Few Good Men From Univac* (1989).

Getting the users themselves to put intelligibility into computer systems via their own trial and error was the standard approach during the early years of computers in the 1950's. In fact, a jargon word, which luckily has since been lost, to explain how to learn about computers was called "Mickey Mousing" a system—early users of computers would try one procedure after another and realize what was the right approach and what was the wrong approach by observing the black smoke billowing out from the machine or observing the number of vacuum tubes blown because of different actions. If that represents the early days of computers, defensive programming represents the future of computers. The use of the improved defensive programming seen in such techniques as windows-icons-mouses-and-pointers (WIMP) has vastly improved the penetration of computers into the general populace.

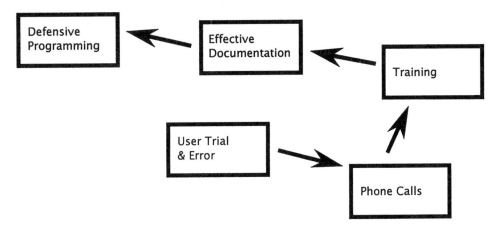

Figure 3. Historical trend in instilling system intelligibility.

In summary, we have many ways to get intelligibility into a system. I don't want to be a documentation chauvinist and suggest that it's only paper and on-line documentation that can put intelligibility into a system. Defensive programming, training, phone call support, and user trial and error are all available to give intelligibility to computer systems.

Why Is Inadequate User Documentation Produced?

Why does poor user documentation occur? Seven factors go a long way to account for these problems:

- The change from centralization to decentralization of computer systems

- Institutional limitations

Infoworld had an editorial with this as its title: "Technical Writing in the Computer Industry—The Armpit of the Industry."

- Inadequate design
- The techniques used in user documentation
- Oversimplifying the writing task in many how-to books and professional journals
- Fighting against rather than harnessing the learning behaviors adults spontaneously adopt
- Natural egoism

Beyond Computer System Centralization

There is a time lag in many writers' attitudes toward the place and functions of user documentation. In the 1950's, through the early 1980's, computer systems were centralized, and they existed in a cocoon—a cocoon of software specialists who surrounded the computer and were a human buffer between the machine and the larger organization (Way, 1982). When users wanted to interact with the computer, they dealt with the human cocoon who could translate any user documentation that users didn't understand. In such a situation, documentation did not have to offer self-sufficiency.

However, like a caterpillar in a cocoon, the computer has burst out of its MIS department. Now, computers are spread throughout organizations and geographic locales. The world of computers has shifted to one of vast decentralization. Just as the microcomputers and workstations now stand alone, the documentation also has to stand alone. The problem is, however, that too many writers are writing in the old cocoon frame of mind. This no longer works—not only because of computer decentralization, but because in breaking out of its cocoon the computer and its documentation have come increasingly into the hands of non-software specialists.

Institutional Limitations

Even when documenters are alert to the needs of documentation in a decentralized environment, there is still the possibility that institutional factors will prevent them from producing effective computer documentation. Some of these factors are sketched in Figure 4.

This book will help you with the training and education element of the problem. However, training and education alone will not solve the problem of effective ongoing documentation unless other institutional factors make their contribution. For instance, if company documentation standards do not enhance and support good, effective documentation efforts, no book or training seminar can help.

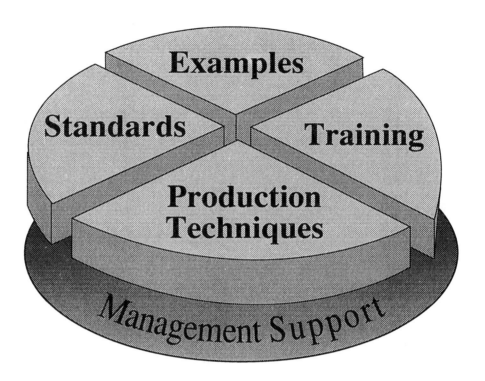

Figure 4. Institutional limitations on documentation.

In the same way, if examples of documentation formally presented in standard development methodologies or informally circulated around an office are not examples of *good* documentation, then training may go for naught. Employees don't learn how to write letters, reports, or memos by turning to a textbook or even to a company book of standards. Instead, they usually learn by opening up the closest file drawer and using the letters, reports, or memos in the drawer as examples from which to develop their own. Therefore, circulating examples of good documentation is crucial to promote good, effective ongoing documentation, and examples of bad

What the *Journal of Systems Management* said about developing computer systems is also true of developing documentation: "You're not gonna get it right the first time. Systems [or in our case, documents] are developed, not created in an instantaneous flash of creation. You're going to do the best you can, then you're gonna do it over...and over...and over...until you get it right" (Mingione, 1983).

cf.

Killingsworth and Jones (1989) point out that even though they and others favor the recursive model, their survey does not show any evidence that this model fosters higher quality documentation.

Stylesheets, templates, or tags are elements in a text file separate from the content. They define the content's positioning on the page, typographical elements such as typesize and typeface, or the use of boxes or rules.

Studies at Bell Laboratories have shown that writers using such aids not only edit more thoroughly, but also learn to edit on their own (Gingrich et al., 1981).

"Hypertext denotes nonsequential writing and reading. Both an author's tool and a reader's medium, a hypertext document system allows authors or groups of authors to link information together, create paths through a corpus of related material, annotate existing texts, and create notes that point readers to either bibliographic data or the body of the referenced text" (Yankelovich, Meyrowitz, and van Dam, 1985) .

documentation may seriously hinder documentation efforts throughout an organization.

Finally, good, effective technological support of the documentation effort enhances the likelihood of good documentation. The various iterations of the document should be done as flawlessly and as quickly as possible. Speed of production is crucial because good documentation is the result of rewriting and rewriting and rewriting. However, if each iteration of a document takes weeks to produce, then few will be inclined to redraft and rewrite. Thus, the more powerful the tools that are put in the hands of the documentation developers, the better the final document will be.

The ideal documenter's tool chest would have these ten items:

- Text input tools such as "document processors" which usually have stylesheet or template capabilities in the document processors to automate standardization of layout, design, and typography; and a text scanner to capture nondigitized text to prevent the errors and time expenditure of rekeying

- Paper documentation automated editing aids such as a speller, an outliner (to aid with large-scale movement of text during revision so as to overcome the implicit focus on small local screen-centered editing), a thesaurus (usually these three are built into most top-of-the-line document processors), a style and punctuation checker (Bates, 1984; Buckley, 1983; Cole, 1985; Daiute, 1985; Glenn, 1983; Heidorn et al., 1982; Holder, 1982; Owens, 1984; Penrose, 1984; Trippe, 1984), and desktop publishing and layout aids (Sylla, 1988)

- Reference aid development tools such as an automatic table of contents and index creators (these are now often built into document processors)

- On-line document authoring tools for hypertext (e.g., HyperTies™, HyperCard™, SuperCard™, Guide™, ZoomRacks™, NoteCards™, and LinkWay™), for demonstrations or on-line tutorials (i.e., DEMO™), or for general interface design (i.e., NeXT Interface Builder™)

- On-line document editing tools (i.e., the Tullis Display Analysis Package™ that critiques screen layout, or Iconer that critiques the design of icons) or on-line guidelines (i.e., HDS™ or NaviText ™ SAM)

- Graphic input tools: paint, draw, and/or CAD software; digital or paper clipart; and scanners

- Standard Markup Language File Translators (SGML)—so that text can be easily reutilized in a variety of situations

- Output tools: for paper, 300 and better dpi laser printers; and for on-line information, WORM drives or magneto-optical drives that can hold up to 800 megabytes of information

- Groupware to automate information gathering, collaborative authorship, and on-line reviewing (e.g., For Comment™ or MarkUp™ which can be used to review document on a local area network)

- CASE tools for the developers

Underlying these institutional factors are management support and encouragement. Good or bad documentation and the climate producing either are largely a management decision (Wiegand and Roguski, 1981).

You can readily observe the effects on documentation in the change in management support by comparing the documentation produced by MicroPro for WordStar™ in 1977 or 1978 with their current documentation package. As Jong originally noted "The original documentation package was so poor that one third-party company alone, Sybex, had three books on MicroPro's WordStar" (Jong, 1984). And yet, because WordStar was so much better than the competition when it was first released—and there really wasn't much competition back then—we were willing to overlook these shortcomings. Now, however, WordStar has some very able competition in the marketplace so they can no longer rely on their inherent market edge. The difference this caused in their documentation efforts is like night and day. MicroPro saw their share

---

Tullis Display Analysis Package, Version 4.0™ The Human Angle, PO Box 3542k, Mission Viejo, CA 92690); see Eisen, 1990 for more information about Iconer.

"HDS now consists of one model Help system and a design aiding system which includes 34 design principles, 191 guidelines, and 200 references in the literature—all linked in a database using HyperCard" (CDC Flyer, 1989) .

NaviText ™ SAM is a hypertext interface to the 450+ page 1986 Smith and Mosier human factors guidelines (see Perlman, 1989).

NeXT Interface Builder, see Thakkar, Perlman and Miller, 1990.

Dots per inch (dpi) is a measure of printing resolution.

At 600 dpi and at normal reading distance, the eye no longer distinguishes the dots that make up the type (Rubenstein, 1988, 87).

Write Once Read Many (WORM) and magneto-optical drives have all the advantages of Compact Disc Read Only Memory (CD-ROM) except that the mastering and replication can be done inhouse

"MicroPro International estimates that 70% of the customers who dial for Help are first-time users who find reaching for the phone easier than wading through pages of instruction" (Elmer-DeWitt ,1986, 51).

"My job has many positive aspects; however, the group manager does not effectively communicate the group's needs to upper management. Hence, although we do fine work, we are consistently understaffed, underequipped, undertrained, and poorly rewarded. Staff efforts to change procedures for better quality and efficiency have been stifled. The work is interesting, but many avenues for striving to do it better are closed" (*Journal of Documentation Management*, Fall 1989—one of the responses of a survey to which more than 300 documentation professionals responded).

of the marketplace declining, and they recognized that a change in their documentation approach was the most direct way to stop this market share loss.

The marketplace, then, not theories, books, or lectures, is what is driving management to put new effort, time, and money into documentation.

We can also see this born-again belief in documentation when we compare the documentation produced by Dan Bricklin in 1986 for his product Demo™ (Software Garden) with the second version in 1987. Again, the product was directed to a new market niche—rapid prototyping and on-line tutorials—there was very little competition in the marketplace, and the price was right—under $100.00. Thus, Bricklin evidently did not feel the need to have adequate documentation—just as earlier he had not felt the need in his first success, VisiCalc™. The original Demo documentation was what the *New York Times* critic called "abysmal":

> "He had done it again with the documentation, too. Like the one accompanying the original VisiCalc, the manual escorting his new software offering can only be described as abysmal. It doesn't even tell you how to start the program....The turgid 29-page manual is presented in all its solitary splendor, sans tutorial, index, quick reference card or anything else resembling the amenities customarily packaged with software today" (Sandberg-Diment, August 1986).

However, the documentation escorting Demo II™ is nearly state-of-the-art. The new version has an index, reference sections, a tutorial, a keyboard template, and terrific layout, format, and typography. One of the most interesting things is that Dan Bricklin himself wrote and produced the new manual on Xerox Ventura Publisher 1.1™—programmers take heart (and technical writers take warning); you don't need to be a professional technical writer to write excellent manuals. Again, it was the competition in the marketplace that drove Bricklin to decide to improve the documentation.

Inadequate Design: The CASE Tool Solution

CASE essentially automates the entire software engineering process. CASE tools run on high performance graphic workstations or PC's, and these tools allow software developers, and even end-users to:

CASE is the acronym for Computer Assisted (var., Aided) Software (var., Systems) Engineering.

cf.

CASE tools are still a technology and methodology that has to prove itself. Many feel it's just a marketing gimmick to sell more computers and seminars.

"Just as the rapid adoption of PC's by the user community was alarming to professional system developers, so may CASE. We're already beginning to see some evidence of users purchasing CASE tools independently of internal MIS departments. Users are finding CASE tools quite comprehensible, easy to learn, and a fantastic way of ordering their thoughts and expressing them in a clear and consistent way" (*The Annual CASE Survey*, 1988, 92).

For a good introduction to CASE tools, QED Publications of Wellesley Massachusetts has three interesting items: *CASE: The Potential and the Pitfalls* (1989), *The Annual CASE Survey, 1988* (1989), and a 20-minute videotape introduction to CASE by the CASE Research Corporation "The Strategic Implications of CASE" (1989).

- Use standardized graphics to design systems
- Develop prototype screens, reports, and the human-computer interface elements of messages, menus, and commands
- Automatically generate new code or reuse old code

The future possible effects of CASE range from truly earth shattering to a hard jolt in the industry. If, as some say, user documentation of computer systems is nothing more than a correction of "aggressive programming" (the opposite of "defensive programming"), or, as others say, it is a translation of computer information to business task-oriented information, user documentation could almost disappear. End-users along with analysts—with technical writer/designer facilitators or even alone—can design systems that employ end-user language, logic, and organization throughout a system. No longer, therefore, will there be the need for lengthy documentation explanations of

- Error messages such as "ILLEGAL SYNTAX"
- Commands such as "&&BDC"
- Systems concepts that require users to "un-delete deletions"
- Menu organizations that scramble the order of system usage

What happens to user documentation and the traditional documentation writer in this use of CASE tools is that writers may redirect their efforts at supporting user needs from writing to system designing. User documentation will be significantly easier to develop because there will be many fewer design errors, and the designs will be written in end-user language, not some machine language gibberish. And, most importantly, user documentation will be able to focus on the business details and strategic planning of a procedure rather than on the keystrokes and menu choices needed to encode it.

But even if these earth shattering effects don't take place, the computer industry and technical writers could still receive a severe jolt with the introduction of CASE tools. To write an effective piece of computer documentation, a writer needs full and complete information on the design of the system or the program. With a solid foundation of design documentation, technical writers can clearly and easily understand a product's design, input requirements, outputs, maintenance, and operator interactions. Without such a solid foundation of clearly written design documentation, technical writer time and effort skyrockets as lengthy, face-to-face interviews with designers, educated guesswork, and repeated review and rewrite processes take place. The lack of complete, accurately written design documents causes many problems for writers and is often the greatest expenditure of documenter time and money.

"Too often, application systems are not documented until the end of a project, if at all, and with varying degrees of completeness and correctness. Too often, the programmers' slogan, 'documentation is fiction, code is fact' is all too true"(*The Annual CASE Survey*, 1988, 79).

Twenty years ago, the lack of design documentation was supposedly solved with the introduction of structured systems design. Structured systems design was supposed to require designers to take a "top-down" approach which would yield a series of rigorously detailed design documents. But the promise of structured design was undercut by the design tools which instead fostered a "bottom-up," microscopic focus on lines of code and which made the production of design documents difficult and time consuming. CASE is the new means by which system designers can finally deliver on their old promise of structured design and rigorously detailed design documents. At the very least, then, CASE tools will finally allow technical writers to spend more time on what they're paid to do—that is, analyzing the user's tasks, procedures, and environment and designing effective user documentation—and less time on investigative interviewing of software developers.

Techniques Used in User Documentation

"A good manual is not a narrative. ...Nobody ever reads a manual cover to cover—only mutants do that" (Greenwald, 1984).

Another source of problems in user documentation is the writing methods required by the users. These techniques differ radically from those we were trained to use in essay writing classes. As you move through this text, you will see that the basic difference between the way you were taught to write and the way you need to write in a commercial situation is the difference between arranging information for sequential access (as in essays, short stories, and novels) and arranging it for random access (as in dictionaries, encyclopedias, and computer manuals). A writer of computer documentation must produce material that can be easily skimmed and scanned—

material that allows itself to be read or not to be read depending on a reader's purpose and reading strategy.

Oversimplifying the Writing Task

This problem of oversimplification occurs when documentation writers turn for help to commercially published instructional texts and are misled about the complexity of their writing task. The texts can be misleading when they do not adequately alert their readers to the effects that audience variations have on documentation projects and products. The origin of this problem can be understood when we consider the development of the template tradition in such texts.

The term "template" (as used in software documentation design rather than document processing) was first used in a 1969 instructional text written by Dorothy Walsh entitled *A Guide For Software Documentation.* According to Walsh, a "template" is

> "...based on simple but fundamental principles ...[which] lead naturally to the development of an outline of all topics that would be required to provide user information for programming systems. The outline is augmented by a generalized commentary describing the content that is related to each topic to provide a guide to the organization and orientation of particular programming manuals and references" (p. vi).

Use of templates, such as those provided by Walsh, appeared to solve problems of content adequacy and of organization. All the individual writers needed to do was fill in set templates with information peculiar to their own system. (The outline processor software mentioned earlier follows Walsh's idea.)

Whether Walsh's text started the template tradition in instructional documentation texts or whether she was just its first published proponent, it is interesting to note the remarkable similarity in texts in the years following the publication of her text. Not only did the texts use the same instructional approach, namely, the template approach, but the content of the templates themselves was also remarkably similar.

As originally conceived and used by Walsh, the template idea included a fairly complete representation of the problem faced by writers. She used templates, but prefaced their use by a consideration of the document audience and the document purpose. However, as the template idea became a tradition, it became a less complete representation of the writing process because it lost the necessary flexibility of content and organization required to cope with the variability in audiences and purposes (Brockmann, 1984). As the template tradition developed after Walsh, it essentially confused sophisticated data processing readers who had sophisticated prior knowledge (text grammar knowledge) of software manuals' formatting, organization, and layout with readers who do not have such knowledge and require much more tailoring and accommodation to their unique needs (Duffy, Curran, and Sass, 1983). Thus, for many years, commercially published books on documentation hindered rather than helped documentation writers.

Now, we have a new, trickier problem with the advent of industry-wide, corporate-endorsed research-based guidelines and user interface standards:

Apple Human Interface Guidelines: The Apple Desktop Interface, 1987.

*Common User Access Panel Design and User Interaction,*1987.

IEEE Standard for Software User Documentation(1988).

ISO (International Organization for Standardization) 6592, *Information Processing—Guidelines for the Documentation of Computer-based Application Systems* (1st Edition, 1985).

> "Apple started it all with the Macintosh Desktop Interface. IBM joined the movement with Common User Access of its Systems Application Architecture. Hewlett-Packard proliferated it with its New Wave environment based on Microsoft Window's environment. And now AT&T is jumping on the bandwagon in partnership with Sun Microsystems in creating the Open Look graphical user interface" (Potosnak, 1988, 14; see also Fraser and Lamb,1989; and Marshall, Nelson, and Gardiner, 1987).

In addition to these interface standards, we also have new paper documentation standards as developed by IEEE and ISO. These standards can cause documenters problems in four ways (Potosnak, 1988):

- First, to be generally applicable, they often fail to be sufficiently specific to the users' tasks

- Second, they can foster a superficial, rather than a deep, consistency, which only a design philosophy can give ("If on the average, users search through 17 pop-up menus before finding the most frequently used function of the system, then consistent design of the individual pop-up menus has relatively little effect on overall task time and ease of use"; Potosnak, 1988, 15).

- Third, research data are currently too incomplete to support all the rules in these standards and so "best guesses" are packaged indistinguish-ably with "soundly researched principles."

- Fourth, and most important, guidelines, rules, and standards invite documenters to forgo testing with real users. Apple admits this need for user testing in its guidelines book: "user testing of the concepts and features of the interface should be a regular, integral part of the design process" (Potosnak, 1988, 15).

At Bank of America, a programmer who had to develop a system for bank tellers was required to take the bank's teller training courses and work as a teller for a month *before* beginning the design of the system. Needless to say, the system was a success.

A content or construction standard for paper or on-line documentation is only as good as the audience-sensitive, context-sensitive, testing-intensive, open-to-innovation-ness of the surrounding methodology into which it's put.

Fighting Rather than Harnessing Learning Behaviors Adults Spontaneously Adopt

A very disturbing fact of life that documenters—be it in paper or on-line—have to face is that "adults resist explicitly addressing themselves to new learning" (Carroll and Rosson, 1987, 101). This doesn't mean that they burn books or begin cursing manuals as soon as they receive them, but they do perform a number of actions that can only be explained by this fact of adult mental life. For example, how does one explain the fact that when given even well-written and well-designed documentation, adult readers constantly skip ahead and begin to try to use the system without reading the whole manual? How do we explain the fact that adults are constantly guessing about what should and should not happen with a new system as soon as they begin learning? How do we make sense of the fact that "learners at every level of experience try to avoid reading" (Carroll and Rosson, 1987, 83)?

Says MicroPro Manager Lee Lensky, "People don't want to read a manual, whether it's a 300-page tome or a clean, well-written one" (Elmer-DeWitt 1986, 51).

A good explanation of these behaviors consists of two paradoxes that John Carroll in his work on "minimalist design" describes as the paradoxes of motivation and assimilation. By the motivation paradox, Carroll means:

> "A motivational paradox arises in the 'production bias' people bring to the task of learning and using computer equipment. Their paramount goal is throughput. This is a desirable state of affairs in that it gives users a focus for their activity with a system, and it increases their likelihood of receiving concrete reinforcement from their work. But, on the other hand, it reduces their motivation to spend any time just learning about the system, so that when situations

appear that could be more effectively handled by new procedures, they are likely to stick with the procedures they already know regardless of their efficacy" (Carroll and Rosson, 1987, 80-1).

And his second paradox, the paradox of assimilation, he explains as follows:

"A second cognitive paradox devolves from the 'assimilation bias': People apply what they already know how to interpret new situations. This bias can be helpful, when there are useful similarities between the new and the old information....But irrelevant and misleading similarities between the new and old information can also blind learners to what they are actually seeing and doing, leading them to draw erroneous comparisons and conclusions, or preventing them from recognizing possibilities for new functions" (Carroll and Rosson, 1987, 81).

Where these two paradoxes become problematic is in the design of documentation that takes a "systems" approach. Such an approach focuses on step-by-step procedures in which the reader is expected to be passive and "color within the lines," just following along (Carroll, 1990, Chapter 4).

Why have we been led into this systems style of documentation? Carroll makes the point that there is a trade-off in training; either training is comprehensive or it is usable. Up to now most documenters have decided, "When in doubt, be comprehensive." But we see the results of emphasizing this side of the equation in how readers really read our documentation—in many cases, they don't. For example, Bell Northern Research claims that only about 30% read standard materials thoroughly (Carroll, 1990, Chapter 9). Perhaps we need to emphasize the other side of the equation—usability—that will work *with* rather than frustrate users.

Natural Egoism

The final factor that can adversely affect documentation is a human flaw affecting all human communication. No matter how well meaning, informed, supported, or trained a writer of documentation may be, the writer will not be effective until they are able to empathize with the readers and recognize that the readers approach software documentation with different backgrounds, expectations, training, and education. A good documenter is one who is able to follow the old Indian adage to "walk a mile in another's moccasins"... or, in our case, to sit in another's seat in front of a computer terminal. In fact, "user-unfriendliness [is] the inability to realize that the [user] sees the [software] in their own terms" (McWilliams, 1983).

Example of Inadequate Paper Manual

Thus far, we've covered the theory of why paper documentation has problems, but let's now turn to a concrete example of inadequate user documentation that is typical in many organizations, Figure 5(a)-(j). As you read the manual, list the features you find that make it ineffective. Then compare your list to the list that follows the manual.

Part 1: The Documentation Problem

The Problems with Paper Documentation:

▶ Theory
Example
Survey Reports

The Problem with On-line Documentation

Theory
Example
Survey Reports

USERS MANUAL FOR UPDATING   .7
THE CENTRAL MATERIALS CHARGE FILE

INTRODUCTION AND OBJECTIVES:

The Central Materials Charge File contains all Central Materials
items, arranged by catalog number. Each record includes price,
inventory, insurance, and locating information on an item. This manual
explains how to--
    Open the Central Materials account
    Call the Charge File Update program
    Retrieve records
    Update the file
        Add records
        Delete records *(at end of fiscal year only)*
        Modify records
    Verify updates
    Abort transmissions
    Exit the program
    Close the Central Materials account

PROCEDURES:
For instructions on how to use a computer terminal, consult the
users manual for the ~~computer~~ terminal. For more detailed information
on individual data items in the CM Charge File, consult FORMAT SPECI-
FICATIONS in this manual.

Instructions to press NEWLINE or XMIT ~~often~~ appear as (NL) or (XMIT).

1.0 Opening the CM account
    Be sure that prev. user has logged out & that
    ~~Be sure~~ you are in the CONV mode.
    1.1 Type HELLO (NL). Wait for: #
    1.2 Type 5,1 (NL). Wait for: Password:
    1.3 Type CM (NL). Wait for: Ready

You are in the CM account.

2.0 Calling the Charge File Update program

    2.1 Type RUN CMMOD (NL). *Wait for: ENTER THE PASSWORD*
    2.2 Type password (NL). (If you make an error, repeat the step,
         as screen instructs.)
    2.3 Press MESG (XMIT), as screen instructs. Wait for blank format
         to fill screen. See Figure 1.

You are in the Charge File Update program.

3.0 Entering the Catalog Number

    The catalog number is the control for this file. In order to
    retrieve a record or create a new one, you must enter a valid
    catalog number.

    Type the catalog number in the catalog number block (XMIT) and wait.

Figure 5 (a) Example of an inadequate paper manual.

.8

3.1 If the system rejects the number, one of two responses will appear in message block:

CATALOG NUMBER IS OUT OF RANGE
meaning: You have entered a number above 2000.

CATALOG NUMBER IS NOT NUMERIC
meaning: You have not entered a 4-digit number.

In either case, you must repeat the step.

3.2 If you have entered a valid catalog number, system will either retrieve the record you called or allow you to create a new one.

To abort transmission, type XMIT; then type ~~D~~ A (XMIT). System will report:

ACTION WAS ABORTED FOR ([record no.]

3.2.1 If you are adding a new record to the file, format blocks remain empty and, in message block, system responds:

ENTER INFORMATION FOR THIS NEW ITEM (xxx

Cursor appears to left of catalog number block.

3.2.2 If you are modifying or deleting a record, blocks fill with information. Cursor appears on command line (Figure 2), which appears at top of message block:

ENTER F=FILE, A=ABORT, D=DELETED FROM MASTER

4.0 <u>Entering Information</u>
Unless you are deleting a record, you will need to enter information. Press HOME. Cursor returns to catalog number block. TAB to blocks and modify or add information according to specifications on pages 5-9. The system will not file information that is entered incorrectly. You may move freely to any block from any other block, and you may return to a block as often as necessary.

5.0 <u>Executing a deletion, modification, or addition</u>

(You may abort ~~at~~ any time before the system executes a command to file (F) or delete (D).)

5.1 To delete a record, type D (XMIT). Wait. In the message block, the system responds:

ENTER YES TO DELETE [record no.]

This is a safeguard against erroneous deletions. Check the record number and type YES (XMIT). (YES must be typed in the first 3 slots of the line, to the left of the arrows. If YES

It only done at end of year so as not to loose storage

Figure 5 (b) Example of an inadequate paper manual.

.3

is not entered in this way, the system will automatically
abort the deletion.) In message block, system reports:

RECORD [record no.] WAS DELETED FROM MASTER

Cursor returns to catalog number block.

5.2 To file modifications or additions made in 4.0, press XMIT.
Cursor moves to command line. Then type F (XMIT). You may
continue to make changes at any time before the system
executes the F command (that is, before you press XMIT).
If you have modified or added information according to
specifications, the system will report:

[record no.] RECORD WAS LAST FILED

If any information was typed incorrectly, one of several
possible ERROR responses will appear in the message block.
Refer to ERROR INDEX and FORMAT SPECIFICATIONS. Correct the
error (XMIT) and again type F (XMIT).

6.0 <u>Verifying a deletion, modification, or addition</u>

6.1 To verify a deletion, type catalog number of deleted record
(XMIT). Wait. The system should ~~report:~~ *Respond*:

ENTER INFORMATION FOR THIS NEW ITEM (xxx

This message indicates that the *old* record was removed and the
catalog number freed. Abort the transmission.

6.2 To verify a modification or ~~deletion~~ *addition*, retrieve the record by
entering the catalog number (XMIT). When format blocks fill,
check the information, correct any errors, and refile the
record.

7.0 <u>Exiting the program</u>

Type EXIT in empty catalog number block (XMIT). Press CONV, as
screen instructs.

You have exited the CM Charge program.

8.0 <u>Closing the Central Materials account</u>

Type Bye Y (NL). Wait.

Figure 5 (c) Example of an inadequate paper manual..

.4

FORMAT SPECIFICATIONS:

Definitions of format blocks are followed by specifications and error
messages related to the blocks. Numbers correspond to block numbers
in Figure 1. Figure 2 illustrates a typical record. Blocks 1-8 are
<u>required</u> blocks. The system will not add, modify, or delete a record
unless these blocks contain information. In required blocks
containing numbers and prices, blank slots must be filled with zeros.

(1) CATALOGUE NUMBER

    Definition--Identifying number for an item carried by Central
             Materials.

    Specifications--Required block; right hand justified; 4-digit
                 number, less than 2000, greater than 0; all slots
                 must be filled.

    Error messages--

        CATALOG NUMBER OUT OF RANGE
        meaning: Number typed was greater than 2000.

        CATALOG NUMBER IS NOT NUMERIC
        meaning: Number typed was not 4 digits.

        ITEM #(IT WAS   )[record no.]
        meaning: Catalog number was accidentally altered after
                 record retrieved, or EXIT attempted with format
                 blocks filled.

(2) DESCRIPTION

    Definition--Description of item.

    Specifications--Required block; left hand justified; maximum 30 ?
                 characters; generic term should be first; use
                 spaces rather than commas to separate.
                 Examples: BELT OSTOMY 26-43 MEDIUM
                          HOLDER PENCIL EZ GRIP
                          RAZOR PREP DISPOSABLE

    Error message--

        DESCRIPTION UNKNOWN
        meaning: Description was omitted.

(3) UNIT

    Definition--Unit in which item is sold.

Figure 5 (d) Example of an inadequate paper manual.

Specifications--Required block; left hand justified.
Unit abbreviations are:

BTL--bottle	GAL--gallon
BX--box	PKG--package
CN--can	PR--pair
CS--case	RM--ream
CTN--carton	RL (ROL)--roll
DOZ--dozen	SET--set
EA--each	TUB--tube
FT--foot	YD--yard

Error message--

UNIT UNKNOWN
meaning: The unit was omitted.

(4) MIN. LEVEL

Definition--Preset minimum quantity that should be in stock.

Specifications--Required block; right hand justified; number;
4 slots; all slots must be filled; check this
block carefully since system does not compare it
with MAX. LEVEL or ACTL. QUANT.

Error message--

NON NUMERIC
meaning: One or more slots are not digits.

(5) MAX. LEVEL

Definition--Preset maximum quantity that should be in stock.

Specifications--Required block; right hand justified; number; 5
slots; all slots must be filled; check this block
carefully since system does not compare it with
MIN. LEVEL or ACTL. QUANT.

Error message--

NON NUMERIC
meaning: One or more slots are not digits.

(6) ACTL. QUANT.

Definition--Quantity of an item in stock.

Specifications--Required block; right hand justified; number
preceded by + or -; 6 slots; all slots must be
filled and + or - must be first character.
Examples: +00315; -00042. This number should
not be changed. In order to produce an audit
trail, all quantity changes must be the result
of an issue, receipt, or adjustment.

Figure 5 (e) Example of an inadequate paper manual.

Error message--

NON SIGNED NO.
meaning: + or - has been omitted or incorrectly placed.

NON NUMERIC
meaning: One or more slots after sign are not digits.

(7) DEPARTMENT PRICE

Definition--Price charged to departments.

Specifications--Required block; right hand justified; decimal is
         middle slot (5th slot from left or right); there
         are 4 slots to left of decimal and 4 decimal places
         Examples: 0014.6432; 0000.7839

Error message--

ERROR IN NON NUMERIC LIKE ####.####
meaning: One or more slots are not digits or decimal has
         been misplaced.

(8) PATIENT PRICE

Definition--Price charged to patients.

Specifications--Required block; right hand justified; decimal is
         3rd slot from right; there are 4 slots to left of
         decimal and 2 decimal places; all slots must be filled
         Examples: 0376.21; 0004.03

Error message--

ERROR IN NON NUMERIC LIKE ####.##
meaning: One or more slots are not digits or decimal has
         been misplaced.

(9) BLUE CROSS CODE

Definition--Alphanumeric code identifying an item paid for by
         Blue Cross.

Specifications--Not a required block; left hand justified; 2
         letters, 5 digits.

(10) BLUE CROSS PRICE

Definition--Price paid by Blue Cross.

Specifications--Not a required block; right hand justified; decimal
         is 3rd slot from right; there are 4 slots to left of
         decimal and 2 decimal places.

Figure 5 (f) Example of an inadequate paper manual.

(11)   INSURANCE SWITCH

Definition--Numeric code signifying which sponsors will pay
            for the item and conditions for payment.

Specifications--Not a required block; each of the 5 sponsors
               is assigned a slot in this 5-slot block:

                    slot 1--Texas Rehabilitation Commission (TRC)
                    slot 2--State Crippled Children's Service (SCC)
                    slot 3--Medicare (M)
                    slot 4--Medicaid (M)
                    slot 5--Blue Cross (B)

               Slots are filled or left blank according to this
               key:

               (blank)--Insurance will pay.
               1--Insurance never pays.
               2--Insurance will not pay if inpatient.
               3--Insurance will not pay if outpatient.

               Example: A block in which the 1st, 2nd, 3rd,
               and 5th slots were blank and the 4th slot con-
               tained a 1 would mean that all sponsors except
               Medicaid pay for the item.

(12)   LOCATION

Definition--Either an alphanumeric code signifying location of
            item in storeroom or W signifying warehouse item.

Specifications--Not a required block; alphanumeric is 1 letter
               and 2 digits: letter=aisle, 1st digit=cabinet,
               2nd digit=shelf.

(13)   TRANS. SLOT

Disregard this block; it is for program use only.

(14)   WAREHOUSE

Definition--Letter code signifying where item is stocked.

Specifications--Required block; slot is filled according to this
               key:

                    W--Item is stocked at warehouse only.
                    S--Item is stocked at storeroom only.
                    B--Item is stocked at both warehouse and
                       storeroom.

Figure 5 (g) Example of an inadequate paper manual.

.10

Error message--

    ENTRY IS NOT "B", "W", or "S"
    meaning: A character other than B, W, or S was entered.

(15) CENTL. SUPP. *PATIENT ISSUE*

Definition--Code indicating items sold to patients.

Specifications--Not a required block; asterisk signifies
              that the item is sold to patients; blank
              slot signifies that the item is sold to TIRR
              department rather than to patients.

Error message--

    ENTRY IS NOT " " or "*"
    meaning: A character other than * was entered.

Figure 5 (h) Example of an inadequate paper manual.

ERROR INDEX   .11

Error messages are keyed to format blocks. ✓ 15.

Message	Block Item #	Page #
CATALOG NUMBER IS NOT NUMERIC	1	5
CATALOG NUMBER IS OUT OF RANGE	1	5
DESCRIPTION UNKNOWN	2	5
ENTRY IS NOT " " or "*"	15	9
ENTRY IS NOT ✗, "B", "W", or "S"	14	9
ITEM # (IT WAS)[record no.]	1	5
NON NUMERIC	4-6	6-7
NON NUMERIC LIKE ####.####	7	7
NON NUMERIC LIKE ####.##	8	7
NON SIGNED NO.	6	7
UNIT UNKNOWN	3	6

Figure 5 (i) Example of an inadequate paper manual.

SUMMARY OF PROCEDURES   *.12*

Instructions to press NEWLINE *or* XMIT appear as (NL) or (XMIT).

Open CM account:	Type HELLO (NL). Type 5,1 (NL). Type CM (NL). Wait.
Run Charge File Update Program:	Type RUN CMMOD (NL). *Wait for:* ENTER THE PASSWORD Type password (NL). Press MESG (XMIT). Wait for format.
Modify:	Type catalog no. (XMIT). Wait for blocks to fill. Press HOME. TAB to blocks and type changes (XMIT). Type F (XMIT). Verify.
Delete:	Type catalog no. (XMIT). Wait for blocks to fill. Type D (XMIT). Check record no. Type YES (XMIT). Verify.
Add:	Type catalog no. (XMIT). Wait for go-ahead. TAB to blocks and type information (XMIT). Type F (XMIT). Verify.
Abort:	XMIT. Type A (XMIT).
Exit:	Type EXIT in blank catalog no. block (XMIT). Press CONV.
Close CM account:	Type Bye Y (NL). Wait.

Figure 5 (j) Example of an inadequate paper manual.

Problems with the Example User Manual

"...a professor learning to use a programmable calculator rapidly came to the conclusion that the manual contained misprints and other errors and could not, therefore, be used: 'at a certain point, you'll go crazy if you don't assume that the book has made a mistake'" (Carroll, 1990, Chapter 2).

"I think not knowing how something ends makes us apprehensive; it prohibits us from understanding how something was done while we frantically try to guess how it might end....While suspense has its place, it does tend to produce anxiety, which is probably not an optimum way to receive new information. If you know the ending, you can relax and enjoy the manner in which something is being presented....An audience will be more receptive to new information if they aren't kept in suspense, made anxious trying to guess where someone is going. Many people can't really listen to an idea until key questions about it have been answered in their minds"(Wurman, 1989, 128-9).

You should have found problems in at least the following seven areas. The solutions to these problems are discussed in the following steps of Part 2.

Layout and Style Problems

The layout of the individual pages and the writing style used in the manual are ineffective because:

- The style is an ordinary prose and paragraph style that is hard to skim and scan.

- The specifics of interactions between the system and the operator are buried rather than highlighted.

- There is an overuse of paragraph numbering.

Organizational Problems

The document is not organized to aid the reader's search for information. For instance:

- There's no preface telling the who, what, and when behind the document.

- The order of presentation of material announced in the "Introduction and Objectives" is not followed.

- The order of the "Format Specs" is not clearly apparent to the reader (it is based on the physical layout of the screen that is never shown).

- *Delete*, *modify*, and *add* are intertwined and not clearly separated.

- After paragraph 3.1 tells you what happens when you have an error, the following paragraph 3.2 tells you what happens when you enter the information correctly—in other words, first they tell you the wrong way of doing it and then the right way.

- The summary of all the procedures is on the last page rather than on the first page.

Audience Analysis Problems

Because there was a poor analysis of reader needs, certain important information is missing. For example:

- There are no screens, even though this is a screen-driven application.

- The diagnostics are not clearly indicated.

- Figures are referenced (Figure 1 and 2), but never appear.

- No reports or source documents are shown so we have no idea where the all-important catalog number comes from.

- The manual assumes that you know how to get in the CONV mode in 1.0, but it never defines this mode.

- In a few places the manual tells you to wait, but it never says specifically how long to wait.

The Macintosh's clock with hands that move while the system is processing information is a simple yet effective way to indicate "wait."

Consistency Problems

The manual was never edited well, thus there are a number of internal inconsistencies. For example:

- Paragraph 2.0 tells you that you have entered the "Charge File Update program." But when you go to exit this program in paragraph 7.0, you are informed that you have exited the "CM Charge program."

- Paragraph 3.1 says there are two responses you will get if you have an erroneous catalog number. However, under "Catalogue Number" in the Format Specifications, you find there are actually three possible error messages.

- The first paragraph under "Format Specifications" says that "Blocks 1-8 are required blocks." However, on close investigation of the later specifications, you find there are more required blocks than just these.

Words to avoid when saying how to press function keys include: "depress" which suggest a less than optimal psychological state of documenter mind; "hit" which invites the user to use brute force; and "mash"...no kidding, one manual asked users to "Mash the ENTER key."

- Sometimes you are told to "Press XMIT," sometimes "Type XMIT," and sometimes just "(XMIT)," all of which mean the same thing.

- The numbering for sections and subsections used throughout the pages is not consistent [e.g., sometimes it's 3.0 and sometimes it's (3)].

- "Catalog" is spelled as both "catalogue" and "catalog."

- In the "Format Specifications," the "Warehouse" block is filled according to the key "W, S, and B." But the message that signals an error is ordered "B, W, and S."

From this manual's lack of consistency in editing, we can derive the first quick documentation QA test—*The Consistency Test.* "Reading is a psycholinguistic guessing game" (Smith F., 1971), and we want our readers to always guess right. Rather than excitement, suspense, or novelty, clarity of presentation becomes the primary guiding principle, and this means that the paper or on-line document should be predictably consistent in its presentation of information: layout should be consistent, transitions from topic to topic or screen to screen obvious, wording of pages or screens changing only when they have to rather than to demonstrate vocabulary dexterity, and organization always announced in advanced. Documentation writers, in contrast to creative writers, have it easy because documentation readers are premotivated; they have a problem, and they look to the manual to solve it.

Poor Reference Aid Problems

There are poor reference aids. For instance:

- There is no table of contents.
- The index on page 9 incorrectly cites page numbers.

Again, from the problems in this manual's lack of reference aids, we can derive a second quick documentation QA test—*The Reference Aid Test.* A good quick indication of the quality of a manual can be had by simply counting the number of these reference aids present in a manual (Pakin and Associates, 1978). The best manuals include:

Reference Aid	Should Include
Table of contents	Two or more levels of detail
List of illustration/figures /tables	Numbers and titles

Preface	Related documentation, how best to use manual
Chapter table of contents	Two or more levels of detail
Headings	Two or more levels with hierarchy clearly indicated
Figure captions	Meaningful summary of graphic (e.g., *National Geographic*-type expanded captions)
Tabs	Titled and printed on both sides
Error message appendix	Should become superfluous if error on-line messages are specific enough for a user to enact the remedy (e.g., **not** the Macintosh's System Bomb #38)
Glossary	Approximately 2% of the total numbers of pages in the book
Index	Approximately 4% of the total numbers of pages in the book; "See," and "See also" should be used.
Quick Reference Card	Summary of major product capabilities

Update Problems

There are ineffective, hard-to-read, handwritten updates suggesting that there was never any plan for updating.

Language Problems

Finally, the document demonstrates a poor choice of language in regard to the audience:

- Words such as *files* and *records* are used without explanation.

- There is no glossary.

- The word "abort" seems inappropriate in the setting of the system.

- The words "execute" and "key" are used interchangeably even though they do not appear to mean the same thing.

- Why is "should" used so often. Either the software performs the task or not; there is no whim involved.

What Led to These Problems

If we could point to a single reason for all the problems in this manual, it would be the inadequate translation of the writer's source material (the software design specifications) to user documentation. It is probably safe to assume that the finished user manual we see here is much like the original software design documentation—documentation written for an audience of programmers and data processing managers. The documenter should have digested the information given to them in the source design documentation, examined how the user was actually going to use the program in their environment, and then reorganized and rewritten that information in a way a user could read, use, and readily reference. At best, the current translation is incomplete.

However, as Weiss noted, good documentation will not make up for poor software design—in fact, good documentation usually shows off how bad the design really is. And this example is a case in point!

- Why is it necessary for the user to left-justify fields with 0's, [Format Specifications (1)]?

- Error messages are too generic (Format Specifications (1): "CATALOG NUMBER IS NOT NUMERIC" can discriminate between both alphabetic and numeric entries as well as entries that aren't left-justified with 0's

- Why must we sometimes abbreviate items for the three-block "Unit" field (i.e., "BX" and "CN" when we should be able to enter "BOX" and "CAN")? Sometimes we don't abbreviate (i.e., "SET" for "set"); and sometimes we are given two options (i.e., "RL" or "ROL" for "roll")

Rather than defensive programming, what we see here is "booby trap" programming that sees how effectively it can ensnare and confuse the user. What we also see demonstrated by this point is that the documenter should be part of the design team right from the very beginning to ensure that defensive programming takes place.

What Surveys Find Concerning Paper Documentation

Part 1: The Documentation Problem

The Problems with Paper Documentation:

Theory
Example
Survey Reports

The Problem with On-line Documentation

Theory
Example
Survey Reports

Thus far we have looked at the theory of why paper documentation has problems, and we have seen a concrete example. But another way to gain insights into the problems of paper documentation is to look at what marketing surveys have found. Note the common reoccurring findings summarized in Table 1.

Maynard (1982) reported on a 15-year survey of users carried out by Xerox, Control Data, and Scientific Data Systems. Beard and Callamars (1983) reported on a parallel survey carried out with military users. Both surveys found that the major complaints were:

• Manuals were software-oriented rather than function-oriented.

• Manuals did not have enough examples.

• The manuals did not have enough reference aids.

Major Consistent Findings For Paper Documentation	Xerox, Control Data, Scientific (Maynard, 1982)	AT&T (1986)	Microsoft (Borland, 1984)	PC-User Group (Wilton, 1985)
More task-orientation	X	X	X	
More tutorials		X	X	X
Improved reference aids	X	X	X	X
More accuracy		X		X
More illustrations		X	X	X

Table 1. Reoccurring findings in user surveys of paper documentation.

AT&T 1986 External Documentation Market Survey

This survey, done in 1986 by an independent market research firm for AT&T, identified documentation features that both users and dealers thought were important factors in selecting one software package over another—what features sell or do not sell a software package. The survey queried 170 users, 40 dealers, and 12 nationally recognized experts.

Some of the major themes were that information in AT&T manuals should be

- Easy to find: better reference aids were recommended

- Easy to understand: not assume too much, have graphics, and be task-oriented

- Complete, accurate, and up-to-date

Some of this survey's findings were unique in that they found that

- Two thirds of the respondents preferred regular page size, although 82% said it was unimportant.

- Over 80% of respondents said that the thickness of a manual does not influence their buy decisions. Experienced users especially said this. We can speculate that the experienced users were banking on the idea of VTM—*virtually thin manual*. They know that a thick manual can be virtually a thin manual if it has good reference aids, and they also know that they will probably never read the whole manual.

- Sample screens, artwork and drawings motivate purchases.

- Only 27% said color was important.

- Absence of an index was a definite reason to avoid purchasing a software product.

cf.

An IBM survey on page size preference (Thing, 1984) found in one test that 90% of those surveyed preferred the small size. Mind you, the survey test was done in such a way that although the the content was identical in the traditional size and the small size manuals compared, the testers were only allowed to put the paper documentation in their laps and not on a table or desk.

Microsoft Corporation Documentation Survey (Borland, 1984)

This survey used four focus groups (each focused on a particular line of products: database management, word processing, programming languages, and spreadsheets), and they totaled 34 members in all. All had at least one year of experience. (What is interesting about this survey is the differentiation in needs between Microsoft application "end users" and "language users" of their programming languages, but I will only report on the end users' comments, since that is the subject of this book.) The survey found that

This survey was done differently from the others because it used "focus groups" that tend to be more far ranging in their comments.

"Spokesman for San Francisco's Exploratorium, the world's finest science museum, 'The exhibit should be equally interesting to a four-year-old or a person with an advanced degree" (Nelson, 1987, DM-38).

- End users wanted task-oriented tutorials. The need for "layered documentation serving both beginners and experienced users was repeatedly brought up.

- End users wanted screen illustrations and terms explained in glossaries.

- End users definitely wanted reference cards which listed first all the commands and then the tasks with commands used to complete them.

- End users wanted a feature-oriented/command index as well as a task-oriented index.

- End users wanted a task-oriented organization

- Everyone wanted a "phone book" (reference manual) that comprehensively described all the features of the product.

- Everyone wanted troubleshooting guides.

PC User Group Survey

Finally, a survey was done of 241 microcomputer owners (Wilton, 1985). In Table 2, observe the contrast between what readers said they wanted and what was actually delivered.

Do You Agree or Disagree?	Agree	Disagree
Manuals should accomodate all users vs. Manuals do accomodate all	86	7
users	16	58
Tutorials are usually helpful vs. Many manuals omit	66	12
tutorials	65	8
Some manuals are too wordy vs. Illustrations are adequate	70	15
in number	18	54
Information is easy to find vs. Manuals bury important	11	67
information	89	4

Table 2. Contrast between what users want and what users get.

Why On-line Documentation?

"CD-ROM is a low-cost publishing medium. This technology makes it possible to replicate more than 500 megabytes of information at a marginal cost of less than $10. To the publisher or printer, this is the equivalent of reproducing a page at a minimal cost—less than a small fraction of a penny. This cost of reproducing information was—and still is—the lowest known to man" (Mathur, 1989, 628).

Part 1: The Documentation Problem

The Problems with Paper Documentation:

Theory
Example
Survey Reports

The Problem with On-line Documentation

Theory
Example
Survey Reports

On-line documentation is defined as follows:

Communication designed to be presented on VDT screens in order to ease interactions between computer software and the individuals who manage, audit, operate, or maintain it.

On-line documentation goes beyond the limits of traditional paper manuals because it integrates text, graphics, animation, sound effects, and database organizational schemas (Brockmann and McCauley, 1984).

On-line documentation will include ever larger portions of the user documentation effort as two different marketplace forces increase. First, with the large-scale digital storage data of CD-ROMs, magneto-optical discs, and other mass storage devices, data can be stored and distributed more cheaply than on paper. Second, the demand for customized, timely, and accurate user documentation of software products—a demand rapidly outstripping the medium of paper— continues to grow.

Additionally, on-line user documentation solves four other problems associated with paper user documentation: their static organization, the massive physical appearance of many manuals, their passive role for audiences, and their inconvenient packaging.

Paper has a problem of static organization. Paper manuals, no matter how well planned and produced, must always adopt the author's structural plan. The structure of a paper manual, as Rosen and Furlow (1983) point out, "determines such interdependent elements as how its sections and subsections are marked, how its table of contents is set up, how things like dividers are used, and so forth." No matter what decision is made regarding the structure of a paper manual, it cannot encompass all possible audience needs. A paper manual inherently cannot be all things to all people.

Paper has the problem of its massive physical appearance. "Apparency" is a word Rosen and Furlow coined to describe many paper manuals' massive physical appearance. If a paper manual is to describe and explain adequately a complex application, chances are great that it will be a physically imposing volume.

This physical size tends to intimidate the reader and makes the manual look "hard to read."

Figure 6. The massive physical appearance of many good manuals.

"Another began the experiment by picking up the Owner's Guide and telling us that his style was to read everything thoroughly. He actually read for less than nine minutes before switching his attention to the system and next referred to the manual almost two hours later" (Carroll, 1989, Chapter 3).

Paper manuals enforce a passive role on audiences. Most readers of user manuals only come to a manual when they have a problem, and most readers employ skimming and scanning techniques that avoid the need for reader motivation devices. Nonetheless, we can increase reader attention and interest in our documentation if we write manuals that have more drama and give the reader a feeling of interaction (Kelly D., 1983). Minimalist design is one technique we will use to increase the sense of interaction, but on-line documentation will increase this sense of interaction even more.

The use of on-line documentation will probably increase due to its convenience:

> "According to Chris Morgan [vice president of the Lotus Development Corp], the Cambridge, Mass. firm decided to offer on-line documentation because 'We foresaw that people would need this kind of help. It allows people to instantly go to the screen without stopping what they were doing to go to a manual. It better serves the needs of users'" (Santarelli, 1984).

Or, as put in a little more pointed manner:

> "Our survey...has made it absolutely clear that even if effective documentation is provided, it will not be read by the majority of users. They will naturally expect all the

information to be in one place and that place to be the interface with the computer" (James G., 1981).

Thus, on-line documentation can answer many of the shortcomings of paper manuals.

Why Should Paper Manual Writers Care About On-line Documentation?

The Marketplace Change

The first major reason why we should care about on-line documentation is the simple fact that a user comes to know about a product primarily through the human communication about the product. This communication is not made up of user manuals alone; it also consists of system messages, system controls, and on-line tutorials. In fact, it is now becoming apparent to those in the computer industry that no product exists for users apart from the communication about it.

There are two alternative views of what a software product is (Talbott, 1983). The conventional view of the relationship of the product to the communication about it can be termed the "No Extended Helping Hand of Intelligibility" view and is illustrated in Figure 7.

This view is a holdover from the days when products were more physical. In that era, the first thing you did with a product was to sense it directly (e.g., feeling the car move left as you turn the steering wheel left, or the toast goes down as you press the lever down). Only later would you read the manual to learn about the available controls. The manual was a totally separate entity. (This approach has probably given rise to the saying, "When all else fails, read the manual.")

On the other hand, software is not a tangible product; it is only experienced through communication about it. We can go one step further, as in Figure 8, and suggest that the product does not exist separately and distinctly from the language, sound, graphics, music, etc., used to describe it—the "Extended Helping Hand of Intelligibility" view. In fact, the product the users employ to solve their business or organizational problems, and for which they are paying is not the software innards—code, algorithms, and structured modules—but the interface options and controls and their introduction to it in user manuals, screens, menus, and on-line tutorials. As Heckel said in *The Elements of Friendly Software Design* (1984):

"The reality of what our programs do is of no importance to the user. Only the mental model of what they do is important. Our task as designers is not so much to design and create software that carries out a function as it is to design and create a believable communication illusion or model for our users."

Windows, Icons, Mouse, and Pointer

Or, as the inventor of the WIMP design Alan Kay wrote in *Scientific American* (1984):

"The user interface was once the last part of a system to be designed. Now it is the first. It is recognized as being primary because to novices and professionals alike, what is presented to one's senses is one's computer. The 'user illusion'...is the simplified myth everyone builds to explain (and make guesses about) the system actions and what should be done next" (54, 58).

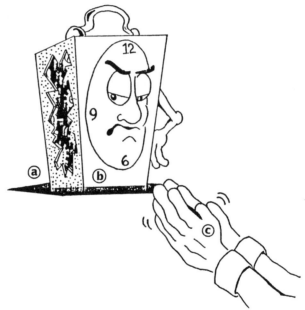

Figure 7. No extended helping hand of intelligibility: (a) software code internals, (b) human/computer interface, (c) system intelligibility.

If these views are correct, products that present themselves with built-in intelligibility are the ones that will survive. Thus the companies and organizations that employ us will require more and more of our specialized expertise in communication forms beyond paper manuals. We will become system designers who supply the necessary communication element to the software.

Redefining the Technical Communicator

"...as more and more people need less and less explanation about computers (and as more and more people work on man-machine interaction), the technical communicator in this high-tech industry must change his orientation; quit thinking so much in terms of print technology...Printed documentation will probably never be eliminated altogether, and its decrease will not necessarily be swift. But the change will come, and as it does, the communicator may still be the writer, but he will 'write' with a new medium" (Young, 1989, 200).

Economically, our profession is at the right place at the right time (Kelley, 1984). But will this growth continue forever, or are we destined to become the unemployed workers of year 2000? A number of trends are appearing and a number of voices are being raised that have disturbing tidings. What should we do when a measure of software effectiveness becomes how little documentation is required to accompany its use (Crenshaw and Philipose, 1983; Kay, 1983)? What we must do to survive the decline of paper manuals is to broaden our area of expertise and our corporate contribution—broaden it to include on-line documentation.

Figure 8. Extended helping hand of intelligibility: (a) software code internals, (b) human/computer interface, (c) system intelligibility.

On-line Documentation Is Like Paper...But

If we are going to be asked to develop more on-line documentation, if that is part and parcel of the coming change in roles for the technical communicator, then one lucky break is that 75% of what we need to know about on-line documentation comes right out of paper documentation. When moving to on-line documentation, we don't need to discard the techniques and ideas of effective paper documentation; 75% of them are perfectly transferrable.

For instance, we still need to plan on-line documentation to be task-oriented, to include visualizations, and to be organized to fit readers' expectations. We will still need to design the format and language to fit the reading behaviors of adults. We still need to edit our on-line documentation and get it reviewed and field tested. Some of the current problems with on-line documentation occur because designers of this medium have forgotten or overlooked just these concepts. Consider, for example, a report on improving the on-line Help messages in a VAX/VMS system (Magers, 1983). The results of the improvements had a

> "dramatic effect on performance in the task. The users of the modified system took less time to complete the task, used more commands (approximately twice as many per minute), made fewer errors in the commands they used, used Help more often, consulted the manual less often, and asked fewer questions" (Magers, 1983, 48).

The quantitative comparison of the original and modified system is shown in the Table 3.

Measure	Original System	Modified System
Total task completion time (min.)	75.6	52.0
Commands with errors (%)	37.9%	17.9%
Number of references to manuals	11.1	1.8
Questions asked of consultant	6.4	2.0
Total number of Helps used	22.4	60.8
Commands used/min.	.99	1.95
Total number of commands used	70.8	98.5

Table 3. Effects of improved VAX/VMS system Help messages.

Of the nine total improvements Magers made, only three were changes that could not be derived from good principles of paper documentation design. The six improvements that could be derived from paper book design included:

- Making the message more task-oriented (see Step 1 in this book)

- Using examples (see Step 3 in this book)

- Providing command synonyms such as we would in using "See" and "See also" in an index (see Step 3, Indexes in this book)

- Eliminating jargon (see Step 4 in this book)

- Adding tutorial information (see Step 1 in this book)

- Scrolling rather than paging (see "Structured Writing" in Step 3 in this book)

The three additional changes Magers made that derived from on-line experience included:

- Replacing a Help command with a Help key so that the knowledge needed to access Help is much less and it's readily apparent

- Making the command syntax more flexible

- Making the Help context-sensitive rather than requiring access by keyword

And, in some cases, on-line documentation is quite consciously attempting to replicate the book on the screen:

"Several systems have advocated a book metaphor so that the on-line version of information closely matches printed formats, even if there is no printed version. The rationale is that systems presenting on-line documents will be easier to learn and use if they match the way books look and work... NaviText™ SAM is like a book, but it attempts to make better use of the information structure needed by power users: the tables of contents with varying amounts of detail are replaced by a dynamic outliner; the index is replaced by keywords attached to structures; cross-references are made dynamic to allow jumps to related information; references to outside sources can be partially expanded or used as a citation index; running headings on printed pages are replaced by context information; format to reflect information type is made dynamic, e.g. information of generally low interest can be made invisible while other types of information can be highlighted" (Perlman, 1989, 71).

However, in the evolution from paper to screen, we need to be sure we do not take our word-processed documents, display them on screens, and call them on-line documents (Price L., 1981; Richier and Thompson, 1974). Such "pseudo-on-line" documents fail both to make full use of the new communication medium of the computer screen and because paper-based methods of displaying information are not 100% transferable to screen displays.

Figures 9 and 10 are two examples of this pseudo-on-line documentation that have many problems. Both were part of an advertising pamphlet that was a collection of photocopies of the application's screens. What you see below is what you would see on the screen.

```
                                                  SCREEN- 18 OF 30
********************************************************************************

        QUESTIONS for the PROGRAMMER ... who LOVES to PROGRAM, PROGRAM,
                PROGRAM, but HATES to DOCUMENT (did I miss anyone?)!!

        1.    Would you LOVE to get rid of that BORING task of writing
              OPERATOR INSTRUCTIONS forever ... by letting the OPERATORS
              do it?  They can do it FASTER, put it where they can FIND
              it again, and then even UNDERSTAND it if they ever need it.
              All you do is EXPLAIN the task ONCE.  TRY "███"!!!

        2.    Will you spend the REST of your natural LIFE having to
              answer questions about an OPERATOR SELECTION since people
              are too LAZY to read your "HARD COPY" guide?  TRY "███"!!!

        3.    Are there TIMES when you program for someone at NITE &/or
              WEEKENDS only to spend the next FULL business day on the
              phone explaining what CHANGES you made?  TRY "███"!!!

        4.    Wouldn't it be nice to have some FREE FORMAT space for each
              MENU# to leave some quick NOTES to yourself on file names,
              specs, descriptions, procedure names, etc.?  TRY "███"!!!


********************************************************************************
```

Figure 9. One of two sample Help screens that exhibit pseudo-on-line documentation.

Descenders are the parts of letters that jut out below the baseline such as the bottom of the letters g, j, y, and p.

With regard to physical problems, both screens exhibit unusually compressed descenders and a minimum amount of space between each line. Neither screen has the necessary white space to compensate for these problems. Also, the white space that is used is only "passive" white space—it surrounds the information

CAMROSE LUTHERAN COLLEGE
LIBRARY

like a picture frame rather than actively separating and discriminating between ideas for the reader (such as the white space on this page which separates the left-side column quotations from the main body of text to the right). And the major method of formatting for emphasis, the use of all upper case words, is done much too frequently.

With regard to organization, you have only one screen navigational aid available, "Screen 20 of 30," to tell you where you are. This isn't very helpful because it only gives a sense of linearity and no sense of the relative hierarchy of information. Also the screen gives you no idea of what to do next, such as how to get to the next screen, or how to quit. With no suggestion of control, users may feel as though the system, not they, are in control of the interaction. And finally, Help information fills the screen, so any previous work is lost.

```
                                                 SCREEN- 20 OF 30
*********************************************************************************

         QUESTIONS for the CRT TERMINAL OPERATOR ......... (OUR HERO!!!):

         1.   Aren't you TIRED of asking QUESTIONS ... that get answered
              at a THOUSAND miles per hour ... in WORDS that don't make
              much SENSE ... by a PERSON who seems PUT OUT that you ASK?
              Wouldn't you rather SIT in your OWN seat, USE your OWN
              terminal to FIND the answers QUICKLY and EASILY, GET the
              INFORMATION in words you can UNDERSTAND, and go back to
              work WITHOUT hasseling anyone?  (YOU DESERVE "███"!)

         2.   Wouldn't your PREFER to spend a FEW minutes each day for
              a while ENTERING what you do on a FREE FORMAT screen that
              is EASY to get to and is FUN to do ... so if you're gone ...
              SICK, VACATION, or PROMOTION ... your REPLACEMENT doesn't
              have to go through what you did when you FIRST tried to
              learn?  (YOU NEED "███"!)

         3.   Wouldn't it be GREAT to get AHEAD in DATA PROCESSING if you
              could LEARN more about what is DONE in YOUR company ... on
              YOUR own time ... and at your own SPEED?  (YOU WANT "███"!)


*********************************************************************************
```

Figure 10. Second of two sample Help screens that exhibit pseudo-on-line documentation.

Beyond these uniquely on-line problems, we can see a problem with false camaraderie and misplaced humor. Numbers are used when simple bullets would do—in fact, the numbers make one conjecture that these are options or menu choices.

Overall, because this material was simply a photocopy of screens, it was neither good paper documentation nor good on-line documentation. None of the capabilities of a screen were used. In fact, we have simply a slavish imitation of paper writing presented on a screen.

Why does pseudo-on-line documentation exist when it is clearly an inadequate approach to on-line documentation? V. Stibic answers this question in the following way:

Marshall McLuhan (1969) noted: "We live in the rear-view mirror."

> "Imitation of old manual techniques or anthropomorphization of techniques—technical solutions simulating human work—arises due to the inertia of human thinking and a limited imagination unable to forsake the old manual methods when trying to mechanize them.... For example, output data displayed on the screen of data processing systems are often nothing more than slavish imitations of preprinted forms; their designers treat the screen as a paper form, characterized by fixed preprinted fields. They ignore the specific properties of a screen, i.e., its flexibility" (Stibic, 1982; see also Gaines and Shaw, 1984).

Part 1: The Documentation Problem

The Problems with Paper Documentation:

Theory
Example
Survey Reports

The Problem with On-line Documentation

Theory
Example
Survey Reports

The solution to this pseudo-on-line documentation is, as Geoffrey James points out, that there needs to be a basic conceptual change as the documentation writer moves from paper to screen (Sickler, 1983; James G., 1985)—our communication model of documentation should become less of a book and more of a "database":

> "To paraphrase, a book is a book, whether it is stored on paper, floppy-disk, or high-density disk. All the inflexibility of having size, format, and content predetermined still remains....Suppose we throw away the idea of documentation as being pieces of paper and model documentation into a database. A database is by its nature fluid and can be dynamically updated as quickly as a software product can be modified. A database is multipurpose, because the reader, not the writer, decides what he wants to read" (James G., 1985).

Example of Inadequate On-line Documentation

Having observed that we will be doing more on-line documentation, that it is very much like paper documentation and yet not a slavish-imitation of it, let us look at two specific screens of on-line documentation. And like the earlier manual we analyzed, imagine you had to use these two screens, and jot down the problems you encounter with them.

Then compare your list to the one presented here. The specific problems are quite typical and will be what we will solve in the following chapters.

The two screens below are from an unnamed company in Sydney, Australia (not Perkin-Elmer, but evidently using its equipment). The situation is that you are sitting at one console and you need to set up a console for processing rainfall data that's alongside. If you were called in right now, what improvements would you suggest the designers make to the screens?

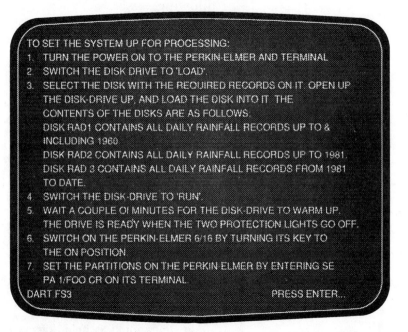

Figure 11. The first of two sample Help screens from Australia .

In Part 1, Step 1, we shall observe that: uppercase lettering slows down the readers speed because it alters the expected shapes of words, and that most serifed typefaces (such as the one used in this text with the little lines drawn across the bottoms and tops of letters) are more readable than sans serifed letters.

Some of the changes you would probably suggest are:

- Get rid of the all uppercase lettering—books are not written that way and neither should screens.

- Use some of the emphasis techniques of a screen such as reverse video to indicate what is text, what is entered by the user, and what is the system's response.

- Use more headings to improve the reader's sense of the text's organization.

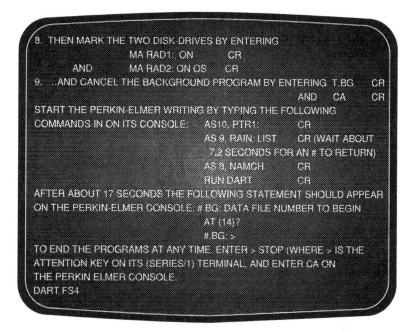

Figure 12. The second of two sample Help screens from Australia.

- Reveal how to maneuver through the information long before its present placement at the end of the second screen.

- Where in the earlier paper documentation we suffered from lack of precision—how long do we have to wait after typing "Bye"—now we suffer from too much precision—who has a watch that will tell you when 7.2 seconds has elapsed?

- Increase the amount of white space by being less verbose, using tables, decreasing the line length ("measure"), and perhaps breaking up the information on more than two screens.

A well-designed screen we shall observe in Part 1, Step 1 has at least 50% white space. "Line measure" is the technical term to describe the width of a line of text across the page. And as we shall observe in Part 1, Step 1, the ideal width is somewhere between 1.67 and 4.5 inches.

- Improve the reader's ability to distinguish between textual commentary and directions and what one is supposed to enter by typing (i.e., **SE PA 1/F000**), what one is supposed to enter by pressing a function key (i.e., **CR**), and what the system's response is to one's actions (i.e., **#.BG**).

- The screens are inconsistent. What happened to the numbered steps after step 9.

- A sense of "where I am" in the on-line documentation, and "how do I get there" are both missing.

- There are no navigational aids such as screen titles or screen numbers.

- There is no evident way to navigate from screen to screen.

- Finally, these two screens are just inconvenient because they wipe out a screen's worth of work that one was working on before asking for Help, and now one has to keep all this information in memory as they toggle back to the application program.

All of these suggestions would definitely improve the design of these Australian Help screens, and they all come right out of our experience with working with paper.

What Are On-line Documentation's Unique Problems?

On-line documentation is user communication designed to be given to an audience solely through the medium of a VDT screen. It can range from fairly simple-looking messages, commands, and menus to complex hypertext documents with hundreds of thousands of screens. The best way, however, to describe this new medium of communication is by comparing and contrasting it with a medium we already know: paper. On-line documentation is different from paper display of user information in three important ways: physical differences that affect any individual screen; organizational differences that can be seen when a number of screens must function together; and rhetorical differences that can be seen when a large number of screens must function together.

Physical Differences Between Paper and On-line Documentation

A user or reader always perceives a page [screen] as being more filled with type than it actually is (Tinker, 1965).

The basic differences between paper and screen presentation of information are the decreased size, legibility, and resolution of screens, and the presence of display features on screens (blinking, color, reverse video, interactive responses) not previously manipulated by many documenters.

There is smaller space on a VDT screen than on an 8 1/2 by 11 inch sheet of paper. Rubens and Krull (1985) note that the ratio of maximum number of characters on a piece of paper to a typical 80-character by 24-line screen is nearly 2 to 1. A well-designed page of printed material usually has a text density (print to white space) of 50%—only 50% of the page should have type on it. Well-designed text screens should employ at least this amount of white space, and for menus or other items that will be quickly scanned, some researchers are suggesting that the text density be somewhere between 15% and 25% (Dancheck, 1976; Reid, 1984; Tullis, 1981). This means that an uncluttered, easy-to-read menu should have around 75 to 80 words, and the rest should be blank space (Hurly, Laucht, and Hlynka, 1985):

> "Not only is the area smaller, the amount of detailed information that can be displayed in that area is less. Contrast the 1250-dot-per-inch typeset paper document with the typical 70-100-dot-per-inch computer screen. For even minimal legibility, text and graphics on the computer screen must be larger than on paper documents. Medieval illuminated manuscripts and children's books average about 200 words per page. An engineering handbook may contain 1500 words per page, along with intricate formulae and diagrams. A typical Help display, incorporating recommended white space and text large enough to be legible, may hold as few as 50 to 100 words" (Horton, 1989, 152).

"The consequences of this difference in the amount of information per page is, first, it increases the amount of information one must sort through to locate relevant facts. Second, the learner will be more likely to read all of the information on the page" (Duffy, et al., 1987, 9).

However, rather than having the suggested density of even a well-designed page, "most studies of on-line information find 77% of the width (80 characters maximum) and 83% of the depth (24 line maximum) being used" (Jackson, 1979). Thus, rather than diminishing the amount of information to accommodate the diminished space available on screen, most designers are crowding information on a screen in order to get it equal in quantity of words to a piece of paper. The problem is that a screen is not a piece of paper. The additional blank space is needed because of the diminished legibility of text on a screen.

To accommodate the new small size of screens, writers will have to chunk information in smaller pieces than currently on paper with its paragraphs. And added to this problem of chunking information in smaller pieces is the sense of "information chunk autonomy." Even though a screen is much smaller than space on a page given to a paragraph, and even though more white space is required to overcome screen legibility problems, users of on-line documentation expect the same type of rhetorical structure, closure, and organization from a screen as from a paragraph. And, if scrolling of text is permitted, creators of on-line documentation will never be able to give the screen any organizational cohesion because they will never know how information will be exhibited to readers.

And not only will these smaller chunks be expected to have the same closure and cohesion of large paper paragraphs, but a paper paragraph can inherently depend on the reader having read prior sections and paragraphs in a book. However, if James is right, and we need to think database not book, and if readers can jump from one chunk in the database to another without reading the intervening document chunks, then each chunk will need to be much more autonomous in its presentation of information. Thus the paradox of on-line document text chunking: it must be smaller than paragraphs, but have the same coherence and closure while also being more autonomous than paragraphs.

The legibility of text on a screen as compared to text on paper is diminished because of the following:

- The descenders of letters are frequently compressed. This alters the shape of letters and denies readers' expectations of word shapes. When we review typography in Step 1, we will see that word shape is an important feature used by readers. Hulme makes the point that word shape is "probably most important in highly familiar words," and it's familiar words that make up most commands and menu choice items (Hulme, 1984). Yet think of how many are presented on a VDT in all uppercase or with their descenders compressed.

---

cf.

"Page size is the amount of text visible at one time. It can affect reading and review tasks by limiting the context for the visible text, thus burdening short-term memory. It can affect writing by impeding reference to recently written text, possibly leading to repetition or omission. If the page is small, the user will have to scroll more often to view the entire text" (Hasen and Hass, 1988, 1082).

- Many screens do not have true proportional spacing; frequently they are "monospaced." Thus fully justified screens are much more prone than paper to the formation of vertical "rivers," and to having too m u c h i n t e r l e t - t e r s p a c i n g which diminishes the readers ability to see word shapes.

- Interline spacing, "leading," is usually held to a minimum. "Research indicates that 30 to 50% of the VDT character height is needed to reduce the effects of irradiation, the blurring of images caused by white light coming through a dark background. For characters 10 pixels in height (average height), 3 to 5 pixels of leading would be required to reduce irradiation" (Rubens and Krull, 1985; see also the Human Factors Society, ANSI Standard, 100-1988). Yet how many screens that you have viewed have that much leading? Thus letters, barely recognizable in the first place, blur into the letters immediately above and below.

- Resolution of characters is also greatly diminished on a screen. On a typeset page, around 17,500 dots are used to create a letter. On a laser printer page, around 1000 dots are used to create a letter. On a screen, around 63 dots are used to create a letter. And the problem is that many of the typefaces used on-line were perfect when they were typeset, but absolutely awful when put on a low resolution screen. Only recently have expert type designers designed for the low density medium of the screen (see Bigelow's design for the Lucida typeface in Step 1).

- In addition to diminished size, shape, leading, and resolution, screens display letters using a type of letter-to-background contrast, "polarity," that is the opposite of letter-to-background contrast on a piece of paper. On a piece of paper, letters are black on a white background (positive polarity), while on a screen the letters are light colored on a black background (negative polarity). This feature can lower rates of understanding and raise rates of error (Hulme, 1984).

"While many characteristics contribute to legibility: font design, spacing, contrast, edge sharpness, anti-aliasing, flicker, resolution..., none is preeminent. As Gould (1984) points out 'each variable contributes...in a small cumulative way'" (Hasen and Hass, 1988, 1082).

All these physical characteristics of a VDT screen combine to slow the speed at which information on the screen can be read (Bork, 1983; Merrill, 1981; Reynolds, 1980; Stevenson, 1984). Some have said that it takes as much as 28.5% more time to read information on a screen to equal the comprehension of reading the same information on a piece of paper (Hulme, 1984):

> "Most studies have determined that reading from paper is faster than reading from computer screens. Muter (1982) showed that reading from TV screens took 25 percent longer than from paper, but produced roughly equal comprehension scores. Wright and Lickorish (1983) also found that paper was faster. Gould and Grischkowsky (1984) studied subjects performing an eight-hour proofreading task. They found that work was done more rapidly on paper, with slightly higher quality than on personal computers" (Hasen and Haas, 1988, 1080).

This lowered reading speed becomes a problem in some systems where the "paging speed" is controlled by the computer. It is a problem not only because readers read screens much more slowly than they read pages, but also the range of reading pace among screen readers varies much more than that among paper readers (Bork, 1983; Stevenson, 1984).

But perhaps it's just that the wealth of new capabilities of this new medium (color, blinking, reverse video, branching, and so on) can cause problems because documenters lacking experience with the screen medium have no intuitive sense of how to use them effectively. On paper, writers have experience with various format devices and have an intuitive sense of how to use them effectively. After all, this intuitive sense has been purchased by us with years of personal trial and error. Therefore, expect to purchase the innate sense of on-line design at the same price through a whole new series of trial and error experiences.

For example, it's only recently that screen designers have made it standard practice to use an extra space before and after a word written in reverse video. By not using these extra spaces, many words written in reverse video had initial and ending letters that were barely discernible. This problem is something unique to the medium of a screen and does not get resolved just by using common sense intuition from paper.

Organizational Differences Between Paper and On-line Documentation

The basic problem here is the either/or quality of screen presentation; if Help information, for example, is present, it totally takes over the screen; your data entry screen is gone. And if your data entry screen is present, your Help information disappears. Paper pages, on the other hand, are still physically present to your eyes even if you are not currently using them or reading them; that is, previous pages in a book can be seen out of the corner of the eye or a number of pages can be placed face up on a desk making them simultaneously available for reading. On-line documentation all too frequently fills a screen with information that "loses'" any work the user was doing, causing them to forget their original problem, or causing them to shift dramatically between a problem solving mode and a learning mode. With a book, readers can simply lay it down on the desk beside the terminal and glance between their work and the Help information alongside (Dunsmore, 1980; Houghton, 1984).

Screens reduce the number of traditional reader "access aids" or as they have come to be called, "navigational aids." For example, readers of a paper book physically compare headings on various pages to understand the level of a heading's depth (e.g., section, subsection, or sub-subsection). On a screen, you have only one screen present. It is nearly impossible to compare headings to determine the level of information. Readers of a paper book often memorize the position of information on a page (e.g., you may know the field delimiter information is somewhere in the manual on the bottom of the left-hand page). Readers of screens have difficulty doing this. And books usually offer room on the page for marginalia whereas screens don't (Bradford A., 1984).

Once you have located yourself in a manual because of its navigational aids, you now need to actively navigate. Good manuals provide a range of methods of navigating. One can read linearly page by page through a book; investigate information in a top-down fashion using a book's table of contents to locate specific sections of a book; go from point to point from a specific word in a book's index to a specific word in the body of the document; or just start flipping through the pages and browse the information by looking at headings or pictures that catch your eye.

But all too often, on-line documents give readers just one or a few methods of navigating rather than the rich multipurpose methods of a book. On-line documents frequently give readers only a hierarchical tree structure of menus (like a table of contents, as we will see in Control Data's "CONTEXT" program), just a keyword search (like an index), or just a browser (like in pure hypertext).

Rhetorical Differences Between Paper and On-line Documentation

The rhetorical problem with screens is probably the most troublesome, and yet it's the least readily apparent. Readers come to any reading task with a great deal of previous experience and skill at handling text. However, screens, especially large groups of screens, seem to frustrate readers' application of their previous experiences to their screen-reading tasks (Gaines and Shaw, 1984), just like digital watches frustrate analog watch readers' actions:

> "Digital time pieces are controversial: in changing the representation of time, the power of the analog form has been lost, and it has become more difficult to make quick judgements about time. The digital display makes it easier to determine the exact time, but harder to make estimates or to see approximately how much time has passed since an earlier reading" (Norman, 1988, 196).

"Books present a clear vision of their boundaries and readers can know when they have read it all, but in the hypertext world other mechanisms must be created to give the reader a sense of progress and closure" (Shneiderman and Kearsley, 1989, 61).

A book's physical appearance is an analog to its conceptual organization and structure. That is, the binding has a front and a back, so we see where we begin and where we end; chapters are differentiated by white space, so readers are kept apprised of their reading progress; progressing three-fourths of the way through a book can be physically verified by the number of pages passed. On-line documentation, however, has no inherent physical analog to its organization and structure. Thus, readers are lost much more easily in the organization of on-line documentation, because they cannot sense its structure or because their past experiences with books have instilled in them an expectation of structure that is not present in the on-line documentation (Bradford A., 1984; Jackson, 1979).

All of these problems add up to what Hasen and Hass call a lack of a sense of text:

"One difficulty users have dealing with documents on computers is in getting a sense of the text. By this we mean the feeling a user may have that he or she has a good grasp of the structural and semantic arrangement of the text—the absolute and relative location of each topic and the amount of space devoted to each. Good sense of text is invaluable to a reader in finding parts of the text, following the thread of an argument, and getting the gist of the material....Poor sense of text can detract from usability, as Mantei (1982) demonstrated with linked networks of pages. Rothkoph (1971) has shown that readers can recall the position of text on paper pages. This may aid sense of text by typing the text to a physical entity which provides visual and tactile cues" (Hasen and Haas, 1988, 1984).

A few years ago a commercial for a new type of cookie showed an elderly couple on a couch discussing a new type of cookie (or "biscuit" as the Australians would have it). The wife kept trying to talk the husband into eating the new type of cookie, but he just kept repeating: "I like the old cookie." However, after once trying the new cookie, the husband ended the commercial with the simple statement: "I like the new cookie."

We can finally add to on-line documentation's rhetorical problems the "I like the old cookie" syndrome. People get set in their ways; they are used to sending, receiving, and studying information in a certain way. On-line documentation disrupts this nice established societal equilibrium:

"Do not forget that the goal is to have people using the system. You may meet some resistance as you try to sell the idea of moving to an on-line environment. These users may be comfortable with their dog-eared versions of manuals or may not have an affinity for terminals as a medium for information gathering. This is where your education process must begin. Even if you sell your management on the cost justification and benefits, if you cannot convince your users that the new system is an improvement and will make their lives easier, no amount of management support or coercion can make your implementation successful" (McGrew and McDaniel, 1989, 17).

"In the first centuries of this era, readers and writers began using the codex format (folded leaves of parchment) of books rather than continuous page or scroll format—even in the face of official government sanctions against codex format—because they found the codex format allowed easier access to information"(Highet, 1967).

And this improvement of on-line over paper documentation cannot be perceived as trivial. Compare the lack of enduring success of teletext and microfiche with the recent success of laser printing, VCRs, and microwave cooking. As Bill Horton once noted, "If on-line documentation is not *at least* 10 times better and easier to use from the user's perspective, it's not going to be successful" (see for example Piskin's critique of the acceptance problems of electronic mail (e-mail) (1989)). It's going to take a time to get people to see and use on-line documentation:

"Significantly, many of those who preferred on-line manuals said they didn't like them at first, but became more comfortable with them in time. Thus, with on-line manuals, as with most new software systems, it seems that a period of adjustment is necessary" (Hasslein, 1986, 436).

Fortunately, these shortcomings in the physical presentation, organization, and rhetorical framework of many past pieces of on-line documentation do not mean that the medium of the screen should not be used to communicate to users. In fact, many of these problems are being solved right now. It does mean, however, that we cannot naively switch from writing paper manuals to writing on-line manuals without some added care, attention, and skill in some new techniques. We will cover the solutions to these three problems in Step 1 of the Standard Documentation Process.

As with paper documentation, we have looked at a couple of specific screens and examined their problems; we have looked theoretically at what the problems are in these three specific areas: physical, organizational, and rhetorical. Now let us see what two surveys reveal about what users think of on-line documentation and how they actually use it.

In 1985, Edmond Weiss noted in his book, *How to Write a Usable User Manual*:

> "The irreducible minimum for paper documentation is an Installation and Startup Guide. If all the user documentation is in the system or on the system, the only external manual we need tells us how to get the system going—at which point the prompts instruct us and the HELP screens solve our problems" (Weiss, 1985).

This is what I used to believe. But in response to a lecture in Silicon Valley many years ago, I was brought up short by a letter I had received reporting the market response to an on-line documentation authoring product from Control Data, CONTEXT (*Control Data On-line Text*). After the product was released, the company performed a marketing survey and, in essence, they found:

> "Our survey showed that readers prefer integrated quick reference information, rather than exhaustive concept and definition information. They cannot cope with as much detail on-line as they can in printed form. The screen produces mental tunnel vision when trying to look something up. Disorientation is far more frequent when using on-line material than when using even poorly organized printed material....Research at a law school

---

Part 1: The Documentation Problem

The Problems with Paper Documentation:

Theory
Example
Survey Reports

The Problem with On-line Documentation

Theory
Example
Survey Reports

What Surveys Find Concerning On-line Documentation

1986 Control Data Survey (Hasslein, 1986)

In 1986, CONTEXT from Control Data allowed users to develop on-line reference manuals, tutorials, and quick reference guides based on a hierarchical tree organization. CONTEXT also allowed for keyword access—although such a feature wasn't well revealed to users and thus many failed to avail themselves of its powers of quick access. It usually took over an entire screen and was not presented in windows or split screens.

indicates that database retrieval experts have significantly less success finding relevant information on-line than similarly trained people using printed sources" (Lori, 1985).

Of course these two studies of on-line documentation do not completely summarize all the published studies to date. For example, Nielsen (1989) reviewed 92 usability benchmarks in 30 published studies focused on hypertext alone.

Later, in 1986, Hasslein reported on the specifics of the survey to which this letter referred. (There were 157 respondents.) The survey asked six major questions. The questions and their responses are presented below.

- Do You Use On-line Manuals? (Yes = 91; No = 65). "Of those who responded "no", many were not even aware that on-line manuals existed. And many of those who were didn't know how to access them and felt no inclination to use them" (436).

There is great interest in on-line tutorials but great dissatisfaction with those of the past. A step-by-step paper manual approach was judged to be more effective (AT&T 1986 market research).

- Do You Prefer Printed or On-line Manuals? (Depends on the situation = 62, Printed = 36, On-line = 15) Those who preferred printed manuals shared a feeling of being uncomfortable with on-line documentation and a feeling that the printed page is simply easier to read than terminal screens. Other responses included:

I don't always have access to a terminal.

I can open several printed manuals at once, but only one on-line manual.

I can open a printed manual without interrupting the current task.

I can clip frequently used pages in a printed manual.

Printed manuals are portable and I can use them when the system is down.

With a printed manual, I can write notes in the margins.(436)

| cf. |

The HyperGate on-line hypertext system and Comment 2.0 (see Figure 45 and 46) allow users to attach electronic "Post-Its" to screens and to insert "bookmarks."

- How Do You Use On-line Manuals? "Most respondents indicated that they used on-line manuals mainly for quick look-up of information with which they were already somewhat familiar....In general they found the reference manuals much too detailed, few were interested in a lot of detail, and still fewer used tutorials to learn a particular software product. Of those who had tried to use the tutorials, most found them to be an unsatisfactory way of learning a new software product. In general, respondents felt that initial learning about new software was easier and more efficient with a printed manual" (436).

cf.

Put as many choices as possible on one menu (a wide menu) rather than on an interconnected menu series (a deep menu). Research has shown that users get lost in the pathways between menus (Snowberry, Parkinson and Sisson, 1983).

"One study (Dunsmore,1980) which compared the performance of users of a database system, found that users of on-line documents were significantly less successful in performing searches than users who had full printed manuals [average success in 30 tries for on-line, 6.5, for paper, 12.5]" (Horton, 1988).

- Do You Get Lost in On-line Manuals? (Yes = 50, No = 54) Of those who responded "yes," most felt that the on-line manuals were too complicated, with too many menus and too many levels in the tree structure. They felt that long, detailed descriptions and tutorial types of information belonged in printed manuals, and that only brief, concise descriptions should be used in on-line manuals. Users seemed to have a feeling of being "out of control" within an on-line manual. Those who responded "no" were more likely to rely on the topic search than menus to locate information.

- "Can You Locate Information Easily? (Yes = 34, No = 34, Sometimes = 17) "Of those who responded "yes," most had made extensive use of and were satisfied with the topic search feature, although some said that it had taken a bit of practice to learn how to use it. Of those who responded "no," a surprising number had used menus only, and were not even aware that a topic search feature existed....Many of those who responded 'no' found the manuals too large and cumbersome; they often had to search screen after screen for specific pieces of information" (437).

- What New Features Would You Like? New features suggested by respondents included: the ability to print selected screens of the manual; concurrent task execution (so that the reader can run a program and read a manual at the same time); windowing (so that several manuals can be open at the same time); better graphics (e.g., different type fonts); a method of annotating screens; a method of quickly going to commonly used screens (i.e., a system that could 'remember' which screens a given user accessed most frequently (bookmarking)" (437).

1986 Survey of Super Computer Users of the DOCUMENT System (Girill et al., 1987, 1988)

Girill's method of "usage analysis" is another valuable way to gather information about users complementing the other methods we've looked at, e.g., AT&T's social survey of user beliefs and Microsoft's focus groups. The advantage of "usage analysis" is that it is less obtrusive in how it observes the user, and it often reveals surprizing findings because actual user behavior does not always coincide with user's expressed beliefs. Carroll's minimalist research findings are so surprizing because he used videotapes of actual usage that showed, for example, that even though a user says they always read a manual throughly, in actual usage, they only read it for nine minutes before giving up and using the system in a trial and error fashion.

In these studies, DOCUMENT, the on-line documentation system at the National Magnetic Fusion Energy Computer Center (NMEFCC), had been running for almost a decade with 19,000 pages of text available, and serving a geographically diverse community of 4,500 people. One long-term finding Girill and his colleagues made is an excellent example of how DOCUMENT demonstrates the overcoming of the "I Like The Old Cookie" rhetorical problem—the inertia of information medium prefernce. In Figure 13, you can observe that the ratio of actual lines printed to lines viewed on CRT's drops over nine years from a ratio of 117 lines printed for every line viewed to a ratio of around 20 lines printed for every line viewed.

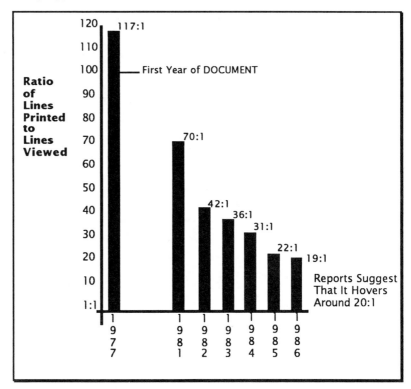

Figure 13. Observed ratio of lines printed on paper to lines viewed on a screen at NMFCC.

But even with this increased relative preference for the on-line medium, the actual numbers of lines printed increased over the same time from 24.3

million lines to 59.3, see Figure 14. Thus even as the on-line medium becomes relatively more accepted (even with the aid of hardware changes during these nine years at NMFECC such as the change from teletype terminals to CRT's and the use of high-speed transmission lines), it does not replace the documentation medium of paper.

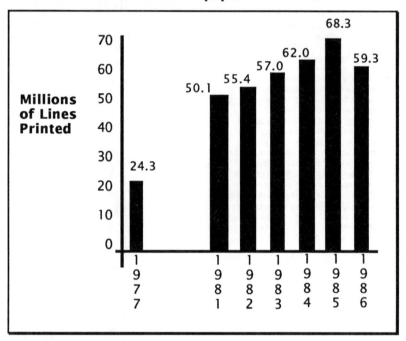

Figure 14. Observed increase in lines printed on paper at NMFCC.

"Past studies of on-line text design sometimes lacked adequate 'enabling' software.[For example, a University of Maryland study reported by Weldon and Shneiderman in 1985] No shortcuts were available to allow the subject to skip a section or turn directly to a specific part of the manual' by exploiting document hierarchy....Past studies of on-line-documentation software [also] often faced the opposite problem of ignoring the relevance of text design to success" (Girill et al., 1987, RET-111).

In a more short-term study, Girill and his colleagues "manually analyzed the 966 transcripts, each capturing one complete interactive session, recorded during January 1986 on NMFECC's CRAY X-MP computer" (RET-112). What they uncovered from this analysis of the DOCUMENT system was that:

- Like CONTEXT users, DOCUMENT users used the on-line documentation "primarily for ready reference rather than for prolonged study or self-tutoring" (RET-112).

- "The most common pattern of index use ...was the sequence document-index-keyword. This is the on-line analog of reference reading off-line:

the searcher answers a specific question by finding a relevant book, checking its subject index to locate relevant passages, then turning directly to that passage for an answer" (RET-113).

- "Most users view text from a single on-line document....The most common on-line reading sessions are small, with less than 100 line displayed....[And,] Few on-line readers even try to scan a whole document from the start" (RET-114).

- "Reference retrieval of focused passages to answer particular questions clearly dominates the use of our on-line documentation.... Hierarchical, example-rich, task-oriented text markedly increases this trend toward reference reading on-line" (RET-114).

The Solution: The Standard Documentation Process

The replication of the best procedures used by the best documentation writers will improve the situation. The Standard Documentation Process (SDP) offers just such method.

Although an in-depth explanation of each part of the SDP will be given in the rest of this book, Figure 15 and the following list give you an overview of what is involved in the SDP.

Develop Document Specifications

In this first step, planning the documentation occurs in two passes. The first pass is the development of a Library Specification that contains a brief description of all the documents involved with a particular software program or system. This plan gives you an opportunity to communicate the "big picture" of the whole writing project to management or clients. The second pass is the development of the Individual Document Specification. This second blueprint follows the Library Specification and communicates the specific plans for a single document to management, clients, and users. Eleven activities are involved in the creation of these blueprints: breaking down the documentation in the library by tasks, using minimalist design principles, planning for an audience, analyzing the purpose of the documentation, organizing the material, developing a product visualization, picking the appropriate media, deciding on page format and layout, planning for updating, considering the competition, and estimating cost and time requirements.

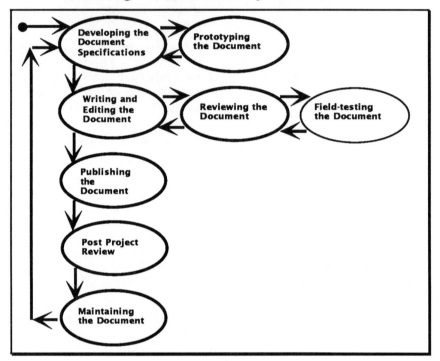

Figure 15. The Standard Documentation Process (Version 2.0).

Prototype the Specification

Since the ultimate test for paper or on-line documentation is usability, document designers should iteratively test their pages and screens with users. Prototyping is repeatedly done with a document as it is being developed, but it basically has four steps: prepare for the test, instruct the testers, run the test, and analyze and apply the results. The results of prototyping should give guidelines to your depth of coverage, vocabulary, readability, and organization.

Draft the Document

Once the specifications have been created, approved, and tested, it is time to draft the document. Seven activities make up this step: overcoming internal and external writing blocks, using a writing style that is designed to match adult reading behaviors, using reader-based writing techniques, developing effective graphics, creating reference aids, developing the documentation packaging, and planning for updates.

Edit the Document

Now that the document is drafted, it is revised so that it effectively and efficiently gets its message across. This is primarily accomplished by using levels-of-edit techniques.

Review the Document

Once the document is drafted and edited, it is sent out for review. To have an effective review, carefully choose reviewers and the time to review, show reviewers how to review, and give them feedback.

Field-test the Document

A part of every document's review should be a field-test of a draft of the whole document. Where prototyping examined the pieces of a manual or on-line document during their creation and assembly, field testing examines how the document works as a whole. Accessibility, navigational problems, and consistency are primary areas of concern here. In conducting a field-test, carefully choose field-testers and the time to field-test, run both an in-house "controlled" field-test and an external field-test, and provide feedback to field testers.

Produce and Distribute the Document

Once the document is drafted, revised, and reviewed, it is time to get it produced in a form suitable for distribution. With paper and on-line publishing mechanisms ranging so widely, and multi-media publishing becoming more and more prevalent, preparing text via SGML-like tagging system becomes absolutely essential. The watch words in these days of media transition is "Be Prepared."

Review the Documentation Project

Once a document is complete, and before beginning a new project, analyze what went right and what went wrong during the process of developing the documentation so that improvements to the documentation process can be implemented during the next project, and mistakes and problems thereby alleviated.

Maintain the Document

Even when the document is distributed, the task is still not completed because the document must be updated. To do this effectively, responsibility for updating a document should be clearly assigned. Distribution of the document should be tracked so that one knows where to send updates. And the changes in the updates should be clearly indicated.

PART TWO:
THE STANDARD DOCUMENTATION PROCESS

STEP 1: DEVELOPING THE DOCUMENT SPECIFICATIONS

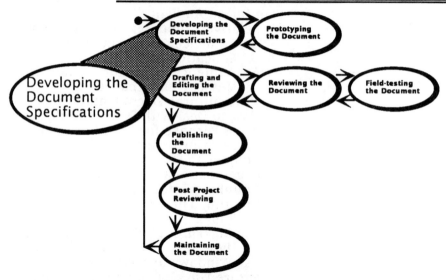

What Are Document Specifications?

Document specifications pass through two stages. First, develop a short preliminary plan overviewing all the documents involved in the documentation of a software system, a Library Specification. Second, develop an in-depth plan for one particular document in this "library." This is called an Individual Document Specification.

What Is A Library Specification?

In a Library Specification, consider all of the paper and on-line documentation needed to form a documentation library. Consider the whole library first so that all activities and audiences receive the documentation they need; production time and effort are not wasted on needless duplication of efforts; and time and money can be allocated accurately.

The Library Specification is a brief report to the manager, client, or reader authorizing your

"We promise no surprises" (Holiday Inn).

documentation work to alert them of your documentation plans. The basic philosophy underlying such a plan is that the fewer surprises to the authorizing agent, users, or reviewers, the higher the frequency of final acceptance of the documentation by readers and management and the easier your job.

What Is an Individual Document Specification?

In the Individual Document Specification, move from the overall Library Specification to consider the plans for each individual document. Notice we are not using the word document "outline" because a document specification goes beyond a typical outline. It covers the document's conception of the audience, content, purpose, graphics, reference aids, format, updating plans, and production cycle—in short, everything that goes into a user manual, as well as ten sample pages on which to run a prototype test.

An Individual Document Specification is divided into three parts. The first part defines the requirements that the finished document must meet:

- Purpose
- Audience
- Layout
- Related publications (or other system intelligibility devices that will be utilized)

For information on updating beyond what is contained in this step, see Steps 3 and 9

- Updating plan
- Production plan or output (i.e., how it will be printed, or on what type of monitor with what kind of typeface it will be displayed)

For information on production beyond what is contained in this step, see Step 7.

For information on testing and reviewing, see Steps 2 Step 6.

- Testing and reviewing plan

The second part defines the content of the finished document as well as Subject Matter Expert (SME) information:

- Organization: headings to be used and their levels

- Reference aids: candidates for the glossary, and what reference aids will be included (i.e., index, visual table of contents, tabs, keyword access capabilities, fisheye lens window, etc.)

- Graphics

- Content

- Style and tone

- Vocabulary

- Information sources (SME) for the various parts as well as their contact number and plans for vacation or other commitments that will take them out of the office during the document development process

- Timing and cost estimates

The third part of the specification will be your sample prototype pages or screens (i.e., a sample procedure page, a sample troubleshooting page, a sample textual introduction page).

How Do You Know When Your Specification Is Complete?

The way to judge whether an Individual Document Specification is complete is to ask, "Can another competent documenter pick up the specification and successfully complete the project without any further information from me?" When the answer is "yes," you are ready to move to Step 2 in the SDP: actually testing the screens or the pages.

Why Develop Specifications?

Specifications Make the Documentation Process a More Professional Endeavor

First, just as flowcharting precedes programming, or blueprinting precedes housebuilding, a specification precedes documentation creation. Too often this commitment to planning has been missing in computer documentation:

"Just as early programming shops emphasized coding to the exclusion of analysis and design, so do present documentation shops emphasize writing to their [analysis and design] exclusion. As with programming, the benefits of analysis and design are not immediate....To writers and supervisors, putting words on paper is reasonably concrete,

"...it is wrong to believe that usability can be substantially enhanced after the draft is complete; the most resistant and elusive usability flaws in a publication are *built into* a draft and are not likely to be ameliorated by after-the-fact testing" (Weiss, 1988, 175; see also, Duffy, T. M., Post, T., Smith, G., 1987).

Keep in mind the truism that people care about those things they help design...and they tend to use those things they help design. This designer/audience shared ownership effect is also a reason for using prototype testing during the design process, see Step 2.

"Because attentional capacity is limited, allocating sufficient attention to collecting, planning, translating, and reviewing is a serious problem for writers. Surveys, interviews, and verbal protocol studies indicate that even skilled adult writers at times find the attentional demands of writing to be overwhelming. If collecting, planning, translating, and reviewing are all resource-limited processes, then failure to devote sufficient attention to any one of them should be detrimental....Adopting cognitive strategies that circumvent attentional overload may be one key to optimum writing performance. Outlining during prewriting and preparing a rough first draft are two potentially useful strategies; each controls the writer's attention to collecting, planning, translating, and reviewing during the various phases of product development" (Kellogg, 1988, 355-6).

while planning to put words on paper seems like a step into the twilight zone" (Perron, 1979).

Specifications Allow Early Interaction in the Design

Second, specifications allow early interaction among the writer and managers, reviewers, and users. By allowing these parties to participate early in the project, the project becomes "their" project as well as "your" project. Their acceptance of the end product is thus much more likely. And, since early involvement is encouraged, specifications help cut the cost of a project. It is much easier to cut a section in an outline than to cut 20 or 30 pages or screens from a final draft. It is easier in terms of time and effort, and it is easier in terms of writer morale; writers are quite willing to let someone else change their plans, but much less willing to let someone throw out 20 or 30 pages they have sweated over.

Specifications Coordinate the Activities of a Number of Writers on a Documentation Project

Third, just as a good architectural plan coordinates the activities of a number of workers on a building project, specifications coordinate the activities of a number of writers on a documentation project. Specifications help avoid the chronic problem of multiauthored documents that require considerable editing to make them internally consistent.

Specifications Diminish the Occurrence of "Writer's Block"

Fourth, specifications greatly diminish the occurrence of "writer's block." The basic cause of writer's block is "attentional overload," and this occurs when writers need to make too many decisions simultaneously. They must decide wording, organization, layout, and what are extraneous details. Ninety percent of decisions regarding a manual can be made in the specifications, so that when writers are presented with the blank paper or the blank screen, they're just not beginning from scratch every time. If you approach documentation in this systematic, specification approach, you will notice that the most interesting and creative part of the entire methodology is the specification stage:

"One of the effects of developing documentation in this structured style is that it reduces the interest of the first draft. Instead of being the most complicated, demanding, and fascinating part of documentation, writing the draft becomes the least interesting" (Weiss, 1985).

Specifications Provide an Economical Opportunity for Trial and Error

Fifth, specifications give document designers an economical trial and error opportunity:

"Prewriting is the secret of planning discourse well. Our minds must create discourse via a feedback loop, that is, we often have to write or argue a thing incorrectly before we realize how to write or argue it correctly" (Tracey, 1983).

Specifications Can Act Like a Contract

Sixth, specifications can act as a contract among different groups as you negotiate agreement on the information and its presentation in testing and reviewing—the sociological context. In fact, developing either paper or on-line documentation using this specification process is very much like the process of developing a charter for an organization. It reveals and balances mutual dependencies among users and designers, reviewers, and testers.

Specifications Can Best Predict Future Performance and Productivity

Seventh, specifications give one the ability to accurately predict future performance and productivity. Records of past performance and costs are the best—and perhaps only—predictor of future performance and costs. No prediction formula or even the "gut feelings" of those with 20 years experience takes the place of specifications in accurately predicting the future.

Specifications Aid Document Maintenance

Eighth, if over 60% of programming now is spent in maintenance, and if the majority of a programmer maintenance time is spent in analyzing the program to be changed—perhaps the same is true of documentation. Specifications could dramatically cut down on the time to do document maintenance because the maintenance documenter doesn't have to study the document to understand how it's designed and how to patch or amend it. The specification spells

"A well-documented technical communication plan is most valuable in the middle of a product's life cycle, when management may wish to alter operating policies without knowing how the different aspects of the communication activity are linked together" (Strassmann, 1982, 236).

"In this writing, there is not one line, not one dot that is frozen. This is the Tao of calligraphy" (Chinese Emperor T'ai-tsung of the calligrapher Wang Hsi-chich).

out the design, and so the maintenance documenter's time can be much more fruitfully spent on actually developing the patches or amendments.

How Long Does It Take to Develop Specifications?

"Most research shows that a writer spends only 30-50% of the day writing. The rest of the day is spent on tasks such as research, meetings, data entry, proofreading, estimating and scheduling, and administration" (Prekeges, 1986, 116).

The drafting of specifications normally takes from 25 to 30% of the entire writing time. This may sound like a lot of time, but probably a great deal of what you now consider writing time is really planning time. And, even if this is a lot of time, the time spent developing writing specifications is much more cost-effective than unplanned time spent in rewriting pages or screens during the testing, editing, or reviewing stages that try to make up for planning mistakes or organization problems. The hidden cost of unexpected problems can be greatly diminished by planning.

How Do I Develop a Library or Individual Document Specification?

Whether it is a Library Specification or an Individual Document Specification, you need to make decisions in three areas: conceptual, physical, and implementation (the only difference is the varying degree of specificity). The first six substeps ask you to make conceptual decisions: what tasks do I document; how can I use my reader's natural impulses to skim, scan, and skip around in my manuals; who is my audience; what is my purpose, etc. The next three steps require you to move from conceptual decisions to physical decisions: what form will the document take; what page layout will be used; how can the document be designed to be easily updated. The last two substeps ask you to review all your previous decisions in terms of what the competition is doing and in terms of time and cost. The 11 substeps consist of the following:

Conceptual Decisions

- Break down the documentation by task.
- Use a minimalist design approach.
- Develop a concept of audience.
- State the purpose for each document.
- Organize the documentation.
- Develop a product visualization.

Physical Decisions

- Pick the appropriate medium for each document in the library.

- Decide on typography, layout, color and page size.

- Design for updating.

Implementation Decisions

- Consider the competition.

- Develop a general timing and cost scheme.

Each of these substeps for both paper and on-line documents is described in detail below.

Break Down Documentation By Tasks

Readers only use documentation to get their job completed when it requires some kind of computer assistance. Documentation is only a tool and not an end in itself (Hauke et al., 1977; IBM, 1983). Thus, the best design for software documentation is the one that fits the reader's method of working and requires the least attention and learning. This self-effacing design for documentation is where we need to begin, and this type of design is called a task orientation.

A task orientation to the design of documentation can be most easily understood by contrasting it with a non-self-effacing design, the software-internals orientation.

Don't Use A Software-Internals Orientation

Widely used in the industry until recently, a software-internals orientation approach to documentation design concentrated on the structure and facilities of a program rather than on the reader's use of that program. Thus, you might design a documentation library for an operating system that consisted of one manual each for the job control language, the file manager, the linker, the loader, and so on.

The software-oriented approach to design received extensive criticism in a 15-year survey of users carried out by Xerox, Scientific Data, and Control Data corporations and discussed in Part One of this book. Users almost always preferred function(task)-oriented rather than software-internals oriented manuals, because a software-internals orientation forces readers to center their business duties around the software rather than vice versa.

Step 1: Design The Specifications

Break Down Documentation
 by Tasks
Use a Minimalist Design
Plan for an Audience
State the Purpose
Organize Information
Develop a Product Visualization
Pick the Appropriate Medium
Decide on Typrography, Layout,
 Color and Page Size
Plan for Updating
Consider the Competition
Develop a Timing and Cost
 Scheme

A few years ago a publisher of children's books had one of their company's books about penguins returned in the mail. It was accompanied by the following note in a young child's scrawl:
"Dear Sirs: I am returning your book because it told me more about penguins than I wanted to know" (Morgan, 1980). This information overload problem in manuals is called the *Penguin Syndrome*.

"Task-oriented" writing has at least three roots. The most obvious is the "task work" and "instruction cards" of Taylor's turn of-the-century management technique, "scientific management." A second older root is the drill manuals and standard operating procedure (SOPs) manuals of the military. Military manual writers themselves wholeheartedly embraced "task work" methods in the 1950s and have carried it on in their manuals in the 1990s. The third root is the least proximate but certainly the oldest: the tradition of "how-to" instructional manuals and pamphlets ranging from Franklin's 1744 instructions on how to properly use his newly invented fire-place, to McCormick's 1851 reaper assembly instructions, to the Model T user manuals of the 1910s and 20s.

In addition, to use this orientation, you must already be familiar with the structure of the system. Thus, those readers who are reading the documentation to learn about the structure of the software cannot read the document until they know the structure of software—an excellent example of a Catch-22.

And finally as a writer, there's no way in a software-internals orientation to know how much is too much. Since knowledge of the software internals only very indirectly transfers to tested, observable activities, a software-internals orientation greatly complicates, if not confounds, prototype and field testing. The tendency, therefore, is to provide every piece of information time allows and hope that the readers have all the information they need and that they will know how to discriminate between necessary and unnecessary information.

Why, in the face of all this criticism, have writers persisted in using a software orientation? The reason is because software orientation is the orientation of the writer's source materials (the design documents), and the writer has allowed this previously established orientation to prevail rather than translating the material for users using the task orientation. It is, in fact, the easiest way to write manuals because it calls for the least amount of "translation;" the least amount of knowledge about users, their business problems, and their environment.

Use a Task Orientation

A task orientation is a much better approach; it is based on an analysis of the user's use of the program and is limited to what information is required to do a specific task using the program. Information that is not needed to do a specific task or tasks is not provided. And, since the information in the documentation explicitly mirrors observable user actions, prototype and field testing are supported and more easily performed. In developing task-oriented documentation, ask these questions (Sederston, 1984; Simpson A. 1986: Ward, 1984; Wight, 1984):

Five Key Task Orientation Questions

- Who performs the task?
- What action begins each task?

A sample application of this task orientation can be seen in the IBM System 36 planning information. All the documents are packaged in a binder labeled *What To Do Before Your Computer Arrives*. Inside are eight booklets. The first is *Your Guide to Planning* which overviews the major planning tasks—it's like a road map charting a path though the other seven booklets. These other booklets are titled *General Planning Activities*, *Preparing a Place for Your Computer*, *Planning to Get Your Computer Up*, *Planning for Data Communications*, *Planning for System Configuration*, *Planning for System Security*, and *Planning to Receive Your Computer* (Waite, 1984).

- What are the specific steps involved in performing the task?

- What action ends each task?

- Are there any variations in hardware or in the general environment in which the task takes place that would alter it?

You can readily see that in asking these questions, we turn from focusing on the system to focusing on the users using the system in their daily work; we are designing self-effacing documentation. We turn from the software structuring of a problem as it is found in a writer's source document to the user's structuring of the problem. You can also see that we have a ready measure of how much information is too much or how much is too little—does the information support this task within these chronological confines? And finally, these questions lead one to organize around a chronological organization—an organization that is most often expected by readers of user documentation.

Test Results Comparing a Software-Internals Orientation to a Task Orientation

There is a price for this type of improved design. It takes more time in planning because more time is being spent on translation and examining the user and their environment rather than allowing previously existing patterns of organization (software structure, menu order, or user titles) to be the organization of the documentation. This orientation will probably require more in pages, because a task approach makes explicit what is only implicit in the other design orientations (Waite, 1984).

A task-oriented manual or on-line tutorial is usually complemented in the documentation library by a product-feature-oriented reference manual or database. The task orientation gets the users going; the product-feature-oriented reference lets them mix and match product capabilities in unique ways appropriate for their environment and users which the original program designers may never have foreseen.

This hunch by Waite in 1984 was further explored by Odescalchi in a study she reported in 1986. Her study compared the productivity of users with a software-orientation manual and others with a task-oriented manual, and her results were as shown in Table 4.

Software-internals oriented manual

- Dissatisfaction rate 79% higher
- Failure rate 310% higher
- Error rate 480% higher
- Ability to follow 88% lower

Task-oriented manual

- Productivity 41% higher
- Amount of time required to produce 42% higher
- Number of words 33% higher
- Number of pages 87% higher

Table 4. Software-internals oriented manual vs. task
-oriented manual (Odescalchi, 1986).

Most of the time, words, and space indicated in the table were needed because of the increased amount of system translation going on. However, don't be discouraged by this increase in time, words, and paper because this one-time-only investment in the documentation gets amortized very quickly over the long term as one user's increased productivity causes them to turn to another user and train them, and so on. It takes energy once to throw a pebble into a pond, but the waves continue to ripple over and over again.

Use a Minimalist Design Philosophy

Step 1: Design The Specifications

Break Down Documentation
  by Tasks
▶ Use a Minimalist Design
Plan for an Audience
State the Purpose
Organize Information
Develop a Product Visualization
Pick the Appropriate Medium
Decide on Typography, Layout,
  Color and Page Size
Plan for Updating
Consider the Competition
Develop a Timing and Cost
  Scheme

Taylor's wound up being investigated in 1910 by a congressional subcommittee, and his ideas remain controversial as illustrated by Shelton's 1989 critique of the use of Taylorism in expert systems.

A task orientation suggested certain fruitful ways a document designer could select content and employ an organization appropriate to a user's work needs. A minimalist design philosophy begins where task orientation leaves off. A minimalist design philosophy suggests how best to present the material a task orientation suggested. A minimalist design philosophy is also a corrective to the manipulative deskilling possibilities inherent in "task orientation." Taylor, who invented "task work" and "instruction cards," did so primarily to break the back of the craftsmen in the steel industry at the turn of the century—he attempted to substitute rote procedures for knowledgeable decision making, passive doers for active thinkers. The minimalist design recognizes the adult learner's active participation and application of knowledge.

The goal of a minimalist design philosophy is to present material in ways appropriate to the actual ways adult learners learn rather than fighting against their natural tendencies in ways that a "systems" design philosophy does:

"It is surprising how poorly the elegant scheme of systems-style instructional design actually works....Everything is laid out for the learner. All that needs to be done is to follow the steps, one, two, three. But, as it turns out, this is both too much and too little to ask of people. The problem is not that people cannot follow simple steps; it is that they do not. People are thrown into action; they can only understand through the effectiveness of their actions in the world. People are situated in a world more real to them than a series of steps, a world that provides rich context and convention for everything they do. People are always already trying things out, thinking things through, trying to relate what they already know to what is going on, recovering from errors. In a word, they are already too busy learning to make much use of the instruction" (Carroll, 1990, Chap. 4).

More specifically, John Carroll's research—he is the principal figure in this design movement—in the last decade has verified and reminded us that adult learners:

- Are impatient learners and want to get started quickly on something productive

- Skip around in manuals and on-line documents and rarely read them fully

- Make mistakes but learn most often from correcting such mistakes

- Are best motivated by self-initiated exploration

- Are discouraged, not empowered, by large manuals with each task decomposed into its subtask minutiae.

How do we accommodate these natural adult learning behaviors? The minimalists basically say, "Get out of the way of the learner as much as possible":

"The key idea in the Minimalist approach is to present the smallest possible obstacle to learners' efforts, to accommodate, even to exploit the learning strategies that cause problems for learners using systematic instructional materials. The goal is to let the learner get more out of the training experience by providing less overt training structure" (Carroll, 1990, Chap. 4).

As you will see from the various applications of the minimalist design philosophy, there isn't a set of specific minimalist guidelines. In fact, Carroll concludes his book *The Nurnberg Funnel* by rejecting the notion that there is a set of minimalist design methods—he embraces the notion of eclecticism. But what does seem consistent in the different applications are listed below.

"The will to learn becomes a 'problem' only under specialized circumstances like those of a school, where a curriculum is set, student confined, and a path fixed. The problem exists not so much in the learning itself, but in the fact that what the school imposes often fails to enlist the natural energies that sustain spontaneous learning—curiosity, a desire for competence, aspiration to emulate a model, and a deep-sensed commitment to the web of social reciprocity" (Bruner, 1966,127).

"Alan Boyd, referring to his company's *Guide* hypertext program for the Macintosh: 'When we write the manual for the IBM PC version, we'll put in longer words" (Nelson, 1987, DM-36).

General Minimalist Design Tips

- Cut secondary features of manuals and on-line documents—overviews, introductions, summaries, etc.

- Focus on what readers need to know in order to immediately apply it to productive work.

- Test repeatedly during design; testing replaces any hard and fast rules and guidelines in the minimalist design philosophy.

- Make it easy for the reader of a page to coordinate the documentation with the screen information via pictures of screens or other graphics.

- Use what the readers already know by continuously linking new information to it (see "Given-New" metaphor approach in Step 3).

- Encourage active exploration of a system via intentionally incomplete information.

In order to see how this design philosophy has been put into action, consider the following four cases.

Minimalist Design Cases

IBM Word Processor Tutorial—The Minimal Manual (Carroll et al., 1988)

In the first application of this design philosophy, Carroll and his colleagues redesigned an IBM word processor's tutorial document. Specifically, he and his colleagues used the following eight unique design elements.

Unique Design Element	Rationale
Slashed 75% of the pages by cutting previews, reviews, index, practice exercises, troubleshooting, "welcome to this application" introductions, and most pictures of screens.	"The rule of thumb in minimalist design is to try first to cut and condense text and other passive components, but the goal of this is to enrich the training experience. The trick is to give the learner more to think about, but less to overcome"(Carroll, 1990, Chap. 4, see also Charney, Reder and Wells ,1988, 55).

Unique Design Element	Rationale
Made iterative testing an integral part of the document design, not just design verification.	"The process of tuning a design by iterative user testing has been found extremely effective, for example, in the development of the Apple Lisa and Macintosh systems, which profited from very frequent user tests conducted by the applications software manager himself" (Laudauer, 1987).
Left procedural details deliberately incomplete to encourage learner exploration, but gave "enabling hints."	"...readers who learned procedures by working exercises that forced them to independently apply the information in the manual performed significantly better" (Charney, Reder and Wells, 1988, 63).
Continually tried to exploit readers' prior knowledge of the task implemented by the computer or analogous noncomputerized activities.	"Many benefits come from encouraging users to utilize their existing knowledge through metaphors. For example, users will tend to know what is happening when the system gives them a certain type of feedback; they will tend to know how to respond to that feedback; they will tend to know how to plan their tasks better; and they will tend to be able to generalize from known, already encountered situation, to new and unknown ones" (Hampton, 1987, 229).
Used open-ended exercises called "On Your Own."	"Procedural knowledge is difficult or impossible to write down and difficult to teach. It is best taught by demonstration and best learned through practice" (Norman, 1988, 58-9)

"The Minimal Manual only covered basic topics, where the commercial manuals covered advanced topics as well. In a later phase of the experiment, Minimal Manual learners were transferred to the sections on advanced topics of a commercial manual. It is notable that they still were substantially faster, but in this comparison their performance on learning achievement tests was better by a factor of eight. In sum, this experiment provided evidence that the final Minimal Manual design was an order of magnitude more effective than comparable state-of-the-art commercial manuals designs..."(Carroll and Rosson, 1987, 106).

Unique Design Element	Rationale
Included manual and system coordination information in such ways as "Can you find this prompt on the display: Enter name of document?"	"What is required is the incorporation of richer implicit and explicit linkages into the training materials. For example, manuals could periodically present a figure demonstrating what the display should look like if all is well" (Carroll, 1990, Chap. 4).
Inventoried principal user errors and then used them in developing specific error recognition and recovery sections.	"A model for giving instructions is the directions you might give someone on how to find a restaurant in the country....All directions should have in them the indications that you have gone too far" (Wurman, 1989, 327; see also Ramey, 1988, 151).
Kept chapters brief (averaging less than three pages).	"The units must be very streamlined so that learners are not likely to skip around within them; the organization of the units must be very simple so that learners can more successfully skip over units or skip among units" (Carroll, 1990, Chap. 4, see also the "chunking" necessary for on-line documentation in "Organization" in this Step, the STOP style and "short blocks and chunks" in Structured Writing in Step 3).

"Holmes: 'You will, I am sure, agree with me that if page 534 finds us only in the second chapter, the length of the first one must have been really intolerable" (Doyle, *The Valley of Fear* (1888)).

Experimental results comparing the Minimal Manual to standard commercial self-instruction manuals found:

- 40% less learning time
- 58% more tasks completed
- 93% more tasks completed per unit of time
- 20% fewer errors and 10% less time in recovering from errors
- 80% more exploratory episodes

Hewlett-Packard Computer-Assisted Design (CAD) Tutorial (Vanderlinden, Cocklin and McKita, 1988)

Vanderlinden, Cocklin and McKita took Carroll's ideas on the Minimal Manual and sparingly added to it specific procedures and prerequisite goals (GP+P). Their work offers some contrast to the IBM experiment because this experiment included a much more open-ended piece of software and a much more knowledgeable and skilled audience.

Comparing the performance of electrical engineers (EE) and printed circuit board designers (PCB) on specific procedures and prerequisite goals manuals (GP+P) vs. traditional self-study (SS) tutorials, Vanderlinden, Cocklin and McKita found that:

- GP+P subjects, whether PCB's or EE's, spent approximately 10% more time working through the GP+P tutorials.

- GP+P subjects had fewer problems completing tutorial tasks and required slightly fewer interventions than SS subjects.

- GP+P subjects completed the post-tutorial test more quickly (2:1) and more accurately (4:1) than the SS subjects.

- SS subjects referred back to the tutorial approximately four times more often to complete the test.

Xerox ViewPoint Electronic Publishing System Tutorial and Reference Documentation (Carroll, 1990)

In the training manuals, Xerox minimalist designers sought to

- Cover only about half the software features and functions, relying on exploration to motivate users to experiment with the system

- Use realistic projects in which users created and manipulated familiar entities, like memos and reports

- Include open-ended pointers to advanced topics in the reference library

- Omit summaries and self-test exercises in order to increase the amount of time spent on realistic activities and decrease the sheer bulk of the material

Later, in their work redesigning the reference documentation (neither Hewlett-Packard nor Carroll had applied this philosophy to reference documentation), Xerox minimalist designers

- Focused on easier access to information by publishing reference manual modules in a consistent order, distinguished through visual layout and graphics.

- Eliminated redundancy. Concepts were defined only once; procedure's descriptions assumed that the user already understood the concepts or could get necessary conceptual information by checking the concept section.

- Employed highly modular sectioning. In each reference chapter, concepts, screen formats, data structures, and procedures were presented as stand-alone components.

So far the work in these two redesigned manuals—the tutorial and the reference manual—seems to have worked for Xerox, "usability testing and initial feedback on the Xerox *Viewpoint* documentation from field test sites have been very positive" (Carroll, 1990, Chap. 9).

Bell Northern Research Norstar Quick Reference Card (Carroll, 1990)

At Bell Northern Research, they decided to produce a single reference card to serve as the principal training and reference documentation for their Norstar telephone system:

- Three 5 by 7 inch panels—the top face was a cover, five faces were used for the documentation, and an additional detachable panel included reference material.

- Buttons names (like Release, Hold, and the dialpad buttons) were presented in boxes to emphasize their linkage to visible system elements.

- Task oriented headings suggested activities users already understand and could find immediately applicable.

- The card did not explain everything; for example, it did not explain that the system provides different dial tones for internal (intercom) calls and external calls. It was assumed the user would notice this correlation through independent exploration.

- Deliberately omitted much conceptual background material about phone systems.

The field trial responses to this minimalist reference card revealed:

- 78% of their users read the card through; the comparison figure for standard materials is no higher than 30%.

- 90% of the users claimed that the cards WERE AS GOOD OR BETTER than standard material AND AS COMPLETE.

- 50% of the user relied only on the card even in cases for which there were back-up manuals.

- Cards cost about a fifth as much to produce as standard manuals.

Problems with Minimalist Design Philosophy

Although we have seen four successful applications of this design philosophy; if you use it, you might do well to anticipate these half dozen problems:

- Learning by self-discovery is less predictable and gaps or lack of depth in learning may appear:

"...even if we assume the availability of appropriate goals, end-product approaches may ultimately impair breadth of learning" (Carroll and Rosson, 1987, 92).

| cf. |

Perhaps the enforced passivity in the designs of playscript and structured writing undermines any motivation on the part of readers to take a more active role.

- This design assumes a motivated audience. However, all the other document designs such as playscript and structured writing that we will examine in Step 3 assume just the opposite. Which is more accurate?

- In allowing the free choosing of goals, some users picked unattainable goals or ineffective goals.

Reviewers unable to empathize with the user's perspective usually urge the more comprehensive rather than usable solutions.

- It's quite different from the ways documenters have traditionally been encouraged to write:

"Fears of 'letting go' of standard procedural techniques when developing GE+P [minimal manual] prototypes was our toughest problem to overcome. As technical writers, we were trained to write specific, clear and complete procedures for end-users. The GE [minimal manual] approach ran contrary to our training in that it required us to write truncated 'hints' which were often left information purposefully incomplete" (Vanderlinden, Cocklin and McKita, 1988, RET-198).

- When does one know when concision becomes cryptic? Will minimalist designers be more open to liability challenges than systematic comprehensive documenters?

- Will designers miss the all-important testing element—the hard work—and just employ the easiest step, i.e., cut out words.

Perhaps the most important lesson to learn from the minimalist design philosophy is that the best solution is an eclectic one. Carroll's two main points—that testing will tell you how much is superfluous and that documenters should get out of the way of learners—are invaluable, but he contradicts many of the other techniques and approaches in this book, e.g., the minimalist idea of cutting overviews and glossaries.

Plan for an Audience

Step 1: Design The Specifications

Break Down Documentation by Tasks
Use a Minimalist Design
Plan for an Audience
State the Purpose
Organize Information
Develop a Product Visualization
Pick the Appropriate Medium
Decide on Typography, Layout, Color and Page Size
Plan for Updating
Consider the Competition
Develop a Timing and Cost Scheme

By using a task orientation and minimalist design in your documents, you have laid the framework for all later design decisions. Now you must plan the tone, style, language, and emphasis of the resulting paper or on-line documents by analyzing your document's audience. We need to consider our audiences in four dimensions, namely with regard to their:

- Relative level of computer sophistication

- General background, training, or education

- Possible attitude toward your message

- Multicultural backgrounds

Each dimension is described inb the following pages.

Relative Computer Sophistication

The number and type of examples or illustrations in a manual depends on a user's computer sophistication. In describing users' varying computer sophistication, we can say that there are five levels of computer user sophistication: parrot, novice, intermediate, and expert (Schneider, 1982). We must add to these one more, the intermittent user. Each of these is defined below (Schneider, 1982; Treu, 1977). But essentially these terms, or the other many varieties of terms used to categorize users, are simply descriptions of various points along the user's learning curve shown in Figure 16.

Parrot

These users have the least experience and knowledge when they approach the software system, and they can handle only the smallest chunk of information, the single character or key; they type only strings of characters or press series of keys. Parrots do not think, question, understand, or synthesize directions. The best form of assistance for parrots is an example or a single choice from a menu.

Novice

"Novices tend to rely on lexical cues and do not distinguish as many command attributes as do the experts. They also do not capture the simple task relationship among [similar] commands. Intermediate users, however, do show a simple task orientation in their grouping of the commands. But like novices, they do not distinguish as many command attributes as do expert users. Finally, experts attend to simple task relationships as well as group commands based on their conceptual understanding of the software" (Palmer J., et al., *Report 39*).

With a little experience, the parrot users begin to understand isolated concepts and are able to choose a specific command or key to perform a specific function. Users now attach meaning to the order of instructions, but the language they read needs to be concrete, not abstract. Novice users rely heavily on the built-in defaults the software provides during the time required to gain additional knowledge and experience. They use simple forms of the services available to them, and they rely heavily on tutorials that guide them through their tasks.

Intermediate

Intermediate users are novice users with a few months experience. Whereas novices concentrate on commands and functions in isolation, intermediate users begin to see the context for certain command choices and options. The intermediate users may link statements into command chains, and they may begin to concentrate on the task rather than its components. The use of the full system is now only restricted by a lack of knowledge. These users begin to understand and know when to use defaults, and they can use a combination of defaults and special options. These users require guidance in the use of services new to them, but rely increasingly on reference information to remind themselves about the use of the services they have tried.

Level of User Computer Sophistication	Requires
Parrot	Ten-minute task-oriented guide; sense of success quickly; practice on immediately practical projects
Novice	Task-oriented tutorial; visualization of whole system or product; practice
Intermediate	Product capability reference manual; visualization; practice
Expert	Quick Reference Card
Intermittent	Visualization; strictly focused; limited; immediately applicable coverage of information; system intelligibility via robust system Help
Transfer	How new system or product differs from what they are used to

Another type of user is the "transfer user." This type of user has had a lot of experience with a predecessor or similar product, and wants to quickly know how and where the new product differs from what they are used to. These users enter the learning curve somewhere near the intermediate level, but these users especially need documentation components with titles such as "What's New About Brand X 3.0," or "Brand X 3.0 for Brand Y Users."

Expert

Expert users evolve from intermediate users over a period of months. While the intermediate users attempt to solve problems via a series of isolated commands, the expert users realize that an interconnected collection of statements can be more productive for certain tasks. Thus, the language read by experts can be very abstract. Experts are facile users and can deal with abstractions at the most global level. They may make use of all the mechanisms the product provides to maximize the performance of their tasks. They mainly require reference information to remind themselves of details about the services they use infrequently.

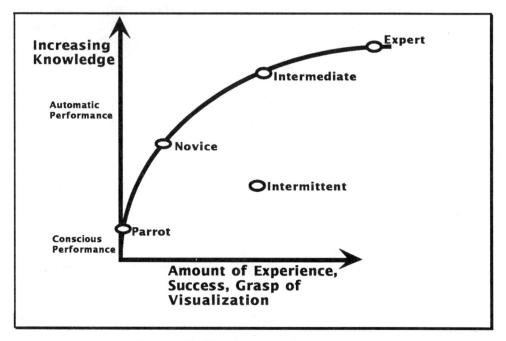

Figure 16. The user learning curve and the location of five user categories.

This difference between automatic and conscious performance also explains why so many reference manuals are written and why so few Ten-minute guides or tutorials are written. As documenters, we are probably automatic performers on the software we are documenting—we don't even know all that we know to operate the software. Reference manuals assume a good deal of unconscious/automatic knowledge. It is **very** difficult to recover the innocence and lack of knowledge we once had in those early learning stages when we were conscious performers and to embody them in a tutorial...but it is also **very** necessary.

What Makes an Expert an Expert, or How to Quicken Users Moves Up the Learning Curve?

Ideally our job is to get users as quickly as possible from the parrot stage up to the expert stage. And now that we understand a little bit about the various levels, we can ask the all-important question: What makes an expert an expert and how can we filter that down to parrots and novices quickly? You will find there are three very important documentation techniques to get parrots up to experts as soon as possible.

First, experts have a sense of success with the software or computer system—they have confidence because they have been successful in the past. Thus quick and easy "Ten-minute"-type guides for parrots or novices quickly give them a sense of success which will encourage continued use and mastery of the system.

Second, as we shall see in the section on visualizations coming up in this Step, experts have a mental map of the material that allows them to easily organize and access information. Thus you should develop a visualization or mental map in the documentation itself—very much like this book's repeated use of the SDP flowchart to give you a visualization of the whole book, or, in this book's longer chapter's, the repeated use of the side "menu" of chapter topics to allow you to visualize the whole chapter.

Third, experts are what's known as "automatic" users and parrots or novices are "conscious" users (Bailey, 1982; Hammond, 1987, 169). The difference between the two is like the difference between how you parallel-parked during Driver's Education classes in school—when you were so conscious of all the subtasks involved in parking that at times you almost lost sight of the end goal—and now when you parallel-park as a much more experienced driver—your performance of the parking subtasks is now unconscious and nearly automatic, so that you attend much more to the goal of the task of parking. To get a user to be an automatic performer, encourage them, force them, make them practice, practice, practice. There is no other activity in learning that improves performance as much as practice. One nice advantage of the minimalist design, therefore, is that its incompleteness forces users to actually use the system instead of just reading about it.

Intermittent Users

Intermittent users are, by definition, different from the four described above. Intermittent users work with the software so infrequently that they do not go through the learning stages. In fact, they may not want to go through the learning stages:

> "These users may not be willing to advance from one learning level to the next and demands upon them to do so generally only breed resentment" (Mozeico, 1982).

In dealing with this particular audience keep these three ideas in mind.

- First, documentation for intermittent users needs to be very brief. Half an hour from nonprogramming professionals' busy lives is about all that they are prepared to give to learning the use of a system that they will

The design of DWIM (Do What I Mean) Help messages is an example of how the software should be designed to accommodate intermittent users. DWIM diagnoses incorrect user commands, and it figures out what users would like to do but failed to do with the incorrect command. DWIM software then calls users' attention to their mistake, and offers users a number of alternatives for reaching their objective in the system (Teitelbaum, 1981).

require so rarely in their business (Martin, 1973). Also, documentation must be brief because intermittent users, who have very little of the reinforcement that comes with practice, retain details very poorly. Therefore, we need to limit the amount of detail in our documentation (Cuff, 1980).

- Second, because the documentation must be brief, intermittent users need a means by which they can easily "discover" additional specific system details when they need them. Intermittent users need a model of the system from which operational details can be discovered—they need a visualization. (See "Develop a Product Visualization"in this Step.)

Another reason such intermittent users need a visualization or model is that if we do not provide it, it is very likely that they will. But their model is likely to be a "ritual magical"model:

"[W]ithout specific guidance, USERs will construct their own models of the system and the methods to achieve goals using them. There is no reason for these models to have any rational, let alone axiomatic basis: such models will be at best, ritual magical systems. When USERs are not computer experts, their models will be overly-complex, difficult to generalize, and most likely of a wildly superstitious nature" (Thimbleby, 1984).

- Third, documentation alone will not take care of the needs of intermittent users. The menus, messages, and commands of a system should be designed to provide a safety net for intermittent users by guiding them along their chosen procedural path, always letting them know what to do next, and helping them to get out of problems.

An Audience's Background, Training, and Education

Knowing the background, training, or education of your audience allows you to decide on the level of language and the type of language to use. For example, a parrot-level accountant should get a different sort of wording than a parrot-level agricultural technician. Audiences should receive their computer system information clothed in the words, phrases, and metaphors familiar to them (McWilliams, 1983 (b)).

An Audience's Attitude Toward the Message and Change

Knowing the audience's attitudes or feelings about the information your manual imparts allows you to know what tone to take in a particular document. And very often, it's not what your manual says as how it conveys change in users' daily work routines. To accommodate these attitudes, your tone could range from reassuring parrot-level users that there is nothing they could do to harm the machine and that they should not be afraid of it, to a tone of no-nonsense directness for expert users.

Judge Mariana Pfaelzer of Los Angeles County sentenced a computer hacker to a rehabilitation center where he would be treated as an addictive personality (*Los Angeles Times*, August 1989, 3).

There is a continuum of user responses to the computer, ranging from computer maniacs:

"It has even been proposed that this [computer addiction] is a new former of mania characterized by 'cruising' computer stores, inappropriate use of computer terms in conversation, social withdrawal, sleep disturbance, physical deterioration, matrimonial difficulties...spending huge sums of money on computers, and anxiety over anticipated separation from the computer" (Van Dyke and O'Neal, 1986, 256).

These folks would probably not need much hand-holding or reassurance; in fact, the more minimalist the design, the better for these folks.

To Handle Computer Phobics or Audiences Resistant to Change:

- Include more hand holding, more reassurances, and more explicit linkage to what the audience already knows and feels comfortable with.

- Use the SDP specification reviews and prototype testing to decrease uncertainty and conflict during the change conveyed by the documentation, and to demarcate clearly the responsibilities and rights of software designers, managers, and users.

- Be flexible in the documentation medium you choose. A trained local expert conveying information orally could allow you to use the office's sociological organization to advantage.

But on the other end of the continuum, we have the computer phobics:

"The other extreme (computer phobia) first recognized over a decade ago, has been widely observed in the workplace.

Note the charter-like character of rights and responsibilities described in ISO (the International Organization for Standardization) Standard 6592, *Information Processing—Guidelines for the Documentation of Computer-based Application Systems (First Edition, 1985—11-15)*: "This [the User Manual] should describe, in a clear and concise way, the rights and responsibilities of both the user and the supplier of the system. The following are examples of what these rights and responsibilities may be: 1) The rights of the user may include: the right to information about usage of the system; the right to information about the system results and correction of errors in data. 2) The responsibilities of the user may include: the correct preparation of input data; informing the supplier of any errors detected in the system. 3) The rights of the supplier may include: the right to revise the system, as supplied; the right to perform continuous testing to ensure that the system continues to function correctly. 4) The responsibilities of the supplier may include: the maintenance of accurate and up-to-date documentation; the distribution of accumulated user experience with the system.

Age seems to be the variable with the most impact on computer phobia. In a study of 500 people, 1150% more younger people (20 years or less) moved from looking at a hypertext system to actually using it (Nielson, 1989, 243).

For instance in a survey of 40 randomly selected hospitals one researcher found that 45% of the institutions had experienced staff resistance to computers, even to the point of sabotage and 'oral defamation'" (Van Dyke and O'Neal, 1986, 257).

(See Brod, 1984, for an especially good discussion of possible negative attitudes or feelings toward our messages.) These people need much more hand holding, many more reassurances, and probably much more explicit linkage of what they are used to doing—working with folders and documents—to the computerized way of doing the same thing—Xerox/Apple's desktop interface is famous for reaching out to computer phobics.

But in addition to thinking about how a single user may react to the computers or to change, we should also consider the sociological context. Mirel, writing in 1988, made a number of observations on this facet of an audience:

"Computerization sets in motion an ever-evolving set of organizational responses. These responses touch on all aspects of organizational life: the restructuring of task responsibilities; the re-allocation of authority; shifts in the channels of communication; and re-conceptions of the interpersonal relations both within and between departments. Overall, these responses create an atmosphere of uncertainty and conflict" (Mirel, 1988, 280).

Such an "atmosphere of uncertainty and conflict" is not assuaged by just changing the tone in the manual. Such a sociopolitical problem of audience resistance means that the documentation process itself must help decrease this "uncertainty and conflict," and it does so by involving all the involved parties (users, management, designers, etc.) in the document development process by making them reviewers of the document specification and testers during prototype testing. Such activity

"conveys the bounds of user and programmer responsibilities and de-mystifies system-related information without championing the interests of any one group. To do so, however, in-house writers need to actively negotiate between the contending demands and goals of users and programmers and document in the manual the outcome of their efforts" (Mirel, 1988, 282) .

Through the review and testing process, the documentation process could reduce user alienation from the computer technology:

> Writers can use the processes of developing and maintaining the documentation to counter this alienation and evoke a greater receptivity to the technology. That is, the manual can make up for missed opportunities in user involvement" (Mirel, 1988, 289).

"When we put a new machine into an office, the entire sociological structure of the office will change. And oftentimes, the effect upon social structure will have more impact than the particulars of the hardware and interface design" (Norman, 1987, 327).

But I think that documenters must also be aware that there is a certain communal inertia that may prevent either paper or on-line documentation from being fully accepted and used immediately upon its production. From whom would you rather get information: a charming colleague over a cup of coffee or a silent cold computer?

> "The mere presence of a manual does not guarantee that users will alter their informal, conversational patterns for accessing information so as to include reference to the manual. Users are frequently reluctant to change their informal channels of communications because these channels provide a sense of social unity in the office" (Mirel, 1988, 284).

Thus, be flexible in the documentation medium you choose to use. As we will soon see in this Step, one medium by which to convey system intelligibility is trained experts strategically located throughout an organization. Using such local experts would allow you to tap into the sociological organization that the users feel comfortable with.

Multicultural Documentation

The following is an example of Japanglish from the preface of a C. Itoh Printer Manual:

> "We sincerely expect that the PRINTER CI-600 will be appreciated more than ever, in the fields of 'data-transformation' by means of human-scale, and the subsequent result of 'fluent metabolism' as regards the artificial mammoth creature—systematized information, within the up-to-date human-society."

It usually takes as much time to adequately translate a user manual as it does to write it in the first place.

Such Japanglish could cause us to smile perhaps, but when I taught in Singapore, I was brought up short when one of the Japanese programmers there explained his theory as to why their products do so well in the United States and why ours do so poorly in Japan.

He said, "When the Japanese send manuals to the United States...they send them in English, even if it is Japanglish as in the above example. And when the United States sends manuals to Japan...they also send manuals in English." In other words, *they* make the attempt to translate, whereas *we*, in many cases don't even try.

In the past we could afford to ignore the global marketplace because of our large domestic economy. But no longer—if a company or a piece of software is going to be successful, it's going to be successful in the global marketplace. There are four document design facets that need some adjustment if you want to develop your manuals for easy translation: vocabulary, different interpersonal relationships, different organization methods, and layout and design. What's most interesting about these techniques is that they are going to improve your documentation long before the product is shipped overseas; these principles are going to make it more accessible for American-English audiences. (Much of this multicultural material comes from Hartshorn, 1987, and Wilhelm, 1987.)

To Prepare Documentation for Multicultural Audiences

Choose appropriate vocabulary:

- Watch the connotative meanings of words.
- Avoid ambiguous terms.
- Be consistent.
- Consider American-English word meanings in other languages.
- Avoid the use of abbreviations, contractions, acronyms, jargon, and idiomatic expressions.

Be sensitive to other cultures' interpersonal acceptable tones:

- Use the imperative voice or familiar "you" in ways acceptable to the culture.

Realize that preference for a linear organization of documentation is a pattern not shared by all cultures.

Plan for an adaptable design and layout of documentation:

- Accommodate the American-English words and space expansion in translation.

- Attempt to use graphics.

Multicultural Vocabulary Decisions and Controlled English

When choosing appropriate vocabulary to use in your manual:

- Watch for the connotative meanings of words or messages. For example, try to imagine what these error messages implied when they were translated literally: "Fatal Error," "Terminal Error," "Illegal Instruction," or the two infamous UNIX messages: "Death in Family" and "Abort The Child." Avoiding such connotative terms in American-English manuals would be a vast improvement.

- Watch for ambiguous terms; especially troublesome words include: "while," "as," "so," "since," and "up to." For example, does "Record Error" mean there is an error in the record or that one should record the error. Such messages are ambiguous in American-English, let alone when they are translated.

- Be consistent in how terms are used or when they are used. For example, when describing how to press a function key don't sometimes say "press," and sometimes "depress," while at other times saying "mash," or "hit."

- Carefully consider the American-English term or name in another language. For example, even though the name for a Chevrolet car called "Nova" works in the United States, it means "Does not go" in Spanish —Chevrolet used it in Latin American nonetheless.

- Whenever possible avoid abbreviations, contractions, acronyms, idiomatic expressions, jargon, and complex indirect sentence construction. For example, what is OOPS ("Office for Operations in Political Systems" or

"The original 1984 translation of UNDO in the Danish Macintosh system was the completely miserable 'glem' [= 'forget'] which many novice users were scared to use according to the experiments done in my laboratory. In the current release, Apple Denmark has changed this to the much better 'fortryd' [= 'regret']" (Nielsen, July 1989, 70).

"Off-line OPerating Simulator") going to mean when it is translated in Hindi?

The best way to write documentation so that its vocabulary is easily translatable is to develop a corporate-wide commitment to an approach to writing called "Controlled English." British companies have long used this technique in dealing with the rest of Europe, and now this technique is even more important because it is the key to the future automation of translation. However, the payoff for the use of Controlled English happens long before the manual is translated into another language; our own American-English readers will have a much easier time understanding the meaning of our documentation.

Some before and after examples of the use of Controlled English are the following (Gustafson, 1988, 93):

Before: The unit includes electronic documentation compensation.

After: The unit checks the total thickness of forms and adjusts the force applied to the print hammer to make sure that all copies are printed.

Before: Overview

After: How to Operate the System

Before: Background

After: What this Program Does

Before: You need to press ENTER

After: Press ENTER"

A Controlled English Program Includes (Gustafson, 1988):

- A limited common vocabulary

- A specialized vocabulary (i.e., product names, tools, routines, instructions, shapes, and geometric terms)

- A dictionary defining the meaning of all words in the vocabularies

- Simple writing rules and strict and rigorous punctuation rules so that translators do not have to deal with variant spelling or punctuation

- A review board or task force would meet periodically to determine the acceptability of new words to be added to the dictionary, old words to be deleted, or new punctuation usage

Already a number of companies employ Controlled English (Gustafson, 1988, 95):

- Kodak's Controlled English system, Kodak International Service Language (KISL), has a vocabulary of about 350 words.

- NCR's Controlled English, NCR Fundamental English, is used to write all types of technical manuals—software manuals, programming manuals, hardware manuals, and field service manuals.

SYSTRAN is also presently being used by the Commission of the European Communities and the German Society for Mathematics and Data Processing, and, according to Lufkin (1989) is the most tested and used translation program throughout the world—it runs on an IBM mainframe.

- But the most ambitious Controlled English program, and the one presently leading to automation of translation, is Xerox's Multinational Customized English (MCE). MCE provides a screened English language input to the SYSTRAN computer-aided translation (CAT) system. SYSTRAN then translates this Controlled English input into the target foreign language. In turn, SYSTRAN's output is then humanly checked for accuracy by a posteditor. The material generated this way is for service and training documentation, and Xerox claims that translation speed was increased 500% by using this process.

Gustafson (1988, 97) claims that the benefits of using a Controlled English approach in documentation go far beyond preparing manuals for translation. Controlled English also:

"One company that uses MT [machine translation] is Perkins Engineering. Since 1986, the company has been using Weidner MicroCAT for batch translation of its English manuals into French, German, Italian and Spanish. Tech-doc chief Peter Pym noted: 'Introducing MT was a logical consequence of using controlled English—which is its ideal input. In the long run, it's cost effective for the type of text we write: factual, non-literary and sometimes repetitive" (*Electric Word*, 20).

- Decreases liability litigation exposure because of fewer possible variant meanings of words.

- Allows for earlier product introduction because production time is cut—it is simply easier to write when the writer's search for an adequate vocabulary word is constrained by this limited vocabulary.

- Saves time and money

- Improves availability of documentation

- Leads to greater accuracy and quality

- Reduces user complaints while increasing sales

Multicultural Tone Decisions

"'We have to produce country-specific manuals though,' explains Mayer. 'Different countries have different laws about things like emission controls, so we have to include very specific warning messages in our documentation'" (Joscelyne,1989, 22–5).

In addition to the obvious necessary changes in vocabulary, there are some multinational issues that are much less apparent, i.e., interpersonal relationships conveyed in the document's tone.

We often use an imperative voice approach to writing instructions (e.g., "Enter the correct amount.") in the United States. However, this tone of command may not be appropriate in certain cultures. One of my Singapore seminar students informed me that this failure to project

This "imperative voice" approach to writing instructions will be seen most dramatically in Step 2, "Writing the Documentation," in the discussion of the playscript and structured writing writing styles.

Also see the use of "you" in Step 3.

an adequate "span of discretion" for the audience would be simply unacceptable in her office.

We also often use the familiar "you" in our documentation (i.e., "First, you should make a backup of your program disk"). However, this tone in Great Britain is deemed too informal (i.e., they would rephrase the example above as "First, the user should make a backup of their program disk").

Multicultural Organizational Decisions

Another less obvious multicultural difference has to do with organization (Dennett, 1988; Kaplan, 1966). As Kaplan pointed out:

> "Speakers and readers of English have a clear preference for a pattern in written communication that is predominantly linear in its development [inductive or deductive in its arrangement]....On the other hand, Arabic language readers and speakers expect predominantly a complex series of parallel constructions, both positive and negative; Korean readers and speakers expect indirection....In French and Spanish many more digressions or introduction of extraneous material is expected" (402–8).

What one does about this problem with different cultures using different methods of organization is unclear. But perhaps it will prepare you for certain misunderstandings other cultures may have of your documentation, and it might prepare you for some type of rewriting tasks in bringing foreign manuals into the United States.

Multicultural Design and Layout Decisions

The final area to consider when dealing with multicultural audiences is the design and layout of the information. In particular, there are two issues you should consider:

- American-English frequently expands in numbers of words and space required when translated, e.g., it usually expands 40–60%, but it can take as much as 800% more words and space to say the same thing about a computer— as in Indonesian—as it does in American-English. (This, of course, has big impact with on-line documentation in windows.)

Some ways in which American firms have sought to handle this translation problem is to leave more white space than is absolutely needed on the English page or in the English message window. In this way, when it is translated, the translated message simply uses up some of the extra white space. John Deere also uses large type sizes in their American-English manuals which simply become a more normal type size when translations expand the space needed.

- Another technique companies have used in dealing with translation problems has meant taking a more graphic approach (see Vogt, 1986). For example, Kodak's KISL writers:

"feel that visual communication is more universally understood and superior to verbal communication, so it's more widely used" (Gustafson, 1988, 96).

Consider how little, if any, translation is required by the diskette manufacture (Wabash) who prints Figure 17 on the back of their diskette protection sleeves. Is any translation needed at all?

John Deere tractor documentation writers use a graphic approach to documentation called the "minimum word method." See also the "Super Comic Book" writing style in Step 3.

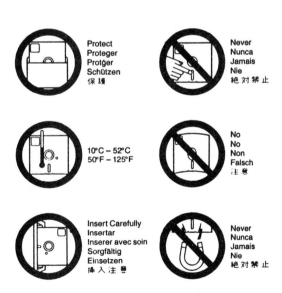

Figure 17. A Graphic approach to documentation.

How to Deal with Diverse Audiences

"Look Me in the Eye When You Write That User's Guide."Pfeffer, Australian Bulletin Board Poster (1969).

First, you need to get first-hand, specific knowledge of your audiences by meeting your users. You could, for instance, try Hewlett-Packard's management technique which was described in *In Search of Excellence:*

> "Hewlett-Packard uses the term MBWA—Management By Wandering Around. Wandering around should mean listening to the user in a direct, not in an abstract or shorthand form. A general manager who designed a major new computer, as sophisticated a person as I know, did a neat trick: 'I bought my uncle a computer store. I spent my nights and weekends working there. My objective was to stay as close to the ultimate user, observe his frustrations and needs firsthand, incognito.' His learning was reflected in the eventual design in a thousand little ways and several big ones" (Peters, 1982).

Perhaps we should develop documentation using DBWA—*Documentation By Wandering Around.* If direct meetings with users are not possible, you could try using phone or written surveys (Horton, 1984 (b)).

The four major types of users—parrot, novice, intermediate, and expert—actually are stages that every user passes through when learning your software. Good documentation should grow with users and allow them to access the type of documentation appropriate for their particular stage of learning. Thus we need to develop a document library designed to accommodate each user's evolution from parrot to expert. Users are not static, and our presentation of information should not be either (Mozeico, 1982).

Parrot users, for example, might benefit from a small pamphlet entitled "A Ten-Minute Guide To Using X." The information in the pamphlet is minimal, has few alternatives, and yet would give parrot users a sense of success when they can use software, albeit a simplified version, in ten minutes.

To Best Handle Diverse Audiences

- Develop a documentation library with documents for every type of audience along the learning curve so that the documentation can grow as the audience grows in knowledge and expertise.

- Include a "How Best to Use This Manual" in the preface that suggests how different levels of readers should read the manual in different ways.

- Explicitly label sections as to their intended level of user sophistication, or use consistent placement of information pertaining to different audience needs, e.g., the STOP writing style.

- Use the query-in-depth approach to on-line documentation so that readers can go deeper into a subject on-line that in fact custom-fits the information to their needs.

Once users are interested in your software because of this ten-minute success, they have become novices and have acquired the motivation to read section one of your manual, your lesson-by-lesson task-oriented tutorial.

When users reach the intermediate stage—usually after 60 days of using your software and reading your documentation—they need something more comprehensive, something organized like an encyclopedia so they can quickly find what they need. Thus, these users are ready for the second section of your manual—the product-capability reference section.

Finally, they have mastered your software and find that even the reference manual is too wordy and has too much extraneous information. This is where a quick reference card, with an overview list of software capabilities, commands, etc., comes in.

Designing a documentation package to include a ten-minute guide, a task-oriented tutorial, a product-capability reference manual, and a quick reference card is designing a documentation package to grow with users. It also gives readers the freedom to access information in the form they find most appropriate. M. L. Schneider's concept of types of audiences in many ways outlines the various parts of our documentation library.

We can accomodate large-scale differences among users in separate documents, or, if we do not have the opportunity to use multiple documents or modules, we can accommodate small-scale variations in our audiences by the following (Gleason, 1984):

- Explicitly directing readers to the text portions meeting their needs, (such as in the Introduction of this book).

- Labeling sections in the text according to their target level of sophistication—this was done by IBM in their recent VM documentation.

- Designing pages or screens consistently so that particular audiences always know that the information they need and the way they need it is always presented in the same location on each screen, i.e., overviews for knowledgeable audiences are always presented in a window on the top left of a screen while detailed textual description always appears on the bottom left (see the STOP and FOMM writing styles in Step 3).

State the Purpose for Each Document

The technical purpose for a document is often obvious, e.g., the user manual for an IBM 3741 emulation program should tell the user how to run the emulator. The subtler business purpose for a document is often not so obvious. For example, the business reason for documenting an IBM 3741 emulation program is that the company wishes their non-IBM system to be viewed in the marketplace as an IBM-compatible product. This has to be a key marketing ploy in a marketplace dominated by IBM, and it is an image that the writers of such documentation should be careful to conjure up as they are describing how to run the emulator.

To state the purpose for a document effectively, you need to answer two questions (Mathes and Stevenson, 1976):

- What is the specific technical problem?

- What is the general business background problem that needs an answer?

Responding to the second question often requires involving a number of people participating in the software project. People with varying perspectives will probably keep you from falling prey to tunnel vision.

You should not start writing until you can state your purpose on an index card. Stating it so succinctly ensures that the purpose is conceptually clear to you.

Step 1: Design The Specifications

Break Down Documentation
  by Tasks
Use a Minimalist Design
Plan for an Audience
▶ State the Purpose
Organize Information
Develop a Product Visualization
Pick the Appropriate Medium
Decide on Typrography, Layout,
  Color and Page Size
Plan for Updating
Consider the Competition
Develop a Timing and Cost
  Scheme

Post the index card near your writing area so that you can continually glance from your writing to the card to monitor your faithfulness to the stated purpose.

Organize Information

There are two primary principles to follow in effectively organizing text material in documentation:

- Make the organization of material apparent to readers
- Organize documentation in ways expected by readers

The first principle is that the organization must be apparent. This means that the writer must "tip off" the reader with words, graphics, or layout regarding how the information is to be organized. Making the organization of information apparent is exemplified by the first rule of all public speakers:

> Tell the folks what you're going to tell' em, before you tell'em.

"The best performance on a post-test consisting of realistic tasks was obtained from the general-to-specific and explanation-to-specific conditions....Here [general-to-specific inferences] the instructions state a general procedure or rule and the users must infer how the general procedure is applied to the specific context. For example, when making field declarations the user might be told that field length should be large enough to allow for most values that could go in the blank, but not larger than is necessary. From that the user would have to infer how many spaces to reserve in the current instance" (Black, Bechtold, Scott, Mitraini, and Carroll, 1989, 81).

The second principle stems from a recognition that readers bring generic expectations of text organization to the task of reading our manuals (reading scientists call these expectations "schemas" (Anderson, 1978)). Therefore, we need to acknowledge and use these expectations if we are to communicate our information effectively (Bach, 1981; Crenshaw and Philipose, 1983; Thorndyke, 1977).

If we use readers' expectations, we need to teach the readers only our new facts; we can rely on their expectations to anticipate the text's organization and to digest the material smoothly.

If we do not user readers' expectations, we must not only teach our readers our new information, we must also teach them how we organized the material—in fact, we must teach them to read. Such a dual task has been imposed by writers of modern fiction such as William Faulkner and James Joyce. Neither of these authors, however, had as their primary purpose the conveying of specific facts or procedures.

"Opaque wordsmith James Joyce is quoted as saying: 'to understand my work you must devote your life to it'" (Nelson, 1987, DM-25).

An example that shows the confusion that can result when the reader's expectation of organization is denied can be seen in the following report by an insurance investigator. It seems that the investigator was looking for facts about an insurance applicant's occupation:

> Applicant is employed by a car dealership. He does no manual-type work, no mechanical work, no delivery work, and no sales. He is the manager.

When material is organized like this—very much like a riddle—the readers do not know what to expect. Therefore, they must assemble the seemingly isolated facts and then guess how all the facts fit together. This method of processing information has been shown by reading research to be very poorly adapted to reading and recalling behaviors—two behaviors we want to simplify, not complicate (Meyer B., 1980). Therefore, we need to organize the text in ways expected by readers.

Next, we need to consider specifically the expectations that readers have of text organization. These include:

- Chronological order. Material is presented from the events or items that occur first to those events or items that occur last. This is the most powerful way to organize material because it is most like the way we experience our daily activities.

- Most important to least important order. Material is presented in descending order of importance to the reader.

- Order of need. Material is presented in descending order of the frequency with which readers will need to use it.

- Order of difficulty. Material is presented in increasing magnitude of its difficulty in terms of use or understanding.

The final four ways to organize material are ways still easily understood by readers and expected by readers. These, however, are less powerful ways to organize material because the organizing principles are becoming more arbitrary and imposed—these principles are not necessarily self-evident to readers.

These ways of organizing material are as follow:

- Question/answer order. This was the organization used by Ford in the 1919-1925

Step 1: Design The Specifications

Break Down Documentation by Tasks
Use a Minimalist Design
Plan for an Audience
State the Purpose
Organize Information
Develop a Product Visualization
Pick the Appropriate Medium
Decide on Typrography, Layout, Color and Page Size
Plan for Updating
Consider the Competition
Develop a Timing and Cost Scheme

edition of their Model T user manual; see Figure 18.

The Rear Axle Assembly

How is the Rear
Axle removed?   *Answer No. 77*

Jack up car and remove rear wheels as instructed in Answer No. 89.   Take out the four bolts connecting the universal ball cap to the transmission case and cover. Disconnect brake rods.   Remove nuts holding spring perches to rear axle housing flanges.   Raise frame at the rear end, and the axle can be easily withdrawn.

How is the Universal Joint dis-
connected from the Drive Shaft?   *Answer No. 78*

Remove two plugs from top and bottom of ball casting and turn shaft until pin comes opposite hole, drive out pin and the joint can be pulled or forced away from the shaft and out of the housing.

How are Rear Axle and
Differential disassembled?   *Answer No. 79*

With the universal joint disconnected, remove nuts in front end of radius rods and the nuts on studs holding drive shaft tube to rear axle housing.   Remove bolts which hold the two halves of differential housing together.   If necessary to disassemble differential a very slight mechanical knowledge will permit one to immediately discern how to do it once it is exposed to view.   Care must be exercised to get every pin, bolt and keylock back in its correct position when reassembling.

How is the Drive
Shaft Pinion removed?   *Answer No. 80*

The end of the drive shaft, to which the pinion is attached, is tapered to fit the tapered hole in the pinion, which is keyed onto the shaft, and then secured by a cotter-pinned "castle" nut.   Remove the castle nut, and drive the pinion off.

How is the Rear Axle
Shaft removed?   *Answer No. 81*

Disconnect rear axle as directed in Answer No. 77, then unbolt the drive shaft assembly where it joins the rear axle housing at the differential.   Disconnect the radius rods and brake rods at the outer ends of the housing.   Take out the bolts which hold the two halves of the rear axle housing together at the center and remove the housing.   Take the inner differential casing apart and draw the axle shaft out.

After replacing the axle shaft be sure that the rear wheels are firmly wedged on at the outer end of the axle shaft and the key in proper position.   When the car has been driven thirty days or so, make it a point to remove the hub cap and set up the lock nut to overcome any play that might have developed.   It is extremely important that the rear wheels are kept tight, otherwise the constant rocking back and forth against the keyway may in time cause serious trouble.

If the rear axle or wheel is sprung by skidding against a curb, or other accident, it is false economy to drive the car without correcting the trouble, as tires, gears and all other parts will suffer.   If the axle shaft is bent, it can, with proper facilities, be straightened, but it is best to replace it.

38

Figure 18. Ford's question/answer organization of the Model T user manual (1919–1925 edition, reprinted by permission from Polyprints, Inc., Nashville, TN).

- Comparison/contrast order. Material is presented on two or more items exhibiting their similarity or contrast.

"For the individual who knows what command he or she wants, the alphabetic structure will typically be most effective....More typically, however, users will not be well practiced nor will they have an overlearned organization of the knowledge domain (as would be found with popular databases). For this more typical case, a functional organization will be more effective when the user does not know exactly what command is required—as is often the case with novice and intermediate users. Indeed, our results suggest that the greater the user's uncertainty about the desired command, the more effective the functional organization will be" (Mehlenbacher et al. 1988).

- Spatial order. Material is presented on the basis of some illustration (e.g., an illustration of a data entry screen is shown, and then the fields are explained from left to right or top to bottom).

- Alphabetical order. This is the least powerful means and is used only as a last resort. Even for reference material written like an encyclopedia, the writer should still seek to group and order the material.

Microsoft documenters, however, have gone to a modified alphabetical arrangement in their reference manuals, and it must be working for Microsoft because

"...a Griggs-Anderson study of Microsoft Excel users cite an 89% satisfaction index with the alphabetic organization" (Slivinski, 1989, WE-88).

Techniques to Overcome On-line Organizational Problems

This is our first attempt at directly solving the problems of on-line documentation we discussed in Part One. In each of the succeeding sections focusing directly on on-line documentation, my major effort is to demystify the handling of such problems. You will soon observe that most of the solutions come from knowledge about writing for paper documentation. But not without some modifications.

To Overcome On-line Organizational Problems:

Don't scroll. Break everything into discrete screen size chunks so that the on-line documentation developer can have some control over the structuring of information. This will allow you to achieve the structural cohesion expected by readers of a paper paragraph (Control Data , 1983).

- Chunk on-line information into smaller pieces as has traditionally been done in paper documentation.

- Provide readers with a richness of local and high-level navigational buoys so that they know where they are.

- Offer users a number of different ways of navigating through on-line information.

- Present information via windows and split screens.

Chunking Information

First, the atomic particle on which all interlinking of screens is based must be on a much smaller chunk of information than has thus far been found in books which had a letter size or A4 metric size "canvas" to display information. Most current computer screens are much smaller "canvas," and they call for new organizational skills. For example, in a study of expert on-line documentation writers in 1988, Gomoll et al. found that a majority of the experts stressed the importance of chunking the information into screen size, standalone units (Gomoll et al., 1988, 9). This majority noted that chunking the information into screen size, standalone units could encourage writers to be more concise, more visual, and produce more pleasing information (Gomoll et al., 1988, 9).

One problem with chunking, however, is how to decide on what principle you will chunk. Should you chunk information based on the content—the so-called "functional units" (Girill, 1984; Price L., 1982)? Or should you chunk information based on the physical constraints of the screen (Girill, 1984; Ridgway, 1983)? The only problem with this latter solution is that the size of the screen is changing with each new workstation—and in some cases now, screen size is "user-configurable" so that the window sizes and shapes cannot be determined by the document designer.

Perhaps the best way to chunk information in this on-line medium is based on a hybrid of the two; the chunks could have a variable number of lines dynamically changing to fit the physical constraints of the screen, but they would be centered around a content-sensitive keyword somewhat like the presentation of information in a KWIC (key-word-in-context) index (see Step 3, Indexes, and Kehler and Barnes, 1981; Sander, 1982).

Once we have designed our text into these chunks, we need to be sure that there are enough navigational buoys that users can know where they are. Like paper pages, on a local level of organization, each screen should be numbered and titled:

> "Getting lost in a hypertext database is a common and serious problem....Disorientation occurs because users do not have enough information about their current location relative to the overall structure of the database. Most hypertext systems provide little in the way of location cues. On the other hand, books provide page numbers and chapter headings as well as thickness that help readers determine where they are (or where they were)" (Shneiderman and Kearsley, 1989, 49).

> "The writers in the group were very positive about using the hypertext technology for writing technical manuals. To paraphrase from a discussion about modularity: 'Lots of technical writers have tried for modularity; having it enforced by the environment is very different. It helps you isolate units and pushes you in the direction of thinking things through logically...' Basically the writers felt that being able to *see* the modular structure of their documents as they were writing contributed significantly to the ease of doing their job" (Walker, 1989, RT-178).

> "An experiment ...using the Hyperties system in which the same database was created as 46 short articles from 4 to 83 lines long and as 5 articles of 104 to 150 lines. Participants in the study were asked to answer multiple-choice questions using the database during a time limited to 30 minutes. The 16 participants working with the shorter articles answered more questions correctly and took less time to answer the questions" (Shneiderman and Kearsley, 1989, 72).

Creating The On-line Navigational Buoys

"System designers should provide users with a 'You Are Here' map similar to the diagrams we see when we enter new buildings. Such a map can provide answers to four essential orientation questions that users ask: Where am I? What can I do from where I am? How do I get out? How do I get to other places I have either been or know about?" (Stahl, 1986). An archetype example of this is the NoteCards Browser (Conklin, 1987; Halasz, 1988).

But on the macrostructure level, another navigational buoy is needed to give the reader an overview, or a sense of the whole "text" and where the various pieces of the "text" fit in—a kind of view of the forest and view of the tree concept that on-line specialists are calling the "fisheye lens" view (Furnas, 1986). This buoy would mean that in one window you have a verbal or graphic map of the whole document, and in another window you present the specific information. That way readers always see information in context. This technique was used to great advantage in a new system called SuperBook:

> "The second SuperBook enhancement is a type of fisheye viewer. Large amounts of text present severe navigation and disorientation problems for users. The fisheye viewer counters such problems by displaying hierarchically structured information according to a 'degree of interest function.' The fisheye viewer permits a user to examine detailed, low-level information in the focus of a display while it maintains successively more global, higher-level information on the display periphery" (Egan, Remde, Landauer, Lochbaum, and Gomez, 1989, 205-6).

This technique seemed to work. When the researchers tested the SuperBook on-line documentation against conventional paper documentation, they found SuperBook had a large advantage in search accuracy and search time compared to conventional documentation (Egan, Remde, Landauer, Lochbaum, and Gomez, 1989, 209):

"Pat Wright [British psychologist from the Applied Psychology Unit in Cambridge and an expert on the technology of text] performed an on-line organization experiment in which she put information about organization first in a separate window and then in the same window. She found that subjects who used the first design—all the navigational information was placed in a separate window—rated 48% of the items as suitable while the users of the second design rated it as only 20% suitable for electronic presentation" (Nielsen, October 1989, 45).

- When users were given questions that included words taken either from the appropriate topic heading or from the text in the vicinity of the answer, SuperBook users had a 10–40% advantage in finding target information.

- When given open-book essay questions that required gathering information from more than a single page of text, students using SuperBook wrote essays whose scores averaged 61% higher than those written by students using the conventional documentation.

- The ease of use and overall superior performance of SuperBook probably led to users' enthusiastic subjective evaluation.

- SuperBook's advantage over conventional documentation appears to be greatest for dealing with questions that are not anticipated by an author's organization of a document

Moving Through On-line Information: Hypertext and Keyword Search

"Hypertext systems are often confused with text search systems that find keywords in context. Such 'brute force' search methods are relatively easy to implement but are only partially successful because it is difficult to determine which of the 'hits' are relevant. This process is like trying to read a book from the index. You may be catapulted into the middle of the database and may become disoriented" (Shneiderman and Kearsley, 1989, 11).

At the very least, give users control over screen paging and over exiting the system. The ability to quit at one's own discretion introduces a quality of experimentation that increases a learner's willingness to use trial and error to learn about a system. The user knows that there is always a way to exit from the system without doing irreversible damage (Gaines and Shaw, 1984). Possibly even give them an "undo" facility (Monk, 1984).

The simplest way to organize chunks of on-line information is by using nested layers of information. Layers of information can be nested, so that although each individual screen is short, the reader has the ability to call up additional information on a particular concept from other screens. This is called query-in-depth. This query-in-depth customizes the level of detail in an on-line document to an individual reader's need (Bork, 1983; Frenchel, 1981; Patterson, 1981; Relles and Price, 1981; Rothenberg, 1979).

Beyond these simple methods of moving forward, backward, deeper, and quitting, users can be given control over information retrieval by either targeted means (e.g., keyword searches and indexing) or navigational means (i.e., hypertext links):

"In targeted searching, the user provides an a priori specification of what is required. The specification typically consists of one or more words or terms found in the database....A further, significant characteristic of this implementation of targeted retrieval is that it tends to encourage failure. If the search specification contains only a few words, many documents will be found, and the user becomes frustrated while scanning through much irrelevant material. Conversely, a very explicit specification containing many words typically ends up finding nothing. Either way the user can easily become discouraged and give up....In contrast, navigational searching (frequently referred to as hypermedia or hypertext access) requires no prior specification. Instead, the searcher navigates into and through the database, using links and structures created by the database author....Navigational, or hypertext systems,are intrinsically easier to use than targeted systems, but provide a characteristically narrower view of the database" (Holmes, 1989, 299-302).

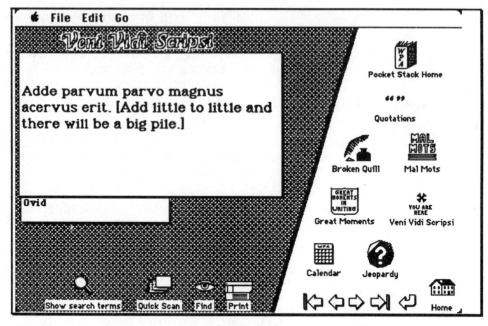

Figure 19. Combining targeted and navigational access: sample screen from hypertext document, *The Writer's Pocket Almanack* (Brockmann and Horton, 1988). Hypertext link buttons are displayed to the right, and targeted keyword search buttons are shown with at the bottom.

"Researchers have found an inverse relationship between recall [thoroughness] and precision [retrieving only relevant documents]" (Zoellick, 1987, 67).

Targeted movement via keywords is a possibility—in many cases what books used to do with indexes with "see" or "see also" to overcome scatter in usual book index parlance. For example, in the SuperBook hypertext, "rich indexing" was used:

> "Research has shown that search success rates can be increased from 20-80% if multiple names are allowed because research has shown that people experience difficulty in finding information in large text databases. The root problem is that users try to find information using words different from those selected to index the information" (Egan, Remde, Landauer, Lochbaum, and Gomez, 1989; see also "aliasing" from Shneiderman and Kearsley, 1989, 43).

But such targeted keyword searches have their problems:

> "An article by Blair and Maron (1985) received a great deal of attention because it raised fundamental questions about

the usefulness of many contemporary document retrieval systems. Part of the article's notoriety, no doubt, is due to its closing sentence: 'Full text-searching is one of those things, as Samuel Johnson put it so succinctly, that'...is never done well, and one is surprised to see it done at all.' Robert Carr (1986) expressed the same sentiment: 'There is no doubt that keyword searches of CD-ROMs will be a standard tool. But unassisted, the user exploring the CD-ROM with only a keyword search facility is left in the position of an ice fisherman dangling his line through a small hole in the ice. He must guess what fish might be in the water below, set the appropriate bait, cast through the small hole in the ice, and hope to hook a fish" (Zoellick, 1987, 66).

For a taste of sample hypertext projects see Brockmann, Horton, and Brock, 1989; Bush; 1945, Yankelovich, Smith, Garrett, and Meyrowitz, 1988; or Cook ,P., 1988.

And what users have thought of using the alternative navigational method of accessing information is mixed. On the positive side,

"Perhaps the only direct comparison of hypertext and paper materials to date has been done with the Hyperties system (Marchionini and Shneiderman 1988). Those studies showed that Hyperties typically resulted in longer task completion times with no gain in accuracy compared to paper materials. Users did, however, prefer the Hyperties system to paper " (Egan, Remde, Landauer, Lochbaum, and Gomez, 1989, 205).

And a report about the LOCATOR hypertext project also showed a successful use of this hypertext-linking method of organizing:

LOCATOR was developed in Great Britain in a joint project of the University of Kent and ICL Computer Company using GUIDE from OWL International. LOCATOR is used by ICL service technicians to respond to hardware fault calls phoned in by customers.

"The LOCATOR experience was that diagnosis was 20% better than when done from a a paper form of the information. The proportion of customer calls handled correctly had changed from 68% correct when using paper to 88% when using the hypertext, even rising to 92% after some use of the system....The primary advantages of hypertext are better information and quicker access to the information. A further advantage is that when hypertext comes into a company it provides an opportunity to standardize the information "(Nielsen, October 1989, 43).

On the other hand, some of the of the concerns mentioned by researchers are

| cf. |

"Overall the results indicate that for less-complex tasks, solution times were significantly faster when subjects were provided the HyperCard user's manual [paper]; however for complex tasks, subjects were faster performing the information-retrieval tasks when provided with the on-line HyperCard Help...Thus, it appears that the hypertext structure is better suited for the retrieval of complex information than it is for simple data retrieval" (Barfield et al., 1990, 26).

- The user's cognitive costs of using hypertext links:

"In her conclusion, [Pat] Wright said that the cognitive costs of using hypertext are not yet well known with respect to non-hypertext solutions or with respect to which of several alternative navigation styles would match users' tasks. She also feared that the cognitive demands on authors could be excessive as long as we do not have better tools" (Nielsen, October 1989, 66).

- The hand-craftedness of hypertext navigational links:

"Hand-crafted links are created individually by the hypertext composer. The exact method for creating links varies between composers and programs, but in all the programs that use this type of linking, the decision to link is in the hands of the composer" (Alschuler, 1989, 344).

And, perhaps it's not just the hand-craftedness of the links that leads to inconsistent on-line structures, but the fact that the links find their value and effectiveness in a particular reader's task focus, prior knowledge, and method of synthesizing information. Links that conflict with such a reader's context give use the "used textbook problem:"

"Like a used textbook, some of the highlighting and margin notes may be useful to another student, but they may be distracting or misleading at other times" (Glushko, 1989, 58).

- And finally, using hypertext links that allow the user some control over organization does not excuse the documenter from thoughtful, difficult, time-consuming attention to effective organization:

"One thing that does bother me, however, is the belief that hypertext will save the author from having to put material in linear order. Wrong. To think this is to allow for sloppiness in writing and presentation. It is hard work to organize material, but that effort on the part of the writer is essential for the ease of the reader. Take away the need for this discipline and I fear that you may pass the burden on to the reader, who may not be able to cope, and may not care to try. The advent of hypertext is apt to make writing much more difficult, not easier. Good writing, that is" (Norman, 1988).

Which on-line method of moving through information should be offered to users? The best answer to such a question is that we should probably combine all these methods of retrieving information because which access method is used depends upon the user's level of expertise—and this level of expertise grows and changes:

---

cf.

Work on automating link creation has recently been reported by Jordan, 1989.

Other methods of retrieving and moving through on-line information can include bookmarking and automated retracing of one's steps. HyperGate, for example, has facilities for bookmarks, as well as margin notes, note cards, and copy machines (Bernstein M., 1988)). Our own hypertext, *The Writer's Pocket Almanack* (see Figure 19) has similar properties available to the knowledgeable HyperCard user—by choosing the Recent command from the Go menu, the user is offered a kind of bookmark in the way Recent shows miniature representations of the 42 most recent screens traversed; and users of our hypertext can add their own links, buttons, and text fields as annotations to suit their own special interests. And hierarchical menus (as seen in NOS CONTEXT in Part One) replicate the top-down method of accessing in tables of contents.

"Experienced users of NaviText™ SAM orient themselves in a novel information space using browsing strategies with a hierarchical outliner and by following cross-references. The same users choose the more direct keyword search to access information in familiar information spaces...Experienced NaviText™ SAM users avoid getting lost in hyperspace by using bookmarks to formulate a breadth-first-search rather than follow cross-references and effectively use a depth-first-search" (Perlman, 1989, 79).

Use Windows or Split Screens

Studies by Tombaugh, Wright, and Lickorish at Cambridge University have shown the advantage of multiple windows in text reading tasks" (Shneiderman and Kearsley, 1989; see also Seabrook and Shneiderman 1989).

Use windows or split screens in presenting organized, chunked information to readers. When users call up on-line documentation while working in a problem-solving mode, they switch modes from problem-solving to learning. This mode change can "undercut the effectiveness of the on-line documentation, so the on-line documentation should be presented in "windows" or "split screens." Also, windows simulate the multiple and interactive tasks we perform in our real world. Thus windows solve a mode problem and give us another opportunity to build a real world analog to our software (Clark H., 1981; Dunsmore, 1980).

Future Ways of Organizing On-line Documentation: Hypertext Intelligent Assistants

In summary, we have replicated the navigational buoys of books—indexes have reappeared as keyword searches and links; verbal tables of contents have reappeared in windows as fisheye lens views while headings, titles, and page numbers are now screen titles and screen numbers. The navigational methods of books have been replicated, automated and enhanced in some ways. But there are ways that on-line documentation organization could in the future go further than paper documentation could ever go. For example, in an article entitled, "As We May Learn," Weyer suggests that the links of hypertext could use some help from an "intelligent assistant":

"Hypertext systems now coming into use hold the promise of letting us look at the library shelves to perceive neighborhoods of information and many interesting connections within and between subject areas (for example, cross-references between encyclopedia articles or bibliographic references to books)....However many problems must be overcome. Without help, browsing through everything in an information system can be as ineffective as searching blindly, creating a higher level of 'information gridlock.'...Browsing through this universe of information directly, without intelligent filtering to create

Develop a Product Visualization

An example of a paper visualization is the bubble flowchart on the cover, title page, and each step's first page in this book. An example of an on-line visualization can be seen in our screen from the hypertext version of the *Writer's Pocket Almanack* in Figure 19 on the right.

Step 1: Design The Specifications

Break Down Documentation
   by Tasks
Use a Minimalist Design
Plan for an Audience
State the Purpose
Organize Information
Develop a Product Visualization
Pick the Appropriate Medium
Decide on Typrography, Layout,
   Color and Page Size
Plan for Updating
Consider the Competition
Develop a Timing and Cost
   Scheme

---

smaller neighborhoods or guidance to prioritize trail selection, will be frustrating" (Weyer, 1988, 98).

A document visualization is a picture that functions like the outside pieces of a jigsaw puzzle and which provides a structure on which to hang all the individual aspects of the product description (Jonassen, 1982). Without a visualization, a software product can easily remain a shapeless blob with a thousand pieces.

Visualizations Aid User's Learning, Retention, and Mastery of Documentation Information

Visualizations help users better learn our information by being able to see the "whole" as well as the "parts." Lehner and Zirk (1987) compared the performance of two groups of users in an expert systems task. One group was provided with a description of how the expert system worked, whereas the other group was not. The group that was provided with the appropriate mental model performed much better than the group that had to make up their own models.

Visualizations help users remember information:

> "Graphically-based text organizers can determine how quickly and easily a user navigates through a manual or interactive program, and they may even help retention of the material. Bernard and Peterson (1981) found that two weeks after reading a text with graphic organizers, subjects performed much better on a comprehension test than their counterparts who used text without organizers" (Lewis, 1988, 241; see also Smith D., 1977; Gardiner, 1987, 157).

And finally, it's through the use of visualizations that the experts become experts—as we saw in our analysis of the various levels of users. For example, expert chess players could recall chess positions with a 90% accuracy because they had put them into relational structures.

Examples

Many products owe their success in a large part to visualizations. The visualization for Visicalc and the other "Calc's" is "an electronic spreadsheet." The visualization for the Xerox Star and all its Apple Macintosh descendants is the physical business office with in-boxes, wastebaskets, file drawers, and cluttered desktops (Gaines and Shaw, 1984).

"The experimental groups that learned from a model learned procedures faster, retained them more accurately, executed them faster, and simplified inefficient procedures far more often. They could infer the procedures much more easily, which would lead to more rapid learning and better recall performance" (Kieras and Bovair, 1984, 255; see also Lewis, 1988).

"[W]hat began as the conceptual model [visualization] for the documentation quickly acquired a life of its own and repeatedly suggested consistent directions for various aspects of the design" (Ledgard, Singer and Whiteside, 1981, Chapter 3, "The Annotated Assistant").

It is interesting to note, then, that all competing software packages developed since FirstDraft have called themselves "outline processors," a term both visual and more appropriate to the target audience's experiences.

Using Visualizations to Overcome On-line Rhetorical Problems

Another good example of a product visualization is the "frame" in Ashton-Tate's *Framework User Manual*, Chapter 1, "What Is Framework?" begins by defining frames:

> "Frames are containers that enable you to organize and store information. You can nest, and relocate frames anywhere on the screen" (p. 1-3).

This definition is then followed later in the book by sections carrying out this visualization: "Anatomy of a Frame," "Types of Frames," "Levels of Frames," "Selecting Frames," "Styling Frames," and so on.

How to Develop an Effective Visualization

- Present your visualization in the library specification because it will influence all later documentation, no matter what the audience or the medium.

- Keep your visualization consistent across all documentation so that the reader is not confused by different visualizations requiring different perspectives or understandings of the product.

- Be sure your visualization uses items or concepts familiar to the readers (e.g., a stack of index cards for a hypertext interface).

FirstDraft, a writer's software aid, offers an example of what can happen when the visualization is not familiar. FirstDraft claimed it was a "writer's spreadsheet." The metaphor of a "spreadsheet" may be effective for accountants who have worked with either the paper or the computerized spreadsheets. However, it is probably worthless as a visualization for a target audience of documentation writers who have no experience with spreadsheets.

As we saw in Part One, in addition to physical and organizational problems, there were rhetorical problems related to on-line documentation. Essentially this new on-line medium did not act like the old paper medium with which people were accustomed, and they described their problem as a "loss of a sense of text." And, just as we abstracted from paper documentation to develop some on-line documentation solutions, so too let us abstract from

"These results support previous findings by Dunsmore (1980) who showed that a decrement in performance for users with an on-line information system. Again, the on-line subjects may have taken more time than the manual group to form a mental model of the system's features..." (Barfield, et al., 1990, 27).

the paper documentation concept of visualization to develop some solutions to this "loss of a sense of text."

First, use a visualization in the on-line documentation just as we did in the paper documentation. This visualization in the on-line documentation, however, is even more crucial since there is no inherent analog of an on-line document's structure; we must invent it, teach it, and use it. In doing so we must remember that software is "theater" and must provide a coherent user illusion:

> "Critical to the success of each system is the appropriate use of a user's model, the conceptual model formed by the user of the information he manipulates and of the procedures he applies to this information" (Newman and Sproull, 1979; see also Kay, 1984).

Pick a visualization that is obvious to users such as the scroll control "elevators boxes" in Figure 20 which not only control scrolling through a file; but, just as importantly, give the user a sense of beginning-ness, middle-ness, and end-ness to a text—recovering the overall sense of text often lost in on-line documents.

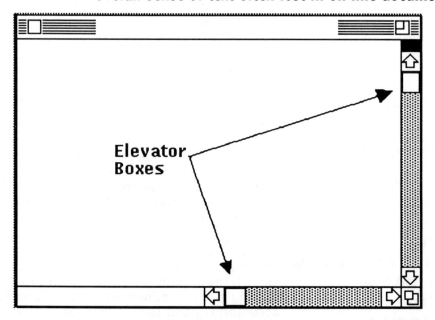

Figure 20. On-line visualization of scrolling elevator boxes to show beginning-ness, middle-ness, and end-ness of an on-line text file.

Be sure to teach users your structure before allowing them access to the on-line documentation. And remember to be consistent in your use of the structure. For example, if using a tree structure that uses "up" and "down" to move up and down the hierarchy of information, don't respond to a "down" command at the lowest level of the tree by switching to a "rolodex" model that shunts the user back to the main menu. If you do, the entire structure analog, illusion, or visualization built up in the reader's mind will be undermined (Control Data Corporation, 1983; Gaines and Shaw, 1984).

Also, to ensure consistency in all user documentation, both on-line and paper, consider creating such documentation out of a common database. The on-line documentation, although not identical to the paper documentation, should be consistent with it. Ideally, both the written and the on-line documentation should come from an identical database (Houghton, 1984). Honeywell's Computer-Assisted Publication (James G., 1985) accomplished this.

Having made all our conceptual decisions regarding the documentation, it is now time to begin making physical decisions. The first physical decision to make is what media should contain the documentation. In general, we can say that there are three primary media for documentation: aural media including trainers, telephone support, and expert users strategically placed in an organization to provide aid; paper media including manuals, brochures, reference cards; and on-line media in which our primary emphasis here will be on CD-ROM. Each medium has different strengths and weaknesses, and perhaps by the end you will see that because different readers have different learning styles (and sometimes the same reader at different times has different learning styles), we need a mix of media. No one medium is sufficient.

Choosing Between Different Media

We could try and fit the media to the learning styles of our audiences (Smith and Stander, 1981). These learning styles are aural, visual, and experimental. Aural learners "like someone to tell them what to do. They would rather not read instructions. They enjoy classroom courses or simply having another person sit down beside them, guiding them as they work" (Casey,

---

"With THUMB, an author enters the unformatted text corresponding to each of the finest divisions of an outline. These passages can be concatenated by the THUMB processor and run through a document formatter to produce a printed copy of the document. In addition, the passages can be individually processed and retrieved by an on-line documentation system" (Venezky, Relles, and Price, 1980).

Pick the Appropriate Medium

Step 1: Design The Specifications

Break Down Documentation by Tasks
Use a Minimalist Design
Plan for an Audience
State the Purpose
Organize Information
Develop a Product Visualization
▶ Pick the Appropriate Medium
Decide on Typography, Layout, Color and Page Size
Plan for Updating
Consider the Competition
Develop a Timing and Cost Scheme

For information on audio-visual media, see *Journal of Education and Industrial Television,* Lee and Misiorowski, 1978, Laurillard's *Interactive Media: Working Methods and Practical Applications* (1988), or Guillermo's excellent *Interactive Digital Video* (1990), a one-hour videotape supplement to the *Communications of the ACM* July 1989 special section on interactive technologies.

At a recent software documentation convention documenters from Microsoft pointed out that they offered users a library of documentation: a paper Getting Started/Roadmap to the documentation library, a paper ten-minute guide, a computer-based tutorial, a paper sampler book demonstrating via examples how the software could be used, a paper alphabetic reference manual (the phonebook) that repeated much of the CBT's content because not everyone uses the CBT.

1985; see also Cook K., 1983; Sandler, 1983; Wines, 1983). These users would probably best use audio or video media. Visual learners "want to have a clear picture of what the software product is, what it can do, and how it is used before doing anything with it" (Casey, 1985; see also Rosch, 1983). These users would best use the paper documentation (manuals, brochures, or reference cards). Experiential learners "like to learn by doing. They try something and if it doesn't work, they try something else" (Casey, 1985; see also Garvey, 1983; Myers, 1984). Perhaps these users would best use on-line documentation in the form of help messages that would appear as they are using the software.

Matching Media to User Learning Styles

- Aural learners prefer audio-video media or training courses with trainers.

- Visual learners prefer paper documentation (manuals, brochures, or reference cards).

- Experimental learners prefer on-line documentation in the form of help messages.

We could also choose various media based upon survey responses. In a 1985 survey, experienced users and writers of on-line documentation ranked their preferences for four instructional media (1=most preferred and 6=least preferred). The rankings were (Bradford A. and Rubens, 1985) as follows:

Ranking Media Preferences

- On-line tutorial   (average 2.58)
- Classroom course   (average 2.65)
- Hardcopy tutorial   (average 3.0)
- Trial and error   (average 4.0)

We could choose media that best fits documenters' experience. A survey of 85 technical communicators (Kirsch, 1989) found that they have written or rewritten three or more of the following documents types:

- 77% had experience writing printed software documentation manuals.

- 37% had experience writing sales material (data sheets, brochures, newsletters).
- 33% had experience writing reference pamphlets or quick reference cards.
- 19% had experience writing "system text" (menus, commands, messages).
- 15% had experience writing on-line documents (Help, computer-based training, demo).

And we could also consider choices between various media according to the table below illustrating the trade-offs between cost and benefit (Dell, 1985).

Cost vs. Benefit of Media

	Least			Most
Cost and Development Time	Manual	Video	On-line tutorial	Interactive videodisc
Updatability	Interactive videodisc	Video	Manual	On-line tutorial
Learning Retention	Manual	Video	On-line tutorial	Interactive videodisc

Paper Media Example: Quick Reference Cards

"...the Mitre Corporation is currently exploring hypertext technology for job aids to be used in the NASA Space Station. Due to the complexity of the equipment and procedures involved in operating the Space Station, and the fact that crews will have limited training, job aids will probably play an important role" (Shneiderman and Kearsley, 1989, 110).

There has long been a movement among professional documentation writers in favor of the adage, "Less equals more." And the minimalist design philosophy is simply the most recent incarnation of this belief. According to this way of thinking, 90% of the time 90% of the needs of 90% of the readers can be covered in a simple summary card or fanfold rather than in the customary bulky three-hole binders (Pakin and Associates, 1981; see also, Lawson, 1988; and Griffith, 1987).

Reference cards can be either of the abbreviated type or the full-disclosure type. The abbreviated card (an example of which concludes this book) assumes the reader is trained and has fully digested the information to which the card refers. (Akin to this abbreviated reference card are the plastic keyboard templates you fit over your control keys. Both act as system reminders, not complete explanations.) The

"Using performance aids [reference cards] to help achieve acceptable levels of human performance is not a new idea. The Incas of the 14th century in Peru used a device called a 'Quipu' (pronounced KEE-POO). The quipu was used by runners who carried messages from town to town concerning the trade of livestock, goods, births, deaths, and other such information. This device was simply a colored length of rope with a series of knots in it. Each knot, depending on its shape and position along the rope, enabled the runner to recall information such as who sent the message, the subject of the message, and the number of items involved" (Bailey, 1982, 446).

Active white space separates units of information and allows the reader to discriminate between sections. Passive white space is the white space ring around the perimeter of the page. It doesn't help the reader separate and discriminate between units of information.

Note: Optimal point size for legible type is dependent on viewing distance; see Horton, 1990,158–60.

Tyvek, a very durable plastic paper, is perfect for use in possibly wet or continuous use conditions in which ordinary paper would deteriorate

full-disclosure card does not assume as much on the part of readers and tends to continue explaining and training. Either type of card can be one- or two-sided, and can be posted under a keyboard or designed in a fanfold that fits into a pocket. It should serve one audience and one purpose. A summary of the qualities of a good reference card—be it abbreviated or full disclosure type—appeared in a book by Houghton-Alico (1985).

A Good Quick Reference Card Should:

- Contain only relevant information because it is very selective in its coverage and in the audience it addresses (an audience with some background or previous experience).

- Have adequate white space in its design—a good paper page or bitmapped screen usually has about 50% white space, a well designed green screen needs at least 50% "white" space to compensate for irradiance effect (more about this in the next substep). Readers believe that ample margins are justified in terms of both aesthetics and improved legibility. In fact, research has shown that well-designed pages have a "print density"of 50%—only 50% of the page has print on it (Dancheck, 1976). Also, the white space used on a page should be active white space rather than passive white space.

- Use a legible typesize—usually this means 10 point or 12 point with 8 point and less becoming progressively less readable (more about this in the next substep).

- Have a design with effective headings that logically group the information and that are easily decipherable by contrasting page placement, typeface, boldness, or size.

- Fit the environment—consider how the card will be physically used on the job in determining its size, paper type, binding, and placement (e.g., will the reader be able to use their hands to turn pages or to hold the card? If not, perhaps a wall poster presentation of the information would be best).

On-line Documentation Example: Optical Discs

CD-ROM

On-line documentation is, of course, much broader than just the information packaged in optical discs. On-line documentation can be packaged, transported, and transmitted in media ranging from standard floppy disks, the way most Help systems are currently published, to telecommunications, the way the DOCUMENT™ system worked in Part One of this book. And the optical disc technology of CD-ROMs could soon become obsolete because of the much lower mastering and publishing costs of other types of optical disc technology such as magneto-optical disks. But CD-ROM is the best current optical disc example to explore the possibilities and documenter responsibilities of cheap, large-scale, digital storage.

It's really only been in the last two years that on-line documentation stylebooks have been written for technical communicators (Horton, 1990; Kearsley, 1988).

What is a CD-ROM and why are many people so excited about it as a documentation medium? Convenience is certainly one of CD-ROM's primary advantages:

> "Formally introduced in 1985, CD-ROM combines PC power with laser technology and easy-to-use multimedia software. Users search large databases from their local workstations without high telecommunications costs or problems connecting with on-line services" (Bangasser, 1989, 6).

Coming CD-ROM subspecies: CDI is being designed as an interactive home information medium; CD-ROM-XA is being designed to use a microcomputer to offer reference applications with increased multimedia capabilities for professionals (Pogson, 1989, 44).

But it's not just the convenience for the reader, it's also that CD-ROMs cost less than paper documentation. As Mathur noted:

> CD-ROM is a low-cost publishing medium. This technology makes it possible to replicate more than 500 megabytes of information at a marginal cost of less than $10. To the publisher or printer, this is the equivalent of reproducing a page at a minimal cost—less than a small fraction of a penny. This cost of reproducing information was—and still is—the lowest known to man" (Mathur, 1989, 628).

"*CD Data Report* surveyed several production companies asking for bids on a hypothetical contract to produce 12 disks during a year with 250 disks per run. The bids were typically $1500 for the master disk, and around $2.50 per pressed disk in a jewel case with a label" (Press, 1989, 786).

CD-ROM Examples

- Boeing Aircraft and 757™ maintenance documentation

"Until recently, high-tech had stayed away from this part of the shop, where maintenance personnel refer to a 14-volume, 140-pound set of manuals. But CD-ROM has changed all that. A CD-ROM maintenance manual, developed for Boeing by KnowledgeSet and Sundstrand, combines a high-resolution personal computer display with vector graphics to bring 757 maintenance into the modern age. The manual offers all of CD-ROM's traditional advantages—large amounts of information in a small space, fast search and retrieval, powerful searches, and data integrity. It is presently being used by British Airways. When used commercially, Boeing will update the disc every 90 days at first, then over longer periods as the product ages and new procedures and notes become less common" (Strukfoff, 1989, 218; see also Johnson L., 1989).

• Engineering Data Compendium Design Textbook

"The *Engineering Data Compendium* is four volumes including nearly 3000 pages of text and more than 2000 figures, tables, and illustrations....The compact disc version of the Compendium contains all of the text and graphics from the printed version. The text of the Compendium occupies about 20Mb, with the graphics requiring another 150Mb. In addition, the disc contains another 40Mb for various indexes" (Glushko, 1989, 293, 295).

• Reference Guides for Tax Professionals

"1200 Arthur Andersen tax professionals now have Toshiba portable computers with CD-ROM drives in their briefcases....The disk contains more than 150 reference guides with proprietary procedures, software, and guidelines as well as published information like the SEC regulations" (Press, 1989, 785).

cf.

"CD-ROM disadvantages include: lack of currency—most CD-ROM databases are not updated as frequently as on-line databases; relatively high data preparation costs; lack of reliable data about the shelf life of optical disc media; and data access that can be slow and inefficient compared to magnetic media and on-line information retrieval" (Bangasser, 1989, 8).

"HP publishes roughly five million pages of documentation. Two million pages are really active, and 1.2 million are appropriate for CD-ROM. They are now producing over 3000 disks per month with 193 databases of product information, manuals, and other publications. To simplify production and presentation, diagrams are stored outside the text and accessed by clicking on icons embedded in the text" (Press, 1989, 785).

What do current users of CD-ROM think of it? Hewlett-Packard surveyed 80 software developers and operations and MIS managers who had been using CD-ROM documentation for nine months on the average. HP found user reactions to their CD-ROM documentation so favorable that they are now considering making CD-ROM the default method of publishing HP-3000™ minicomputer documentation and charging extra for paper editions. Here's why (Press, 1989, 785):

• 83% rated the overall usefulness of CD-ROM as medium or high.

• 75% of use is reading on screen rather than printing hardcopy.

• 63% indicated a willingness to give up paper manuals completely.

• 40% save from 2 to 5 hours per month compared to manuals.

- 21% save over 5 hours per month compared to manuals.

So we see that we can have a very inexpensive, convenient way to display data, and early users are claiming that CD-ROM is superior to their older paper documentation.

In general, what do you need to do if you already understand the other more general discussions we have been having about paper and on-line documentation? For example, writing is still writing whether it be on paper or CD-ROM/hypertext.

To Develop CD-ROMs

- First, develop your "texts" and use a markup language such as SGML so that you are device- and medium-free (we'll talk more about SGML in Step 6, Production).

- Second, use good indexing tactics in the development of your links (which we will discuss in Step 3). One should plan for a 20% overhead of memory, time and effort for indexing and other accessing aid development.

- Third, be humble enough to recognize that effective CD-ROM/hypertext with graphics, text, animation, etc., probably requires a group effort:

"These mixed-media scenarios now demand cross-discipline skills, understanding, and language from producers, engineers, programmers, and other communications executives" (Traub, 1989, 618).

"Just as desktop publishing de-mystified the publishing process, desktop optical will allow publishers to enhance and transfer their knowledge from print to optical. Many of the same tools and approaches to design are involved in both technologies. Additional knowledge in databases, indexing, digital audio, animation, interactive design, and CD-ROM pre-pressing will be needed to bring a desktop publisher into the optical domain" (CasaBianca, 1989, 638).

"At present, we seem to take visual literacy as a given despite the fact that our entire educational process aims at verbal literacy at the expense of the visual" (Rubens, 1989, 7).

Decide on Typography, Layout, Color and Page Size

Format is a crucial element in the creation of simple, effective, printed materials, but unfortunately, only recently has format been investigated and guidelines developed. British psychologist Pat Wright wrote:

"Increasingly it is being recognized that effective communication depends not only on the content of what is said, but on the way it is physically presented. Illegible or badly presented information can reduce the user's efficiency and may result in negative reactions to the information and its perceived source" (1981).

Typographic Considerations

There are ten typographic design elements to consider when developing either paper documentation or on-line documentation. It used to be that most of these

Step 1: Design The Specifications

Break Down Documentation
   by Tasks
Use a Minimalist Design
Plan for an Audience
State the Purpose
Organize Information
Develop a Product Visualization
Pick the Appropriate Medium
Decide on Typography, Layout,
   Color and Page Size
Plan for Updating
Consider the Competition
Develop a Timing and Cost
   Scheme

were the province of printers and typesetters, but with document processors, desktop publishing, and the ability to manipulate screen design characteristics, these have now become our area of focus. These eleven elements and their recommendations are as follows:

Typographic Recommendations

Element	Definition	Recommendations
Typeface	The look of the letters' presentation on the paper or the screen	Use serifed type for extended reading purposes; chose an appropriately toned typeface; use typefaces with a large x-height, keep the number of typefaces used to a minimum
Type size	The vertical size of the letters' (their point size)	Use 10 or 12 point, but be aware of typeface size variations
Family branch	Within the letters' typeface family, letters can be bolded, condensed, outlined, shadowed, etc.	Minimize typeface shape variations
Letter posture	Within the letters' typeface family, letters can be roman (straight up and down) or *italic*	Use roman for extended reading; use italic for rare occasions for contrast
Letter composition	Within the letters' typeface family, letters can be ALL UPPERCASE or a mix of upper and lower case	Use a mixture of upper and lower case
Leading	What we used to call double space or single space between lines	Use 1 point lead on paper; 15% of character stroke width on-line

Line measure	What we used to call the width of lines on a page	Keep line length between 4.5 inches and 1.67 inches
Appointment	Decisions on column justification or raggedness come within this element	Use ragged right
Wordspacing	Distance between words	Use less space between words than between lines
Letterspacing	Distance between letters	Use proportional spacing
Rulers, leaders, punctuation marks, and paragraph indentation		Leave behind typewriter practices and use proper typesetting marks

Typeface

There are four concerns you should keep in mind when choosing your document's typeface: Should you use a serif or sans serif typeface? What is an appropriate typeface for the audience, writer, and content? How can you make letters look large without sacrificing page or screen real estate? How do you avoid readers spending too much time noticing your typeface rather than your content?

Sumerian cuneiform type of writing in the third millennium B.C. was written top-down, Egyptian hieroglyphics were written top-down, the Chinese still write top-down, and it is only with the influence of Western writing systems that the Japanese are beginning to write horizontally.

Serifs are the little tops and bottoms of letters such as you can see in Figure 21 on the left. The reason that writing tends to be more legible when using serifs is because the human eye's natural tendency is to read from top to bottom vertically. Serifs tend to emphasize horizontal-ity and thus bind the letters into letter groups; they help move the eye horizontally rather than vertically down the page.

cf.

"Serifs suffer from reproduction processes that cutoff the thin serifs. Thus especially for on-line presentation, one wants to use slab serifs—the serif lines are 90 degrees to the verticals rather than serifs which curve on a diagonal which pixel densities on the screen make difficult to read "(White, 1988, 13-5).

This book uses a Lucida serifed typeface for the primary text. Many computer manuals use such serifed typefaces as Times, Schoolbook, Bookman, or Palatino as seen in Figure 22.

Figure 21. Serif (serifs are circled) and sans serif typefaces.

Another reason why many computer manuals use these particular typefaces is because they are *appropriate.* The typefaces in Figure 22 fade into the background, don't call undue attention to themselves, and generally could be called conservative.

> Times
> Schoolbook
> Lucida
> Palatino

Figure 22. Appropriate serifed typefaces.

Compare the typefaces in Figure 22 to those in Figure 23 which contain what many would consider inappropriately fancy, elegant, or clownish typefaces.

> *Chancery*
> Camelot
> Woodstock

Figure 23. Inappropriate typefaces.

Another reason why sans serif type generally was not recommended on legibility grounds is because the sans serif type usually had all the strokes of the letter identical and because the letterspacing tables associated with sans serif typefaces weren't as sophisticated as the serifed typefaces. However, two typefaces (Futura and Optima) have been developed to overcome just these legibility deficiencies, and, in fact, show very little difference in legibility when compared to serifed typefaces.

cf.

AT&T in their 1989 corporate-wide documentation standards and guidelines is now requiring serifed type (Caslon) for headings, and sans serif type (Helvetica) for body copy.

In addition to considerations of serif or sans serif, appropriate or inappropriate, you should also consider how the design of the typeface affects how the *reader perceives the type size* to be. For instance which one of the groups of letters in Figure 24 looks larger to you?

hdgxk   hdgxk

Times (24 point)   Lucida (24 point)

Figure 24. Which group of letters looks bigger to you?

The group of letters on the right looks larger not because of a type size difference—both are 24 points high—but rather because of their design. As you can see in Figure 25, letters are made up of ascenders, descenders, and x-heights.

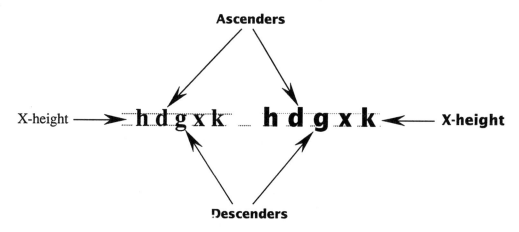

Figure 25. Typeface parts: ascenders, descenders, and x-heights.

Large x-heights work well with low-resolution printers or screens: "This fact accounts in part for the popularity in desktop publishing of versions of Times New Roman and Helvetica, two traditional faces with larger x-heights" (Rubinstein, 1988, 90).

When more of the typeface is devoted to the x-height than ascenders or descenders, the letter looks bigger even though it takes up no more physical space. This "optical illusion" is especially important on-line when, as we have noted many times, there is much less space to display information than on a piece of paper. Thus we need a compact typeface that can squeeze a great deal of information in and yet look large to the reader's eye.

But perhaps the best principle to use in choosing typefaces is to keep things simple. Choosing a number of typefaces and a large number of typeface size changes draws the reader's attention to how you are giving them the content of the manual rather than directly to your content (Dencker, 1984).

Type Size

"Typesize has connotations just as does the typeface (e.g., large typesize connotes grade school readers while small typesize connotes adult reading" (Rubinstein, 1988, 206).

Even though type size is relative to the reader's viewing distance, we can generally say that the old 10 point or 12 point (such as in the body text in this right column) will be appropriate for most reading situations.

However, type size is not type size, is not type size! Observe how the lengths of the lines set in different typefaces change in Figure 26 even though each line is 12-point size.

Lucida:

Watch how the quick brown fox jumps over the

Schoolbook:

Watch how the quick brown fox jumps over the

Helvetica:

Watch how the quick brown fox jumps over the

Times:

Watch how the quick brown fox jumps over the

Figure 26. The varying lengths of lines all using 12 point type size.

This, of course, would be especially troublesome in the presentation of on-line documents. Always be aware of what type sizes and faces your audience has available on their computers, design for their limitations, and always test your design in the users' environment.

Family Branch, Posture, and Composition

The decision you need to make in this typographic element is what typeface branch you want your type to be (i.e., normal, bold, outline, shadow, etc.); what posture you want your type to take (i.e., italic or roman); and what composition you want of your letters (all upper case or upper and lower case mix) (see Figure 27).

Fog	*Fog*	FOG
Normal, roman, mixed upper and lower case	Italic	All Uppercase
F⊙g	<u>Fog</u>	Fog
Shadow	Underline	Outline

Figure 27. Typeface variations.

Lateral inhibition also explains the irradiance effect problem of CRT screens where because of poor resolution of letter edges, the letters appear to bloom, spread out, and melt into one another (Rubinstein, 1988, 60).

Two perceptual facts will allow you to make some decisions as to whether or not to use these variations. First, *word shape* is an important clue for readers in deciphering words. Second, in deciphering word shapes, the retina is primarily physiologically wired to detect edges—in our case, the edges of words and letters—because of an effect termed *lateral inhibition.* Thus, if the edges of words or letters are tampered with in any way by—slanting them in italics or altering them in using shadow or outline—legibility decreases (Rubinstein, 1988, 32).

The bottom line, then, is to maintain the reader's expected word shape of letters and words if you want to allow the reader to easily recognize the letters and words. This concept is violated in all upper case lettering; all words become similar rectangles of various lengths rather than the dissimilar shapes we expect, and thus reading speed decreases (Peterson, 1982; Spencer, 1969; Tinker, 1967; Vartabedian, 1971). Reading speed decreases have also been found by researchers in the use of italic, and underlining—underlining blanks out the descender information.

A similar problem is the one created by the "squeeze" some VDTs put on letters, destroying their descenders, and thus greatly altering word shape and causing screen readers to slow their reading speed (Reynolds, 1980; Stevenson, 1983).

Of course, you can use the concept of word shape altering reading speed to your advantage. Perhaps all danger, caution, or note information should be in an alternative word shape so that the reader is forced to attend closely and look at it twice because it contrasts with the surrounding type. (However, a better way to distinguish such information could be by setting it off with white space or boxes.)

Thus, although your fancy desktop publishing software and hardware give you lots of type shape alteration possibilities, allow your reader to forgo the experience of altered type shape.

Leading (linespacing)

Type with small x-heights needs more leading. Imagine how much leading is needed for the large ascenders in the Camelot typeface in Figure 23 and how much less for Woodstock at the bottom of Figure 23.

To separate lines of type, typesetters physically inserted strips of lead . In the days of typewriting, we could simply choose single or double space; but now with desktop publishing and screen design we need to recover some of the leading technique that typesetters use. In general, one usually adds a lead size that is one point more than the type size that is used. Leading usually isn't a problem in paper documentation because, as you see in Figure 28, we usually use single- or double-space leading.

(a) *Normal Leading (single space).*

The mood of text varies with the leading; very tight leading seems to imply scholarly-ness, while loose leading seems to imply extravagance and arti-ness (Rubinstein, 1988, 158).

(b) *Large Leading (double space).*

The mood of text varies with the leading; very tight

leading seems to imply scholarly-ness, while loose

leading seems to imply extravagance and arti-ness

(Rubinstein, 1988, 158).

(c) *Negative Leading*

The mood of text varies with the leading; very tight leading seems to imply scholarly-ness, while loose leading seems to imply extravagance and arti-ness (Rubinstein, 1988, 158).

Figure 28. The effects of leading: (a) The reader has no problem distinguishing between the ascenders and descenders of lines, and the clumping together of paragraphs is enhanced; (b) The reader has no problem distinguishing between the ascenders and descenders of lines, but the clumping together of paragraphs is decreased (this leads to quadruple space between paragraphs to have the paragraphs visually clump together); (c) The reader may have problems distinguishing between the ascenders and descenders of lines.

Line measure, leading, and type size are, of course, all interrelated; the larger the type size, the larger the leading, and the larger the measure.

However, there are problems to be overcome in on-line documentation because the default on many display screens is the zero leading (much like the negative leading of Figure 28 (c). In on-line presentations, this zero leading usually leads to squashed descenders. Thus when designing on-line documentation, increase the leading or line spacing using such ANSI guidelines as (1988):

- Space lines two times the stroke width of the character

- Space lines 15% of the character width

Line Measure and Appointment

"Surprisingly, for most books, the main body of the text only occupies 50% to 60% of the page. Thus the ratio of text area to page area is about 1:2. A visual illusion creates the impression of greater coverage of text. People shown pages with 50% text coverage estimated that about 75% of the pages were actually text" (Rubinstein, 1988, 168).

When considering line measure, we want to decide how wide our text lines should be. Although this is relative to how far from the text the reader is reading (Horton, 1990), for the normal reading distance from a screen or piece of paper of 18 inches, the eye with all its peripheral vision usually scans 4.5 inches of text (10–12 words in length, or roughly 2 alphabets printed out in the typeface used). This 4.5 inches width is not exact, but it is a dimension to keep in mind, as are widths narrower than 1.67 inches which are too narrow (Rubinstein, 1988,177):

> "...from about 2 inches to about 1.67 inches, in two steps, resulted in a significant reduction in reading speed. This result suggest that column widths can be too short for optimum legibility. Tinker also found that long lines slow reading because more eye fixations are lost to tracking errors and to undershooting the beginning of the next line"

It also winds up that having text widths of between 4.5 and 1.67 inches (such as in this book), headings can be dramatically set off by white space to the left and the overall amount of white space on a page can be increased.

We need to thank a monk by the name of Alcuin (his Feast Day is May 20th) who was Charlemagne's Education Prime Minister, and who *invented* lower case letters, and, even more importantly, space between words.

Making choices when it comes to appointment or alignment means that you must choose whether you want your on-line or paper text to be ragged, centered, or justified as shown in Figure 30. But before we get to making a choice, and understanding why to make one choice rather than another, we need a little history lesson.

In Figure 29, you will see Western Civilization's first-draft attempt at making decisions in this area. This is the type of writing that was practiced by the Greeks prior to 300 B.C.; it was all upper case; there was no space between words (although sometimes word separation was indicated by dots or bullets; and there was no punctuation. No wonder Plato and Aristotle distrusted writing; I would, too, if I had to read this simple little nursery rhyme written like this.

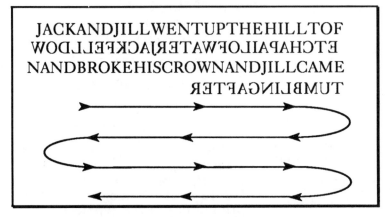

Figure 29. Greek writing prior to 300 BC: boustrophedonic, all uppercase, no space between words, and no punctuation.

But even more disruptive was that fact that the writing was arrayed bidirectionally; first left to right, then right to left, alternatively throughout the entire text. This was called boustrophedonic writing (meaning "the way of the oxen" because this was the way a farmer would follow their oxen while plowing across a field—thus again we see power and the problem with analogies), and it was changed somewhere around 300 BC. Boustrophedonic writing made the *eye tracking* from one line to another very easy because one just dropped down vertically and there was the next line to read and the next letter to read.

However, luckily as well as unluckily for us, someone in ancient Greece suggested that each line be read from left to right and that the human eye needs to track from the end of a line back left to the beginning of the new line—it made it easier to read and write, but harder for the eye to track from line to line. Thus, we can make our primary decision in this area on

whatever appointment best aids our readers' tracking
to the next line.

(a) Jack and Jill went up the hill to fetch a pail of water. Jack fell down and broke his crown, and Jill came tumbling after.	*(b)* Jack and Jill went up the hill to fetch a pail of water. Jack fell down and broke his crown, and Jill came tumbling after.
(c) Jack and Jill went up the hill to fetch a pail of water. Jack fell down and broke his crown, and Jill came tumbling after.	*(d)* Jack and Jill went up the hill to fetch a pail of water. Jack fell down and broke his crown, and Jill came tumbling after.

Figure 30. Appointment: (a) right ragged, (b) right
(fully) justified, (c) right justified and left ragged,
and (d) centered.

We can quickly get rid of right justified, left ragged,
Figure 30(c)—unless of course you are writing
documentation to audiences in Israel, the Middle East,
or in Hindi in India, all of whom read right to left with
the eye tracking back to the right—for the body text.
Such an appointment for text makes it hard for the
reader's eye to track back to the beginning of the next
line because the lines are so uneven.

We can also get rid of centered text, Figure 30(d),
because it will make it even more difficult than the
right justified, left ragged to track to the beginning of
the next line.

That leaves us, then, with Figure 30(a), justified left
and ragged right appointment, or Figure 30(b),
justified text on both the left and right. I will suggest
that we use (a), justified left and ragged right
appointment, for the following reasons. Ragged right
margins don't force cheaper justification algorithms
used in many popular microcomputer word processors
to insert irregular spaces or hyphens [e.g., look at the
odd wordspacing in line four of Figure 30(b)].
Although right justification with such word processors
may give typescript a typeset appearance, full
justification of text can actually cause "rivers"—
accidental white spaces [as you can observe in Figure

30(b)] lining up in a text causing the reader to read vertically rather than horizontally (Promptdoc, 1983).

Fully justified text on the right and left can also increase the chances of hyphenations being inserted. This is a situation we want to avoid as much as possible because you may remember that readers read by recognizing the shape of words; hyphenation would greatly disrupt this reader strategy.

Right ragged text is also better because

- When your eye looks away from the page for a moment, it is easier to relocate your original location because there is so much variety.

- The ragged look decreases an unnecessary tone of formality in the documentation; it's hard enough to read the manuals without making them seem overly formal in their bearing.

- Fully justified text was initially used by everyone when first using word processors because fully justified text seemed to make documents appear more important—in the pre-word-processing ages, only the very high bosses could have their texts fully justified because it could only be achieved through the expensive process of typesetting. But now anyone with the cheapest laptop computer can fully justify text. Thus, the meaning has been lost in the great overuse of it.

- Finally, there are some readability studies that claim there is less eye fatigue in reading ragged right text because the eye sees more variety in measure length.

Wordspacing and Letterspacing

The primary problem we want to avoid when making decisions regarding wordspacing is rivers. As I noted earlier in the discussion of serifs, the human eye's natural tendency seems to be to read up and down (i.e., the following were all read up-and-down: Sumerian cuneiform, Egyptian hieroglyphics, Chinese calligraphy, and, until only lately, Japanese), and serifs aided the learned eye behavior of reading horizontally across the page.

cf.

The only good reason to use fully justified appointment—after all, aren't all magazines and newspapers fully justified, and don't people in journalism who give desktop publishing seminars suggest we use fully justified text? —is when you are using multiple columns of text. It winds up that fully justified text columns can be set closer to each other, and thus a great saving in space is achieved.

Avoid widows and orphans: "A *widow* is an isolated line set at the top of a new page, the last line of the paragraph on the previous page. An *orphan* is a single line left alone at the bottom of a page. Orphans can be the first line of a new paragraph, or a title or a header line associated with the next paragraph."(Rubinstein, 1988, 235).

However, if the space between words becomes irregular and too large—say, when the word processor in attempting to implement full justification clumsily inserts irregular spaces between words to get the lines to line up—then a diagonal line between words—a *river*—may appear to the readers' eyes, and their eyes may begin to move diagonally rather than horizontally.

The way to avoid the development of such problems is again to use a ragged right appointment and to remember what typographers have long known that in general there should be less space between words (interword space) than between lines (leading or interline space).

"Interletter spacing is much more critical than interword spacing" (Rubinstein, 1988, 155).

With letterspacing, remember that the reader is recognizing words by their shape. T h u s w o r d s t h a t h a v e t o o m u c h s p a c e b e t w e e n l e t t e r s d o n ' t a l l o w t h e w o r d s t o e f f e c t i v e l y "c l u m p t o g e t h e r" t o t h e r e a d e r ' s e y e—such as in this sentence. To avoid this, try always to use proportional spacing in which the space devoted to a letter is in proportion to its width; i.e., fat letters such as "w" gets a lot of space, and a thin letter like "i" gets significantly less space.

"Numerous experiments have verified the superiority of proportional spacing over monospacing" (Rubinstein, 1988, 37).

Even more problematic is the use of "monospace" as the default letterspacing on computer display screens using "character cell displays." In monospac spacing, each letter, no matter whether it is fat or thin, gets exactly the same amount of display space and space between adjacent letters. If you examine words on such screens, they fail to clump for the expected word shape to the reader's eye; in fact, some of the thin letters at the ends of words appear to be flying off into interword space. Such monospace is yet another explanation of why it takes readers so long to read text on some computer screens.

Rules, Punctuation Marks, and Paragraph Indentations

When using rules (thin horizontal or vertical lines), minimize the use of vertical lines because it may give the reader's eye yet another excuse not to read horizontally across the page. Also make sure that rules are used in a consistent way with standard thickness or point size throughout a text.

Leave behind, as Rubinstein says, your "typewriter habits"—habits for a monospace world—when using desktop publishing—a proportionally spaced world—for paper documentation or when designing bit-mapped screens. For example, he and others suggest (Rubinstein, 1988, 168; see also Kleper, 1987, 31–2, and White, 1988, 55–9):

cf.

Putting punctuation inside quotes could leads to problems, e.g., publishing PRESS: "DELETE." rather than PRESS: "DELETE". could lead the user to actually type the period as part of the command.

- Don't double space after periods—laser printing gives us much crisper word shapes so that sentences don't need extra interword space for their distinctions to be seen, plus the extra space could contribute to the formation of rivers

- Put most punctuation inside quotation marks— "not only is this good style, but it also avoids odd spacing."

- Don't add extra lines between paragraphs; they are unnecessary. "Most books are set with indentations to indicate a new paragraph, but without extra vertical space except after headings."

- Don't underline; instead use italic or bold, which were never available to us on typewriters and which don't cut off the descenders of letters as underlining does.

- Don't indent paragraphs or indent them 1/5 as much as paragraph tabbing on a typewriter.

Finally, like typesetting, laser printed documents should use " ", ' , and not " or '.

Typographic Choices Made in this Book

To summarize, let me review for you the typographic decisions I made in regard to typography for this book. I chose Lucida serif *typeface* for my primary column's body copy and Lucida sans serif for my headings off in the left column, my side quotes, and my indented quotes. I chose Lucida for specific use in laser printing because, as Rubinstein points out,

"Bigelow's entry into the superfamily category [a font in both serif and sans serif, roman, italic, bold, proportionally spaced and monospaced] was a set of fonts based on his Lucida typeface—a font specifically designed for readability on a cathode ray tube screen—and the Pellucida variation used for laser printers...a variation he called Lucida Bright has been adopted by *Scientific American*" (Rosenthal, 1989, 16).

"Lucida is characterized by a large x-height, short ascenders and descenders, and relatively open interletter spacing, all properties that improve its appearance on the screen [as well as on paper]" (1988, 203*).

"Unfortunately, many typefaces have the nasty habit of disintegrating when faxed. So to help improve the legibility of your faxed documents, we conducted a little test....We printed the same letter twelve times, then the letter was faxed across the street and across the country. Using volunteer judges, including members of Adobe's Type Development department, each fax was ranked on secret ballots by how well the typeface maintained clarity of its letterforms and legibility of the text. The winners were clear. Lucida Roman and Lucida Sans, two faces designed specifically for low resolution electronic publishing finished first, and second, respectively" ("Face Fax," 1989, 12).

It is also a "collateral design" because it results in good legible results on both high- and low-resolution printers (Rubinstein, 1988, 111). Lucida was also designed in both serifed and sans serifed versions so they mix very well. Thus I would avoid any possibility of typeface clash such as might happen when two similar but different serifed or sans serifed typefaces are used for headings and body copy. Unlike the heading type used in Version 1.0 of this book, Helvetica, and one that is traditionally used by many desktop printers, Lucida sans serif has strokes which are differentiated from each other and thus more legible.

My *appointment* is right ragged. I used a roman *posture* for my letters except when discriminating quotes or special words which used italic. The *type size* for the main column's body copy is 10 point, in the side quotes, 7 point, and the headings up to 24 point—all point size differences are larger than 4 points because the human eye has great difficulty distinguishing smaller point size variations. I did not use an additional line between paragraphs, but customized the document processor to insert 6 points of lead after each paragraph; this would tighten the text and present a "darker" page than the default leading for 10 point type. *Leading*, *wordspacing*, and *letterspacing* were all left up to Adobe's type defaults for the Lucida typeface.

Layout

Now that we have covered all the major aspects of typography that are under our control, we need to think about how they all go together, and that is called *layout*. Layout can contain a myriad of concerns and considerations for a page ranging from page size (metric A4 or U.S. legal size or letter size), to "pull quotes" and initial caps, to headers and footers, to portrait mode or landscape mode, etc. To cover all such items would mean a book dedicated to layout, and there are quite a number of good ones already; see White's (1988) chapter, "Page Ingredients," or Parker (1988). What I am more interested in are the two or three principles that can direct someone who is more interested in content than design to at least design the most readable layout.

When Designing the Layout of Documentation:

- Pull the reader's eye to the fallow areas of attention by contrasting typographic elements because the reader's eye naturally moves across the page or screen following the Gutenberg diagram.

- Be consistent in your layout by using grids or templates because the reader quickly parses your layout, and expects such parsing to be consistently followed.

- Use type size (at least 4 points in differentiation) or boldness to indicate relative importance or weight.

First, we've already learned that the reader's eye naturally wants to move from top to bottom. And if we combine that with the learned behavior of reading left to right in Western European styles of writing, then we get what's known as the Gutenberg Diagram (Arnold as in Wheildon, 1986) shown in Figure 31. Basically the diagram shows that there is a certain visual gravity pulling the reader's eye from their arrival point at the top left to their departure from the page point at the bottom right. Researchers have found that the reader's eye resists moving to the left of the page in the middle and to the top right corner. However, we cannot afford to have the reader's eye skip half our page of text; thus we have to do something to guide the reader's eye away from going down this visual slide to the bottom right.

We also must recognize that the reader's eye is drawn to those things on a page which contrast with the rest of the page. We can use such contrast to our advantage as I will point out in a moment.

Finally, and most importantly, we need to realize that our reader seeks to learn how we have laid out information and then seeks—like the reading process in general—to correctly guess what the design is going to be on each successive page. If your design is consistent—whether it's visually elegant or not—your reader will be able to learn your layout and spend

This is an odd moment in the history of document design very much like the moment when color televisions were first sold to the public. In those early color television days, one often had to manually adjust the hue, brightness, and redness nobs for each station and sometimes for different shows on the station—sometimes one got the colors right, and other times Mr. Ed turned out to be slightly green. Now, television color adjustment is all done automatically. Desktop publishing gave the means of typographic and layout control to documenters who were not typographers. And with this opportunity came the responsibilities for many choices and their interactions—sometimes it worked and other times we had four column screens. And, even if a manual or set of screens were designed well by an individual desktop publisher, they might not be consistent with every other manual and with every other screen produced by the organization. To ensure consistency and quality of design, companies will soon be taking the responsibility and freedom to choose out of the hands of the individual documenters and handling such options automatically by having corporate grids, templates, style sheets, layout tags, etc., developed in-house, or buying them from outside vendors (Aldus' PageMaker, for example, has a manual's layout package of grids and stylesheets for sale). (See Brockmann, 1988 (b)).

little time deciphering page parts and more time attending to your information:

> "People learn easily by example. By seeing a few combinations of the basic spaces on the page, readers absorb the plan of the book. They parse subsequent pages using this 'grammatical' information.' And once people see a few pages of your layout, and have effectively parsed them for a few pages, they 'absorb the plan of the book,' and using this 'grammatical' information, easily parse the rest of the text. This suggests one should be consistent in their layout" (Rubinstein, 1988, 165).

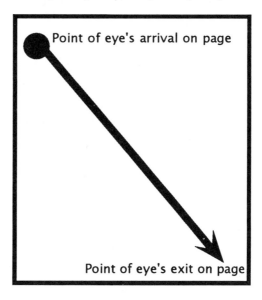

Point of eye's arrival on page

Point of eye's exit on page

Figure 31. The Gutenberg diagram.

A page grid was invented in the 1920s by Dusenbury, Bradbury, Thompson, and others who superimposed it on a page.

By consistently using text size, placement, indentations, paragraphing, captions, graphics, etc., we can allow readers to effectively guess what's going to come next (Rubinstein, 1988, 163). Thus always be sure to develop a page grid and stick with it. Choosing an effective page format is an important decision, but not one that needs to be done for each and every manual in a product library or even for every product library in an organization. The company or organization ought to develop a page grid to which all writers adhere:

> "Using this grid allows you to move about, add, delete and rearrange elements on a single page with comfort....No matter what configuration you select for text presentation,

you remain within the framework of a 'constant form'"
(O'Neal, 1983).

What's particularly advantageous about using grids these days is that the document-processing and desktop publishing tools of today have grid presentations and designs of text built right into them, i.e., PageMaker by Aldus and Microsoft Word 4.0 when using the "Page Preview" mode.

For example, using the grid to lay out a single page with text and headings, you could use the template in Figure 32. This is the new "traditional" asymmetric page layout template of the early 1990s. Using this template (as used in this text), you would put your body copy in the right-hand column—it will probably be less than 4.5 inches so that the reader's eye will easily track to the next line. And to bring the reader's eye to the fallow portion of the page not natively attended to, the left, we will put our contrasting headings, pull quotes, side quotes, danger and caution, notes, etc.—their contrasting type sizes will tend to bring the reader's eye over to the left.

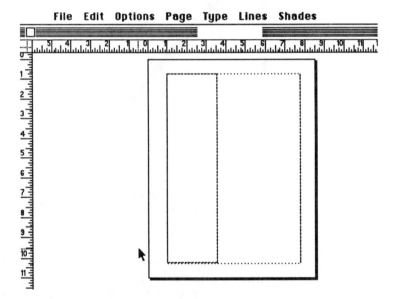

Figure 32. Typical standard 1990's template for manuals.

Finally, in addition to directing the reader's eye byconsistently using grids such as in Figure 32, direct the reader's eye by using contrasting type sizes. Remember that the reader's eye assumes that equal sized type is equal in importance and required attention, and that larger sized type is more important and denotes higher levels in heading hierarchy than smaller sized type. Also keep in mind

Color—Use for Coding, Not Comprehension,

When I say the word "color" in this section I mean polychromatic color—i.e., red vs. blue vs. green—and not achromatic black and white. Technically speaking, black and white are color just as are shades of grey. It's just that these "colors" vary from each other by luminance rather than by hue. "Although the term color is generally used to describe object attributes such as redness and greenness, the term actually extends to neutral colors (black, gray, etc.) as well. An object that exhibits a specific hue, such as red or green, has a chromatic color; an object that stands out from its background on the basis of lightness, such as black or gray, has an achromatic color" (Murch, 1986, 1).

that the eye finds it very difficult to discriminate type size differences less than four points.

Sometimes advances in technology open a trap-door for writers rather than a real door of opportunity. Color is the newest trap-door that technology is seductively offering. By simply glancing around the office, you will surely see a large percentage of color computer monitors, and, if you glance at the covers of all the leading PC magazines, you will see that color laser printers are invading our desktop publishing systems.

Why should you be so suspicious regarding the introduction of color in computer documentation on paper and on-line? On the one hand, marketing and advertising have successfully used color for over a generation:

> "Spot color can do wonders for advertising revenue. This is unassailable. US research tells us about one advertiser who paid a loading of 70% for spot colour and drew nearly 400% more sales. Spot colour generally adds to the cost of an advertisement by 20% or more, but the advertisement is noted by 63% more people and results in 64% more sales" (Wheildon, 1986, 20).

More recently, a market survey for Hewlett-Packard revealed that

> "...businesspeople are quite ready and willing to face up to the extra expense. Of those customers, 55% use a color monitor, 83% believe color adds impact to presentations, 60% see color as increasing productivity, and 30% claim color hard copy is currently required" (Reveaux, 1989, 106).

Don't "colorized" movies of the 1930s and 1940s consistently pull in larger viewing audiences than the same movies in black and white? And, finally, hasn't marketing used color to put us in the "mood" to purchase more items in grocery stores or eat more in a restaurant?

Problems with Color for Readers

But if color is measured by the comprehension standards of documentation, then color fails miserably. The confusion stems from confusing aesthetics with performance:

> "Looking good is being good. The disease of looking good is confusing aesthetics with performance. A piece of

information performs when it successfully communicates an idea, not when it is delivered in a pleasing manner. Information without communication is no information at all. It is an extremely common, insidious malady among graphic designers and architects to confuse looking good with being good. The cure obviously is to ask how something performs" (Wurman, 1989, 125).

The preponderance of research has noted that color either on paper or on the computer screen does not improve reader comprehension of extended text. In fact, the bulk of research reveals that color undermines comprehension.

"An even more fundamental and philosophical issue underlies color on the Mac—the very nature of the color model itself. The current Picker is designed after an image-processing model and is based upon the mathematically derived RGB system. These standards are color spaces obtained from the consistent, incremental subdivision of visible spectral bands. Based upon the physics of light, RGB is used most often for CRT and video displays in this country. A perceptual model like the Munsell color system, based upon the physiology of human vision, shows you only the colors that your eye can differentiate. Interpreting our subjective perception of reflected light, this model is used widely in government and industry and is the one most familiar to artists and designers" (Reveaux, 1989, 104).

In the early 1980s, Colin Wheildon in Australia realized that many of the rules of typography were "largely ancient maxims, with very little empiricism to support them." So from 1982 to May of 1986, he conducted a series of studies on these maxims. Three of his studies examined the influence of color on reader comprehension: relative comprehension and colored headlines, colored text, and text on colored backgrounds. He concludes these studies with the following observation:

> "It's impossible to avoid the fact that comprehensibility of coloured text increases as the colour gets closer to black" (Wheildon, 1986, 27).

Problems with Color for Desktop Publishers

Color screen designs will be quite difficult if not impossible to produce on the new color laser printers because there is no mathematical relationship that can be established between colors on a screen (produced additively) and colors on a page (produced subtractively):

cf.

One possible solution to this problem is now being offered by Tektronix in a product called TekColor™. Even though all the colors that can be shown on a monitor cannot be reproduced by a color printer, nor can all the colors produced by a color printer be displayed on a screen, there are some colors that are shared by specific monitors and specific printers. These shared additive and subtractive colors are called "color gamuts." TekColor automatically narrows down the colors it offers on the screen to these "color gamuts," and thus offers a guarantee of accurate color reproduction—but only for these select few colors (Yi, 1990, 18.

> "Although the color you see on your computer screen is improving by leaps and bounds, it will never precisely match the color you see on the printed page. One reason for this is that the screen colors (red, green, and blue or RGB), being created by a light source, are additive—as you add more colors the image lightens toward white, just as the colors of the rainbow add up to white light. Colors created by printing ink (cyan, magenta, and yellow, or CMY), though, are subtractive—as you add more color, the image becomes darker and tends toward black (actually a dark brown)" (Eckstein, 1989, 46; see also Thorell and Smith, 1990, 44).

Forget about color WYSIWYG desktop publishing (What You See Is What You Get) and be prepared for color WYSIOSWYG desktop publishing (What You See Is Only Somewhat What You Get).

Problems with Color for Writers and Designers

When writers are trying to produce quality documents, they must simultaneously control many communication variables such as tone, structure, layout, vocabulary, typography, etc. This attention to so many variable during the writing process leads to *attentional overload*:

> "Attentional capacity is overloaded when people attempt to do too many things at once. Writing attention may be divided simultaneously among the processes, rapidly alternated among them, or primarily focused on one process while others are executed automatically. Difficulties arise when insufficient time and effort is devoted to planning and sentence generation because of competition from other processes. Effective writing presumably requires sustained concentration on each process. Consequently, overloading attention by trying to plan, translate, and review at the same time [and effectively handle polychromatic color, we might add, which is so 'attractive' to the eye] probably hinders writing performance" (Kellogg, 1988, 61–2).

Color is perhaps just one too many factors to control. Color can, in fact, mislead and befuddle the writer trying to control all the complexities of effective communication.

In a 1985 AT&T marketing survey discussed earlier in Part One, only 27% of the respondents felt that color was important in paper documentation. And a year later at the 1986 International Technical Communication Conference, a survey of technical writers' thoughts on color on-line documentation found that:

> "The respondents thought color was not only unimportant but also relatively unworthy of further research; this sort of 'not now, not ever' response may arise from a view that use of color is an aesthetic 'frill' without communication power, or it could indicate a deeper belief that color actually works against communication, perhaps by overpowering the information itself or by otherwise distracting the user from the message" (Fisher, 1987, 151).

cf.

"When should you put color in documents? Here's my rule: When the informational and/or aesthetic value of doing so is greater than the sum of (1) the cost in time required to put color in, including the time needed to make appropriate color choices that achieve you informative or aesthetic goals, and (2) the cost incurred in using the color file, which will take up more disk space and time than a monochromatic document" (Swaine, 1990, 251–3).

Perhaps another reason for this reticence in discussing color or using color is its cost–$200 to $300 for a single four-color separated image (Roth S., 1989, 199). Color could add as much as 40% to the cost of a document (Willoughby, 1988, VC-23), and require untold hours of working closely with color separation experts to get color into a document.

Cautionary Facts About Readers and Color

"In the standard interface part of applications (menus, window frames, and so on), color should be used minimally or not at all; the Desktop Interface is very successful in black and white. You want the user's attention focused on the content of the application, rather than distracted by color in the menus or scroll bars" (Apple Computer, 1987, 32–3).

- Nearly 8% of the male population (and 0.4% of the female population) has some form of color blindness primarily in their red-green receptors. Can you be sure none of your readers is color blind?

- Older readers require brighter colors in order for the colors to be recognizable. Yet younger readers find bright colors distracting and fatiguing to the eye. What brightness of color, therefore, should one use?

- When one views a painting or colored picture, one's eyes sweep broadly across the canvas, but when one reads text, one's eyes must proceed linearly across a page with frequent stops and tracking from the end of one line to the beginning of the next. But when the eye behaviors of readers of colored on-line text were examined, researchers found them using a broad sweeping "paint mode" of viewing rather than a precise linear mode of reading (Krull and Rubens, 1986). Do we want readers of on-line text to appreciate the colors of on-line text or to read and comprehend the text?

"Using these programs [Illustrator 88, Aldus Free Hand, LaserPaint II, QuarkXpress 2.0], you can bypass several steps traditionally relegated to specialists. Not surprisingly, you can also make a mess of things. Those specialists are there for a reason, and bypassing them puts all the responsibility on your shoulders. The same is true with black-and-white publishing, but color adds a layer of complexity that many will find daunting" (Roth S., 1989, 200).

- The interactions of different colors on paper or screens is difficult to predict and can cause optical illusions (the Bezold effect). And too many colors can overwhelm readers who easily forget the defined meanings of colors. Do we really want readers to put in extra effort to read colored texts to feel they have to EARN the meaning of our messages?

- Experts on text say never rely on color alone to communicate a message; always redundantly communicate with color. Consider, for example, how traffic lights convey "stop" and "go" to viewers by color, by positions of the lights, and, color blind friends claim, by different intensities of light.

When You Should Use Color

Keeping all the problems and cautions in mind concerning color and continuous text comprehension, the difficulty of color production, and the possibility that color may exacerbate a writer's attentional overload, you should note one role for which color can be used effectively—coding information.

Researchers supporting the effective coding function of color include Horton, 1990; Thorell and Smith, 1990.

There is much good research to show that color can effectively aid readers' searching activities if it is used sparingly, i.e., the hypertext links on a screen could all be green in contrast to the black-and-white presentation of the rest of the screen, or dangers, cautions, or warnings could be printed in red on a page, again in contrast to the black-and-white presentation of the rest of the page. This research has shown that when readers are quickly searching for highlighted items or trying to group distant items on a page or screen, color is superior as a visual code to shape, brightness, size, and typeface.

To Use Color Effectively

"Use no more than five when their meanings must be remembered" (Thorell and Smith, 1990, 214).

- Be consistent in your use of color codes, and use a minimum number of colors so as to make your use of color predictable, and so as to not overload the audience's short-term memory.

- Avoid putting colors from the extreme ends of the color spectrum (i.e., red and blue) next to each other. Doing so makes it very difficult for the audience's eye to perceive a straight line, and the boundary between the two seems to shimmer—like heat coming off a radiator.

- Use familiar color coding such as red for "hot."

Watch out, however, because colors and their associations not only change between professions (i.e., green for process control engineers means "nominal or safe," for financial managers it means "profitable," and for health care workers it means "infected" (Thorell and Smith, 1990, 13), but also between cultures (i.e., blue for Americans means "masculinity" ("true blue"), in Japan it means "villainy," and in Egypt it means "virtue, faith, or truth" (Thorell and Smith, 1990, 12).

- Redundantly signal; don't rely on color alone to discriminate between items:

"You should design your application first in black and white. Color should be *supplementary*, providing extra information for those users who have color. Color shouldn't be the only thing that distinguishes two objects: there should always be other cues, such as shape, location, pattern, or sound" (Apple Computer, 1987, 32–3).

To use color properly in designing screens, turn off the color screen design of a screen and use light intensities or gray shades to discriminate features. Then, since you can never totally plan for how users have the colors set on their VDTs, you can always rely on light intensities to convey your messages of information discrimination (Rubinstein, 1988, 68).

- Finally, get the advice of a professional.

Page Sizes

cf.

However, we also saw in the Part One's review of the 1986 AT&T Documentation Survey two-thirds of the respondents preferred regular page size, and 82% said page size was relatively unimportant.

Just when page size for documentation seemed to be standardizing on a 5.5 x 9 inch size page, along comes the NeXT's 1989 manuals using a 8.5 x 11 letter size page. If the history of automobile user manuals can give any guidance, expect to see page sizes continue to shift and alter; consider Table 5. Why use a page size smaller than the normal letter size, legal size, or A4 metric size? Consider some of the following reasons:

- It looks less foreboding to readers than the standard 8.5 x 11 inch page format. In an informal study done by some writers at IBM in Kingston, NY, test subjects were asked to rate an assortment of manuals on ease of use solely on the basis of external appearance. They gave the smaller manuals the highest ratings (Thing, 1984 (a)).

	Chevrolet Manual's Sizes		Ford Manual's Sizes	
1910	9 x 5.5	(49.5 sq. in.)	6 x 3.75	(22.5 sq. in.)
1920	8 x 5.25	(42 sq. in.)	8 x 5.25	(42 sq. in.)
1930	8.25 x 5.25	(43.3 sq. in.)	7.75 x 5.5	(42.6 sq. in.)
1935	8.25 x 5.25	(43.3 sq. in.)	7.5 x 5.5	(41.3 sq. in.)
1940	8 .38 x 5.25	(43.9 sq. in.)	6.25 x 4.5	(28.1 sq. in.)
1950	8.25 x 5.25	(43.3 sq. in.)	6 x 4.5	(27 sq. in.)
1960	5.25 x 8.25	(43.3 sq. in.)	4 x 9	(36 sq. in.)
1970	5.25 x 8.25	(43.3 sq. in.)	4 x 8.5	(34 sq. in.)
1980	7.25 x 5.25	(38 sq. in.)	7.5 x 4	(30 sq. in.)

Table 5. The changing sizes of automobile user manuals over the last seventy years (from "Have You Read A Ford Manual, Lately?" in *Historical Considerations of Technical Writing* (Brockmann, forthcoming)).

- The small size is physically easier to handle when working at a VDT on a crowded desk.

- The small size automatically decreases the measure, the width of the text, thus making the pages more readable.

- The small size is more difficult to photocopy and pirate because photocopy automatic loaders have difficulty handling this size.

If you are going to use an unusually small page size, most of the the format suggestions given in the past few pages still hold true. The only alteration you will need to make is to use hanging headings rather than a true two-column format. To use white space and format to make your headings stand out, simply have the headings begin a few spaces to the left of the body of the text. There simply isn't enough room on the page to use two columns.

Techniques to Overcome On-line Physical Problems

Getting Some Ideas From Effective Paper Design

First the good news. As with the earlier solutions to organizational and rhetorical on-line problems, most of what needs to be done to solve the physical problems of on-line documentation can be abstracted from what we have learned in paper documentation. For example, in the layout area of paper documentation, we learned that readers develop "page parsing" expectations from our layout and that we need to be consistent in our layout. The exact same thing is true of on-line documentation;

"More than any other aspect of design, consistency is the key to usable on-line information" (Bradford A., 1988, 204).

From Paper Typography, Layout, Color, and Size Principles, Use the Following Principles On-line:

- Maintain a consistent layout using templates and grids that allow for all screen elements to be clearly distinguished.
- Be circumspect in any use of color.
- Use screen fonts that have large x-heights.
- Don't fully justify text.
- Increase the leading or line spacing.
- Keep your measures or line lengths between 4.5 and 1.67 inches.
- Use layout of the screen to suggest the organization of its content.
- Use emphasis devices sparingly.

Always clearly indicate what relates to what (Galitz, 1981; Heines, 1984).

Galitz (1981) suggests an interesting way to determine if a screen is structured properly:

> "Are all display elements (captions, error messages, etc.) identifiable without reading the words that comprise the element?"

If they are, the screen is structured properly. And Reid similarly suggests, "It is important that the [screens'] wording and the order in which they are displayed corresponds to the user's expectancies" (Reid, 1984).

To develop this consistent screen presentation of information, use screen capabilities to set off navigation aids from text or items to be manipulated. Also, use contrasting display features to call attention to different screen components, e.g., items being operated on, and urgent items.

Another way to achieve this screen layout consistency is by adopting the use of grids from paper page formatting to screen formatting. For example, Mehlmann suggests using the grid format for screens displayed in Figure 33 (Mehlmann, 1981; see also Heines, 1984; and Hurly, Laucht and Hlynka, 1985).

Figure 33. A sample screen design grid.

Even though you should be wary of the misuse or overuse of color, "color coding is better than size, angle, or shape for identification purposes, and easier to locate than alphanumerics" (Reid, 1984).

As we saw in paper documentation, be wary of using color to present extended textual information that is to be continuously read (not just scanned). As Rubinstein points out, and as Wheildon (1986) alluded to in his research in paper, it's the achromatic channel of vision that is ultimately responsible for the detection of shapes—the shapes of letters and thus words—and is the primary factor in determining the legibility of a screen:

> "In choosing foreground and background colors, it is important to remember that high intensity contrast is required for good-quality text. Contrast of color alone does not work well. Research shows that the visual system detects edges based primarily on intensity rather than color. In fact, one model of the perceptual system, opponent color theory, describes three information-processing channels that work with the same input signal (light acting on the retina) but use the information differently. The light-sensitive cones in the fovea are of three types—those that respond to red, green, and blue. Two color channels deal with color, transmitting a red-versus-green signal and a yellow-versus-blue signal....The remaining channel, the achromatic or luminance channel, ignores color and communicates only intensity. In opponent color theory, the achromatic channel is responsible for edge detection and ultimately for the decoding of shape" (Rubinstein, 1988,, 68).

Also as with paper documentation typography, we want to use large x-height fonts to improve the readability:

> "Designs with relatively large x-heights are attractive at lower resolutions because they make better use of the available space, and simultaneously appear larger on the screen with the same line height, than designs of smaller x-height" (Rubinstein, 1988, 90).

We'd also like to justify text items on the left and leave them ragged on the right so as to avoid the formation of rivers—this is especially true on monospaced screens. We also want to watch the leading on screens since the default leading on many screens is zero—nearly a negative leading (review again Figure 27). And along with appointment, letterspacing, font choice, color, and design consistency, we need to be especially sensitive to line length or the measure of a screen. This is especially important because the screen's aspect ratio is different from that of a paper page—and it's just the wrong ratio for simplifying the sweep of the eye across the screen:

"Most terminals have an aspect ratio of 4:3. This means that most terminals present text in a landscape mode with the line length being longer than the depth of the text on the screen. However, most books use portrait orientation where the depth of the page is greater than the width. There is good reason for this. The human eye scans left and right in very small increments when reading. If the deflection angle becomes too great several things happen: reading becomes physically tiring; the eye loses sight of the left side of the page. This causes tracking errors when a return to the next line is made. The left edge should never leave the peripheral vision of the reader; losing place and tiredness increase the frustration level with the material being read. Consequently, retention and understanding may be severely reduced" (McGrew and McDaniel, 1989, 140).

Two more techniques can help overcome the physical problems generally associated with on-line documentation. First, the user should not be confronted with a solid block of text; such inadequate use of white space is neither helpful nor reassuring. The on-line document should be styled in such a way that the user can recognize the relative significance and hierarchy of information at a glance. This can be achieved by using some of the "printing information" concepts from playscript and structured writing that we will learn about in Step 3. It can also be achieved in several other ways:

- Chunking information on a screen so that there are about three lines per paragraph and blank lines between paragraphs

- Using short lines (less than 60 characters)

- Highlighting critical words, or positioning lines so that they break at the ends of "natural" phrases so that the format supports organization (Bork, 1983; Clark H., 1981)

Second, emphasis devices (blinking, color, reverse video, word-phrase spacing (displaying text with more than normal spacing either horizontal or vertical)) should be used carefully. Blinking, flashing, and color especially draw a reader's eye; therefore, they should be used sparingly (Heines, 1984). Overuse of any device destroys its usefulness (Bork, 1983; Bradford A.,

1984), and the overuse of blinking is extremely troublesome:

> "We advise you to avoid blinking text except where absolutely warranted—that is to say, almost never" (McGrew and McDaniel, 1989, 60).

Unique On-line Typography and Design Techniques

"The results of several experiments using anti-aliased characters of paper-like fonts produced by the IBM Research YODA system have led to the identification of CRT-display conditions from which people read as fast as they read from good paper. This evidence also suggests that variables associated with the image quality of the CRT characters themselves account for the reading-speed difference" (Gould, , Alfaro, Barnes, Finn, Grischkowsky, and Minuto, 1987, 298).

As we turn to those unique on-line physical problems, technology is beginning to give us a bit of luck. The bottom line appears to be that on-line legibility problems are rapidly becoming a thing of the past as more and more workstations use higher resolutions and improved font technology:

> "... there is good and growing evidence that higher resolution displays, techniques to improve fonts (such as anti-aliasing), and larger displays (more lines of text) can substantially reduce or eliminate the disadvantages associated with on-line reading" (Shneiderman and Kearsley, 1989, 38).

and have larger screens:

> "...legibility and page size make it easier to review one's text on the workstation and paper than on the personal computer" (Hansen and Haas, 1988).

Another new technology beginning to have an effect legibility is the use of *anti-aliasing* in letterforms. By using anti-aliasing, the jaggedness in the curves of letters (*aliasing*) can be minimized and more subtle shapes can be created by using varying gray levels at the edges of strokes:

> "This technique works because of the eye's ability to enhance edges when viewing shapes. Instead of seeing a soft edge, as actually displayed, a sharper one in an intermediary position is perceived" (Rubinstein, 1988).

Use the Newest Technology to Solve On-line Design Problems

- Higher resolution monitor
- Larger screen sizes approximating paper
- Anti-aliasing fonts

Improvements in the legibility of type, the size of the screen presentations, the factors of measure, leading, appointment, and consistency all need to be dealt with simultaneously. But even then, there's more to do to make it easy to read on-line documentation:

> "Reviews of decades of reading research on typeset materials...show that most physical variables, when studied

individually, have only a modest effect (10% or less), even when varied over a large range. These include line width [measure], line spacing [leading], margin size, print size, and font type" (Gould, Alfaro, Barnes, Finn, Grischkowsky, and Minuto, 1987, 297).

<table>
<tr><td>

cf.

Interestingly, the effective use of windows to solve organizational problems on-line gets one into deeper problems with the amount of white space on a screen. Damned if you do, damned if you don't.

</td></tr>
</table>

So far on-line is just replicating the effectiveness of page design. Perhaps it can go beyond what paper pages can do by being dynamic in its design. For example, we observed on paper that bright colors are required by older people for effective presentation but that bright colors cause eye fatigue for younger people. We also noted that color coding changes from culture to culture. Could we design the interface so that after the user answers a series of questions about age and culture, the appropriate colors and brightness are used...and, if they are color blind, even more energy is put into luminance?

Plan for Updating

In a software environment, changes are an everyday occurrence. If a document is to be useful, it must be updated as needed. To ensure that a document is easily updated, you need to begin thinking about updating in the planning stage of a document.

cf.

A few of my seminar students from Hewlett-Packard have advanced the idea of abolishing the concept of single-page updates. They said they have found that it's more expensive than simply reissuing the whole manual, and that most of the user's complaints they receive center around this single-page updating.

First, you need to be sure that readers know in which manual and where in a particular manual to insert any page sent out as an update. You can ensure this by including the document title and the page number on every page. (A page date should only be put on update pages as an additional signal of an update. Thus, any page without a page date is considered an original page.)

Step 1: Design The Specifications

Break Down Documentation by Tasks
Use a Minimalist Design
Plan for an Audience
State the Purpose
Organize Information
Develop a Product Visualization
Pick the Appropriate Medium
Decide on Typography, Layout, Color and Page Size
▶ Plan for Updating
Consider the Competition
Develop a Timing and Cost Scheme

Things to Do or Not Do During Document Design to Prepare the Way for Updating

- Consider abolishing the idea of single-page updates in favor of reissuing entire manuals.

- Consider using on-line transmission of documentation so that many of the problems of updating disappear.

- Put a document title and section-page number on each page.

- Pick the type of binding that fits the frequency of your updating.

- Include a Page Change sheet and Reader Comment endsheet.

You may also want to use a binding that fits the anticipated frequency of your updates; the lower the frequency of the updates, the more permanent the binding. Thus use comb or perfect binding only for those manuals that will be totally replaced rather than updated by single-page updates. Use looseleaf binders for manuals that will be updated with single-page updates.

To minimize the number of changes caused by a change on any one page, number pages with the chapter number and the page number within the chapter (e.g., part 2/Step 1-37). With that done, if any one chapter is changed, the required page number changes are limited to that one chapter, rather than necessitating changes in page numbers throughout the manual. This type of pagination functions somewhat like a ship that uses watertight compartments to contain flooding.

In addition, plan to add a Page Change sheet to the front of your document and a Reader Comment endsheet to the end of your document. Page Change sheets added to the front of your manual are simply a central place to record updates so they are easily noticed by readers. They indicate your commitment to systematically updating the manual. (In the last step of the SDP, we'll cover how to effectively use these Page Change sheets.) Reader Comment endsheets solicit user help with later updating and offer readers a way to feed comments and suggestions back to you. Endsheets indicate your responsiveness to the reader. These endsheets can only roughly simulate a feedback loop from reader to documenter. Honeywell's Computer Assisted Publication software package, on the other hand, with its on-line methods of collecting and responding to readers' comments, can actually be a feedback loop (Sickler, 1982).

Step 1: Design The Specifications

Break Down Documentation
  by Tasks
Use a Minimalist Design
Plan for an Audience
State the Purpose
Organize Information
Develop a Product Visualization
Pick the Appropriate Medium
Decide on Typrography, Layout,
  Color and Page Size
Plan for Updating
▶ Consider the Competition
Develop a Timing and Cost
  Scheme

Consider the Competition

Now that you have made all your conceptual decisions regarding tasks, audiences, purpose, organization, and visualization, and after you have made all your physical decisions regarding medium and page layout, you need to consider your decisions in the light of what the competition has produced. As Digital points out in their internal style guide:

"Your competition can have useful ideas on content, format, layout, and access methods you might use in your book.

Part of your job is to know what competitive products do (and do not) exist so your manual can be 'state of the art'" (Digital, 1983).

Competitors' manuals are a good place to begin...and a good place to end a documentation project. One manual writer noted that he checked both the adequacy of his index and the completeness of his coverage of material by comparing his manual's index with his competitors' indexes. If a particular bit of material was covered in his manual, but the word his competitor's index used to access it was not, he would consider adding the word to his index. And if a competitor indexed material that was not in his book, he would consider adding such material to his book.

Develop a Timing and Cost Scheme

With all the output of the documentation effort generally defined in terms of its organization, audiences, and media, you now need to complete your specifications by including the time and cost requirements for the work outlined.

Step 1: Design The Specifications

Break Down Documentation
  by Tasks
Use a Minimalist Design
Plan for an Audience
State the Purpose
Organize Information
Develop a Product Visualization
Pick the Appropriate Medium
Decide on Typrography, Layout,
  Color and Page Size
Plan for Updating
Consider the Competition
▶ Develop a Timing and Cost
  Scheme

To Break Through the Page-a-Day Documentation Productivity Barrier:

- Have the best publishing technology support.

- Use specifications reviews and prototype tests with real users.

- Be part of the design team right from the beginning of a project.

- Write the user guide first.

- Work in a team.

Breaking the Productivity Barrier

Until recently, one could feel secure in stating that it takes about a page a day to plan, write, test, review, edit, and publish a manual:

1981—In a survey of a dozen or so computer documentation departments in New England, Firman found that the average time to produce a 100-page manual was 999 hours—9.9 hours per page—and $239.00 per page (Firman, 1981).

1984—Ringland in England publishing in the journal *Software Practice and Experience* stated

NCR observes that only 25% of a writer's time is actually spent in writing. The remainder is spent in preparation (50%) and in final production (25%) (McKinley, 1984, 77, see also Microsoft's experience in Prekeges, 1986, 116). In addition, Digital Equipment Corporation notes in their internal style guide (1983) that 25% of the total scheduled time is "often consumed by illness, vacations, slips, machine down time, developer recalcitrance, and natural disasters." Digital suggests that, if possible, a planner should try to add "fat time" to a project schedule to cover unforeseen problems and difficulties.

On estimating cost and page size, see the "Special Issue on Productivity Measurement and Enhancement in Technical Communication" *Technical Communication* 34 (4) Fourth Quarter 1987: Shultz, 1987; Corbett, 1987; Strassmann, 1987; Doebler, 1987; Reily, 1987; and most especially Stultz's 1984 book.

"The technical editor becomes a part of the design team very early in the project (more than a year prior to release). As the product develops, the editor understands it and the writing of the documentation is a team effort. This eliminates most of the Engineer/Tech Writer conflicts. It works well for us" (Killingsworth and Jones, 1989, 219).

that the average for producing user documentation was 20–30 pages per man-month (less than a page a day).

1985—Digital Equipment Corporation was claiming in their internal documentation that they expected 1.5 pages per day productivity.

1985—*InfoWorld* interviewed Mike Allen, CEO of Trademark Software (maker of the "Dow Jones Accounting System"), who won acclaim in the magazine for his company's documentation and who, when asked about what percentage of overall software development costs were devoted to such an award-winning documentation effort, noted that 25–30% of software development costs were dedicated to documentation efforts. In the same *InfoWorld* interview, Evan Moltz of International Data Corporation claimed that the national average of software development costs dedicated to documentation efforts is 10%.

But then in 1987, the page-a-day "productivity barrier"—like the "sound barrier" and the "light speed barrier"— began to be broken in computer documentation. Hewlett-Packard's Information Technology Group claimed 4–5 pages per day, and their INDCI Group claimed to consistently produce 4 pages per day.

What happened between 1981 and 1990 is that computer documentation writers began to

- Have the right tools. On-line hypertext authoring systems including tools to effectively produce and display text on-line; desktop publishing tools such as PageMaker and document processing tools such as WordPerfect along with improved spellers, style checkers, indexers, table of contents creators, etc.

- Have the right methodology. Specifications and prototyping (see Step 2) allow documenters to surface problems earlier in the design of documentation when they are inexpensive and easy to handle.

- Work as members of the design team.

Documenter-as-Part-of-Design-Team Approach Case

The documenter-as-part-of-design-team approach was used at both AT&T and IBM.

"Our company is unique in that the technical writers are on the software development staff, rather than in a separate department....[The] programming staff is cooperative in teaching new system and enhancements to technical writers, and in reviewing the writer's work for technical accuracy. Also, the development staff calls on the writing staff for help in organizing menus, displays, editing on-line help, editing prompts and comments, and presenting effective screen formats....We feel that our documentation procedures result in manuals which are both technically accurate and accessible to users" (Killingsworth and Jones, 1989: 219).

- AT&T reported using this approach in 1986:

"About 20 months ago, AT&T's Denver Technical Publications Department and one of the software development groups it supports embarked on an innovative journey into the product design process. The approach, strongly supported by upper management, was simple: if a product design is difficult to document, it is probably poor design. That in itself was a breakthrough, but it gets better. Upper management further asserted that, to ensure product and document quality, a technical writer should be part of the human interface design teams developing new products" (Mohr-Callahan, 1988, 159).

The benefits an AT&T documenter experienced by being included as part of the design team were: better early planning, better document design, better rapport with subject matter experts, shorter learning curve, easier document organization and faster documentation development, earlier document testing and validation(Mohr-Callahan, 1988, 161–3).

- Saar, commenting on her observations as an academic associate in IBM-Kingston's Information Development group, noted five differences between "information development" at IBM and traditional "technical writing" (Grice, 1988, 138): (1) the developer tends to get information from people rather than from books; (2) the developer works as part of a team; (3) the developer tests the information for its usability; (4) the developer may put the final written product into a variety of forms; (5) the developer is responsible for the form of the presentation of the final product (layout, graphics, binding, etc.)

Timing the Documentation Process

Another reason why documenters should be part of the design team is because, ideally, documentation should be done first:

"In the best of worlds, the manuals would be written first, then the design would follow the manual. While the product was being designed, potential users could simultaneously test the manuals and mock-ups of the system, giving important design feedback about both" (Norman, 1988, 191).

One way to have the documentation design actually happen first is to have the designer simulate the program on the system for the user:

Simulating the final system by a human play-acting behind the scenes seems very similar to the classic "Turing Test" (Rheingold, 1985) and Carroll's "intelligent help" (1989, 1990).

"The user says what action he would take and the product designer says how the product would respond. Back and forth they go; the user learning how to use the product, you learning how to write the instructions, and the product designer learning how to improve the product" (Horton, 1984, WE-198).

Another way to have the documentation precede final product design is to give the user the product and have them dictate the manual:

You'll also have some great headings for your documentation.

"Give the user no written instructions. Have him learn to use the product solely by asking you questions. With you tape recorder running have him paraphrase your answer to each question. Keep the tape and any sketches you may have made, and you'll have a complete first draft in the user's words" (Horton, 1984 (b), WE-198).

(See also, Knapp, 1984; Maynard, 1982; McAusian, Armstrong, and Francoise, 1984).

However, your own environment may not be as "user-sensitive" or you may have little control over the final implementation of the product or system. In either event, the following suggestions on timing warrant consideration:

- See writing as dynamic and incremental in its development as it moves from specification to finished document; do not rush pencil to paper nor finger to word processor. See the document as being rather like a pearl that only slowly develops from the grain of sand to the finished pearl. That is, realize that the document will slowly assume shape as the product assumes shape. Documentation efforts should begin as soon as the product or systems development begins so that there is time for maturation. And if the document remains in outline form until coding—until the program or system is fully developed—altering the specification because of software or system enhancements is easy to do.

- Begin documentation efforts early so you have time to analyze the users' tasks in their own

"Quality in software documentation is a matter of discipline. You set your standards, and you have to stick by them no matter what. That's easy for most engagements, but it's another thing when you're bumping the high end of your estimate and your client is impatiently demanding receipt of your draft so it can be publishing and distributed. That's when you really earn your reputation for quality" (Pakin S., 1988).

environments, to do the necessary prototype testing, and to send documentation out for a field test when the system or product goes out for a system test.

Beyond these general guidelines, little can be said about timing. Each documentation situation is unique in its content, format, and production so that no magic formula for timing is likely to prove successful all the time. You should be cautious about accepting at face value any magic formulas that purport to give exact cost of documentation. They are probably as scientific as snake oil. However, there are several suggestions that are appropriate and likely to increase your accuracy in estimating costs:

Budget for documentation. All too often the costs of documentation are higher than expected because a budget for it was not included in the original system proposal. All cost related to documentation and under the control of the documenter should be included in a budget for documentation (American Institute for Professional Education, 1981).

Commit yourself to adequate planning and the development of document specifications. Spending time in planning will prevent unplanned time and, therefore, prevent unbudgeted money being spent on "editing" or reviewing"—correcting problems not caught in the original document design. In addition, committing yourself to planning specifications will allow managers or clients to catch errors early while they are still in the specification stage rather than after 20 or 30 useless pages have been written.

Keep your information sources informed. Tell them what type of information you as a writer will need and in what form it can best be used by you. Then when information comes to you, you will need to spend less time compensating for the idiosyncrasies of each information source. This could even be automated by using some of the "outline processors" noted in the last section. Use software writing aids such as spell checkers and style and punctuation guides.

One Note of Caution Regarding Specification Flexibility

Every builder or contractor follows the plan of a specification closely. But a good builder or contractor knows that changes in the final plan can and should be made when unforeseen difficulties or opportunities occur during the building process. Of course, they explain these changes to the original architect, but nonetheless, they allow unique occurrences in the building process to help shape the final product. The same practice should be followed for a specification. When you, the writer, come on novel ideas or unforeseen problems while writing from the library or individual document specification, don't be afraid to change the specification. The best specification is a flexible specification.

STEP 2: PROTOTYPING THE DOCUMENT

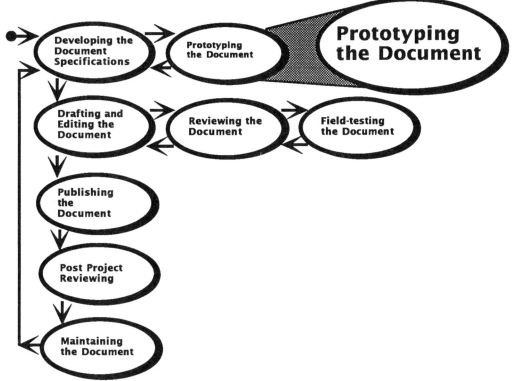

What Is Prototyping?

Prototyping has only recently come into computer documentation. Over the last decade, it has swept through systems analysis and systems design aided by structured design as a methodology and the rapid development of CASE tools. The Xerox Star™ and its descendants, the Lisa™ and Macintosh, all were the products of user prototyping:

> "The process of tuning a design by iterative user testing has been found extremely effective, for example, in the development of the Apple Lisa and Macintosh systems, which profited from very frequent user tests conducted by the applications software manager himself. Notice that

But prototype testing and design precedes computers by many generations. For example, consider the history of the typewriter:

"One device after another was conceived and developed until twenty-five or thirty experimental instruments were made, each succeeding one a little different from and a little better than the one preceding. They were put into the hands of stenographers, practical persons who were presumed to know better than anyone else what would be needed and satisfactory. Of these, James O. Clephane, of Washington, DC, was one. He tried the instruments as no one else had tried them; he destroyed them, one after another, as fast as they could be made and sent him, till the patience of Mr. Sholes was exhausted. But Mr. Densmore insisted that this was the very salvation of the enterprise; that it showed the weak points and defects, and that the machine must be made so that anybody could use it, or all efforts might as well be abandoned; that such a test was a blessing and not a misfortune for which the enterprise should be thankful" (Mares, 1909, 42-3).

See Kearsley, 1988, Appendix B for software tools that can be used for on-line prototyping.

Joseph D. Chapline, history's first computer user documentor in the late 1940s and early 50s with the Eckert-Machuly Computer Corporation, tells the story that he was stumped as to how to write the BINAC operations and instruction manual in 1949 until he had to teach the BINAC to a group of actual users in a class. It was their questions and their understanding or confusion with the class notes and lectures that convinced Chapline what to write and how to write it.

features found at fault in such a process are identified in a context that is very realistic and includes most of the complexity under which the user will actually operate" (Laudauer, 1987).

In many ways, prototyping is based on the age-old observation that people are good at telling you what they don't want *after* they see your work, but very poor at telling you ahead of time what they want. The document specification does the best it can in packaging what the users, managers, clients, etc., say they want ahead of time. On the other hand, a document prototype checks this design by giving users a taste of what they said they wanted before proceeding into full drafting of a document. As with systems design, documentation prototyping has become more of a possibility with the document automation tools of recent years—desktop publishing for paper documentation and design tools for on-line documentation.

Document prototyping has also become more of a possibility as documenters truly become egoless documenters and realize that they can only discover the proper design for documents from actually users using their documents. A document prototype better places the readability tools as part of document design rather than as part of the document verification where any readability problems are identified too late to be corrected simply and inexpensively.

A document prototype is a group of sample pages or screens from a document. It need be no longer than a single chapter or a dozen screens. But the part of the document that's chosen for prototyping should best illustrate the layout/format/design, writing style, tone, and reference aids to be used later in the production of the full-scale manual. This representative chapter, or group of screens, is then given to typical users who use it while performing a task; activities and reactions are recorded; and the document design is reconsidered in the light of these actual user reactions.

Prototype Testing Is Similar to Field Testing, But...

Prototype testing and field testing (Step 6) are nearly identical in their techniques. However, prototype

"We measure documentation validity against two general goals: a tutorial goal and a reference goal....We measure tutorial validity by: observing test users to determine whether they learned the critical material, and asking test users to perform basic tasks and observing how well they are completed. The reference goal is the need to enable the user to find specific information quickly" (Margolis, 1989, 2).

Note: Not only can testing precede complete first drafts, but testing can even precede completed program or system design (see Step 1).

cf.

"The benefits of user involvement have not been strongly demonstrated. Of 22 studies included in Table 3, eight claim to demonstrate a positive relationship between user involvement and various measures of system success, seven others present mixed results, and results from the final seven are negative or insignificant. Having reviewed these studies, however, the authors must conclude that the consistent lack of rigor in research to date seriously limits an understanding of the nature of user involvement in development. Positive results frequently may be attributable to common method variance, 'halo' effects, or statistical artifice" (Ives and Olson, 1984, 600).

testing is part of the design process, and it focuses on local issues of usability and readability because it uses only small portions of the final document. Another difference between the two types of testing is that prototype testing—to realize its biggest benefits—is performed iteratively as the document is refined:

> "...approximate the real needs, and then, through successive refinements, pinpoint them exactly. It is the iterative nature of prototyping that provides the benefits" (Boar, 1984).

Field testing, on the other hand, focuses on the same issues but with a more global perspective because the entire document, not just portions or sample pages, is used in the test. It especially focuses on accessibility issues related to accessibility of information within the document.

One test of test does not replace the other, although effective prototype testing will greatly decrease the number of problems field testing uncovers. Prototype testing is also cheaper than field testing because design problems are revealed early in the process where they can do the most good.

Why Prototype?

You can write leaner.

"I can say the bare minimum about a product or feature, knowing that testing will reveal areas that need more detail or an in-depth discussion" (Margolis, 1989, 7).

Prototype testing lets you know how a real reader reacts to your text—you don't have to second guess.

"...I can observe patterns of usage, learn what works and what doesn't, and polish my skills based on real information about how customers use my manuals and what they like and don't like. I can generalize from what I learn. Testing lets me avoid mind-reading. I don't have to guess what readers want or anticipate their needs on an uncanny sixth sense" (Margolis, 1989, 7).

People support that which they help to design, and it eases the sociopolitical element of documentation by allowing documents to evolve with the participation of all involved.

"Users of prototype systems reported greater satisfaction with the design process and lower conflict between users and designers" (Guillemette, 1987, 137).

Designers know too much—they are too close to be effective testers.

"Designers have become so proficient with the product that they can no longer perceive or understand the areas that are apt to cause difficulties. Even when designers become users, their deep understanding and close contact with the device they are designing means that they operate it almost entirely from knowledge in the head....Innocence lost is not easily regained. The designer cannot predict the problems people will have, the misinterpretations that will arise, and the errors that will get made" (Norman, 1988, 156-7).

Prototype testing is the best way to settle arguments between documenters, reviewers, and managers.

"Validation of computer manuals, like validation of instructional manuals, makes the user/student a court of last resort and, thus tends to cut down on arguments about what will or will not work" (Margolis, 1989, 1).

How Do You Go About Prototyping a Document?

First, prepare your testers and the test. This process includes:

- Choosing a typical audience of readers or simulating an audience if the former is not possible
- Developing a task problem scenario for testers to solve using the system and the paper and on-line documentation
- Putting in a Help phone connected to the author stationed in another room so as to

The most accurate readability test to use as part of the prototype test is the "Cloze test"—also known as the "Five + Five test." The Cloze test works perfectly with the small samples of the manual that may be available in a prototype test. (1) Take five paragraphs at random from all the material available and print them. (2) Delete every fifth word and insert a blank, and then (3) give these five paragraphs with deleted words to the user. (4) If the user can supply exactly the right word or a very close synonym, your document is on the right readability level. If they can't, then evidently your document is not at the right readability level. Although it appears to be less scientific than other readability tests such as the "Gunning index," "Fog index," or "Clear River index," the Cloze test is the most accurate test because it uses real users rather than representing them mathematically as in all the other tests. It's also more accurate because it brings into the readability analysis the reader's use of sentence and paragraph context which is largely ignored by all the other tests' foci on the length of individual words, phrases, or sentences. The Cloze test also brings into the analysis the reader's vocabulary developed from their unique backgrounds, training, or education. None of the other readability tests allow for such individual vocabularies.

simulate the phone support available to actual users

• Making them feel comfortable

• Cautioning them that it's the document not them that's being tested

• Having the field testers use the software and documentation according to your instructions

Use one of three ways of capturing the user experience. These vary in their sophistication and the amount of time, money, and effort they require. The three types are the "educated observation and debriefing method" (Heines, 1984; Horton, 1984), the "reading protocol" method (Swaney et al., 1981; Flower and Hayes, 1981), and the "playback" method (Neal and Simons, 1984).

The "educated observation and debriefing method" is the easiest and the cheapest of the three methods. To use this method, watch the testers and try to find out where they have problems. If you have trouble picking out their confusion, use the "two-together: method:

> "[T]ry letting two ... [users] work through the ... [documentation and system] together. This is an excellent technique for achieving verbalization, because the ... [users] usually talk to each other and try to achieve consensus before trying any actions. Listening to their conversation will let you trace their thinking processes and provide insight into just where they were led astray" (Heines, 1984).

The "reading protocol" is a bit more scientific because it asks the testers to record their thoughts into a tape recorder when they are working on the assigned task (Barton, 1984; Winkler, 1984). After about 5 different subjects have worked for 2 or 3 hours on the task, listen to the tapes to ferret out possible problem areas in the documentation.

The most sophisticated technique is the "playback" technique—currently the basis for much of IBM's usability testing (Casey, 1984; Cunningham, 1984; Grice, 1984 (b); Hernandez and Wilder, 1984; Shufelt, 1984; Thing, 1984). In this technique, when a user is working with a system and its accompanying documentation, the keyboard activity is timed and recorded by a second computer. This material is later

"One of the important points about this method [thinking aloud protocols] is that the protocol is produced at the same time as the experience it describes. Thus we do not ask participants to summarize their reactions to the task of learning a computer application (that is what you might read in magazine reviews of a computer product), we asked them to verbalize the experience itself. This method produces vivid glimpses of human problem-solving and learning, and a very rich qualitative survey of phenomena and problems in a task domain" (Carroll, 1990, Chapter 2).

A terrific videotape overview and demonstration of this whole process can be seen in NCR's *Validating Information Products* (1989).

played back for analysis (Neal and Simons, 1984). This technique also uses videotape cameras to monitor the testers' use of the documentation. This is a much more sophisticated system than "educated observation," and it is a less invasive method than the "reading protocol." It is, however, much more expensive.

Next, debrief the testers after the test is over to capture their feelings about the entire process:

> "In debriefing sessions with users testing an on-line HyperCard presentation, Barbara Harvie of Software Publishing Corporation asks these questions [to get at reader attitude]: did you feel stupid or frustrated at any point; do you feel that you learned anything; were you surprised by anything; did the organization seem clear and logical; were you bored at any point; how do you feel about the level of the information—too much—too little—not relevant—useless; how do you feel about the overall metaphor" (Margolis, 1989, 6).

Finally, summarize your findings and meet with the rest of the design team to see how the test findings should be implemented.

One Company's Approach to Prototype Testing

In Tandem Inc.'s in-house technical writing newsletter, Dennise Brown had the following additional suggestions about how prototype/usability testing should proceed (1989):

> "Q. The articles I read about usability talk about elaborate labs with two-way mirrors. Do I really need all that equipment to get started in usability testing?
>
> A. No. The minimum requirements for usability test are one item and two people: something to test (your manual), someone to give the test (you), and someone to take the test (your test subject).
>
> Q. OK, OK. I have my first draft of a complete procedure. Now what?
>
> A. Now you start on the testing sequence: design the test, give the test, and evaluate the test.
>
> Q. Design the test? What's involved in designing the test?
>
> A. Write your problem statement. This is where you define what you want to get from the test. Selecting the right part of the manual, one that outlines as specific a task as users should be able to accomplish, is the key to a clear problem statement. If you have trouble writing

the problem statement, you may need to choose another part of the manual to test.

Create your test documents. I'd suggest keeping these to a minimum so the test doesn't sink in a sea of paper. However, in addition to copies of the chapter you're testing, and a tracking list to record the changes you decide to make, you'll need four types of documents for the test itself: a description of the test environment, instructions for the monitor, and a scenario and task description for the test subject; a debriefing questionnaire.

Prepare for the test: prepare the test environment, select and invite test subjects, rehearse the test, train the monitors, and prepare the test packets.

Q. So tell me what's involved in actually giving the test?

A. Usability testing is like fixing Thanksgiving dinner: it takes a lot more time to plan and prepare than it does to serve and eat! The tasks involved in giving the test are: welcoming the test subject, getting the test started, monitoring the test, and debriefing the test subject.

Q. What's left?

A. After the test comes the important part: evaluate the test process, compile the test results, and incorporate changes into the manual.

Q. So is this a cure-all?

A. Usability test won't tell you if all the information in your manual is technically accurate. It won't tell you if there are typos. It will, however, give you information about a very specific, very important class of problems: problems that users encounter when they try to use your product. Usability testing is an important tool in a writer's toolkit, but it's up to the writer to choose when and where to use it!"

When You Prototype Test Your Document Design:

1. Prepare the test, the testers, and the location.

2. Have testers perform the test and capture their responses.

3. Debrief them to capture their overall feelings.

4. Analyze and apply the findings.

STEP 3: DRAFTING THE DOCUMENT

This step and the next step, editing the document, although separated here for convenience of coverage, probably proceed almost simultaneously and iteratively until the final draft is finished.

In the third step, we turn from the planning and prototype testing stage to the execution stage of the SDP, writing the first draft. The following seven substeps are involved in drafting the document:

- Overcome writer's block.

- Use an appropriate style.

- Employ reader-based writing principles.

- Develop effective graphics.

- Create your reference aids.

- Consider your packaging.

- Plan for updates.

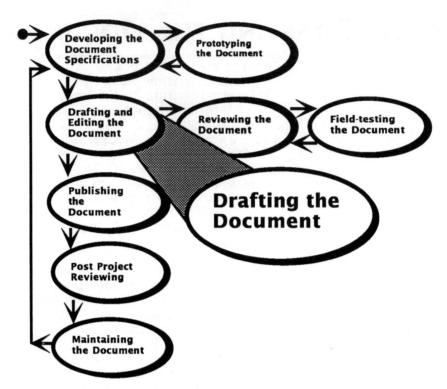

Overcome Writer's Block

Writer's block can occur at three different junctures:

- Between your thoughts and your fingers on the keyboard—the inability to produce text because of internal, psychological factors

- Between yourself and your information source—the inability to produce text because either your information source "can't" find the time or won't talk to you

- Between team members—the members of a team cannot function together effectively to produce the document

Step 3: Draft the Document

Overcome Writer's Block

Use an Appropriate Writing Style

Employ Reader-Based Writing Techniques

Develop Effective Graphics

Create Your Reference Aids

Consider Your Packaging

Plan for Updating

To Overcome	Be Sure To
Internal writer's block	• Plan to write poorly but edit well
	• Don't start in the beginning
	• Always stop at the end of the day in the middle of a page or screen
	• Talk it out

Writer's block from information sources	• Build your creditability with subject matter experts
	• Offer sources alternative ways of getting information to you
	• Use management leverage
Team writing blocks	• Build cohesion and participation
	• Use storyboards
	• Keep teams small

Internal Writing Block

Decision overload is often a cause of internal writer's block. Therefore, the best way to overcome internal writer's block was covered in the last step: develop document specifications. Developing such blueprints prevents decision overload from occurring because you have already made 80% of the decisions regarding a text. With these decisions made, the drafting of a text is more a function of crafting words and paragraphs.

However, if you have done your document specifications, and you still have an internal writer's block, try one of the following strategies:

Studies have shown that the amount of material produced by someone who writes "perfectly" the first time and the amount of material produced by someone who brainstorms and then edits is similar for a given amount of time. The psychological toll, however, on the "perfect writer" is much greater than that exacted from the two-phase brainstormer/editor (Mack and Skjei, 1979;see also Elbow, 1981, and Green's discussion of Flower's weak and strong writing strategies). However, Glynn, Britton, Muth and Dogen (1982) counter that such first draft/final draft writers produced less quality and less quanity writing.

- "Plan to write poorly and edit well" (Promptdoc, 1983). Don't try to write anything "perfectly" the first time. The more you try to say it perfectly, the more you forget what you wanted to say. Hold back from editing anything when you first begin. Just try to get material down on a page, then go back and edit it. You can implement this idea by telling yourself that you will keep writing on that blank page or keep typing on the keyboard for 5 minutes straight without stopping and without using the eraser or backspace key. Don't even look at the screen of your word processor when you are doing this, so that you will not be tempted to slip into the editing mode.

- Don't start at the beginning. The introduction, overview, or summary is always the hardest part of the document to write, so don't begin there. Begin, rather, in the middle of the manual where things are more procedural and straightforward and thus easier to write. Then you can build up a head of steam and write through to the end of the manual. Eventually,

Beware of the "instant fix" problem—correcting surface errors on the screen may interrupt creative brainstorning: "A curious feature of computers, as opposed to pencils and typewriters, is when you ought to be writing something more interesting than a nearly perfect sentence. Since it is easier to revise and edit with a computer than with a typewriter and pencil, this amazing machine makes it very hard to stop editing and revising long enough to write a readable sentence, much less an entire newspaper column" (Baker, 1986, 30; see also Feno, 1986).

External Writing Blocks from Information Sources

If you were not part of the design team, one aspect of writing preparation might be to study the design documents of the system or software (Digital, 1983). This might include some of the following documents (Zaneski, 1982):

The requirements analysis document may answer your questions regarding the general business and specific technical purposes of the system.

The basic project plan explains how the basic goals and objectives of management have been carried out by the software.

The functional specification isolates and describes key areas of a system.

The system specification describes how the system handles errors, what the screen messages include, and security considerations.

Additionally, an examination of code listings, notes and memos, and minutes of design meetings could also prove helpful.

take the end of the manual and work it into the overview or summary.

- Stop drafting the document or screen at the end of the day halfway through a paragraph or sentence. In this way you'll have something easy to get started on the next day (Horton, personal communication).

- When you are in the midst of a highly specialized, sophisticated, and complex problem, it is sometimes difficult to draft material for outsiders. If so, try taping a monologue on a tape recorder to an imaginary member of your target audience or actually explaining it to a friend or other "outsider." Consider this a preamble to the actual writing.

Besides internal writer's block, there is also the more insidious *external* writer's block. Its source lies in individuals other than the writer, and is, therefore, less open to the writer's control. To overcome this type of writer's block, use these techniques:

- Build your creditability with subject matter experts.

For one thing, you can do your homework concerning the technical area you are trying to document. If your manual deals with data communications, study it before you go to your information sources. Don't expect them to educate you in the whole technical field in addition to giving you the specifics of the software package about which you are asked to write. Also, take on the role of the users. Walk in their shoes...or rather sit in their seats in front of their VDT's. Try using the software. Try to recapture the feeling and frustration that goes on early in the "learning curve." Very often these experiences will lead you to the questions for an information source. It will give you and the information source some common experience on which to build. It will also give you a way of establishing empathy in your manual with the user's early learning frustrations.

If, after you have done your homework and tried using the software, you still don't understand, ask for further clarification. Most subject matter experts are much more cooperative once they realize you have taken the time to learn and use their program or system; you've "paid your dues" in ways that glancing over the design document just doesn't.

Reveal the business or usability reasons for the documentation to information sources who are outside of marketing or management. Frequently, the software designers and engineers fail to see the need to participate in a documentation project that seems to them to be only fulfilling a distant bureaucrat's requirements.

- Use alternative ways to collect information.

  We've all known one or two people who function best in a critical mode rather than in a positive mode. If your information source is one of these people and is unable or unwilling to give you the information you need, try using the review process as one of your information-gathering techniques.

  Some people honestly do not have the time to talk with you, or they are so shy that they avoid talking. If your information source is like one of these two, present them with a list of questions and a tape recorder and ask them to dictate their information into the tape recorder when they are commuting home, waiting at the airport, or taking a coffee break. (Other ways of collecting information that would not require face-to-face meetings also include electronic mail or questionnaires.)

- Finally, if nothing else works, seek diplomatic ways to use management leverage to support your efforts and to break down information barriers (Pakin and Associates, 1984).

External Writing Blocks in Team Writing

The written product of groups has long been disparaged by such stock phrases as "a camel is a horse that was assembled by a committee." And, the concept of a writing team seems to be very unsettling to writers who are accustomed to the traditional "lone gun" lifestyle of documentation writers. However, the productivity demands made on writers are making

A psychologist from the Royal Australian Army suggested to me the acronym PUB to guide team building:

P should remind you to make sure the team clearly understands the purpose of the team. When the purpose is clear to all, a team is efficient.

U should remind you to understand that different people have different capabilities and, thus, should be charged with those portions of the project that best fit their capabilities.

B should remind you to balance the resources so that all member of the team receive the resources, e.g., hardware, software, supplies, artwork, to perform their portion of the project.

Storyboards are an improvement over the typical outline because storyboards make all plans explicit, thus, they provide a clear focus for debates and reactions from team members. Storyboards provide mass access to the document plan, rather than the sequential access arrangement of the typical outline; since all the parts of the plan are simultaneously visible to team members, the parts are kept in perspective by team members and are kept interconnected. And, although storyboards are a clever way of planning paper documentation, they will become an absolute essential for on-line documentation when multiple reader pathways through a document can only be shown through storyboards and not ordinary outlines. Finally, storyboards are excellent for management reviews of the team's documentation plan. The manager can be brought into the room and "walked through" the plans for the documentation by observing the storyboards on the wall (Tracey, 1983; Barkman, 1982, 1984; Andriole, 1989).

companies take a new look at writing teams and are making documenters question the effectiveness of continuing the "lone gun" lifestyle. Teams offer a psychological edge over the "lone gun" lifestyle. Teams can perk up writers and challenge writers when their own individual head of steam seems to run out. Teams can bring divergent perspectives or divergent backgrounds to bear on a project. And, for those who watch the bottom line, an effective team can produce a document in less time than a lone writer.

If you go with a writing team, here are some suggestions on how to avoid writing blocks within a team:

- Build team cohesion and participation.

  Don't be democratic. There should be a benevolent dictator responsible for setting priorities and responsibilities.

  Don't enact solutions by voting. Voting always leaves a disgruntled minority. Come to decisions by consensus so that all members feel involved in a decision. (Remember that the solution the team develops is not the perfect solution, but only the solution which works best within the given constraints. Realizing you are not striving for absolute perfection usually allows the team to come to compromise more easily.)

  If you need to avoid having one person dominate the brainstorming session, use a "round robin" method; give each team member two minutes to lead the brainstorm session, and then go to the next person, and the next, and so on, until each person has had a chance to lead the discussion. Only once everyone has had an opportunity to speak should anyone be given a second chance. And on this second turn, and henceforth, everyone should again be systematically given an opportunity to speak. Doing this draws each member into the team and doesn't allow them to withdraw from active participation.

- Remember that people have short attention spans so use storyboards (blackboards or large flip chart paper as posters) to record the ideas and suggestions of group members. Place these storyboards on the walls clearly visible to everyone in the group and make everyone responsible for recording their own ideas or suggestions. Thus, no one will repeat an earlier person's ideas just because they forgot them; in other words, no more out of sight, out of mind.

- Keep the team to an optimal size: at least three members to avoid suffering from tunnel vision, but not more than five. When a team gets as large as five members, a team becomes less of a team and more of a *horde*. (However, teams developing interactive on-line media could require the team work of slightly larger teams including programmers, designers, artists, writers, managers, human factor testers, etc.)

The size in documentation teams where time spent on coordinating and organizing begins to noticeably diminish time spent on producing documentation is five (Brooks F., 1975).

Brooks in *The Mythical Man-Month: Essays on Software Engineering* pointed out that above a certain size, a team spends more time coordinating and organizing itself, and less time on producing the end product. He called this problem the "mongolian horde syndrome"—above a certain number the team becomes more of a horde rather than a cohesive unit, and thus requires a greater and greater percentage of time and effort just to coordinate itself.

Use an Appropriate Writing Style

Reading scientists studying how adults read have broken the activity of reading into continuums of two reading types and five different reading strategies (Pugh, 1975).

How Do Readers Read Documentation?

Reading to Learn	Reading to Do
"In reading to learn, the reader must integrate and store information in long-term memory so that it is available for later use" (Sticht et al., 1977; see also Duin, 1988).	"In reading to do, information is gathered for immediate use and typically does not require either the integration of large segments of information, nor the long-term retention of that information. Additionally, in reading to do, the purpose for reading is well defined" (Sticht et al., 1977; see also Duin, 1988).
"They interviewed civilian and military high school students, technical school students, technical school instructors, and regular workers asking them how they used information in school versus on the job. A large percentage (66%) of the students' reading was for reading to learn something" (Sticht, 1985).	"The largest percentage of the regular workers reading (78%) was for reading to do" (Sticht, 1985).

Critical Reading	Receptive Reading	Search Reading	Scanning	Skimming
Reading for evaluation purposes.	Reading for thorough comprehension.	Scan with attention to the meaning of specific items.	Reading quickly through a text with the purpose of quickly finding specific items.	Reading for the general drift in a text.

Studies of adults reading in a business or commercial environment reveal that they read to do; their purpose for reading is usually well defined in advance (e.g., how to solve a software problem), and they retain the information only long enough to perform the task. They also employ the reading strategies of skimming, scanning, and search reading; they need to find specific pieces of information quickly (Digital, 1983; Pugh, 1975; Thomas, 1976). These studies also show that the adults approach data processing documentation in a random access method; they turn to the information they want, no matter where it is in a document, without necessarily reading the information leading up to it or the information immediately following it.

Luckily, there are alternative writing styles that accommodate readers who are "reading to do," who employ the reading strategies of skimming and scanning, and who require a random access arrangement of information. Basically these styles unite in a single package much of the individual design areas discussed in Step 1: tasks, organization, layout, visualization. Some are already fairly familiar to most readers (Wright and Reid, 1973): logic tree or flowchart (both are graphic or pictorial styles that substitutes predefined symbols for specific functions), or text flowchart (uses the straightforward succinct approach of the flowchart but adds the explanatory information that only text can give). The others (text picture or "Super Comic Book," FOMM, STOP, Playscript, and Structured writing) are not so familiar and will be discussed in greater depth.

The common element in each of these styles is that the writer takes on more of the interpretive work than does the reader. Each of these methods predigests the information and uses not only words and graphics, but also page formats to present interpreted information. These styles follow the idea that "text is diagram" and use macropunctuation devices such as headings, boldface, and other layout and typographic devices to make a text more understandable (Jonassen, 1982 (b); Hartley, 1980). In fact, a byproduct of this writer-interpretive work with its attention to white space and format is that "clarity in layout equals clarity in content, because this process requires clarity of thought" (Hartley, 1980).

Step 3: Draft the Document

Overcome Writer's Block

Use an Appropriate Writing Style

Employ Reader-Based Writing Techniques

Develop Effective Graphics

Create Your Reference Aids

Consider Your Packaging

Plan for Updating

Reader-Engineered Writing Styles

Micropunctuation devices such as commas and full-stops are sentence-level icons revealing the organization of a sentence. Macropunctuation devices such as tables or indentation and headings are passage level icons revealing the organization of an entire page.

Reading to Learn			Reading to Do	
Critical Reading	*Receptive Reading*	*Search Reading*	*Scanning*	*Skimming*
Traditional Methods of Writing:			*Documentation Methods of Writing*	
Continuous prose unmarked or only occasionally marked by macropunctuation. Usually found in fiction. Text structure is conveyed within the text itself by transitional words and phrases (Bernhardt, 1986).			Text structure is visually conveyed by macropunctuation such as tables, indentation, rules, frequent headings, etc. (Martin, 1989, VC-32; see also Watzman, 1987 (b)).	

"Often, though, designers focus on a single approach to usability problems (e.g., the use of visual metaphors). We argue that they should be encouraged to incorporate complementary or even contradictory principles into their analysis" (Carroll and Rosson, 1987, 81).

A number of styles rather than just one style are presented here, for like a good painter with a palette of colors, you need a number of different styles to use at different times with different audiences—don't be afraid to be eclectic. In addition, you may create your own style by combining ideas and techniques from all the different styles.

The text picture style tries to present as much information as possible in pictures. One of the earliest examples of the text picture style was developed by the Pratt and Whitney Aircraft Company. This company started using text pictures because no matter how simple the words and how short the sentences, aircraft mechanics were still misreading directions and causing tremendous damage to aircraft. John Deere Tractor Co. also used this style because they wanted to minimize translation costs; a picture doesn't require expensive translation. (IBM has used this style in their *IBM 5080 Graphics System Setup Manual* (Gange and Lipton, 1984; see also Vogt, 1986.)

FOMM (Functionally Oriented Maintenance Manuals)

Why Was It Invented?

By analyzing the work patterns of maintenance technicians, the FOMM designers made three important observations about the reading styles or preferences of technicians:

- They needed to know the functionality of groups of hardware components first rather than the components' physical layout in the computer.

- They appeared to use a top-down approach in pinpointing hardware faults; they first asked general questions concerning hardware functionality, and then progressively narrowed down the area of their search much like the children's game of "Twenty Questions."

- They seemed to derive more information quickly from graphic displays of hardware components than from verbal descriptions.

To Use the FOMM Technique

- Use functional schematics.

- Organize the content in a top-down manner so it's visually easy to scan across a high level description in order to zoom in on the specifics.

- Keep the text to a minimum by using tables, charts, and schematics.

How to Use It

FOMM designers:

- Use functional schematics (block diagrams with simple arrows for directions) rather than physical schematics (symbols for transistors, capacitors, and gates in a highly sophisticated flow) (FOMM, 1974, 14).

- Organize the presentation of schematics, troubleshooting charts, and text in a top-down approach as seen in Figure 34.

"A FOMM manual presents information in three hierarchical levels as follows: (1) the overall information level that shows and identifies the 'functional' makeup (major functions) of the equipment or system, and provides that information necessary to determine whether or not each of the major equipment functions is operating properly; (2) the major function level that provides information necessary to isolate an improperly operating major function to an item of hardware, and (3) the hardware level that provides for each unit or assembly of hardware that information necessary to isolate a fault to a defective component (or group of components), and effect a repair" (FOMM, 1974, iv).

- Use charts, troubleshooting tables, and schematics with text kept to an absolute minimum:

"Basic to the FOMM philosophy is that one picture is worth a thousand words. Therefore, the Troubleshooting/Repair volume has a maximum of graphs, charts, and diagrams with a minimum supporting text" (FOMM, 1974, 2).

From FOMM We Can Learn

Although we may never write hardware documentation, the most important lesson to learn from the FOMM writing style is that it is designed for one purpose only: to fit the way the reader needs and uses the information:

"In the development of most technical manuals, all too often there is usually one concerned group that does not have a voice in manual content. This group consists of the ultimate users; the technicians who must use the manual as a source for preventive and corrective maintenance information....The FOMM concept is one attempt to focus the writer's attention on the needs of the technician, and to ensure that all the information necessary for understanding and maintenance is included" (FOMM, 1974, 1).

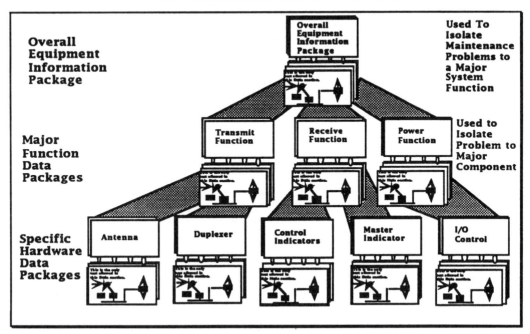

Figure 34. The top-down design of FOMM.

And one way they fit the technician audience was through scan-zoom:

> "In the functionally oriented maintenance manual, we want to maximize communication efficiency by providing a concept of visibility that, for lack of a better name, we refer to as *scan-zoom*....What we need is a technique that will allow a person to scan the whole system, then zoom in on the level of detail he needs at the moment while being able to zoom back out and maintain his system perspective" (Macindoe, 1985, 8).

STOP (Sequential Thematic Organization of Proposals)

Weiss' book, *How to Write a Usable User Manual* (1985), describing a GOTO-less structured documentation style, is largely based on STOP.

Hughes Aircraft Company invented STOP along with FOMM in the late 1960s in order to improve their proposal writing style. Prime Computers, Texas Instruments, NCR, and IBM have adopted variations of this technique for some of their user documentation.

STOP's essential concept is that the page format should structure the content so that the information is more easily grasped by readers.

To Follow the STOP Technique

- Break information into two-page components.
- Use a substantive title.
- Put a thesis statement on the top left.
- Use less than 500 words on the left-hand page.
- Have a graphics, example, or summary table on the right hand page which summarizes the text page.
- Use an extended caption beneath the graphic.

This style has these six simple rules (Weiss, 1985; Tracey, 1983):

- All information must be broken down until it can fit on a double-page layout. In this way, when a reader physically turns the page, a reader is also conceptually moving to a new topic. It also recognizes that paper documentation readers see a two-page spread when they look at the open pages of manual, and thus a designer should plan for a double-page spread of information.

- Develop a headline which defines one double-page spread; it can contain themes, ideas, assertions:

"The traditional heading used in outlines and tables of contents contains only nouns ('LOGON Procedure,' 'Power Redundancy,') or nouns and modifiers ('Alternative LOGON Procedure,' 'Multiple Power Source Redundancy'). These traditional headings give little clue to the actual scope or intent of the section....Neither the author who must write the section of the outline nor the reader who is searching the table of contents really knows what the writer of the outline had in mind" (Weiss, 1985).

- At the top of the text page there must be a "thesis statement" that summarizes the main idea of the two pages to follow.

The use of a headline and thesis statement in STOP and the overview block in structured writing is especially useful in tutorials where the type of reading being employed is reading to learn (Hauke et al., 1977). In reading to learn, readers must integrate and store information in memory. The thesis statement and the overview block function as advanced organizers that greatly aid readers performing this integration process (Meyer R., 1979).

See Step 1, Dealing with Diverse Audiences

"We discovered a natural passage structure marked by subheadings, transitions, keywords, conclusions, etc., already at work in technical discourse. The average passage length was 500 words, and 90 percent had fewer than 750 words. Since the two-page module holds 750 words and one figure, the format appeared to have a practical capacity" (Tracey, 1983).

This thesis statement is also useful for readers only interested in general details. By designing text with the STOP method, the reader is given the opportunity to read only the statements written on a generalized level because the thesis statement, which is on a general level, has been visibly set apart by format.

- The left-hand page has text on it. All text, according to this style, must be broken down to 500 word units.

- The right-hand page is the graphic page. Prime Computers and NCR used this style, but put examples, even text examples, rather than graphics on the right-hand page.

In popular magazines, figure captions are read by more people than any other part of the articles except the main title.

- The figure or example should have an expanded caption of as many as three or four lines of text, much like those used in *National Geographic* or *Scientific American*. With such extended captions, a reader could receive much of the information in a two-page passage just by looking at the figure and reading the caption.

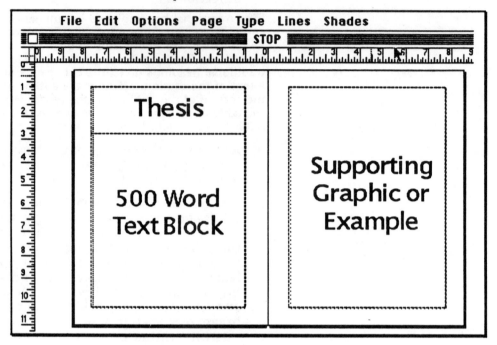

Figure 35. The grid behind the STOP design (using PageMaker 3.0™).

Criticisms of STOP

Two frequently heard criticisms of the STOP style are as follows:

- By making each topic only two pages long, the hierarchy of topics in a manual can be obscured.

- It can lead to a use of graphics and examples that is redundant—they merely restate the content of the text page.

Weiss responds to the first criticism by suggesting that each two-page module be assigned a module number, e.g., 12.1. In doing so, he claims that "the hierarchy can not only be preserved but made clearer to the reader" (Weiss, 1985).

In answer to the second criticism, Weiss points out that these graphics and examples are intentionally

Carroll and the minimalists would claim that such redundancy just gets in the way of streamlining documentation. Additionally, quick reference cards can be so quick and short because the documenters can rely on users' prior knowledge and experience. Thus the need and usefulness of redundancy is inversely proportional to the experience readers have.

redundant in order to compensate for careless reading. Using an analogy from thermodynamics—the universe of energy and matter tends toward a state of disorder or entropy—we could say that redundant graphics and examples combat the problems of entropy in information:

> "Norbert Wiener of M.I.T., the father of CYBERNETICS, the science of maintaining order in a system …[stated] that 'Information is Entropy: Due to entropy, corrections in message transmission are constantly required. The problem is separating the messages from the noise. In nearly all forms of communications, more messages are sent than are strictly necessary to convey the information intended by the sender. Such additional messages diminish the unexpectedness, the surprise effect of the information itself, making it more predictable'" (Turner, 1985).

So rather than the graphics and examples being unnecessarily repetitious, these graphics and examples minimize information entropy and ensure that the reader gets the message in each two-page module.

However, give paragraph numbers an inch and they'll take a mile; see Structured Writing's example from the Australian Department of Defence.

Playscript

Playscript was originally developed in the early 1960's by Leslie Matthies (1977) to show how to integrate the activities of a number of people involved in one project. Its two-column formatting of information promotes readers' ability to skim and scan—the major reading strategies of our target readers. A sample of a classic playscript procedure from Matthies' book is shown below:

Actors	Action
Executive secretary	1. Upon receipt of time-cards (received daily from Accounting), sort them by department, and place in Form 683 Time Summary Envelope.
	2. Deliver to department clerks.
Department clerk	3. Distribute time-cards to all employees.
Employees (all)	4. Prepare time-cards as instructed in Procedure No. 71, Daily Time Tickets.

5. Sign time-cards at start of each day as well as writing the department number after the signature, enclosing the department number within parentheses, such as (12), (15),(17), etc.

6. Send to department clerk.

Department clerk   7. Collect all time-cards at end of shift.

8. Calculate regular time and overtime by jobs.

9. Check each time-card for inclusion of department number.

10. Post totals, with grand total for each job, on Summary Envelope. (Jobs are listed in numerical sequence.)

A variation on playscript's layout that is especially useful for our purposes is shown below (see also Simpson and Casey, 1987, who discuss playscript and show a matrix version of the style used by Apple Computer Co. in the *Macintosh Plus User's Guide*, 1986, 167). In this variation there is only one "actor"—the operator—and the important purpose of the text is to reveal the interaction between the system and the operator:

User Action	System Response
1. Be sure that all disks are out of all drives	Drives emptied
2. Turn system on	Red indicator light illuminates
3. Put WORDSTROKE disk into drive 0	ENTER TIME AND DATE
4. Type: tttt, mm/dd/yy [Enter]	TOSDES READY
5. Type: FORMS {R=66,L=66}[Enter]	TOSDES READY
6. Type: BASIC WORDSTROKE-F:1 [Enter]	COMMAND: SCROLL: HALF appears at top of screen with blinking cursor
7. Begin your word processing	

Notice how by representing the function keys or special keys as visually different, ([Enter] , [⊡], [Return]), from the keyboard keys, or words typed by the keyboard keys, readers will be less likely to confuse typing RETURN and [Return]. It also means that we don't need to discriminate between the two by using the initial verb of "Type" for entering information on the keyboard as on a typewriter, and PRESS when we want them to use a special function key. Visually representing the function keys or special keys as different is simply an easier and more elegant method. It's also more memorable, see Graphics Rules in this step.

Although there are a large number of rules associated with playscript (see Matthies, 1977, and now the Playwrite seminars), the four key techniques used in playscript are listed and explained below:

- Playscript is written in the *who does what when* arrangement because these are the questions a reader of a procedure would be asking of a text. "Who" are the positions or roles appearing in the left column; "does what" are the present tense verbs listed after each of the numbers; and "when" are the numbers running down the middle of the page. Notice that when an actor performs more than one action, his title or role is only written once so that the left-hand column doesn't become cluttered. And because it is understood by the reader that the name directly opposite the verb or the last one stated in the left hand column is the doer of the action listed in the verb, we don't need to include all the "and then's," "and also's," and "finally's" as connectors of the actions. The actions are interconnected to subjects by format.The page layout grid behind the playscript style is shown in Figure 36.

For instance, the typical milk carton says "Open Here"—present tense—not "You will open the top when required"—future tense.

- Write in the "work mode" (imperative voice). This means using action words in the present tense, "plain English," and active voice.

  Action words begin each step. By beginning each step with an action word, you get right to the point. For example, in the two sample playscript procedures:

"7. Collect all time cards at the end of shift."

"1. Be sure that all disks are out of all drives."

Remember to be sensitive to non-American audiences who would find such imperative voice presentations rude.

Each verb is in present tense in order to make the action more of an order than a description of an action. It's more of an order because the interpretation of activities isn't left up to the reader. Some activities don't require giving the reader the option of a choice. It may feel odd to write about an action that will take place in the future by writing in the present tense. However, it will seem perfectly natural to the readers when they are simultaneously reading and performing the action. Finally, the present tense gives the reader a greater sense of certainty than the future tense, which denotes some tentativeness.

Use plain English, which means using the words to the right rather than those to the left on the next page.

CAUTION: There is only one absolute unchanging rule in computer documentation, everything else is only a suggestion. The only unchanging rule is that the audience is always right. Therefore, if your audience analysis reveals that the words in the right-hand column are more appropriate, use them. Always use the appropriate vocabulary, but, when in doubt, use the words in the right-hand column. For 90% of the people, 90% of the time, they are the appropriate words.

Rather than	Use
Ascertain	Find out
Originate	Start
Advise	Tell
Compile	List
Forward	Send to
Expedite	Rush
Disseminate	Spread

The reason for use of the words in the right-hand column is not because the left-hand column words are morally wrong or semantically incorrect. It's just that we have used the words in the right-hand column for a much longer part of our lives and are therefore more familiar with them. On the other hand, the words in the left-hand column are more recent acquisitions in our experience and are thus less familiar. They may be more difficult to recognize and, therefore, may delay our reader's understanding of our text.

There is a place for using passive voice—namely, a sentence in which the subject of the sentence is the receiver of the action rather than the doer of the action, when there are no doers of an action, and when the focus is to be on the receiver of the action. A similar observation regarding the passive voice can be made for saying things negatively. The reader can better understand sentences when they are phrased in the affirmative (Anisfeld and Klenbort, 1973; Clark and Chase, 1972; Palermo, 1973; Sherman, 1976).

Use active voice rather than passive voice. Passive voice is often over-used as shown in the example below (Barnett, Lentzner, and Prono, 1979):

"LLL has been designated by ERDA to head up a 2-year study."

takes longer to say and longer for the reader to understand than :

"ERDA has designated LLL to head up a 2-year study."

- Actions should be linked together like a chain. Tell readers explicitly how to get from one step to the next. Don't ever think it's obvious. It probably isn't. (Margolis, 1982).

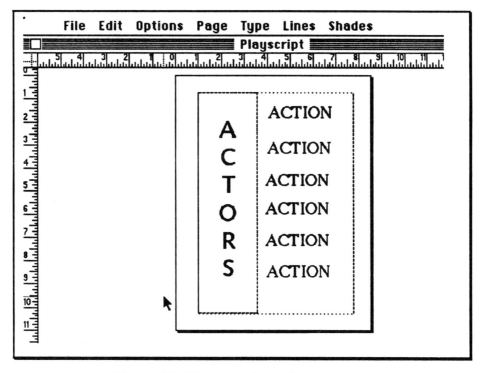

Figure 36. The two-column (unequal columns) grid behind the Playscript layout (using PageMaker 3.0™).

To Follow Playscript Techniques
- Use a two-column arrangement displaying who does what when.
- Write in the work mode.
- Link actions.
- Block actions with white space so that steps are visually segmented.

- Block the actions by using single spacing within an action and double spacing between actions. This format makes it easy for a reader to see where an action begins or ends. It also uses white space actively to separate and differentiate.

Structured Writing   Structured writing (Horn, 1969) is a style that could almost be called the child of STOP and playscript. From the STOP style, structured writing borrowed the idea of a thesis statement at the top of the page. Structured writing requires an overview block at the

Of course, the FOMM, STOP, playscript, and structured writing styles have a substantial portion of their handbooks devoted to analysis of the documentation situation similar to Step 1 in this book. We are, therefore, in this step just examining their various notions of text format and layout.

beginning of its double-page format. Also, structured writing borrows the two-page format from STOP as seen in Figure 37.

Like playscript, structured writing makes use of a two-column format, but where playscript divides the page into actors and action, structured writing divides it into headings and text. With a two-column format we ease the task of skimming and scanning, and we use white space to make the headings stand out. Where playscript uses double-spacing between actions, structured writing makes use of horizontal lines drawn between paragraphs. In fact, these horizontal rules are the hallmarks of this style.Thus far we have seen how on-line documentation can learn from paper documentation. In structured writing we have the first instance of information flowing from on-line documentation to enhance paper documentation.

Structured writing also takes its form from on-line documentation. The inventors of structured writing were originally involved in developing computer-assisted instruction modules. When they moved from the medium of the screen to the medium of paper, they discovered that the discipline of writing for paper was much less stringent than writing for a screen presentation and could easily lead to sloppy organization. Therefore, they brought much of the discipline of chunking information for screens to paper. Thus as we move from paper to screens in on-line documentation, some of the best ways to make that transition are already outlined in structured writing.

There are a large number of rules associated with structured writing (see Horn, 1969, whose version of structured writing also goes under the trademarked name of "information mapping"™). However, the key techniques of structured writing are listed and explained below in a variation of the structured writing format.

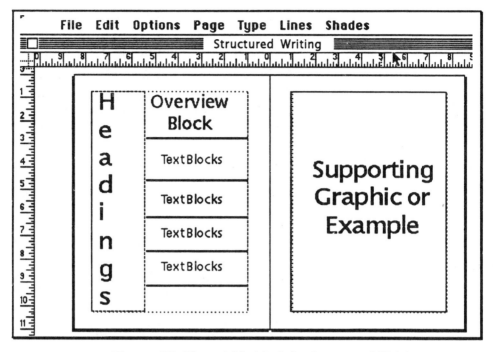

Figure 37. The grid behind the Structured Writing layout (using PageMaker 3.0™).

Sample Structured Writing Double Page Layout

Overview	Break information into double-page maps with information in visible blocks. Label each block and keep them short, and the sentences (chunks) short.
Break Information into Maps	Start each new map (a passage or chapter) at the top of a page, and try to fit a map on a double-page spread: a left-hand side text page and a right-hand side page with a supporting graphic or example.
Use Blocks	Present information in visible blocks (paragraphs) that are outlined. This makes information bite-sized and localizes all the information on one topic or aspect of that topic in one physical place. For example, the information on "DPBS" in Figure 38 is all centered in one location so that it is easy to find.
Label Blocks	Standardize labels and their locations on the page. Side labels are restricted to the left column and do not cross over into the text column on the right. This type of label allows the reader to read the text uninterruptedly, whereas conventional cross-headings interrupt the text and strongly imply borders.
	Structured writing's use of such left-hand column labels coincides with the research that suggests that "the left half of the page has a strong influence on reader attention" (Rubens and Krull, 1985). You can speed retrieval of information and improve readability by using such side labels (Hartley and Burnhill, 1976).
Use Short Blocks and Chunks	Within a map, many blocks are preferable to one long one. Within a block, many short chunks of information (sentences) are preferable to one long chunk. Break up the longer blocks and chunks of information. Note how the content of Figure 38 is broken up into four discrete smaller blocks.

Sample Structured Writing Double Page Layout

Sample Page of Structured Writing

PBS TERMINAL OPERATOR'S GUIDE

PBS OVERVIEW
‾‾‾‾‾‾‾‾‾‾‾‾‾‾‾‾‾‾‾‾‾‾‾‾‾‾‾‾‾‾‾‾‾‾‾‾‾‾‾1.0

The Professional Billing System (PBS) is an on-line
system created by the Service Computation Center (SCC)
for the Department of Professional Billing Services
(PBS). With proper instruction, the system will
automatically handle all phases of billing patients
for professional services rendered by approved
physicians at the University ▮▮▮▮▮▮▮▮▮▮▮▮▮
Hospitals. The system can be used for billing by
sixteen different departments. It can also be used
for inquiry by the hospital and Emergency Room.

MANUAL
‾‾‾‾‾‾‾‾‾‾‾‾‾‾‾‾‾‾‾‾‾‾‾‾‾‾‾‾‾‾‾‾‾‾‾‾‾‾‾1.1

This manual is designed to be a training guide for the
new data entry operator, and a quick-reference manual
for the experienced operator. Its contents include a
brief description of the subsystems of PBS; detailed
procedures for using these subsystems; screen
illustrations and field requirements for each; and a
glossary of DPBS and data processing terms the
operator will need to know to effectively use the
terminal. Operating instructions for the following
subsystems are given in this manual.
          *Account Load/Update;
          *Abbreviated Account Load/Update;
          *Institutional Account Load/Update;
          *Financial Information Update for an
           Account;
          *Insurance Load/Update for an Account.

DPBS
‾‾‾‾‾‾‾‾‾‾‾‾‾‾‾‾‾‾‾‾‾‾‾‾‾‾‾‾‾‾‾‾‾‾‾‾‾‾‾1.2

The abbreviation, DPBS is a mnemonic originally
created to access the PBS system. Use of the term
since its origin, has necessitated it being adopted as
a synonym for the PBS system. Hence, in this manual,
the two terms are used interchangeably.

NOTE: Throughout this manual, the word "she" is used to represent
both men and women. This is used for convenience and does not
reflect preference or condition.

PBS TERMINAL OPERATOR'S GUIDE

PAGE 1-1

Figure 38. An introduction designed using Structured
Writing. Notice how the page violates the layout
grid to display better the bottom note on
pronouns.

Sample Structured Writing Double Page Layout

Overview

Use overviews at the top of each new map and use bold or italic to set off words that change the meaning of sentences. Use a portrait layout to display pages.

Have an Overview for Each Map

Overviews are used at the top of each map. Their function is to relate new ideas to previously discussed concepts, to familiarize audiences with the nature and importance of any new ideas, and to provide a transitional and cohesive element to a map (MacDonald, 1979).

Technical writing in general and computer documentation in specific, has long been accused of being *cobblestone writing*. Just as a cobblestone street bounces and jostles all those who drive over it in a car, so too, can technical writing bounce and jostles readers as they go from one fact or topic to another if smooth transitions or cohesive elements are left out.

Consider how the overview block at the top of Figure 39 introduces all the information to follow.

When to Use Bold or Italics

Always bold or italicize the word not. Bold or italicize such words as

> If, Nor, Nothing

> Unless, Never, Refuse

> Unable, Either/or Except

if they change the meaning of the whole sentence. Bold or italicize to stress significant words. Readers of directions often overlook key words which signal abrupt turns in the logic of a sentence.

Display Pages Using Portrait Layout

Pages should be read vertically (portrait). A reader should not have to turn the book sideways to read a diagram (landscape). Transform horizontal tables into vertical ones. Figure 44 violates this rule.

Sample Structured Writing Double Page Layout

Same Document — The Structured Writing Version

```
How to Run the Daily Equipment Location Run

When          Do this run every morning.

Input         • Daily Equipment Run tape
              • data cards from the previous run
              • update cards
              • lead cards

Output        • updated Daily Equipment Run tape
              • daily Equipment log
              • daily Equipment Location Change Report
```

Procedure	STEP	ACTION
	1	Fill out the lead card with today's date
	2	Separate the cards with a punch in col. 10 from the rest of the sorted "PERMEQUIP" cards
	3	Verify the following • all cards have a 'F9' in col. 79-80 • a code is punched in col. 18 • all cards have a valid equipment type number in col. 14-15 • col. 22-28 has a valid department code
	4	Enter the word DAEQLOC on the typewriter and push RUN
	5	Check upper right hand corner of first page of report to see if there are rejects
	6	Verify that the Report Date is the same as the lead card date
	7	Separate punched output and send all cards with a missing equipment type number to Coding Department
	8	Send all cards with invalid codes in Col. 14-15 to Equipment Verification Department

Figure 39. A Structured Writing page with a procedure. Do we really need all the vertical lines?

Sample Structured Writing Double Page Layout

Overview	Minimize the use of vertical lines; tabulate long series of items; use vertical bullet lists for most lists and numbers only for steps in a procedure.
Using Rules and Lines	Minimize the use of vertical lines; they tend to break up the flow of a page. In fact, vertical lines are usually the page element to which the eye is most powerfully drawn. Figure 40 illustrates the most complex use of vertical lines in all the examples. Its use of vertical lines almost turns the page into a giant checkerboard.
How to Handle a Series	Tabulate long series of • Words • Verb phrases • If, then clauses • Clauses • Sentences of similar construction rather than bury them in prose paragraph form.
Using Numbers, Letters, or Bullets	Use numbers only for steps in a procedure; bullets for most other lists; and letters if a bulleted list doesn't sufficiently denote priorities or orders of importance. Computer documentation often includes far more numbers than necessary. For example, in one Australian Department of Defence manual this heading appeared: "3.3.12.3.2.2.10 POINTER SEQUENCE (DS124LI)" followed by a section which consisted entirely of "See paragraph 3.3.12.3.2.2.1.12." The U.S. Army's manual designed to teach better manual writing techniques makes the point that overnumbering is more distracting and confusing to the reader than it is useful (Hauke et al., 1977). The Army advises all their manual writers not to use numbers beyond two levels ("7.4").

Sample Structured Writing Double Page Layout

```
Financial Information Update

                                                                    5.2
PREREQUISITES      To use this function, the account must have previousl·
                   been established through one of the Account Load
                   functions.  Valid information for financial class,
                   patient type and statement code must be provided
                   before an account is established.  Appropriate codes
                   may be selected from the codes table.
                                                                    5.3
PROCEDURE          Assuming you have logged on to the PBS system and
                   accessed the Financial data screen, proceed as
                   follows:


I  STEP  I  OPERATOR ACTION...           I  TERMINAL ACTION...            I
I_____I_____I_____I
I   1    I  Type in Unit History number  I                                I
I_____I_____I_____I
I   2    I  Press *ENTER*                I                                I
I        I                               I                                I
I        I     I  IF...          I  THEN...                I              I
I        I     I_____I_____I              I
I        I     IPatient has ONE  I  Financial Data         I              I
I        I     IGUARANTOR on file Iscreen will appear.I     I              I
I        I     I_____I_____I              I
I        I     IPatient has more I  Acct Selection         I              I
I        I     Ithan one Guarantor I  screen will appear I    I              I
I        I     Ion file          IProbe one guarantor I    I              I
I        I     I                 IFinancial Data          I              I
I        I     I                 Iscreen will appear.I     I              I
I_____I     I_____I_____I_____I
I   3    I  Type in changes in valid     I                                I
I        I  codes for financial class,   I                                I
I        I  patient type, statement      I        N O N E                 I
I        I  code, collection level,      I                                I
I        I  freeze account and satellitel                                 I
I        I  accounts. (Accounts may be   I                                I
I        I  forced to Bad Debt status    I                                I
I        I  through this function.       I                                I
I_____I_____I_____I
I   4    I  Press *ENTER*                I  A review screen will appear   I
I_____I_____I_____I


                      continued

PBS TERMINAL OPERATOR'S GUIDE

                                            PAGE  5-2
```

Figure 40. A Structured Writing page with an overuse of vertical lines. Most of these lines can be replaced by the implied left line of left justified text. Also, the future tense "will appear" should be replaced by the present tense "appears."

Employ Reader-Based Writing Techniques

We need now to infuse some reader-based writing techniques into these writing styles and patterns of organization:

- Examples and metaphors
- Interrelated examples called cases
- A conversational style
- The scenario writing principle
- Avoidance of humor

Using Examples and Metaphors

"Yoder investigated the relationship between an individual's cognitive style as measured by the Myers-Briggs Type Indicator and their performance on two task using the IBM VM/SP and VM/CMS operating systems....Perhaps of more importance, was the finding that most participants performed better with formats based onexamples and poorly using help messages involving abstract explanations" (Norman, 1988, 54-5).

cf.

"The power of an analogy or metaphor will be increased if examples of where it holds true, and where it does not, are given" (Hampton, 1987, 230).

"Many benefits come from encouraging users to utilize their existing knowledge through metaphors. For example: users will tend to know what is happening when the system gives them a ertain type of feedback; they will tend to know how to respond to that feedback; they will tend to know how to plan their tasks better; and they will tend to be able to generalize from known, already encountered situations, to new and unknown ones" (Hampton, 1987, 229; see also Wozny, 1989).

In Part One, a 15-year survey of users and their complaints regarding user manuals was cited (Maynard, 1982). One of the three major complaints was that there were not enough examples in user manuals. Examples, if nothing else, serve to specify the theoretical or abstract content of many user manuals (Gilfoil, 1982). In addition (if you remember our discussion of readers in the first step of the SDP), less knowledgeable audiences, parrot and novice audiences, rely heavily on examples.

When Using Examples:

- Place examples physically near the text they exemplify—a double-page spread on paper or multiple windows can be most efficient ways to do this.
- Make examples stand out from the rest of the text by boxing or italicizing them. Doing this ensures that readers will not confuse specific examples with general information.

Metaphors are closely akin to examples. This is so because they usually employ a concrete idea that is known to explain an abstract concept that is unknown.

A wonderful example comes from the first attempt at a user-friendly computer manual, the UNIVAC I Operation Manual in 1954. The first page of the first chapter endeavors to explain what a computer is, and it does this by showing a picture of a payroll clerk with a stack of time cards and hourly rate cards to the left, a mechanical hand calculator in front, and the ledger book to the right:

"In order to make clear the function of each component of the computer and its relationship to other components, let us consider the operation of a payroll clerk....This payroll process can be thought of in terms of four basic operations: Input, Output, Arithmetic, and Supervision. As shown in the figure, the time cards and hourly rate cards are the input data, the calculator is the arithmetic unit, and the output is the net pay entered in the ledger. The whole operation is supervised and executed by the clerk."

Providing Interrelated Examples Called Cases

The first principle is obvious, but sometimes we overlook the second one. In one manual produced by a large U.S. mainframe company, the examples for a spreadsheet software package all contained accounting and financial information as examples. It worked well. On the other hand, a manual developed in a government research facility to explain a word - processing package used a consistent but inappropriate set of examples. The example centered on Edgar Allen Poe's poem, "The Raven," a topic and example not very relevant to the working lives of scientists and engineers. Not surprisingly, the manual was not very successful.

You have already seen how examples should be an integral part of user documentation. The case method, however, urges a more sophisticated use of examples by suggesting that examples be interrelated and consistent. For instance:

- All the examples of input forms for a piece of software should come from a single scenario.

- This same information should then be transferred to all examples of screens in the manual.

- Then it should be used in all examples of the output.

By keeping examples consistent, readers can see how material entering the system in one form is modified by the software into output. By keeping the examples consistent, you avoid one fragmenting element— isolated examples—in your material, and gain an additional device to enable readers to put the information manuals together for themselves. This interrelated set of examples is called a case study (Pakin and Associates, 1980). (Case studies are especially useful for tutorial readers who are "reading to learn" and who need to integrate text.)

Step 3: Draft the Document

Overcome Writer's Block

Use an Appropriate Writing Style

Employ Reader-Based Writing Techniques

Develop Effective Graphics

Create Your Reference Aids

Consider Your Packaging

Plan for Updating

To Develop an Effective Case Study:

- Maintain continuity with all examples.

- Fit the case to the audience.

If you are using a team writing approach to your documentation, make sure that all members of a team need to draw from a common case (Holden and Winter, 1984). If this is not done, a writer using a company making widgets and directed by a Mr. Feversham in chapter 1 of a manual can be contradicted by another writer in chapter 3 who transforms the company into a telecommunications giant that employs Mr. Feversham as the janitor.

Using a Conversational Style

The British strongly object to this informal tone; see multicultural documentation in Step 1.

A conversational style can be defined as a style in which you write to readers as though you were talking with them. Second person pronouns and contractions are common in this style of writing. This style can be contrasted with what is described as the impersonal scientific style that communicates to readers as if human readers don't exist. The writer who adopts a scientific style never uses contractions. Some of these writers use passive voice and nominalization as much as possible (e.g., the nominalization of *optimize* would be *optimization*) in an attempt to sound more "scientific." Such writers frequently employ the third person point of view.

cf.

Conversational tone can cause problems for on-line text: contractions can be misread because apostrophes may be composed of only one pixel; people expect more formality and dislike chatty machines; and first person pronouns can anthropomorphize the machine (Horton, personal correspondence; Shneiderman, 1986; Brockmann, forthcoming).

Instead of	**Write**
After the user receives the listing, he or she should check its accuracy.	After you receive the listing, check its accuracy.
One hundred people were interviewed during the system test.	We interviewed one hundred people during the system test.

Use the conversational tone in your documentation to soften the alienness of the software. Naisbitt, in his book *Megatrends*, makes this point when he discusses the concept of high-tech/high-touch. He describes a subtle societal backlash against computers—witness the letters to *Time* magazine when they declared the computer the "Man of the Year." This alienness can only be coped with by clothing the alien computer in "user-friendly" terms. A conversational tone is a good way to do this in language.

Avoiding the Use of Humor

The use of the conversational tone in documentation is quite effective. But some writers take the concept too far and introduce humor in their manuals:

> "[M]any writers have mistaken cuteness for friendliness...[which] comes in the form of a book written in conversational slang or from the point of view of the machine. Instead of capturing the essence of user friendliness, many have mastered something closer to user-patronizing or user-obnoxious" (Chavarria, 1982).

Some texts that describe how to write documentation recommend the use of humor (Spear, 1984). But humor has many more opportunities to fail than to succeed. First, humor is usually local and culture/subculture specific. Second, humor is temporal:

> "It [humor] depends on surprise for its appeal and diminishes in effect with repetition. In a work likely to be referenced as often as the well-written and well-structured tutorial, humor can become an impediment to usability and can flaw the user's concept of the source" (Bradford D., 1983).

Consider whether you think the following are funny ("Manual Madness," 1981). If even one does not seem funny to you, would you want to take the chance that your documentation could be that one unfunny one to your readers?

Cases of Humor(?) in Documentation

One section of *Apple's DOS 3.2 Manual* was subtitled "Do's and Don't's of DOS." It offered the following explanation for an error,

> 'What happened was this, your Apple II went on a fruitless, unending search for information on a blank diskette (on a clear disk you can seek forever...)."

In the *Xerox Data System's Expanded Fortran IV Reference Manual*, the following appeared:

> "Instead of referring to pi as 3.14159265358 at every appearance, the variable pi can be given that value with a DATA statement and used instead of the longer form of the constant. This also simplifies modifying the program should the value of pi change."

In the *DECsystem-10 Hardware Reference Manual*, under the heading entitled "Cleaning the Equipment," this section was presented:

> "It is alright to use spray cleaner on exposed vertical surfaces....The 'alright' in this caution applies to the sheet metal. Whether the carcinogens that come out of aerosol cans are alright for your lungs is up to you to decide. It has never been shown that the presence or absence of fingermarks or other stains has any effect whatever on the operation of the system. And anyway, it is probably much healthier to get a little exercise using something like Spic and Span."

And, in what must have been written late on a Friday afternoon, the *IBM APT-AC Program Reference Manual* had this passage in its syntax section:

> "The CONTIN statement is an executable statement, and when it is executed, it performs no operation, provides no

> output, hums not a note, taps no foot, and it don't care what's ahead of it or, for that matter, what's behind it. It is as solid as a redwood tree and as wispy as a cloud, for none can remain there very long. It is N/C's 'Ole Man River': it don't do nothin', it just keep rollin' along. It is, in effect, a neutral statement, a shady spot, a point of quietude in the midst of a busy thoroughfare..."

Using the Scenario-Writing Principle

This principle originated in research that sought to find out how people interpreted very abstract material during the reading process (Flowers and Hayes, 1983). The researchers asked the participants to report aloud their thoughts as they digested the material. The researchers had hypothesized that the subjects would take large sentences and break them into smaller sentences. But this isn't what they did. The researchers also thought that perhaps the participants would take long words and break them into shorter words. But they didn't do that either.

What the subjects did do was to take the theoretical material and weave it into concrete scenarios. For example, when they examined some governmental tax code material, the participants might say:

> Oh, I see what's going on. It's as if I backed my car out of the garage and in the process ran over the next door neighbor's kid's bicycle. I would have to pay for it.

Thus, the subjects consistently provided themselves with concrete examples and illustrations in order to understand the exampleless and illustrationless text. The researchers called this the "scenario principle."

Flower and Hayes suggest that rather than waiting for the readers to supply such a scenario, effective documentation writing should supply the scenario to readers in the first place. Specifically, they suggested many of the things we have already mentioned: the use of examples, the use of metaphors, and the use of cases. Additionally, they suggested that writers observe the following points:

The headings in the introduction to this book illustrate how this heading principle can be used, but they also illustrate how difficult it is to carry throughout a document.

To Use the Scenario Principle:

- Organize material around actions not terms. For example, a discussion organized around the decision, "How to decide if the defaults values should be used," will be much more understandable than a discussion defining "defaults." The information would probably remain the same, but its comprehensibility to the reader would increase.

- Organize material around readers' questions. (This in fact was the strength of Mr. Ford's Model T automotive user manual in 1919.) Good writing creates a context for its information, introducing new facts in light of old ones, answering questions, and fulfilling expectations. With software documentation this is particularly important since readers normally come to it with a purpose; they read to find answers to their own questions.

We could imagine that there is a general set of questions people bring to documents such as: What is this document about? To whom does it apply? What do I have to do? What does this assume I already know? Are there other sources of further information? (These are the sort of questions a good preface page in a manual should answer.)

Why Use Graphics?

There are basically five reasons for using graphics. Graphic devices can:

- Emphasize points in a text.

- Increase readers' interest in the material. With an appropriate graphic, you can take something boring and make it interesting and alive to the reader (Pakin and Associates, Spring 1979).

- Replace, clarify, or simplify a technical discussion of software. This follows the old adage that a picture is worth a thousand words. Upper level managers in organizations know the importance of this third advantage of graphics:

"The higher one looks in administrative levels of business, the more one finds decisions are based on data analyzed and presented in tabular or graphic formats" (Enrick, 1980).

And, it is not just upper-level managers who can use more graphics. In examining how to design most effectively a telephone line testing system, Tullis (1981) compared VDT displays of information in the following formats: narrative, table, black-and-white graphics, and color graphics. He found that

Research into the needs of actual users can often reveal many questions that are specific to a particular document. For example, Siegel and Gale, a firm that specializes in writing and designing commercial documents, conducts such research before revision. On one loan agreement, they discovered that one of the questions borrowers most frequently asked was "Can I repay the loan early?" However, because it was not critical to the writer who wrote for the bank, this information was buried in the form. It's these kind of questions that can be uncovered during prototype testing.

Develop Effective Graphics

"More graphs and charts to explain complex ideas (like the US deficit) and shorter copy are the newspaper predictions of Alvah N. Chapman, chairman of the Knight-Ridder newspaper chain. 'We are not in the business of manufacturing paragraphs. We are in the business of moving ideas into the minds of people'" (Harris, 1986).

"This is the story of the trial of John Gotti, the alleged Mafia leader in New York who was acquitted in 1988. The jury had met for several days and then they asked the court to let them take another look at a piece of evidence that Gotti's lawyers had introduced. They saw the chart again and then immediately voted to acquit John Gotti and his colleagues" (Tufte, 1989, 343).

Step 3: Draft the Document

Overcome Writer's Block

Use an Appropriate Writing Style

Employ Reader-Based Writing Techniques

▶ Develop Effective Graphics

Create Your Reference Aids

Consider Your Packaging

Plan for Updating

"1. Never draw what you can copy.

2. Never copy what you can trace.

3. Never trace what you can cut out and paste down" (McKay, 1984).

"4. Never cut out and paste down what you can electronically merge from your electronic clipart on your hard disk" (Brockmann and Horton, 1988).

"response times were considerably shorter for the two graphic formats and that fewer training sessions were required to achieve the accuracy criterion." And he found that the graphic presentation of information for the testing system was particularly effective with users with little experience.

- Increase the skim- and scan-ability of a text by being used as access devices much like headings.

- Respond to the consistent demand in user surveys (see Part One) for more illustrations.

The Most Popular Type of Documentation Artwork, Line Art

Line drawings, such as shown in Figure 41, are the easiest, most widely used, and least expensive type of graphic (sample forms, reports, or screens are a form of line art). The best line drawings are ones that conform most closely to the reader's perceptions of what the object looks like in reality. Line drawings are the most widely used because they are the easiest to produce [see for example the *Picture This™* series of computer documentation clip art books (1986, 1987) from The Write Words].

Line drawings are also popular because they are easily scannable and because they reproduce well on photocopy machines—the usual printing press of choice. For example, you can digitize photographs or

vendor-produced line drawings using a scanner, trace your digitized photographs using an autotrace tool (to leave out unnecessary details in the photographs or to focus attention on important aspects), insert them into your text via your "desktop publishing package," and print them out on your laser printer or insert them into your magneto-optical on-line document. The biggest advantage of this type of artwork is that it gives you time to try different options, layouts, and positions before finally deciding on the way you want your graphic to look. In essence, this type of artwork allows for the same evolution in design that the specification allows for text.

Line art can also be used as text signs or emblems that symbolizes repeated headings or concepts in a text

(Pakin and Associates, 1980). In fact, this type of artwork serves as an access device that signals the location of specific information to readers who skim or scan. For instance, one manufacturer's manual used a simplified keypad to symbolize the section describing

Figure 41. An example of computerized line art—click art.

"Simple, realistic line drawings can be identified as easily as photographs, and their information is better retained. In a recent investigation, Biederman and Ju (1988) compared viewers' abilities to perceive and recognize objects when they were represented by color photographs or by line drawings. They found that simple line drawings could be identified as quickly and accurately as fully detailed, textured, color photographs. These researchers also suggest that instructional materials for assembling equipment are more easily followed when the parts are drawn instead of photographed. They argue that the advantage of drawings is not due to any intrinsic perceptual superiority, but rather to the poor quality of photographic reproduction" (Lewis, 1988, 239; see also, Beiderman,1987).

how to key in the information in the program (see the symbols used to indicate function keys in the playscript example). Such visual signs can make a manual more attractive and visually unified for readers. To develop good sign or emblem consider the following:

- Choose symbols that are clearly related to the concept or heading that you wish to symbolize.

- Use no more than seven different spot art symbols in a text. When you do have more than seven different symbols the reader loses the ability to remember them and they tend to clutter rather than simplify the format of a page.

An Example of a Graphic Symbol

A simple example of a piece of line art as symbol or emblem comes from *Texas Instruments Model 707 Data Terminal User's Manual* (1983):

"At certain times in the text we will use the following symbol in the margins:

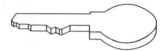

Pay particular attention to the information next to these keys. They're used to denote"key" information" (Texas Instruments, 1983 p. vi).

Icons

A new piece of software titled Iconer can critique the design of icons (Eisen, 1990).

Why use icons? First, icons decrease the burden on the user's memory by making visible everything relevant to a task . Second, icons make the software's analogs real:

> "A subtle thing happens when everything is visible; the display becomes reality. The user model [visualization] becomes identical with what is on the screen. Objects can be understood purely in terms of their visible characteristics" (Smith D. et al., 1982).

"One solution to icon ambiguity is to combine encoding systems. That is, to join icons with written labels. This form of redundant encoding can help reduce interpretation errors for icons representing objects and actions. Bewley, Roberts, Schroit, and Verplant (1983) found that users made 25 percent fewer errors when icons they were seeing for the first time were accompanied by labels. Palmer P. (1986) found that labels combined with icons produced more rapid, accurate visual search of computer menus than did the label alone" (Krull, 1988, 261).

By making everything visible and by making the display real, the user can learn to use the system using a scientific hypothesis-testing approach. In this approach, commands are individually testable, verifiable, and expandable. When the software doesn't conform as closely to the real world, and commands and menus often don't, users need more intermediary instruction; they can't find things out directly by experience (Smith D., 1977).

In designing system control icons, keep the rules of line art symbols in mind, use icons that look like the action they represent and that are readily recognizable by your target audience. And avoid any attempts at humor—especially with icons that will be used over and over again (Heines, 1984; see also Hemingway, 1982; Krull, 1985, 1988; Lindgaard et al. 1987; *Simply Stated*, 1987; Seeing, 1989). You might also consider using some of the new automated icon design "checkers" that are becoming available such as "Iconer" (Eisen, 1990).

Principles Behind Effective Graphics

There are seven principles to follow in developing effective graphics:

1. Keep your intended audience in mind. What is true for words and sentences is also true for graphics (Pakin and Associates, 1979). Decide what you want to say and then choose the graphic that best communicates that idea. Remember that there's always more than one way to inform a user. Think about using familiar objects as metaphors for new objects; for example, when Hayes Microcomputers wanted to "explain" to the user on a computer what their modem was doing digitally during the call connecting process, they showed a series of illustrations from a typical human-to-human phone call.

   To develop a varied repertoire of graphics and graphic formats, consider keeping a scrapbook of good advertising graphics or copies of good graphics from other manuals you've seen. Then when it comes time to develop a new graphic, you have a number of ideas available to stimulate your thinking. (Note: Do not copy these graphics verbatim because you may violate copyright.)

To Develop Effective Graphics For Documentation:

- Analyze your audience.
- Plan for graphics in your specification.
- Have a clear focus.
- Balance your graphic.
- Use contrast to set off your graphics.
- Increase the dimensions of your graphic.
- Guide the reader's eye.

2. Plan for graphics from the very beginning. Give your authorizing personnel an opportunity to review your graphics when they review your specification. They can review the graphics for appropriateness, clarity, and accuracy.

"At present, we seem to take visual literacy as a given despite the fact that our entire educational process aims at verbal literacy at the expense of the visual" (Rubens, 1989, 7).

Some good books to get you thinking "visually" are two from von Oech: *A Whack on the Side of the Head*, and *A Kick In The Seat of the Pants*, and Tufte's classic *The Visual Display of Quantitative Data*.

3. Establish your focus and purpose clearly. Omit all extraneous details and information. This is especially easy to do in line drawings and especially hard to do in photographs. Just as good sentences have no unnecessary words, so good graphics should have no unnecessary features to distract the reader from your intended purpose.

4. Balance your graphic. You should be able to pick out the visual center of graphic quite readily. If you can't, it isn't balanced.

5. Create a graphic that contrasts in line, color, or shading with the surrounding text. For example, sample screens, reports, and forms should be boxed or shaded so that they stand out from surrounding material.

6. Add more dimensions to your graphic. The more dimensions your graphic has, the more memorable it is (Horton, 1983). A one-dimensional graphic is the least memorable. An example of this would be:

"Press the RETURN key."

A simple two-dimensional graphic would be memorable and would revise the example above:

"Press `return`

A three-dimensional graphic would revise the example to:

`return`
"Press

A fourth dimension can be simulated by indicating action:

"Press

7. Guide the reader's eye to the intended message. Remember when you went to the county fair in your younger days and you beheld such marvelous sights that you tugged and pulled on your parent's hand to take you here, there, and everywhere all at once? Well, a good graphic is like your parents response, "First we'll go here, and then we'll go there."

Two examples illustrate controlling the reader's eye along a certain path.

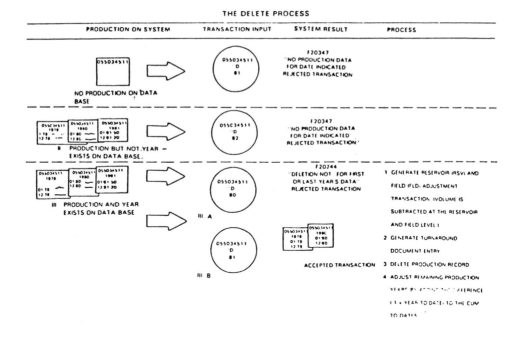

Figure 42. A graphic that fails to guide the reader's eye.

Figure 42 fails to achieve that end. It uses a type size that is nearly identical throughout. For example, the heading at the top is nearly the same size as the footnote material at the bottom right. The arrows and circles it contains make it appear as though there are four possible processes being discussed when actually there are only three. The distinction between each of the three different database inputs is difficult to see.

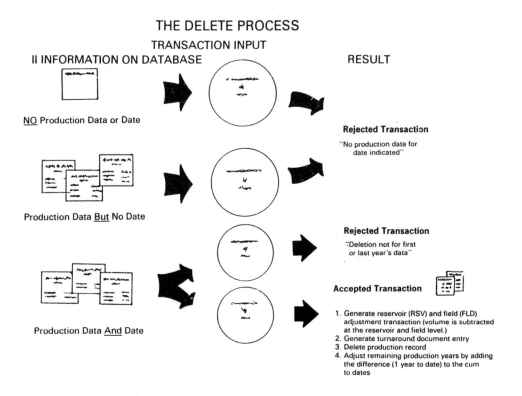

THE DELETE PROCESS

TRANSACTION INPUT

II INFORMATION ON DATABASE   RESULT

NO Production Data or Date

Production Data But No Date

Production Data And Date

Rejected Transaction

"No production data for
date indicated"

Rejected Transaction

"Deletion not for first
or last year's data"

Accepted Transaction

1. Generate reservoir (RSV) and field (FLD)
   adjustment transaction (volume is subtracted
   at the reservoir and field level.)
2. Generate turnaround document entry
3. Delete production record
4. Adjust remaining production years by adding
   the difference (1 year to date) to the cum
   to dates

Figure 43. A graphic that guides the reader's eye.

The graphic in Figure 43 reworks Figure 42 so that it guides the reader's eye to a single correct interpretation. This is achieved because of the following:

- The size and boldness of the print indicate that the headings are clearly more important than the footnote material to the bottom right.

- The solid arrows direct you to the three important distinctions between the inputs.

- The differences between each of the inputs are underlined.

Create Your Reference Aids

One of the common findings of all the surveys on paper documentation reviewed in Part One was the need for improved reference aids. Because software documentation is read using a random access style of reading, this is a very serious criticism. Therefore, reference aids have the same high level of importance for manuals as directories have for databases. Reference aids are the readers' key to your information.

Some question the need for more than a good table of contents and an effective style, such as playscript or structured writing, to enable readers to access a manual's contents randomly. The problem is that readers random accessing strategies vary. For example, if readers are familiar with a particular text or topic, they scan the text directly, using layout and format devices. Or, if they are familiar with the major topics in the manual, they scan the table of contents. Or, if they are looking for a specific piece of information, they scan the index (Sullivan and Jenik, 1984). In short, you cannot know all accessing methods readers are going to use on a document (for example, review the research findings in Step 1 on how NaviText ™ SAM users changed their use of particular access methods as they became more expert (Perlman, 1989, 79)). Therefore, to accommodate all possibilities, use a variety of reference aids.

Step 3: Draft the Document
Overcome Writer's Block
Use an Appropriate Writing Style
Employ Reader-Based Writing Techniques
Develop Effective Graphics
▶ Create Your Reference Aids
Consider Your Packaging
Plan for Updating

"They use the index about twice as often as the table of contents to search for information" (Ramey, 1988, 153).

As we saw in Part One's Reference Aid Quick Quality Test, a good quick indication of the quality of a manual can be had by simply counting the number of these reference aids present in a manual (Pakin and Associates, 1978). The best manuals include nine or more of these aids, while inadequate manuals usually contain considerably fewer:

- Table of contents (with two or more levels of detail)

- List of illustration/Figures or Tables (numbered and titled)
- Chapter table of contents (with two or more levels of detail)
- Headings (two or more levels with organizational hierarchy clearly indicated)
- Figure captions
- Tabs (titled)
- Error message appendix
- Glossary
- Indexes
- Reference card

Glossary

Since manuals are read using a random access approach, and even though a word may have been defined in parentheses when first used, a glossary is needed for readers who have been reading only the middle of a section. Thus, a glossary provides the reader with the meaning of a word at any point in the text.

A rough target for glossary length is 2% of the total number of pages in a document.

Remember that the content of a glossary must be appropriate to the audience in terms of what words are defined and the technical level of the definitions it contains.

Tips on Glossaries (Digital, 1983):

- Don't define a word by using a variation of it. For example, don't write:

  QUIESCE: The process by which one quiesces a system.

- If two terms are defined separately, don't define the combination unless it has a special significance. For example, if you define *memory* and *address*, don't define *memory address*.

- Don't define procedures in a glossary. They belong in the text.

- Use examples.

Also consider that if a manual is more a tutorial than a reference, a glossary may be more appropriately placed in the front. There, it can introduce readers to new words before they are used in the text.

Indexes

An index, either arranged alphabetically or by function, command, procedure, topic, and so on, is one of the most important parts of a good user manual. An index is a reader's most important key for finding information in a manual that is read using the random access style of reading.

This important component of a successful user manual has been all too often assigned as a clerical task to a subordinate of the documenter or, even worse, to the brute force of an automated computer listing. Rather than a simple clerical task or the focus of a large number cruncher, index creation is a very creative activity involving trade-offs among the following:

- Exhaustiveness (How many of the words in a book should I include in the index?)

- Precision (How much interpreting should I do in developing an index? How much culling of indexed items should I do?)

- Faithfulness of text wording (How much should I let the text's arrangement and wording dictate the arrangement and wording of index items?)

- Usability (How should the manual be arranged to make it easy for readers to find information?)

In discussing indexes in general, Thomas Caryle said, "Publishers of any index-less book ought to be damned ten miles beyond Hell, where the Devil could not get for stinging nettles" (Boorstin, 1983).

Exhaustiveness and Precision

The exhaustiveness of an index can be a quick predictor of the quality of a document. One "Index Test" (Pakin and Associates, 1978; see also Boston, 1986, 214–7, "How to Recognize a Good Index") suggests you do the following:

1. Choose one or two items from each alphabetic section of the index and look them up in the document.

2. Then choose one or two items from selected pages and look them up in the index.

"If you don't find it in the Index, look very carefully through the entire catalogue" (Sears, Roebuck and Co. *Consumer's Guide*, 1897).

If the index fails to help you find items easily, or if the index is incomplete, it is unsatisfactory. This simple test can serve as a strong indicator of the quality of other portions of the manual that are not so apparent (Pakin and Associates, 1978).

"All acronyms and abbreviations should be indexed twice. This approach is important because you never know if the user will look up the acronym and abbreviation or the full names that they stand for" (Swain, 1987, WE-141).

"Manual indexing is time-consuming and the results are inconsistent, either between different trained indexers or for the same indexer over time. Automatic indexing is usually based on word frequency; it can be improved by grouping words into index phrases. Current systems do not collapse synonymous references to a single term, handle proper names properly, or suggest terms that do not occur in the document" (Weyer, 1988, 97).

"Limit page references to no more than two pages per subject; otherwise create secondary or tertiary subentries for the page references" (Swain, 1987, WE-141).

However, exhaustiveness for the sake of exhaustiveness is not the solution. Early automated KWIC (Key word in context) and KWOC (Key word out of context) index programs were very exhaustive ...but not very useful. KWIC programs, for example, alphabetized every word in a manual and presented them in a list with the words immediately before and after an indexed item as well as the page number. A KWIC index program, for instance, might produce the following index for just the "A" and "B" lettered words in this paragraph:

immediately before and	after	an indexed item
programs, for example	alphabetized	every word in
before and after	an	indexed item as
in a manual	and	presented them in
words immediately before	and	after an indexed
word in context)	and	KWOC (key word
an indexed item	as	well as the
item as well	as	the page number
the solution. Early	automated	KWIC (key word
the words immediately	before	and after an
	But	exhaustiveness for the
were very exhaustive	but	not very useful.

This would pass the index test, but the reader will suffer from information overload. The old automated KWIC and KWOC indexes just don't make the reader's task of finding the items easy (Cleveland and Cleveland, 1983).

However, new KWIC and KWOC automated indexes have solved this problem by adding another step in their index production; they compare their alphabetized list to a "stop list," a list containing the 200 or 250 most often used words in English such as: as, the, these, is, are, and so on. If an item in their alphabetized list matches one of these words, the item is excluded from the final printed index. Thus the new KWIC and KWOC automated indexes can be both exhaustive and much more precise.

In addition to being complete, a good index should be as specific and analytical as possible. For instance, observe the following examples:

Format, 20, 99, 152, 166

This isn't nearly as helpful as the next example:

Format

    default parameters, 166

    footers, 152

    headings, 99

    two-column format, 20

Faithfulness to Text Wording and Usability

There are a number of automated index programs to help you with indexing, and most document-processing programs come with such facilities already built-in (Cole, 1985; see also Daiute, 1985).

A word of caution is necessary. Automatic indexers tend to direct writers to use only words from the text; they don't necessarily include all the "generic" terms a reader might use when first approaching the index. For instance, suppose that an organization wanted operators to use the word "quiesce" when shutting down the system. If only the automated indexer were used, "quiesce" would be the only word that would appear in the index to guide readers to information about shutting down the system. Clearly, however, the index in its final form should also include the following entry:

Shutting down system (see quiesce).

The word "see" when used in an index is a one-headed arrow that directs the reader from a less precise "generic" term that the reader might think of to an exact term as used in a manual.

Also using words directly out of a text without any analysis or translation for the sake of the reader can lead to the problem of *scatter* (Borrko and Berneir, 1984). Scatter occurs when information of like ideas is put among diverse headings and various synonyms. The reader must know to look in various places for all the information on any one topic. For example, information on a particular data communications protocol could be listed under the following:

""A major cause of search failures [in using a hypertext system] is that people use different terms than the assigned name of the item. Research has shown that search success rates can be increased from 20-80% if multiple names are allowed. This technique is called 'aliasing'. For best results, aliases should be determined empirically by discovering what alternate names users actually try to use. Aliasing capability can be built into the system so that it displays or asks for alternate terms when a search fails and automatically assigns to the original term the term selected or provided by the user" (Shneiderman and Kearsley, 1989, 43).

"In terms of safety and avoiding major problems, indexing restrictions and warnings is very important. All readers must be able to locate any rules, limitations, incompatibilities, and cautions or danger warnings. Unfortunately, many of these types of subjects are not listed as such or set apart in the text. Thus the writer-indexer must be familiar with the text and analyze it for these index subjects" (Swain, 1987, WE-140).

```
BSC, 3-41
Communication, 1-1, 1-9, 1-14
Data communications protocols, 7-11
Protocols, 1-2, 3-4, 5-6, 7-8
Sending and receiving, 9-3
```

Two points help to remedy the problem of scattering:

1. Analyze your audience and find out which term is the single most appropriate pointer term. Look in competitors' manuals to see which single terms appear most often in their indexes.

2. Put "See also" beneath index words to direct the reader to synonyms that point to closely related information. "See also" is a two-headed arrow. For example:

```
BSC, 3-41
(See also Communication, Data communication
    protocols, Protocols, Sending and receiving)

Communication, 1-1, 1-9, 1-14
(See also BSC, Data communication protocols,
    Protocols, Sending and receiving)

Data Communications Protocols, 7-11
(See also BSC, Communication, Protocols, Sending
    and receiving)

Protocols, 1-2, 3-4, 5-6, 7-8
(See also BSC, Communication, Data
    communication protocols, Sending and
    receiving)

Sending and receiving, 9-3
(See also Communication, Data communication
    protocols, protocols, sending and receiving)
```

Creating Your Own Index

So, as you can see, indexing is quite a complex activity. For example, Borrko and Berneir (1984) suggest the following:

- For the average book of 282 pages, 1045 lines of index are developed.

- The typical index contains 3.7 lines per page indexed.

If you don't want to hire a professional indexer (consider contacting The American Society of Indexers), here are the steps to producing an index using a document processor's automatic indexing options:

1. When you are inserting copyedit or reviewer corrections—when you are thus beyond the substance of the document and just looking at individual words or sentences—paragraph by paragraph find substantive items in the document that are meaningful to your audience; look for cross-references.

2. Play "word games" and think of all the synonyms with which readers may try to access your information—or variant word orders (e.g., initially I may insert the index term "additive color," but you may try to look up "color, additive." Thus I should index both word orders).

2. Analyze your entries to make sure they are both important and understandable outside the immediate context.

3. When you are done with a large section in your document—i.e., the first large chapter—print your index. It will of course only cover these few pages, but it will give you guidance in choosing the phrasing of index words in later chapters or sections of the document (PageMaker 4.0™ has a facility built right into it so that you can preview previous entry's wording as you develop later index entries, see Roth and Kvern,1990, 48).

4. Cull out words or phrases in this same preliminary index that link to the same information, but are just slightly different in spelling or punctuation (e.g. using "HP," "H-P," "Hewlett Packard," and "Hewlett-Packard" to access the same information will just bred confusion—let alone the fact that correctly spelled, H-P is always hyphenated).

4. Continue to index paragraph by paragraph for the rest of the book.

6. Print the index out at the end in a manner consistent with the concepts of active white space.

7. And, check the final index. No matter how careful you are page by page, spelling, punctuation, and grammar errors always creep in. Always proofread your "automatically" generated indexes.

A little trick of the trade to check the completeness of both your index and your text is to compare your index to a competitor's index. If the competitor has an index word or term you don't, check to see whether it is because you haven't included the word in the index or your manual doesn't contain it.

Headings

Headings are useful because they act as signposts that point the way to sections and areas of interest. They enable a reader to skim and scan a text. They can also be used by automated indexers or by software that automatically generates a table of contents.

If the writer has used a specification, most headings can be taken directly from the specification. To make them particularly effective, follow the nine rules listed below (Boomhower, 1979). Headings should:

- Emphasize important divisions within the text.

- Be brief but understandable out of context.

  For example: "Available Methods of Transferring Data from Main to Secondary Storage" should be better stated as "Moving Data from Main to Secondary Storage."

- Use parallel syntax in a series.

- Add a practical flavor.

See also Weiss's STOP concepts of headings and HOrn's structured writing rules on headings

  For example, "Cross-Talk Linkage Conventions" could be much better written as "Linking from One Task to Another." Similarly, "Scope Procedure for Vertical Sensing Mechanism Adjustment" could be much better written as "Using the Scope to Adjust Vertical Sensing Mechanism."

- Avoid using long series of nouns or adjectives.

For example "Control Program Preprocessing Initialization Requirements" would be better written as "Initialization for Control Program Processing."

- Do not let readers confuse nouns for verbs.

  For example, do not use "Select Parameter Table Format" when you mean "Format of the Select Parameter Table."

- Do not take on unwanted meaning.

  For example, does "Mutilated Card Feed" mean "How to Feed Mutilated Cards" or "What to Do When the Card Feed Has Been Mutilated?"

- Be meaningful and specific.

  For example, "Appendix B" is not enough; make it "Appendix B: Control Card Formats." Similarly, "Preface" may be rewritten as "How to Use This Manual."

·Consider Your Packaging

The best packaging of user documentation depends on the audience and the way they will use the manual. If a data entry person is entering data while using a tutorial user manual, consider using an "easel" packaging for the manual so that it stands up by itself and is easily readable by a person working at a keyboard. If the manual contains a group of reports with their fields and attributes defined at some length, consider running the pages horizontally, not vertically.

Beyond audience considerations, there is one specific packaging concept to consider, modularization. Borrowing a concept from structured programming in which programs are considered to be built of replaceable, transferable modules, we can also consider chapters as modules. Conceptualizing chapters as modules doesn't require you to change the way in which you do your writing. A module is simply more "standalone" than a chapter—a module will perhaps have its own binding, its own table of contents, and its own index. All the modules that make up a total package will have a master index and a master table of contents.

Why go to all the trouble to create modules? Actually, modules make a documentation project easier by

Step 3: Draft the Document

Overcome Writer's Block

Use an Appropriate Writing Style

Employ Reader-Based Writing Techniques

Develop Effective Graphics

Create Your Reference Aids

▶ Consider Your Packaging

Plan for Updating

making it bite-sized for all involved (Pakin and Associates, 1980). Modules allow writers to juggle more apples simultaneously. The writer can have one module out for review, one in a specification stage, be drafting one, and have one in word processing. Life is easier for reviewers because they get only one module at a time rather than a whole manual. Production turnaround time decreases because production people work on only one module at a time.

Most importantly, for the reader, modules make the manual bite-sized. Decreasing the amount to digest at any one time reduces the problem that a complete, large manual always has—that is, that it looks impossible to tackle. Different readers can work with different modules depending on the tasks they have to complete. Therefore, you also save paper by giving readers only what they need.

The key to the modular development of a manual is centralized management of the project using a complete document specification.

Plan for Updates in the First Draft

> **Step 3: Draft the Document**
>
> Overcome Writer's Block
>
> Use an Appropriate Writing Style
>
> Employ Reader-Based Writing Techniques
>
> Develop Effective Graphics
>
> Create Your Reference Aids
>
> Consider Your Packaging
>
> ▶ Plan for Updating

Developing a document database or having an exhaustive index could alleviate the need for an update checklist.

Programmers are always accusing other programmers and analysts of not leaving sufficient information behind to decipher how their program runs. Unfortunately, there is no easy way to patch a program or to update a program without such information.

Some documenters are equally remiss in not leaving behind sufficient information to allow others to update their document after they have finished writing it. To avoid this problem, you can create three pieces of information just in case you will not be doing the updating or revising. The information you need to leave behind includes a list of important cross-references, any special procedure used in writing the manual, and any special method used in producing the manual (Pakin and Associates, 1981). The following three documents can take care of these bits of information:

- Update checklist. This lists all areas of a manual that need to change if any one section changes. This checklist makes explicit what is implicitly interrelated in the text. (An example of such a checklist is shown in Figure 44.)

REPLACES		MANUAL OF PROCEDURES		TEXT	
SEC	SUBSECTION	WORK IN PROGRESS SYSTEM		SEC 08	SUBSECTION 06
SHEET OF		TITLE MANUAL OF PROCEDURES BULLETIN		SHEET 7 OF 7	
DATED		SUBJECT GENERAL		DATED 4-9-76	

* INDICATES CHANGE OR ADDITION

EXAMPLE

CHART SHOWING SECTIONS CHANGED BY CHANGES TO A MANUAL.

SECTION CHANGED	MASTER FILE DESCRIPTION 08-003	CODES 25	INPUT 55	INQUIRIES 60	OUTPUT 75	CONTROLS 80	ERROR CORRECTION 85
MASTER FILE DESCRIPTION	X	X	X	X	X		
CODES	X	X	X				
INPUT	X	X	X		X		
INQUIRIES	X	X	X	X	X		
OUTPUT	X	X	X	X	X		
CONTROLS			X		X	X	
ERROR CORRECTION	X	X	X		X		X

Figure 44. Update checklist. (Notice that this example violates the structured writing rule about display of portrait pages.)

These notes could be avoided if the Document Specifications were available to update documenters— the specifications should have a description of unique writing styles used.

However, if SGML-like tags are used to format the text, then simply making available the tags and their definitions would greatly help updaters.

- **Author's notes.** This lists all those special techniques used in writing the manual (for instance, your own amalgam of playscript and structured writing).

- **Production instructions.** This lists all those nonstandard methods used in producing the manual.

With these documents available, revision is easy because the new writer will know what to write (because of your update checklist), how to write it (because of your author's notes), and how to produce it so that it looks identical to the original (because of your production instructions).

STEP 4: EDITING THE DOCUMENT

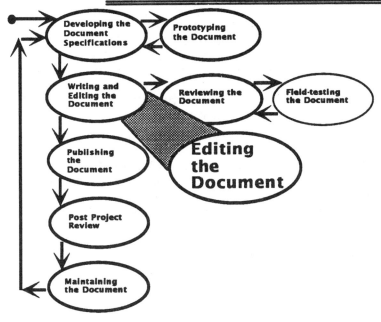

In this fourth step, we turn a draft document into a finished document ready for review and field-testing. As mentioned in Step 2, the writing and editing steps are iterative and are separated here only for clarity.

General Editing Principles

Editing

- Involves more than a hunt for grammar, spelling, usage, and punctuation errors.

- Is a collection of multidimensional tasks. Just as attentional overload can lead to writer's block in the drafting stage, so too can attentional overload in revising lead to an editor's block.

- Cannot be accomplished using automated spellers and style guides alone.

- Cannot be completed efficiently by an author working alone.

- Cannot be accomplished wholly on the VDT screen.

"Attentional capacity is overloaded when people attempt to do too many things at once. When writing, attention may be divided simultaneously among processes, rapidly alternated among them, or primarily focused on one process while others are executed automatically....Flowers and Hayes noted that '...writing is the act of dealing with an excessive number of simultaneous demands or constraints. Viewed this way, a writer in the act is a thinker on full-time cognitive overload'" (Kellogg, 1989, 61-2).

Editing involves more than a hunt for grammar, spelling, usage, and punctuation errors. As you have seen in the SDP so far, drafting a document is much more than stringing words together on a page. As you write, you need to consider your audience, and you need to develop an effective style, format, tone, etc. You need to consider all of these factors in the task of revising. Often this means "getting some distance" from the draft by letting it sit for a day or two before you begin revising.

Editing is a collection of many multidimensional tasks. Any attempt to perform all the tasks simultaneously is doomed to failure. We pointed out above that editing is more than the eradication of sentence level errors. Because of this, we need to develop a methodical way of considering each revision activity in turn. If we are not systematic in our editing, we may encounter *revision overload*.

Editing cannot be accomplished by using automated spellers and style guides alone. In Part One, the advantages of automated documentation aids were noted. These aids can include automated spellers as well as style and punctuation software. However, these aids can be misused. For instance, depending on automated spellers to do all proofreading can be dangerous because homonyms and typographical errors that result in valid words still slip through. Similarly, using automated readability indexes and style aids without critical evaluation of their suggestions is dangerous because of the inherent limitations of such systems. For example:

"Because readability scores are widely assumed to reflect word familiarity and sentence complexity, Duffy and

For those who must be their own editors, Lanham in *Revising Business Prose* has a paramedic editing process with two especially good suggestions: (a) Say your writing aloud as if it's a speech—this speaking of the text will give you a little distance from the text and allow your ear to pick up long-winded or badly phrased sentences. (b) Always ask of a sentence, "Who is kicking whom"—this will lead you to be sure the subject, verb, and direct object in a sentence are all perfectly clear.

"Even the largest screens now available can display no more than about two full printed pages of text. The result is that corrections tend to be made locally, on what is visible. Large-scale restructuring of the material is more difficult to do, and therefore seldom gets done. Sometimes the same text appears in different parts of the manuscript, without being discovered by the writer" (Norman, 1988, 211; see also Heim, 1988, 314). However there are ways in which the computer itself can aid you in overcoming its overly localized focus during editing. For example you can use the document processor's outliner function to view and manipulate large sections of text

Specific Editing Principles: Levels Of Edit

Kabance (1982) modified sample material in a well-defined way intended to lower the readability formula score directly, by using higher frequency words and shorter, simpler sentences. These changes, which produced very large improvements in the readability score, made little or no difference in people's ability to recall the information, or to answer questions of the sort found on standard comprehension tests" (Kieras, 1989, 153; see also Coke, 1982; see also Boston, 1986, 53—9).

Editing cannot be completed efficiently by an author working alone. No matter what technique you use to edit, you'll always overlook something that is obvious to any pair of eyes other than your own. Therefore, ask a colleague or friend to look over your manuscript before sending it on to your superior or your final editor. As Edmond Weiss points outs in this regard:

> "Editing, like most difficult jobs, works on the 80-20 principle. You can do 80% of the work in the first 20% of the time. After that, diminishing returns set in, and it becomes increasingly harder for you to find anything more to fix" (Weiss, 1982; see also Elbow, 1981).

Editing cannot be accomplished wholly on the VDT screen because the screen cannot give you a sense of the "flow" of a document beyond a rigid boundary of 24 lines. In fact, Lutz (1984) discovered in research with student writers using word processors that the "linearity of scrolling focuses attention to the local [sentence level] problems rather than with more global [organizational, audience] level problems" (Lutz, 1984; see also Marcus, 1983). We need to correct and revise from a much larger perspective. Long-term memory alone cannot make up for the portions of the copy that aren't visually present.

Keeping these general editing principles in mind, an excellent system for the editing process can be found in the "levels of edit" concept developed at the Jet Propulsion Labs in Pasadena, California (Buehler, 1982). This concept breaks the activity of editing into a number of discrete steps that are listed and explained below. These steps not only illustrate that editing involves more than sentence level concerns, but they also demonstrate one way in which the overall editing activity can be broken into its components (Elbow, 1981).

"Certain studies by Wright (1985) suggest that correcting text according to a set of guidelines is, in fact, a very difficult and complex skill. She found that there was little consistency between professional editors in their evaluations and revisions of a manuscript...the majority of the writing problems in the text were left unchanged even by those subjects who had the guidelines before them at all time. This is a startling result; it suggests that guidelines do not help because it is very difficult to detect problems in writing. But this follows from the currently accepted idea that much of the reading process is highly automated. In order to spot a comprehensibility problem, an ordinary reader would have to notice that the normally subconscious automatic reading mechanisms were having difficulty....Detecting comprehensibility problems is a difficult task for a writer, because it involves undoing or modifying the highly developed and automated skill of reading" (Kieras, 1989, 144-5).

There is no necessary order to the steps in editing. They can be done in any order that seems to be most effective to you or to your organization. However, they all must be done.

The eight steps in editing are as follows:

- Coordination Edit. In this step you coordinate people, budgets, schedules, etc., to bring a document to press. As you carry out this step, you are acting as a middleman to expedite the movement of a manual through production and distribution.

- Copy Clarification Edit. In this step you ensure that the instructions to the compositors for typesetting or to the graphic artists for graphics are clear. (Desktop publishing largely does away with the need for this coordination between different roles in an organization since these roles are combined now.)

- Policy Edit. In this step you examine your manual to be sure that the specific rules of your institution's or company's style guide are followed. Each style guide is unique to the organization or company in which the document is written. For example, one organization's style guide did not allow writers to put an apostrophe "s" after a program name. So in performing a policy edit in this organization, a writer would go through his entire document making sure there is no apostrophe *s'* after program names.

- Integrity Edit. In this step you make sure that all cross references are clear and accurate. For example, wherever the text reads "See Figure 1," you would make sure that the Figure 1 referred to is present in the document. Or, whenever an overview gives the names of sections to follow, you would make sure that the names of the following sections on later pages are identical in phrasing and format with the names in the overview.

- Format Edit. In this step, inspect the layout of material on the page to see if it is effective. A good way to do this is to hold an individual page out at arm's length. If the format and layout of the page reflect its conceptual organization, then you have an effective format. Techniques drawn from structured or playscript writing can help you in this step.

- Mechanical Style Edit. In this step make sure that similar units of meaning are treated consistently in spelling, graphic, and typographic terms. For example, if "Reference 1," "Ref. 1," and "reference 1" are all used in the same document, the inconsistency should be corrected at this stage.

- Substantive Edit. All the other steps can be completed without considering the content. In this step, look at the content in the manual to ensure that the organization of the manual is appropriate, that any contradictions are resolved, and that the presentation is complete and coherent.

- Language Edit. The language edit ensures that the paragraph and sentence level concerns of parallelism, usage, clarity, and coherence are addressed. Because the language level of edit is particularly complicated, it is discussed at some length below.

cf.

To edit the user interface, IBM added a *usability edit* (which we have put in prototyping and field testing) to the Levels of Edit (Brooks T., 1988); Editorial Experts used two broad categories of editing: *substantive editing* and *copyediting* (Taylor, 1981); ARINC Research Corp. uses *thorough editing* and *cursory editing* (Boston, 1986, 74); the National Center for Health Statistics (NCHS) of the Department of Health uses *production editing*, *copyediting*, and *substantive editing* (Boston, 1986, 76).

Language Edit

The elements of language edit proceed from larger to smaller units—that is, from paragraph or information chunk units to the individual word. A complete language edit includes the following elements:

- Edit contextually.

- Maintain coherence.

- Weed out abstractions.

- Minimize sentence complexity.

- Eliminate nonessential preliminaries.

- Break up dense writing.

- Watch out for fuzzy words (jargon, abbreviations, and acronyms).

Edit Contextually

When we discussed organizing text in Step 1, we noted a number of ways to cue the reader to the content of a portion of text. This cuing was done in order to avoid microprocessing of a text and to allow the reader to guess what was going to happen next. In those earlier cases, we achieved this by format, layout, and organization. There is, however, another way to achieve this same end in the language itself: contextual editing.

Remember for a moment children singing the song "99 Bottles of Beer on the Wall." One of the terrible aspects of that song is that the same words were repeated over and over again to boring effect. Good contextual editing is something akin to that song.

Contextual editing is based on two premises (Mathes and Stevenson, 1976). One is that no one reads single sentences or single words. Rather, they are always reading words and sentences in the context of many words and many sentences. The second is that, in the context of many sentences and many words, readers want to be able to guess what is going to happen next so that they can efficiently process the material. Contextual editing combines these two premises by suggesting that you develop a pattern to your multiple paragraph chunks of information.

To Edit Contextually:

1. Look for a core sentence or paragraph that establishes a pattern for the segment; if one is not there, supply it.

2. Determine whether the pattern is appropriate for the purpose of the segment. If it's not, change it.

3. Make sure that the sentences following this core sentence or paragraph carry out the pattern by following consistent noun and verb chains.

4. Justify any variations in the pattern.

5. Signal the pattern with connective words and phrases.

The next paragraph demonstrates contextual editing.

"PIREX (peripheral executive), a component of the UNICHANNEL-15 (UC15) Software System, is described in Chapters 3 and 4 of this manual. PIREX is a multiprogramming peripheral processor executive executed by the PDP-11. It is designed to accept any number of requests from programs on the PDP-15 or PDP-

11 and process them on a priority basis while processing other tasks concurrently (e.g., spooling other I/O requests). PIREX services all input/output requests from the PDP-15 in parallel on a controlled priority basis. Requests to busy routines (tasks)) are automatically entered (queued) onto a waiting list and processed whenever the task in reference is free. In a background environment, PIREX is also capable of supporting up to four priority driven software tasks initiated by the PDP-ZS or the PDP-11" (O'Rourke, 1976).

The subject of each sentence (save one) is the word "PIREX" or a pronoun referring back to PIREX:

PIREX (peripheral executive)... .

PIREX is a multiprogramming... .

It is designed... .

PIREX services all input/output requests... .

... . PIREX is also capable of ... .

Only one sentence does not begin with the word PIREX; "Requests to busy routines ... ." However, it does repeat the word "requests" in the sentence immediately prior. "Requests" is a little minipattern within the larger pattern. This paragraph is quite easy to follow. Since this is a list of attributes of PIREX, the pattern of noun plus "verb of being" is entirely appropriate.

Much technical writing has been accused of being "cobblestone writing," or writing in which the writer gives the reader one fact after another without explaining how to get from one fact to the other, or how all the facts fit together. The need for coherence refers not only to the need for the smooth flow of thought in written material, but also to the need for connective words and phrases that signal the way in which readers are to interconnect each of the individual facts in their minds. Without appropriate transitional words or phrases, we open our writing to multiple interpretations by readers, thus making our writing unpredictable or inconsistent.

With the following techniques you can increase the coherence of text:

- Using pronouns that reflect preceding sentences or repeating key words or phrases as in contextual editing

---

"Spelling is a basic, neuromuscular ability—a kind of eye-hand coordination, like hitting a golf ball. It's nothing to feel guilty about. It's not a matter of morality. What, then, is it a matter of? There are as many theories as there are spellings of 'medieval.' One well-accepted notion holds that poor spellers have a mild form of dyslexia, but that doesn't explain why some very competent readers can't re-create the words they see. Another school of thought blames the English language itself, that orthographic melting pot which has mixed so many different traditions that phonetic rules scarcely apply....it does not correlate with writing ability. F. Scott Fitzgerald was a notoriously bad speller. His longtime editor, Max Perkins, was not much better..." (Beck, 1988, 52).

Maintain Coherence

- Using transitional words or expressions, such as:

Also	Another way to	Instead of
And	As well	More specifically
In brief	Furthermore	What's more
Too	In summary	Eventually

Particularly useful resources for editors include: Editorial Expert's journal *Editorial Eye* and the "best of *Editorial Eye*," *STET!* (Boston, 1986), Plotnik's *Elements of Editing* (1982), and Judd's *Copyediting: A Practical Guide* (1982) with its copyright guidelines.

Transitional words and phrases not only provide smooth semantic links for the thoughts in a passage, but they also provide conceptual links, as shown in the next paragraph:

"(1) **When** speaking of memory locations, it is very important that a clear distinction is made between the address of a location **and** the contents of that location. (2) A memory reference instruction refers to a location by a 12-bit address; **however,** the instruction causes the computer to take some specified action with the contents of the location. (3) **Thus, although** the address of a specific location in memory remains the same, the content of the location is subject to change. (4) **In summary,** a memory reference instruction uses a 12-bit address value to refer to a memory location and it operates on the 12-bit binary number stored in the referenced memory location" (Digital, 1983).

The "however" in sentence 2 not only semantically links the comparison of "address" and "contents" with sentence 1 (where they were connected by an "and"), but the "however" in sentence 2 signals that the expected unity of "address" and "contents" does not occur. The "Thus, although" in sentence 3 continues this idea of the expected unity of "address" and "contents" being denied. If we had substituted "and" for "however" in sentence 2, deleted the "although" in sentence 3, and inserted "and" before "the content" in sentence 3, we would still have a pair of semantically correct English sentences, but the meaning would be quite different.

Thus coherence isn't just a semantic nicety but a real necessity in conveying the meaning of a passage.

Weed Out Abstractions

The problem with abstract words (as with text missing coherence elements) is that they allow multiple images to be conjured up in a reader's head—images that cannot be predicted with accuracy. An illustration can be found in the story of an applicant seeking a job with the late Senator Everett Dirksen.

During the interview, the applicant was asked about his grandfather. Seeking to cover up a skeleton in the family closet, he said, "My grandfather died while participating in a public ceremony when the platform gave way." This abstract statement allowed the senator to conjure up his own interpretation as to the cause of the grandfather's demise, and the applicant hoped the senator's interpretation was not the correct one; the applicant's grandfather was hanged for a crime.

Advertising frequently uses abstract words because such words can mean anything to anybody. Thus, advertising can make an advertised product look like the panacea for problems ranging from athlete's foot to lung cancer. Abstraction makes good advertising, but poor computer documentation.

Minimize Sentence Complexity

In a famous psychological experiment, researchers showed that short-term human memory can store seven different items plus or minus two items (Miller D., 1956; see also Chase and Simon, 1973). In the act of reading, this aspect of human memory is physically demonstrated when you have to reread a sentence that taxes your short-term memory capacity. For instance, you would probably have to reread the following sentence:

> "Systems for digitizing and storing analog data, sorting and averaging multiple analog signals, and sequencing processing events are all examples of laboratory problems where DIGITAL has knowledge independent of scientific disciplines" (O'Rourke, 1976).

The main reason you would have to reread this sentence is not because of its length, but because of its structure. In an English-speaking environment, we expect a sentence to contain the subject in the subject slot, at the beginning of the sentence, with the verb following in the verb slot as soon as possible afterward. When a sentence denies such traditional expectations, we are forced to microprocess the sentence, remembering each unit of information as an independent item in short-term memory, rather than processing the sentence as a whole. For instance, the subject of the preceding example "Systems" does come in the subject slot of the sentence, at the beginning of the sentence, but the verb "are" doesn't come until

16 words later. Readers, therefore, have to keep these 16 words in short-term memory overloading their memory's capacity. The key to less complex writing, then, is to fulfill readers expectations.

To Minimize Sentence Complexity

1. Put the subject in the subject slot of the sentence as close as possible to the beginning of the sentence.

2. Put the verb in the verb slot of the sentence as close as possible to the subject.

Once the subject and verb are read, the reader forms a general structure of the meaning of the sentence and stores it in long-term memory, which has far greater storage capacity than short-term memory. The reader can then fit in any phrases and clauses that follow the verb regardless of the sentence's length. For instance, the sentence above can be rewritten as follows:

> "DIGITAL has systems which can digitize and store analog data, sort and average multiple analog signals, and sequence processing events. All these capabilities exemplify DIGITAL's knowledge which is independent of scientific disciplines."

Thus, we see the word "DIGITAL" in the subject slot at the beginning of the sentence. The verb "has" comes as soon afterward as possible. The first sentence has 20 words, but is not difficult to process because it fits our expectations.

Involuntary muscles are excellent for keeping us alive; they breathe for us, they cause our blood to circulate, and so on. Writing can sometimes work in a similar involuntary, unthinking way, as when a clump of words comes tumbling out onto the written page as a unit rather than as carefully thought out single words that would express the same meaning. Examples of such automatic, rather than clearly thought out, clumps of words are as follows:

This language-editing technique is dependent on the expectations of language users. If you are writing in Punjab, Apache, Japanese, or Farsi, for instance, you would put the verb at the end of the sentence because that is where users of these languages expect it. Always remember that there is only one absolute rule in computer documentation: "The audience is always right. Give the audience what they expect."

Eliminate Nonessential Preliminaries

"I apologize for the long letter, I didn't have time to shorten it" (Pliny the Younger).

Automatic Clump	Rather than
In an effort to improve	To improve
All programmers	Programmers
Any programmer	Programmers
In the event that	If
In view of the fact that	Because, since
In order to	To
In a manner similar to	Like

Using such unnecessary "deadwood" words is clearly a problem if we realize that every extra word causes our readers to expend energy, unwanted and unnecessary energy. For instance, the following sentence contains 37 words:

> The programming office will perform an evaluation or system study, as discussed in previous paragraphs, on each requirement, or recommendation to provide the headquarters staff directorate information to render managerial decisions on the validity of each requirement" (Harper, 1981).

"It is harder to boil down than to write" (Sir William Osler).

The sentence can be shortened to read:

> The programming office will evaluate each requirement, as previously mentioned, to let the headquarter's staff directorate decide the requirements' validity (20 words).

Thus, when audience, organization, style, reader-based writing techniques, and so on have been controlled, cut out the deadwood words—words that add nothing to the meaning of a passage.

Break Up Dense Writing

Dense writing occurs when we follow the maxim of freshman composition that "Everything must be written in full sentences and full paragraphs." By writing in that style, we are apt to turn out paragraphs such as the following:

> "The 1440 is the smallest of the five systems. The typical configuration of this system has a KA10 central processor, 32 to 64K high-speed ME10 core memories, the RP026 disk system with up to two disk packs, the TM106 magnetic tape system with up to two drives, and low-speed peripheral equipment including a CR10F card reader, an LP10A line printer, and local DC10 lines. This is an excellent system for the scientific research lab where multiple real-time tasks and general computing are required, and also for small colleges where there is a need for handling administrative, student, and faculty workloads simultaneously. This system is easily expandable with most equipment on the DECsystem10 Equipment List" (Digital, 1983).

This type of writing disrupts the reader's normal reading speed, because the sheer number of items overwhelms his short-term memory, because it is nearly impossible to skim and scan. Since you know about structured writing and playscript, it probably will be unusual for you to fall into such a writing trap. You would have probably written the paragraph as follows:

> The 1040 is the smallest of the five systems. Its typical configuration includes the following:
>
> - One KA10 central processor
> - One 32 to 65K high-speed ME10 core memory
> - One RP026 disk system with up to two disk packs
> - One TM106 magnetic tape system with up to two drives
>
> It also includes the following low-speed peripheral equipment:
>
> - One CR10F cord reader
> - One LP10A line printer
> - Local DC-10 lines
>
> This is on excellent system for the scientific research lab where multiple real-time tasks and general computing are required. This is also an excellent system for small colleges where there is a need for handling administrative, student, and faculty work loads. This system is easily expandable with most equipment on the DECsystem-10 Equipment list.

In Western Civilization, we claim that a picture is worth a thousand words; in China, they claim it's worth a million. Perhaps the best revision to this paragraph's dense writing is a graphic.

The solution to the problem of dense writing, then, is to remember that there are alternative writing styles such as structured writing mentioned earlier in this book.

Watch Out for Jargon, Abbreviations, and Acronyms

Jargon can be defined as words that are unfamiliar to the intended audience. There is rarely a jargon word that is jargon to all audiences. For instance, an "objective correlative" is perfectly meaningful to a literature major who specializes in T. S. Eliot, but is incomprehensible jargon to anyone else. By the same token, a "MUX" would be totally meaningless to a literature major.

The key to avoiding jargon has already been clearly stated in the first step of the SDP as one of the substeps of planning for an audience. By analyzing and knowing the audience from the beginning, you know what is and what is not jargon for that audience.

"Jargon is like rhetoric. It always describes what the other guy does. We argue; he indulges in specious rhetoric. We make ourselves clear; he speaks jargon" (Lanham, *Style: An Anti-Textbook*).

"Coined" words are a more difficult type of jargon, because they are created by someone without regard to any audience. An example of coined words as jargon can be seen in the following "Instant Buzzword Generator." Both the Royal Canadian Air Force (1967 newsletter) and a U.S. Public Health Service official (Philip Broughton in *Newsweek*) claim authorship, but as you read through the following, surely you will be reminded of a half dozen writers in your own offices who might claim authorship—if they only recognized what confusion their words were creating.

Instant Buzzword Generator

Technology has created a new jargon that is as incomprehensible as it is sophisticated. With the Instant Buzzword Generator to help master this jargon, you can generate a variety of intelligent sounding technical terms. Merely select a digit from each of the three columns below and combine the words into your own technical jargon.

"No one will have the remotest idea of what you're talking about when you use these expressions," says Broughton, "but the important thing is that they're not about to admit it."

For example, select A-3, B-8, C-1, and you generate "parallel incremental options"—an expression bound to command instant respect...and confusion!

Column A	Column B	Column C
1. integrated	1. management	1. options
2. structured	2. monitored	2. security
3. parallel	3. reciprocal	3. mobility
4. functional	4. digital	4. programming
5. responsive	5. logical	5. software
6. optional	6. transitional	6. time-phase
7. synchronized	7. fifth-generation	7. projection
8. compatible	8. incremental	8. hardware
9. balanced	9. analog	9. firmware
10. total	10. organizational	10. communication

"One Benjamin Pitman offers a magnificent program in FORTRAN to generate textual garbage. It's so good it can be used to expand proposals by hundreds of pages. He calls it Simplified Integrated Modular Prose (SIMP), and it sells for $10 (c/o Computech Systems, Inc., 1819 Peachtree Rd., Atlanta, GA 30309)" (Nelson, 1987, CL-53).

Honeywell Australia has developed an advanced edition of the buzzword generator (a buzzphrase generator) called "Simplified Integrated Modular Prose" (SIMP for short). Picking numbers randomly from the four columns of their apparatus—much as you would from the Buzzword Generator—could yield such gems as the following:

(A-1) Based on integral subsystem considerations

(B-0) a primary interrelationship between system and/or subsystem technologies

(C-0) adds overriding performance constraints to

(D-7) the philosophy of commonality and standardization

The best way to combat such coined expressions in our writing is to keep our audiences uppermost in our minds (Bureau of Land Management, 1966).

Abbreviations and acronyms are often used in computer documentation. If there are any unknown or rarely used abbreviations, the reader may have to struggle to translate them. To avoid problems in a document that contains abbreviations or acronyms, remember:

SMASH [Southeastern (Asia) Multisensory Armament System for Helicopters)] (Nelson, 1987, 49).

- The cover-to-cover reader of documentation should be able to tell what abbreviations mean the first time they are used. This is normally done by spelling the term out the first time it is used and following it with the appropriate abbreviations or acronyms, usually in parentheses.

- For the random access reader of documentation, the meaning of abbreviations or acronyms should be clear each time they are used. This is done by providing an index or, more importantly, a glossary.

Again, remember that exactly which abbreviations and acronyms need to be defined depends on your audience, their background, and their knowledge. Also, in our modern age, some abbreviations or acronyms are becoming accepted words. For instance, how many people can easily supply the words contained in ASCII, FORTRAN, BASIC, or even IBM—or understand the complete version if it is given. Again, consider your audience.

PageMaker's on-line hypertext Help (GUIDE from OWL International) does a terrific job of handling glossary terms—one simply clicks on an unknown word and a definition pops up in a small window to the side. The real beauty is that one pop-up definition could be called by twenty different locations of the word, so that random access readers are served quite well.

Rules of Editing Best Forgotten

Now that we have gone through tested and sure ways of editing computer documentation, we need to note what not to do in editing. Shaughnessy, in her book describing the errors made by neophyte writers, points out that one source of error is the teaching of writing principles that amount to old wives' tales. Below is a list of rules which you may have learned, but which are best forgotten because they have nothing to do with good computer documentation (Price J., 1984):

- Never start a sentence with *because.*

- Use a comma whenever you want the reader to take a breath.

- Don't use *may* or *might.*

- Never use *about.*

- Don't use *then* so often.

"The fundamental problem with both CRES [Computerized Readability Editing System developed by Kincaid et al in 1981] and WWB [Writer's Work Bench developed by Bell Laboratories in 1981] is that they are not based on the actual psychology of comprehension, but rather on traditional writer's intuitions, many of which are incorrect or inapplicable in terms of current knowledge of comprehension" (Kieras, 1989, 146).

Bernstein in *Miss Thistlebottom's Hobgoblins* (1971) takes aim at some other sacrosanct writing "rules" because he notes that we've been victimized by many editing rules that are nothing more than superstitions:

> "...prohibitions deriving from mere personal prejudice or from misguided pedantry or from a cold conservativism that would freeze the language if it could" (Introduction).

Some of these sacrosanct writing "rules" include:

- A paragraph cannot contain one sentence:

> "It [a paragraph] is a means of grouping thoughts, but much more it is a visual device. Much depends on the subject, the typography, the purpose...the readers to whom it is addressed, and the conditions under which they are likely to read it" (174).

"A tabulation of errors found by professional proofreaders provides the following 'most frequent' errors in written copy: letters omitted (14.5%), substitutions (14.1%), space omitted (10.7%), punctuation mark omitted (10.5%), transpositions (6.6%), word omitted (5.9%), small letter for capital (2.9%), full line omitted (1.7%), spelling error (1.6%), and capital for small letter (1.1%)" (Boston, 1986, 227–8).

- Never put a preposition at the end of the sentence—"you just don't know what rules are for!"

> "The fact is,' says Fowler, 'that the remarkable freedom enjoyed by English in putting its prepositions late and omitting the relatives is an important element in the flexibility of language'" (178).

- Never split an infinitive—"he tried to quickly get to the main menu":

"From about the fourteenth century on, the adverb began to take its place after the 'to' and ahead of the verb and was so used by good writers" (116).

There is a lesson underlying this list; writers should be critical in the editing principles they apply. The ultimate criterion on editing principles should always be whether or not the principle, when applied, eases the reader's task of understanding the text. What we need to overcome is the presence of many editing rules that reflect blind linguistic prejudices learned in the past. Perhaps this small story makes the point best:

"This is the story of a professor who went off to England to give a talk. He was a philosopher, and he spoke about the use of language. He had studied the world's languages and said that in some of them, a double negative means a negative—a reinforced negative. For instance, when the President of the United States said, 'There ain't no smoking gun,' he really meant that there wasn't one. The double negative was a reinforced negative. And sometimes, of course, a double negative is a positive; the signs cancel each other out. But, the professor said, though the meaning of a double negative might vary depending on context, one thing was for sure: In absolutely none of the world's languages did a double positive ever mean a negative. Well, sitting in the back of the room was a feared 'counter-example' person, Sidney Morgenbesser. He heard the theory that in none of the world's languages did a double positive ever mean a negative come floating to the back of the room. And without missing a best, Morgenbesser said, 'Yeah, yeah'" (Tufte, 1989, 353).

Step 5: Reviewing the Document

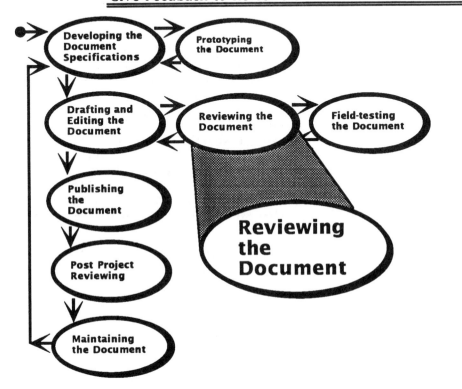

In this fifth step, we turn from writing and editing to the review step of the SDP. In the book *The Psychology of Computer Programming* (1971), Weinberg made the following observation concerning the need for egoless programming—programming in which the programmer asks for second-party criticism and review:

> "Programmers who truly see their programs as extensions of their egos are not going to be trying to find all the errors in their programs" (Weinberg, 1971).

For documentation, this quotation can be rephrased to emphasize the needed professionalism of documenters:

Documenters who truly see their documents as extensions of their egos are not going to try to find all the errors in their documents.

As egoless documenters, we need to include a review stage in our plans so that we can better perfect our documents for our readers.

When Getting a Document Reviewed:

- Choose reviewers and the time to review.
- Show reviewers how to review.
- Give feedback to reviewers.

Choose Reviewers and the Time to Review

You may be fortunate enough to have on your staff someone who can take multiple perspectives when reviewing the same document. Most of us, however, require several different people to bring different perspectives to the same document. Each reviewer should respect deadlines, stick to his or her review responsibilities, and understand that compromises may need to be made. The number of perspectives that should be included follow (Pakin and Associates, 1981):

- A technical perspective can be used to examine a document for technical accuracy and completeness.

- A management perspective can be used to examine how well a document meets its overall objectives, how well it projects a positive image of the company, how well it fulfills any legal commitments, and how well it protects proprietary information.

- An editorial perspective can be used to examine a document for departures from accepted writing style.

- A user perspective can be adopted to examine a document for its usability by the intended audiences.

The timing of the reviews should be coordinated with the activities of the SDP as follows (Pakin and Associates, 1983):

- During the document specification creation, reviewers who have been asked to examine the document from the management and user perspective can check the specifications for conformity to corporate requirements. The technical reviewers can review the specifications for completeness, while the editorial reviewer can examine the specifications for organization, format, and layout, completeness of audience definition, clarity of purpose, and effectiveness of proposed graphics.

- During the document-prototyping stage, test your document's readability with actual users.

- During the review of the drafts, the technical reviewer can examine the document for accuracy and detail. User reviewers can examine the document for accuracy, detail, language, and usability. At the same time, the editorial reviewer can apply the entire "levels of edit" apparatus to the document. Management reviewers can examine the document to see how well it fulfills legal liabilities and obligations, how well it conforms to standards, and how well it meets corporate needs.

Review Copy-Circulating Strategies

When you send out a document for review, you can be guided by one of two strategies concerning how many copies of the document ought to circulate.

Circulating multiple copies of the review document decreases the amount of calendar time required for review because several people are reviewing simultaneously. However, with this approach to circulating a review document, you can get caught in a conflict between two reviewers who disagree about your document.

Circulating one copy of the review document increases the calendar time required for review because every reviewer is performing his or her task serially. However, the probability that you will get caught in a cross-fire between two reviewers who disagree on your document decreases dramatically; the two conflicting reviewers can readily see their area of disagreement without you having to mediate. If you elect to send out multiple copies, and if you have reviewers who disagree, let them resolve such disagreements in a general review meeting. In that meeting, set out all areas of disagreement, and ask reviewers for their help in resolving the disagreement.

See Hayhoe, 1989, "No Desktop is an Island: Groupware Needs of Publications Departments," for a discussion of ODMS/DocuShare™ that allows file sharing on Macintosh and Digital VAX systems.(See also Rosenthal, 1990)

Another way to "circulate" and collect user comments is using some of the new groupware on a Local Area Network (LAN) such as Comment 2.0™ on the Macintosh. Figure 46 shows what the last page in this step might look like if it had been published over a LAN for a review.

When the reviewers receive this file and scroll to the last page, they make comments in small "note windows" and then send the annotated file back to the original author. When the original author gets the file, nothing has been deleted or changed, but the reviewers' comments can be seen in the "note windows" automatically popping up as the text is scrolled through—comments you can see in Figure 47, and they can be easily collated and kept track of. (Perhaps a good idea to avoid being caught in a cross-fire between contradictory reviewers is to let them see all the comments of all reviewers before you act on them.)

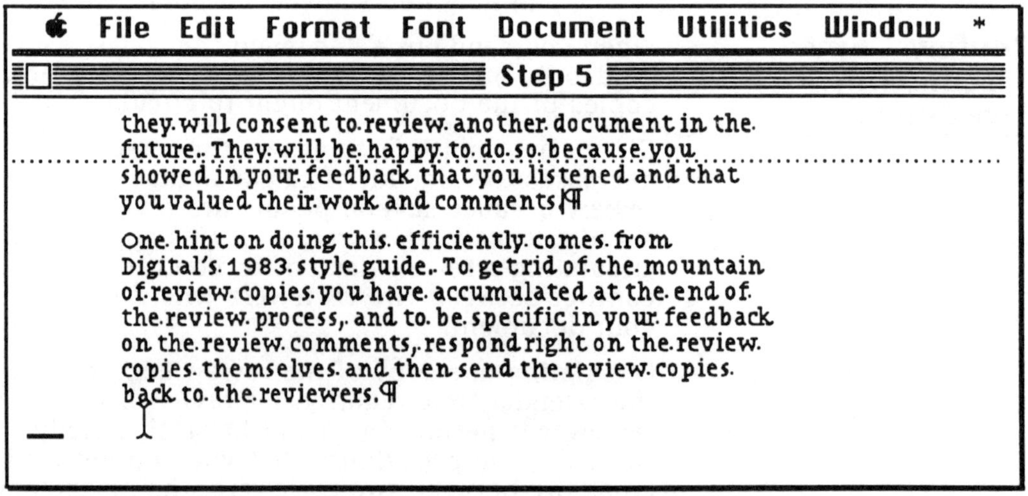

File   Edit   Format   Font   Document   Utilities   Window   *

Step 5

they will consent to review another document in the future. They will be happy to do so because you showed in your feedback that you listened and that you valued their work and comments¶

One hint on doing this efficiently comes from Digital's 1983 style guide. To get rid of the mountain of review copies you have accumulated at the end of the review process, and to be specific in your feedback on the review comments, respond right on the review copies themselves and then send the review copies back to the reviewers.¶

Figure 45. A page published over a LAN for reviewers to review using groupware.

Show Reviewers How to Review

No one has ever been taught in school how to review a user manual effectively. Thus the quality and quantity of the reviews you receive are directly related to the amount of time and effort you expend in spelling out what is needed from reviewers (Elbow, 1981).

Reviewers should be prepared for reviewing your document in a general initiation meeting or in a general initiation letter. In this meeting or letter, you need to apprise them of the general picture: what your purpose is, who your audience is, what special techniques your manual uses, and so on. In addition, specific directions should accompany each document.

All too often reviewers who are supposed to be commenting from a technical perspective take on the work of the editorial perspective, while those who are supposed to be commenting from the management perspective take on the work of the technical reviewers.

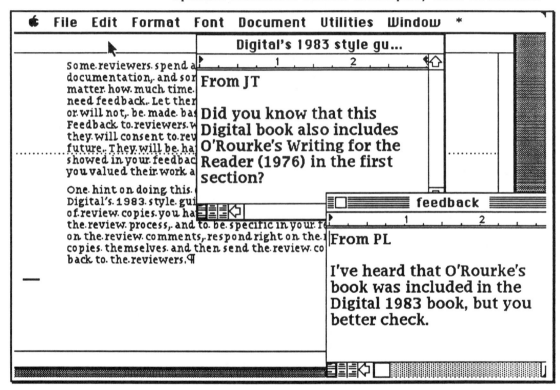

Figure 46. With groupware, reviewer's comments automatically pop up when the documenter scrolls through the document.

Reviews are better and faster if you can put your directions in checklists that are supplied as coversheets to your document or blueprints. For example, on the coversheet, you might ask these questions in the form of a checklist:

- Is the purpose of the material clear and accurate?

- Is the definition of the audience's needs and experience complete and accurate?

- Does the product visualization in the material suit the audience?

- Has all required information been provided?

On a coversheet accompanying the draft document, you might group the activities required for each reviewer in a box. The management box could have such checklist questions as the following:

- Does the material show accurately the benefits of the system?

- Can all promises made in the document be kept?

- Does the material protect the confidentiality of corporate information?

If you find that even after all this substantive and psychological preparation your reviewers still seem to criticize and change things simply for the sake of changing things, just remember George Orwell's proverb:

"Man's greatest drive is not love or hate, but to change another person's writing."

Simply handing content checklists to reviewers, however, is not enough. You also need to prepare them psychologically for their task (Daoust, 1983). The psychological problem many reviewers have is that the last, and perhaps only, time they ever personally experienced a review of their own writing was in grade school or high school when their writing confidence was low. Many well-meaning criticisms by teachers were seen in those days as personal attacks rather than as constructive criticism of their written product. Thus many adult reviewers of documentation confuse criticism of a document with criticism of the document creator.

The letter below represents one attempt to prepare reviewers psychologically and to help them separate criticism of a document from criticism of the document creator (Daoust, 1983):

"Dear Reviewer,

If you see a statement that is dead wrong, don't be surprised or upset. Misstatements generally result from a lack of correct information. When the writer has no information or incomplete information, the writer must often simply "take a shot at it." Don't assume the writer is grossly negligent or untalented. Statements based on incomplete information are trial balloons.

Never add an exclamation point to your comments. There's no need to shout. Whenever you are tempted to add an exclamation point to your comment, bite your pen and count to 10.

Be constructive and specific. The writer is on your team. Suggest better ways to present the material. If you have a manual with a good example of how you would like the information presented, show it to your writer. One concrete example is worth a whole afternoon of discussion.

Thanks"

Think about giving reviewers examples of what you consider to be helpful or unhelpful comments. Show them what you want or don't want.

Once the document has been reviewed, corrected, and is ready to go for printing or electronic publishing, send the document around to the reviewers with a final sign-off sheet. The gist of such a sign-off sheet is that once signed, the signer is approving the manual for production and distribution. Such a final sign-off sheet helps to protect you, the documenter.

Give Feedback to Reviewers

One hint on doing this efficiently comes from Digital's 1983 style guide. To get rid of the mountain of review copies you have accumulated at the end of the review process, and to be specific in your feedback on the review comments, respond right on the review copies themselves and then send the review copies back to the reviewers.

Some reviewers spend an hour reviewing your documentation, and some reviewers spend three days. No matter how much time they spend, however, they all need feedback. Let them know the changes that will or will not be made based on their review comments. Feedback to reviewers will increase the chance that they will consent to review another document in the future. They will be happy to do so because you showed in your feedback that you listened and that you valued their work and comments.

Finally, be sure to thank your reviewers in a short note...perhaps even send a carbon copy of your thank you note to their managers. Maintaining good will among reviewers is an important lesson often learned too late.

Step 6: Field-testing the Document

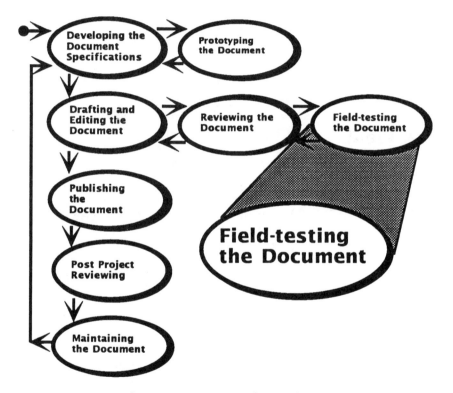

In this step, we turn from the review step to the closely related field-test stage of the SDP.

In field testing, we let the users of the documentation try using a document to see if it is effective and can stand alone. This practice has long been a standard method of testing computer systems and programs. If such an activity has been shown to develop more effective systems and programs, why not apply the same quality control technique to the documentation?

In each context, the purpose of field testing remains the same—let real world experiences improve the writing.

"Our ultimate goal is to increase customer satisfaction, and that satisfaction is based on customers' perceptions of their own usage, not on any separate measurements" (Bethke, 1983).

Many of the specifics of this step have already been covered in Step 2, Prototype Testing. The major difference between this step and Step 2 is that this step focuses on more global issues, especially issues of accessability. This step also measures the effectiveness of the whole manual when it has been almost perfectly put together because a good manual is more than just the sum of its parts.

To Run a Document Field Test:

- Choose field testers and the time to field-test.
- Run the field test.
- Give feedback to field testers.

Choose Field Testers and the Time to Field-Test

Circulate your field test document to a typical audience of readers or simulate an audience if the former is not possible.

Field-test your document when it looks reasonably like the finished product. You don't need to wait until the document is completely finished; it needs to be field-tested before final release. A field test takes at least three weeks and may take six to eight weeks for a complicated system. Thus, the field test documents need have only the following (Pakin and Associates, 1981):

- Graphics that are readable sketches rather than finished prints
- A table of contents at the beginning of the document, but not at the beginning of individual chapters

Run the Field Test

Just as the Prototype Test required sufficient preparation and development of monitoring forms, so too does the Field Test. In the final step of the field test, you need to send your documentation outside your company or department. Because you will not be there to monitor and instruct the field testers on what is required of them, you need to develop directions for them. Just as reviewers are never taught in school how to be reviewers, field testers have never been taught how to field test a document. Therefore, you should prepare them psychologically for their role in a general letter that contains many of the comments made earlier about reviewing. For instance, you need to take the time to inform field testers of the general picture: what your purpose is, what special techniques your manual uses, and so on.

Additionally, a coversheet should accompany the field test document and should include the following (Pakin and Associates, 1983):

"Perhaps the best computer manual ever written was the original manual for the original video game 'Pong:' 'Avoid Missing Ball For High Score'" (Nelson, 1987, DM-36).

- Identify the document as a field test document that is to be used for evaluation purposes only and not for final release.

- Explain the purpose of the test.

- Explain how long the test will take, and indicate that the document should be returned to the documentation writer when the test is over to prevent test documents from "living on" past their useful lives as test documents.

- Explain how changes and suggestions should be made—on the draft, in a meeting, over the phone, and so on.

Give Feedback to Field Testers

Just as it was important to give feedback to reviewers so that they know that you listened and valued their review work, it is important to treat field testers with similar courtesy. If you ever want field testers to help you with future field tests, you have to give them feedback. Such feedback should thank them, summarize their comments, and tell them what will take place because of their comments.

"WordStar is the second hardest video game ever made" (Nelson, 1987, DM-26).

STEP 7: PUBLISHING THE DOCUMENT

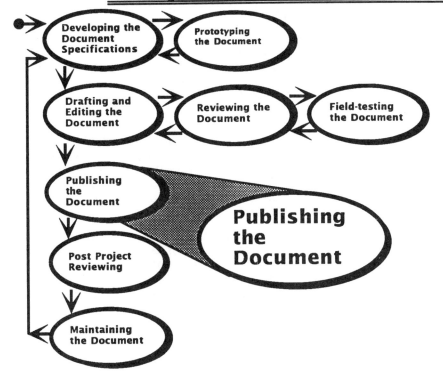

In this seventh step, we turn from the planning, writing, and reviewing stages to the production stage of the SDP.

The Old-Fashioned Way

Activities involved in coordinating the publication of a user manual include word processing, proofreading, illustrating, copyediting, assembling, reproducing, and packaging. To maintain quality, all steps are required and the responsibility for the activities in these steps should be divided among several people, e.g., the word processor should not be the proofreader, nor should the writer be the final editor (Matthies, 1976).

When you use an artist, or a printer, give them specific directions regarding the production of your manual.

You need to take the time to inform them of the overall picture, just as you have done with other members of the documentation team (Pakin and Associates, 1979, 1982, 1983).

Leave adequate time for this stage of the SDP. Projects frequently run into trouble at this stage because the timing and priorities are out of the writer's control. The total elapsed time for this stage is about 25% of the total time given to developing the manual (and that's not counting the time for getting color, typesetting, or any other fancy frills that a printer can provide). The best way to handle the huge block of time required to produce a manual is to send out your requests to graphic artists, printers, word processors, and so on, a chapter at a time (or a module at a time) rather than waiting till the manual is complete. And, just as with reviewing and field testing, the better the specific directions to the word processors, artist, or printer, the better the final product. The time you take to be specific and complete will save you time in the end.

Lastly, so that you don't think the documentation process is an unbroken linear progressive process, Figure 47 is presented on the next page (Krupp, 1979). The game board captures a lot more of the true documentation review and production experience—with its one-step-backward-for-every-two-steps-forward activity—than words could ever convey.

The Way of the Future: SGML

The problem with producing documentation in the old-fashioned way is that it required too much hand-crafting, and because of the hand-crafting, the old-fashioned method of publishing documentation made it difficult to:

- Swap information from paper offline presentation to on-line presentation or to storage on a CD-ROM:

  "...the second consideration in preparing text for CD-ROM is to make sure your data contains the formatting instructions necessary to implement the structure required by your retrieval system and to display the information the way you want on the screen....If the existing structure is well documented and totally consistent across all the files you intend to include in your CD-ROM product, conversion to the structure needed for CD-ROM presentation may be a simple matter...Conversion of poorly documented or inconsistent structures, on the other hand, can take unpredictable amounts of time and eat up huge chunks of product-development budget....The instructions are in the form of codes or tags, that establish the font, typesize, leading, and column width the typesetting machine is to use for any particular element. It is these tags that give the data its structure" (Cox, 1989, 325).

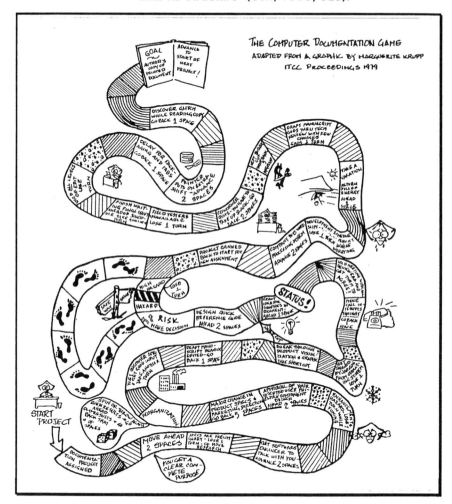

Figure 47. The Computer Documentation Game (Krupp, 1979).

- Reutilize information in updates or new packaging (i.e., taking information from a manual and automatically reformatting it for presentation in a reference card or brochure):

"A carefully designed SGML [*Standard Generalized Markup Language*] tagging scheme can be the backbone of a true publishing database. In other words, a good tagging system can allow a company to treat its information as a resource rather than as just an archive. The tagging system can facilitate sophisticated, flexible information retrieval, extraction and rearrangement of material for producing different publications for different audiences, and presentation of the material on different types of print and electronic media" (Zoellick, 1989, 339).

• Search for items based upon their structure or to use structure to establish hypertext links:

"The beauty of a well-planned publishing system is this ability to have atoms in a data base. The internal structure of the data base allows the publisher to store information in a generic, neutral form, separate from restricting structures or hard-wired links. The result is that atoms can be reused in any number of contexts. If a publisher has astutely identified atoms with tags, editors can create links with minimal effort. Besides functioning as identification devices, tags are useful for tracking and reporting; editors can identify what tags have been 'borrowed' from the data base's library, how many times the atom has been used, and in what modules. In this new, interdisciplinary medium for the marketplace of ideas, tags become the coin of the realm..."(Brunsman, Messerly, and Lammers, 1988, 227).

• Change output devices so that what was wonderfully designed for a dot matrix presentation for circulation within a department now has to be rekeyed and reformatted for a wider circulation throughout the company because it is going to be printed on a typesetting machine.

Standard Generalized Markup Language-like (SGML) publishing techniques go a long way to solving these problems...and to straightening out the loop-de-loop publishing method of the old-fashioned way of publishing visualized in Figure 48.

What is SGML? Well, as the name implies, it is a standard method of marking up text graphics, copy, and layout so that any printing device can replicate the original layout and design. It took twenty years to develop (Dole, 1989, RT-103) but is now:

I use the term "SGML-like" (*Standard Generalized Markup Language*) rather than SGML because the key the declarative formatting techniques exemplified by SGML [document type definitions (DTD's), and tags] have, in many instances, been imported into stylesheet definitions and stylesheet tagging in many document processors such as Microsoft Word 4.0 and WordPerfect 5.0. Thus, don't get the feeling that you have to immediately go out and buy a system called SGML.

"Officially recognized by the International Standards Association (ISO) in 1986, SGML (Standard Generalized Markup Language [Standard Number 8879]) has been adopted by organizations such as the American and Canadian Departments of Defense, the Commission of European Communities, the Library of Congress, and McGraw-Hill" (Fawcett, 1989, RT-59).

To use an SGML-like publishing technique, you must do the following:

1. When it comes time to insert the corrections from reviewers and field tests, in addition to inserting their corrections, begin your text tagging. Keep the content of the document separate in your mind.

2. Much as you must define stylesheets in document processors, identify every distinct item in your document (first level heads, captions, page numbers, headers, boxes around graphics, bullet lists, table of contents, headings, and normal body copy). Once identified, define each item's layout/printing characteristics in a file—usually called the *Document Type Definition File* (DTD). Be sure also to define their relationships to each other (their structure)—very much like decomposing larger boxes which hold progressively smaller boxes (called in SGML, *#PCDATA* (Dole, 1989, RT-103)), e.g., in this book, within a level 1, 2, 3, or 4 heading is normal body copy, and within normal text can be a shadow boxed graphic with a graphic caption:

"The Association of American Publishers (AAP) uses one DTD for tagging books, journals, and articles that are interchanged among authors and publishers. The Department of Defense (DoD) will use MIL-M-2801 as the DTD for electronic interchange of information among DoD agencies and contractors" (Dole, 1989, RT-103).

"The concept is similar to that of using style sheets, with some important differences. Style sheets do not address document structure, and style sheets are software dependent. The document type definition shows the relationship of all the document's elements and specifies the order that these elements can occur. For example, a DTD may be written so that a figure caption cannot occur within another figure caption" (Dole, 1989, RT-103).

3. Once the tags and their structure are defined in the DTD, begin tagging each item in your document with the defined tag (called in SGML, an *instance* (Dole, 1989, RT-103). This can be done by hand, or, more effectively:

"Many existing word processors can be used to prepare SGML-coded documents with the minimum of fuss. All that is required is the ability to strip out any internal coding while converting a marked up document to the ASCII format used by SGML. (Many word processing programs are supplied with this capability as a standard feature.) Where a word processor provides facilities for converting its internal coding scheme to a different format, specific tags may not need to be entered for many of the elements in an SGML document. Provided that an internal word processor code has a unique use, it can be converted to the appropriate SGML tag before output, retaining its internal use until it is recoded for onward transmission" (Bryan, 1988, 18).

"...you can use an SGML-based editor that inserts the tags as you create the document. [Or] If you have text that is already marked in a highly structured way, you may be able to use a code-for-code translator to create most of the SGML tags" (Zoellick, 1989, 339).

And these three steps are the backbone to using SGML-like publishing. The nice thing is that it's not too different from the way we proceed now:

"Users may hardly notice the difference between their current word processors and such advanced SGML-based programs. Both use the same sequences of key depressions to enter and format the text. The main difference will be in the way the text is perceived. Instead of defining a heading as a line of emboldened text it will now be identified as a special element (selected from a list of permissible elements). The physical format of the element will be defined, possibly at a later stage, using a special menu or form, each logical element having its own set of parameters (style sheet)" (Bryan, 1988, 18).

The major difference is:

"Specific markup instructions [such as WordStar's PB to indicate bold] describe the format of a document by use of instructions that are specific to the programs used to generate or output the text. Such instructions normally have immediate effect on the appearance of the text. They can either affect the appearance of the characters or the position of characters or lines. Generalized markup instructions identify the purpose of the following text rather than its physical appearance. They indicate the basic structure of the document by marking where the various components making up the text begin and end. Typically generalized markup instructions identify such features as headings, highlighted material, quoted text, etc. When the text is output the relevant program can then decide how it should present each of these structural elements to the reader" (Bryan, 1988, 6).

You can see this difference in Figure 48.

The Dangers of SGML-like Techniques

But with this new publishing method, comes some new dangers for the documenter . Will the methodology actually make it easier for documenters to do their work? Shifting the emphasis of documenters from creating documents to creating reusable modules looks positive at first glance. As David Hancock notes:

"...all this should be liberating to writers: they are freed from niggling worries about format, appearance, pagination, and product name changes. They are free to concentrate on the information they are producing. Time once spent poring over galley proofs making repetitive changes...can instead go to quality writing" (Hancock, 1986, 67).

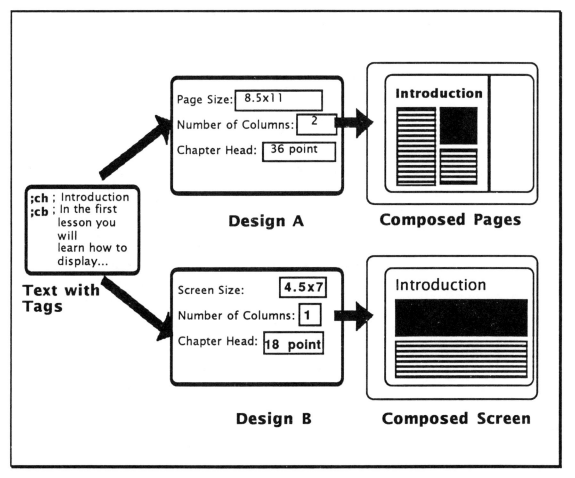

Figure 48. Use of SGML-like tags to produce different presentations of text on paper and on screen (Brockmann, 1988).

However, if documenters totally cut off the text and graphic composition from layout and format qualities—qualities which will be tagged—then they may have a difficult time. They may, in fact, find it more, not less, difficult to create the text in the first place.

Bernhardt (1986) points out that part of what allows writers to produce text and to control their thoughts on paper is the format/headings/indentations they make in their texts on the page. In other words, verbal production of text is crippled without the accompanying visual presentation of its organization. In fact, Bernhardt suggests that a visually informative presentation of information (the way documenters now produce manuals) is composed by writers in a qualitatively different way than nonvisually informative text—the type of format-stripped text that may make up the screen size frames of the document database. Won't tagging, in fact, be blindfolding the documenter just as the knife thrower in the sideshow is blindfolded? Both need to be applauded because neither *should* be able to perform successfully. And, perhaps, one shouldn't be surprised when the knife thrower's assistant, (or a documenter's audience), is pierced on a misplaced throw.

For example, the New Riders Publishing Tec Doc Collection for the Xerox Ventura Publisher package offers" automatic section numbering." Thus just as the documentation profession is getting away from paragraph numbering such as "1.1.1.1.1.1.1," the built-in canned document templates will automatically be inserting them.

In addition to undermining the documenter's traditional method of composition, tagging could possibly put documenters in a new political problem—a political problem analogous to the current European VAT taxes. In Europe, one of the reasons politicians like VATs (value added taxes) is because the taxes generate funds in ways less visible to a taxed population—the taxing all takes place within the manufacturing process itself, behind the walls of the factory and in the counting rooms of the corporate accountants. Because the taxes are thus less visible to the taxed public, the taxes seem less onerous and are subject to fewer voter backlashes. The politicians realize that the taxes will have fewer repeals because no one in the public realizes what the tax is doing ...or that it even exists. Couldn't tagging be like VAT's to documenters? After all, the individual documenters will probably not be the ones who develop the corporate tags, rather such structures will probably be generated by those same people at the corporate headquarters who presently hand out the corporate style guidelines and formats...or perhaps even those outside hardware, software, or consultant companies who are presently developing canned formats for desktop publishing. At least now documenters feel the corporate guideline's bit in their mouths. They know what it is they are complaining about, and, perhaps, what it is they must change. When these corporate guidelines disappear into the digital ether of corporate "tags," the corporate bit in documenters' mouths will become less visible, less questioned, and less open to innovation and improvement. If it has occasionally been revealed that those old corporate guidelines were simply linguistic prejudices of management rather than guidelines derived from studies of readers in a business context (see "Rules of Editing Best Left Forgotten"), couldn't tags simply be new mistaken linguistic prejudices whose errors are simply less visible?

To see possible responses to these worries I am voicing, see James in *Context and Hypertext* edited by Edward Barrett. Cambridge, MA: MIT Press, 1988.

Finally, won't the creation of corporate tags and DTDs undermine the professional stature of documenters? Documenters are already embarrassed by the managers who, in responding to pressure for more documenta- tion, simply go to the word-processing pool and promote a keyboard operator to software documenter. Won't this methodology lead to and even encourage this kind of action because the methodology leads to a deskilling of the documentation profession? By taking away decisions regarding format, layout, design, typeface and size, and even reference aid design, won't this methodology, when married to desktop or workstation publishing technology, lead to a contraction of professional responsibilities and to less of a need to increase documenters' expertise?

A similar process of deskilling in programmer ranks was well described by Kraft (1977):

> "De-skilling is a deliberate effort to transform work made up of separate but interdependent tasks into a larger number of simpler routine and unrelated tasks. Such routinized subtasks can be parceled out to workers who do only one, or, at most, a few of them over and over, and nothing else. Such workers obviously need less skill than the workers who performed all the tasks of the more complex original work."

Thus, William Houze's prediction that 75% of current technical communication positions would be obsolete by 1990 could be coming true. Fewer people will be needed to produce many more manuals. And the people who remain to churn out the manuals will be divided almost along class lines into those who assemble and develop the generic text and graphics and that handful of "superdocumenters" at the home office designing all the corporate tags.

STEP 8: POST PROJECT REVIEWING

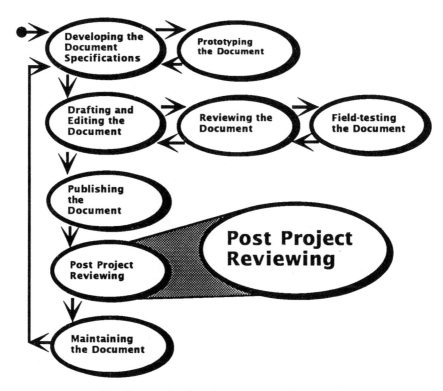

What Is a Post Project Review and Why Have One?

At the end of a documentation project, everyone needs time to catch her or his breath, take pride in a job well done, and learn from their mistakes. Santayana's aphorism is all too true:

> "Those who cannot remember the past are condemned to repeat it."

A post project review accomplishes these objectives in ways ranging from the very simple to the quite complex.

The simplest approach is represented by the form in Figure 49 from Rainier National Bank in Seattle. Denise Brown, who gave me a copy of this form,

In addition to simply filling out a form when a document is done, another very good way to give documenters recognition is to have manuals with signed authorship. If a manual is good, the writer gets the kudos; if it is bad, perhaps complaints addressed to the writer will motivate an improvement in the design process the next time. And even if a manual is a joint effort of many people, don't movie credits credit a number of people? Assigning individual responsibility is one of the best ways of promoting excellence in documentation.

explained that once writers are done with a project at the bank, another writer would interview them to gather information to fill out this form. The very action of the interview provides a recognition that one document is completed. It gives the documenter time to reflect on his or her experiences, and for the entire group of documenters to learn from this one designer's experiences. It also is a way of giving recognition to a documenter who all too often labors in solitude for many weeks on a project only to see the end-product slip unrecognized into another set of ubiquitous black three-ring binders. (See Foti, 1987 for a bit more involved post project review method.)

```
                    DOCUMENT REVIEW SHEET

                                    Writer  _____
                                      Date  _____
                              Project Name  _____
                             Project Phase  _____
                             Document Name  _____
                             Project Dates  _____

    1.  DIMENSIONS  (Tell us about the document.)

        A.   How many pages?              _____
        B.   How many sections?           _____
        C.   How many copies?             _____
        D.   How long to produce?         _____
        E.   How did you print it?        _____
        F.   How did you handle tabs?     _____
        G.   How did you bind it?         _____
        H.   How did you handle the cover? _____
        I.   Any special features?        _____


    2.  PROCESS  (Outline the steps you followed.)




    3.  HURDLES  (What problems did you face and how did you resolve them?)




    4.  SATISFACTION  (What worked particularly well about this document?  Anything
                       you'd do differently another time?)



    5.  HINTS  (What did you learn from creating this document?)


                                                    DCB2268.2
```

Figure 49. Post project review form from Rainier National Bank.

STEP 9: MAINTAINING THE DOCUMENT

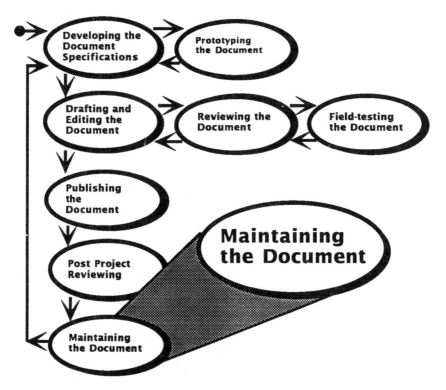

In this ninth and last step of the SDP, we have released the document and must now keep it up to date. Because we have been considering how and when to update the document throughout the SDP, this step is now easy.

It is even easier if you use some of the advanced technologies such as CD-ROM, magneto-optical read-write storage, or an on-line documentation database. Using these methods of publishing would mean that updating and maintenance could be accomplished quite simply by sending out a whole new CD-ROM or magnetic-optical disk rather than groups of pages. And if we don't send the actual disks out, perhaps we could simply transmit our updated manuals over a Local Area Network (LAN) or more distantly over phone lines. Hewlett-Packard is beginning to move in this direction by reissuing rather than sending out groups of paper pages—they find that it's cheaper, and that since most of the user complaints about their documentation had to do with the updating process, such a reissuing process would overcome the largest area of user complaint.

But no matter what technology you use to maintain the document, there are still a number of guidelines to follow.

The most important step in handling updating is to assign responsibility for it. During system acceptance, someone should be given the responsibility for updating the document and for distributing the updates.

When the pages that are updated do not exceed 30%, you can release updates by single pages. When, however, the updated pages exceed 30%, it is time to rerelease the entire document (Digital Equipment Corporation, 1983; traditional military specifications).

During the life of the document, remember the following (Pakin and Associates, 1979, 1981):

- Maintain a master copy of the document that notes all corrections and updated information. Date each correction and change and the reason for it. This master copy acts as an audit trail for documentation changes.

- Maintain a document distribution list. This list should identify all document holders. One way to keep track of document holders is to use the postcard-tracking system shown in Figure 50. Every time someone gets a manual, they fill in one card and send it into the person responsible for updating the documentation. Their name is then entered on the update list. When the manual is passed on to the next person, he or she fills out the next card, and so on. (This, of course, can be automated electronically and would probably vastly improve the list's accuracy.)

Any time this book is assigned to another employee, the Documentation Section should be notified of the change. Please fill in the card nearest the bottom of this page and return to the 3rd floor - Electric Tower Annex. Your cooperation will assure that each person assigned a book will receive the latest revisions.

WIP Procedure Manual _____ MANUAL NO. _____62_____

I am currently the holder of the manual identified above. In the future, please send any revisions to my attention:

NAME: _____

DEPARTMENT: _____

LOCATION: _____

RETURN THIS CARD TO: COMPUTER SERVICES DEPT.
                        DOCUMENTATION SECTION
                        3rd FLOOR - ELECTRIC TOWER ANNEX

3

Figure 50. Sample postcard tracking system for paper document maintenance.

When distributing updates—either on-line or on paper—we must direct the readers' attention to changes so that their procedures or actions will change to fit the new situation. This "calling the reader's attention" needs to be done on a local level (with page dates and change bars) as well as on a global level (with a cover letter summarizing all the changes). We also need to encourage readers not only to insert the modified pages or screens in their manuals, but also to read the changes. In traditional paper manual situations, we have achieved these updating goals by:

- Distributing a full list of all updates every six months.

- Distributing one set of updates on white sheets to be placed immediately in the manual and another set on a contrasting color paper that is just to be read. These dual pages encourage

"Before the blessed event are the trials of labor...And documenters are no more immune to them than are any other professionals. Code that will not freeze, even as your book heads through the wintry air to the printer; developers who won't give you the time of day (even in octal!); mastering concepts only to have them etched into oblivion in the next base level; so many cooks in the broth that...well, it's just part of the Job. You'll never be bored" (Digital, 1983)

users both to read and to file updates (Matthies, 1977).

- Calling attention to the updated or changed sections by adding change bars (as we've done to the outside of the page with this paragraph) and by dating the pages.

- Sending out an acknowledgment card with each update. The receivers of the updates fill out this card signaling that they have received the update page and have put it in the manual.

- Sending out new coversheets with each set of updates to distinguish those manuals that have been kept up-to-date from those that haven't been.

BIBLIOGRAPHY

ACM Computing Surveys. Special Issue on Human-Computer Interaction, March 1981.

Adams, Douglas. "Guide to the Macintosh." *MacUser* 3 (9) September 1987: 144, 146.

Adams, James L. *Conceptual Blockbusting: A Guide to Better Ideas.* NY: W.W. Norton, 1979.

Al-Awar, J.; Chapanis, A.; and Ford, W. R. "Tutorials for the First Time Computer User." *IEEE Transactions on Professional Communications.* March 1982: 30–7.

Alschuler, Loira. "Hand-Crafted Hypertext—Lessons from the ACM Experiment." In *The Society of Text: Hypertext, Hypermedia, and the Social Construction of Information.* edited by Edward Barrett. Cambridge, MA: MIT Press, 1989.

Amanda, Robert E. and Goldman, Mark. "A Renaissance Approach to Technical Documentation." In *Proceedings of the 36th International Technical Communication Conference, Chicago, Illinois, May 14-17, 1989.* Washington, DC: Society for Technical Communication, 1989: MG-39–42.

American Institute for Professional Education. *User Documentation.: A Fundamental Course for Data Processors and Managers.* Carnegie Building, 1981. 100 Kings Road, Madison, NJ 07940: 4–5, 2-1-2-2, 2-15-2-18.

American Society of Mechanical Engineers. *Guideline for Documenting of Computer Systems Used in Computer-Aided Preparation of Product Definition Data.* NY: ASME, 1973.

Anderson, R. C. "Schema-Directed Process in Language Comprehension." In *Cognitive Psychology and Instruction.* edited by A. Lesgod et al. NY: Plenum Press, 1978.

Andriole, Stephen J. *Storyboard Prototyping: A New Approach to User Requirements Analysis.* Wellesley, MA: QED Information Sciences, 1989.

Andre J.,Furuta R. and Quint V. (eds) *Structured Documents.* Cambridge, England: Cambridge University Press, 1989.

Anisfeld, M. and Klenbort, I. "On the Function of Structural Paraphrase: The View from the Passive Voice." *Psychological Review.* (79) 1973: 117–26.

Apple Human Interface Guidelines: The Apple Desktop Interface. Reading, MA: Addison-Wesley, 1987

Arnold. William A. "Learning Modules in Minimalist Documents." In *Proceedings of the 35th International Technical Communication Conference, May 10-13, 1988.* Philadelphia, PA. Washington, DC: Society for Technical Communication, 1988: WE-16-9.

Arnon, Jonathan and Lehrhaupt, Harry. "Software Documentation, An Automated Approach." In *Conference Proceedings of the International Conference on Systems Documentation* January 22-23, 1982. NY: Association for Computing Machinery, 1983: 1–8.

Asinof, Lynn. "Briefs." *Wall Street Journal.* 4/20/89: 1.

Australian Government Publishing Service. *Style Manual for Authors, Editors and Printers.* Canberra, ACT, 1978.

Ayer, Steve J. and Patrinostro, Frank S. *Volume 1–Software Development Planning and Management Documents.* Plant City, FL: TCA Publishing Division (PO Box Drawer E), 1990.

_____. and _____. *Volume 2–Software Development Analysis Documentation.* Plant City, FL: TCA Publishing Division (PO Box Drawer E), 1990.

_____. and _____. *Volume 3–Software Development Design Documentation.* Plant City, FL: TCA Publishing Division (PO Box Drawer E), 1990.

_____. and _____. *Volume 4–Software Program and Test Documents.* Plant City, FL: TCA Publishing Division (PO Box Drawer E), 1990.

_____. and _____. *Volume 5–Software Implementation Documents.* Plant City, FL: TCA Publishing Division (PO Box Drawer E), 1990.

_____. and _____. *Volume 6–Software Configuration Management Documents.* Plant City, FL: TCA Publishing Division (PO Box Drawer E), 1990.

Baceski, Dave. "The Parody Bit." *Computerworld.*

Bach, G. R. *Stop, You're Driving Me Crazy.* NY: Berkeley Books, 1981. ("One of man's most fundamental needs is to have his expectations met.")

Bailey, Robert W. *Human Performance Engineering: A Guide for System Designers.* Englewood Cliffs, NJ: Prentice-Hall, 1982:433.

_____. *Human Errors in Computer Systems.* Englewood Cliffs, NJ: Prentice-Hall, 1983.

Baker, Russell. "Computer Fallout." *New York Times.* 10/11/86: 30.

Bangasser, Thomas F. "The Utility Value of Information." In *Microsoft CD-ROM 1989-1990 Yearbook.* compiled by Salley Oberlin and Joyce Cox. Redmond, WA: Microsoft Press, 1989: 5–8.

Barkman, Pat. "Storyboarding and Writing." In *Proceedings of the 29th International Technical Communication Conference, May 1982.* Washington, DC: Society for Technical Communication, 1982.

_____. "Using the Flowchart in Technical Writing." In *Proceedings of the IEEE Professional Communication Society, October 1984.* NY: IEEE, 1984.

Barfield, Woodrow; Haselkorn, Mark; and Weatbrook, Catherine. "Information Retrieval with a Printed User's Manual and with online HyperCard Help." *Technical Communication* 37 (1) February 1990: 22–7.

Barnett, J. M.; Lentzer, H. L.; and Prono, J. K. *Technical Writing for Scientists and Engineers.* Livermore, CA: Lawrence Livermore Laboratories, 1979.

Baroudi, Jack J., Olson, Margrethe, H., and Ives, Blake. "An Empirical Study of the Impact of User Involvement on System Usage and Information Satisfaction." *Communications of the ACM* 29 (3) March 1986: 232–8.

Barrett, Edward. (ed.) *Text, Context and Hypertext.* Cambridge, MA: MIT Press, 1988.

Barton, Ben F. and Marthalee S. "A Critique of Current Notions of User Friendliness." A paper presented at the College Composition and Communication Conference, NY City, March 30, 1984.

Bates, Peter. "How To Turn Your Writing Into Communication." *Personal Computing* 8 (10) October 1984.

Beard Richard E. and Callamars, Peters. V. *A Method for Designing Computer Support Documentation.* Master's Thesis, September 1983, Report No. LSSR 54-83, Department of Communication, AFIT/LSH, WPAFB, Ohio 45433.

Beck, Melinda. "Can't Spell? Yur Not Dumm." *Newsweek.*, June 6, 1988: 52–3.

Beiderman, I. "Recognition by Components: A Theory of Human Image Understanding." *Psychological Review*, (94) 1987: 115–45.

Benzon, Bill. "The Visual Mind and the Macintosh." *Byte* 10 (1) January 1985: 113–30.

Bergstrom, Delores "Life as a Product Support Technician." In *33rd International Technical Communication Conference Proceedings.* Washington, DC: Society for Technical Communication 1986: 102–4.

Berlitz. *Native Tongues.* NY: Grossett and Dunlap, 1982.

Bernard, R. M., Petersen, C. H., and Ally, M. "Can Images Provide Contextual Support for Prose?" *Journal of Educational Communication and Technology* 29 (2) 1981: 101–8.

Bernhardt, Stephen. "Seeing the Text." *College Composition and Communication* 37 (1) February 1986: 66–78.

Bernstein, Mark. "Hypertext: New Challengers and Roles for Technical Communicators." In *Proceedings of the 35th International Technical Communications Conference.* Washington, DC: Society for Technical Communication, 1988: 33–6.

Bernstein, Theodore M. *Miss Thistlebottom's Hobgoblin's: The Careful Writer's Guide to the Taboos, Bugbears, and Outmoded Rules of English Usage.* NY: Simon and Schuster, 1971.

Bethke, Frederick. "Measuring the Usability of Software Manuals." *Technical Communication* 29 (2) 1983: 13–6.

Bewley, William L., Roberts, Teresa L., Schroit, David, Verplank, William . "Human Factors Testing In the Design of Xerox's 8010 "Star" Office Workstation." In *Proceedings of the CHI '83 Human Factors in Computing Systems Conference, Boston, December 12-15, 1983.* NY: Association for Computing Machinery, 1983: 72–7.

Biederman, I. and Ju, G. "Surface versus Edge-based Determinants of Visual Recognition." *Cognitive Psychology* 20 (1) 1988: 38–63.;

Black, John B., Bechtold, J. Scott, Mitraini, Marco, and Carroll, John M. "On-line Tutorials: What Kind of Inference Leads to the Most Effective Learning." In *'Wings of the Mind,' Conference Proceedings of the SIGCHI (Human Factors in Computing Systems) April 30-May 4, 1989* Meeting. edited by Ken Bice and Clayton Lewis NY: Association for Computing Machinery, 1989: 81–3.

Blair and Maron. "An Evaluation of Retrieval Effectiveness for a Full-Text Document-Retrieval System." *Communications of the ACM* 28 (3) 1985: 289–99.

Blumenthal, Joseph C. *English 3200.* NY: Harcourt Brace Jovanovich, 1972.

Boar, Bernard H. "Alleviating Common concerns of Application Prototyping—The Experience Difference." *Computerworld.* 18 (22) May 28, 1984. 66–7.

Boomhower, E.F. *Guide to Better Writing.* IBM Raleigh Publication Center and IBM FDL Technical Publications, 1979.

Boorstin, Daniel J. *The Discovers.* NY: Random House, 1983: 532.

Bork, Alfred. "A Preliminary Taxonomy of Ways of Displaying Text on Screens." *Information Design Journal* 3(3) 1983: 206–14.

Borland, Russell E. "'Those Silly Bastards': A Report on Some User's Views of Documentation." In *Proceedings of the Second International Conference on System Documentation, April 28-30, 1983, Seattle, Washington.* NY: Association of Computing Machinery, 1984: 11–5.

Borrko, Harold and Berneir, Charles. *Indexing: Concepts and Methods.* NY: Academic Press, 1984. (See also, *Indexer*, Journal of the American Society of Indexers, NY.)

Boston, Bruce O. *STET!: Tricks of the Trade for Writers and Editors.* Alexandria, VA: Editorial Experts, 1986.

Bowman, George T. "Applying Theory to Develop Task-Oriented Documents." In *The Proceedings of the 33rd International Technical Communication Conference, May 1986.* Washington, DC: Society for Technical Communication, 1986: 174–6.

Brace, Colin. "Literatus Turned Computerandus." *Electric Word* (15) September/October 1989: 64.

Bradford, Annette Norris. "A Planning Process for Online Information." In *Effective Documentation: What We Have Learned from Research.* edited by Stephen Doheny-Farina. Cambridge, MA: MIT Press, 1988: 185–211.

_____. "Writing and Using Online Tutorial Information." Paper presented at the College Composition and Communication Conference, NY, March 30, 1984.

_____. "Enhanced User Interface Through Computer Tutorials." Paper delivered at the IEEE Conference on Professional Communications, October 1983, Atlanta, GA. NY: IEEE, 1983.

_____ and Rubens, Brenda. "A Survey of Experienced User and Writers of Online Information." In *Transactions of the IEEE Professional Communication Society, October 16-18, 1985. Williamsburg, VI.* NY: IEEE, 1985: 269–74.

Bradford, David. "The Persona in Personal Computer Documentation." In *Proceedings of the IEEE Professional Communication Conference, 1983.* NY: IEEE, 1983: 136.

Brockmann, R. John "Desktop Publishing—Beyond GEE WHIZ" *IEEE Transactions on Professional Communication* 31 (1) March 1988 (a): 21–9

_____."Exploring the Connections Between Improved Technology—Workstation and Desktop Publishing and Improved Methodology—Document Databases." In *Text, Context and Hypertext* edited by Edward Barrett. Cambridge, MA: MIT Press, 1988 (b): 25–49.

_____.Desktop Publishing: A Critical Bibliography *IEEE Transactions on Professional Communication* 31 (1) March 1988 (c): 30–6

_____.and Horton, William. *The Writer's Pocket Almanack.* Santa Monica, CA: InfoBooks, 1988: 75.

_____, _____, and Brock, Kevin. "From Database to Hypertext Via Electronic Publishing: An Information Odyssey" In *The Society of Text: Hypertext, Hypermedia, and the Social Construction of Information.* edited by Edward Barrett. Cambridge, MA: MIT Press, 1989: 162–205.

_____ "Where Has the Template Tradition Led Us." In *Conference Proceedings on Systems Documentation, April 28-30. Seattle, Washington. edited* by John Browne. NY: Association for Computing Machinery, 1984.

_____. and McCauley, Rebecca J. "The Computer and the Craft of Writing: Implications for Teachers." *The Technical Writing Teacher* 9 (2) Winter 1984: 132.

Brod, Craig. *Technostress: The Human Cost of the Computer Revolution.* Reading, MA: Addison-Wesley, 1984: 51. "In 1983, *Psychology Today* documented the increase in "flaming"—making rude or obscene outbursts—by computer. According to the article, a study of group decision making at Carnegie-Mellon University showed that students were more abusive to each other when the group was linked by terminal than when the students met in person. We are less concerned with one another's feelings when we can't see the face or hear the voice at the other end. . . . Peter, who works in a computerized insurance company office, believes people in the office are no longer as friendly as they were before the office computerized its operations...The electronic memos were brusquer than the old written ones."

Brooks, Fredrick. *The Mythical Man-Month: Essays on Software Engineering.* NY: Addison-Wesley, 1975.

Brooks, Theodore S. "Online Information: Display Panels as a New Editing Challenge." In *Proceedings of the 35th International Technical Communication Conference, May 10-13, 1988.* Philadelphia, PA. Washington, DC: Society for Technical Communication, 1988: WE-3-5.

Brown, C. Marlin "Lin." *Human-Computer Interface Design Guidelines.* Norwood, NJ: Ablex, 1988.

Brown, Dennise. "Discussions with a Skeptical Writer: Questions (and Answers!) on Usability Testing." Tandem Corporation In-House Writer's Newsletter. Cupertino, CA, 1989.

Brown, Judith and Cunningham, Steve. *Programming the User Interface: Principles and Examples.* Wiley-Interscience, 1989: Chapter 8–On Color.

Brown, P. J. "Error Messages: The Neglected Area of the Man/Machine Interface." *Communications of the ACM* 26 (4) April 1983: 246–9.

Brown, Zoe N. "Page Design for Data Processing User Documentation."In *Proceedings of 31st the International Technical Communication Conference, May 1984.* Washington, DC: Society for Technical Communication, 1984: VC-27–30.

Bruner, J. S. *Toward a Theory of Instruction.* Cambridge, MA: Belnap Press/Harvard University Press, 1966: 127.

_____. *On Knowing: Essays for the Left Hand.* Cambridge: Harvard University Press, 1962.

Brunsman, Sally, Messerly, John, and Lammers, Susan. "Publishers, Multimedia, and Interactivity." In *Interactive Multimedia: Visions of Multimedia for Developers, Educators, and Information Providers.* edited by Sueann Ambron and Kristina Hooper. Redmond, WA: Microsoft Press, 1988: 275–88.

Bryan, Martin. *SGML: An Authors Guide to the Standard Generalized Markup Language.* Wokingham, England: Addison-Wesley, 1988.

Buckley, William A. "An Electronic Critic Tells Today's Typist How to Write Better." *Wall Street Journal.* September 19, 1983: 1, 20.

Buehler, Mary Fran. *The Levels of Edit,* Publication 80–1. Pasadena, CA: Jet Propulsion Labs, 1980—also available from the Government Printing Office, Washington, DC See also her article "Defining Terms in Technical Editing: The Levels of Edit as a Model." The Special Issue on Technical Editing.

Bureau of Land Management. *Gobbledygook Has Gotta Go.* Washington, DC: U.S. Government Printing Office, 1966.

Bury, K. F. "Prototyping on CMS: Using Prototypes to Conduct Human Factors Tests of Software During Development." IBM Human Factors Center Technical Report HFC-43. IBM General Products Division, 5600 Cottle Road, San Jose, CA 95143 (February 1983).

Bush, Vannevar. "As We May Think." *Atlantic Monthly* 176 (1) July 1945: 101–8.

Byte. Special Issue on Human Factors Engineering 7, April 1982: 108–22; "Making a Case for CASE." 14 (13) December 1989: 154–71.

Caird, Helen G. *Publications Cost Management: Anthology Series No. 3.* Washington, D. C.: Society for Technical Communication, 1976.

Card, Stuart K. "User Perceptual Mechanisms in the Search of Computer Command Menus." In *Human Factors in Computer Systems Proceedings, March 1982. Gaithersburg, MD:* NY: ACM, 1982.

_____.; Moran, Thomas P.; and Newell, Allen. *The Psychology of Human-Computer Interaction.* Hillsdale, NJ: Lawrence Erlbaum Associates, 1983.

Carr, Robert. "New User Interfaces for CD-ROM" in *CD-ROM The New Papyrus.* edited by S. Lambert and S. Ropiequet. Redmond, WA: 1986.

Carroll, John M., and C. Carrithers. "Blocking Learning Error States in a Training Wheels System. " *Human Factors* (26) 1984: 377–89.

_____. et al. "The Minimal Manual." *Human Computer Interaction, 1987-88* 3 (1978-1988): 123–53.

_____. "Minimalist Design." *Datamation* 30 (18) 1984: 125–36.

_____. "Minimalist Design for Active Users." In *Human-Computer Interaction—INTERACT '84.* edited by B. Shackel. Amsterdam: North-Holland, 1985: 39–44.

_____. et al. "Exploring Exploring a Word Processor." *Human Computer Interaction, 1985* (1) 1985: 283–307.

_____. and Rosson, Mary Beth. "Paradox of the Active User." *Interfacing Thought: Cognitive Aspects of Human-Computer Interaction.* edited by John M. Carroll. Cambridge, MA: MIT Press, 1987: 80–111.

_____. *The Nurnberg Funnel: Designing Minimalist Instruction for Practical Computer Skill.* Cambridge, MA: MIT Press, 1990.

_____. and Aaronson, Amy P. "Learning By Doing with Simulated Intelligent Help." In *The Society of Text: Hypertext, Hypermedia, and the Social Construction of Information.* edited by Edward Barrett. Cambridge, MA: MIT Press, 1989: 423–52.

CasaBianca, Lou. "CD-ROM The Final Countdown." In *Microsoft CD-ROM 1989-1990 Yearbook.* compiled by Salley Oberlin and Joyce Cox. Redmond, WA: Microsoft Press, 1989: 631–9.

Casey, Bernice. "An Information Developer's View of Usability Testing." In *Proceedings of the 31st International Technical Communication Conference, May 1984.* Washington, DC: Society for Society for Technical Communication, 1984: MPD-22-5.

_____. "In Search of the Most Amazing User Interface." In *Transactions of the IEEE Professional Communication Society, October 16-18, 1985.* Williamsburg, VI. NY: IEEE, 1985: 193–7.

"CDC Develops Online Help Systems Using HyperCard." *Communications Design Center Newsletter* 6 (1) February 1988: 1, 4, 5. HDS Demo Disk available for $10.00 from HyperCard HelpWare, Carnegie Mellon University, Communications Design Center, 160 Baker Hall, Pittsburgh, PA 15213. See also, Duffy, 1988; Brown, 1988; Kearsley, 1988; and Horton, 1989.

Chandler, Bob. "Grammar Problems?" *Electric Word.* (15) September/October 1989: 46–50.

Chapanis, Alphonse. "Interactive Human Communication: Some Lessons Learned from Laboratory Experiments." In *Man-Computer Interaction.* edited by B. Shackel. Alphen aan den Rijn, The Netherlands: Sijthoff and Noordhoff, 1980.

_____ "Words, Words, Words." *Human Factors* (7) 1965: 1–7.

Charney, Davida H. Reder, Lynne M., and Wells, Gail W. "Studies in Elaboration in Instructional Texts." In *Effective Documentation: What We Have Learned from Research.* edited by Stephen Doheny-Farina. Cambridge, MA: MIT Press, 1988.

Chase, William and Simon, Herber. "The Mind's Eye in Chess." In *Visual Information Processing.* edited by W. Chase. Academic Press, 1973: 218–81.

Chavarria, Linda S. "Improving the Friendliness of Technical Manuals." In *Proceedings of the 29th International Technical Communication Conference, May 1982.* Washington, DC: Society for Society for Technical Communication, 1982: W-26-8.

Clancy, Frank. "Mac Brings Ancient Philosopher Up To Date." In *Microsoft CD-ROM 1989-1990 Yearbook.* compiled by Salley Oberlin and Joyce Cox. Redmond, WA: Microsoft Press, 1989: 134–9.

Clark, H. and Chase, W. "On the Process of Comparing Sentences Against Pictures." *Cognitive Psychology.* (3) 1972: 472–517.

Clark, Ian. *How to Help 'HELP' Help.* IBM United Kingdom Laboratories Ltd., Technical Report HFO22. December 1981 (a).

_____ "Software Simulation as a Tool for Usable Product Design." *IBM Systems Journal.* 20 (2) 1981 (b).

Cleveland, D. B. and Cleveland, A. D. *Introduction to Indexing and Abstracting.* Littleton, CO: Libraries Unlimited, 1983.

Cohen, Nancy E., Nyhus, Karl A. and Wenstrom, John D."Designing an On-line Interactive HELP System." In *Proceedings of the 36th International Technical Communication Conference,1989.* Washington, DC: Society for Technical Communication, 1989: 69–71.

Cohill, A. and Williges, R. "Retrieval of HELP Information for Novice Users of Interactive Computer Systems." *Human Factors* (27) 1985: 335–43.

Coke, Ester U. "Computer Aids for Writing Text." In *The Technology of Text: Principles for Structuring, Designing and Displaying Text.* edited by David H. Jonassen, Englewood Cliffs, NJ: Educational Technology, 1982: 390–7.

Colborn, David. "Inexpensive Text/Graphics System: A Step Forward For Writers." In *33rd International Technical Communication Conference Proceedings.* Washington, DC: Society for Technical Communication 1986: 21–9

Cole, Bernard C. *Beyond Word Processing.* NY: McGraw-Hill Book Company, 1985. Both this book and Daiute's contain excellent reviews of writers' tools that go beyond word processing in such areas as indexers, outline processors, and so on.

Collier, Richard M. "The Word Processor and Revision Strategies." *College Composition and Communication.* 34 (2) May 1983, 149–50.

Coletta, Barbara; and Oatley, Lorraine. "Online Editing: Is it Worth the Trouble?." In *Proceedings of the 31st Annual Technical Communications Conference, May 1984.* Washington, DC: Society for Technical Communication, 1984: WE-59–62.

Common User Access Panel Design and User Interaction. (CUA guidelines—IBM Publication No. SC25-4351) 1987.

Conklin, J. "Hypertext: An Intrroduction and Survey." *IEEE Computer* 20 (9) September 1987: 17–41.

Connor and Kaplan, Robert B. *Writing Across Languages.* NY: Addison-Wesley, 1987.

Control Data Corporation. *Creating An On-line Manual: For Cyber 180.* 1983.

Cook, K. "In Search of Computer Training."*Personal Computing.* 2 August 1983: 98–9.

Cook, Peter. "Multimedia Technology: An Encyclopedia Publisher's Perspective." In *Interactive Multimedia: Visions of Multimedia for Developers, Educators, and Information Providers.* edited by Sueann Ambron and Kristina Hooper. Redmond, WA: Microsoft Press, 1988: 219–40.

Corbett, John R. "A Method to Measure Productivity: JPL's Product Inventory System." *Technical Communication* 34 (4) 1987: 225–34

Cox, Joyce. "What's Involved in Text Data Preparation." In *Microsoft CD-ROM 1989-1990 Yearbook.* compiled by Salley Oberlin and Joyce Cox. Redmond, WA: Microsoft Press, 1989: 323–8.

Crenshaw, Jack W. and Philipose, Joseph. "Can Computers Really Be Friendly?"*Computer Design.* February 1983: 103–8 ("A good portion of user's responses to a situation revolve not around what happened, by what they expected to happen.")

Cuff, Rodney N. "On Casual Users."*International Journal of Man-Machine Studies.* 12 (1980): 163–87.

Culbertson, Jim. "A Hypertext Interface to CD-ROM" In *Microsoft CD-ROM 1989-1990 Yearbook.* compiled by Salley Oberlin and Joyce Cox. Redmond, WA: Microsoft Press, 1989: 289–92.

Cunningham, William R. "Testing Task-Oriented Publications in a Laboratory Environment." In *Proceedings of the 31st International Technical Communication Conference, May 1984.* Washington, DC: Society for Society for Technical Communication, 1984: WE-144-7.

Daiute, Colette. *Writing and Computers.* Reading, MA: Addison-Wesley, 1985: "Resources," 300–22.

Dancheck, M. M. "VDT Displays for Power Plants." *Instrumentation Technology.* 23 (10) 1976: 29–36.

Daoust, Tom. "Seven Steps to a Better Technical Manual." *STC Austin* (newsletter of the Austin chapter of the Society for Technical Communication) February 1983.

Dehning, W.; Essig, Heindrun; and Susanne, Maass. *The Adaptation of Virtual Man-Computer Interfaces to User Requirements in Dialogs.* #110. Lecture Notes in Computer Science. edited by G. Goos and J. Hartmanis. NY: Springer-Verlag, 1981.

Dell, Sherry. "An Overview of an Interactive Videodisk Project." *Technical Communication* 35 (3) Third Quarter 1985: 210–7.

Dencker, Andrea. "What Is Good Typography?"In *Proceedings of 31st the International Technical Communication Conference, May 1984*: Washington, DC: Society for Technical Communication, 1984: VC-19–22.

Dennett, Joann Temple, "Not to Say Is Better Than to Say: How Rhetorical Structure Reflects Cultural Context in Japanese-English Technical Writing." *IEEE Transactions on Professional Communication* 31 (3) September 1988: 116–9.

Department of Treasury, Internal Revenue Service. *Effective Revenue Writing 1. Effective Revenue Writing 2.* and *Effective Writing: A Workshop Course.* Washington, DC: Government Printing Office, 1977, 1973, 1976.

Desmaris, Joyce. *Computerworld.* January 19, 1981.

Digital Equipment Co. *The Personal Computer Documentor's Guide.* Maynard, MA: Digital Equipment Co., 1983: I-3-2, I-1-11, I-4-23, I-5-8, II-1-5, II-5-7.

"Division of Labor or Integrated Teams: A Crux in the Management of Technical Communication." *Technical Communication* 36 (3) Third Quarter, August 1989: 210–21.

Dobrin, David. "What's Technical About Technical Writing?" In *New Essays in Technical and Scientific Communication: Research, Theory, Practice.* edited by Paul Anderson; R. John Brockmann; and Carolyn Miller. Farmingdale, NY: Baywood 1983: 231.

Document Design Project. *Guidelines for Document Designers.* Washington, DC, 1981. (A free monthly publication is available from them called *Simply Stated* that covers many national topics in the area of "clear writing."American Institutes for Research, 1055 Thomas Jefferson Street, NW, Washington DC 20007.)

Doebler, Paul D. "Productivity Through Electronic Publishing." *Technical Communication* 34 (4) Fourth Quarter 1987: 250–6

Dole, Jeanne. "Standard Generalized Markup Language: An Introduction." In *Proceedings of the 36th International Technical Communication Conference, Chicago, Illinois, May 14-17, 1989.* Washington, DC: Society for Technical Communication, 1989: RT-103–4.

Duffy, T. M., Curran, T. E., and Sass, D. "Documentation Design for Technical Job Tasks." *Human Factors* 25 (2) 1983: 143–60.

Duffy, T. M., Post, T., Smith, G. "An Analysis of the Process of Developing Military Technical Manuals." *Technical Communication* 34 (4) Second Quarter, May 1987: 70–8

_____., et. al. *Learning With On-line and Hardcopy Tutorials.* Communications Design Center Technical Report No. 32. Pittsburgh, PA: Carnegie Mellon University, January 1987.

_____. and Kebance, P. *Testing the Readable Writing Approach to Text Revision.* (Technical Report) Naval Personnel Research and Development Center, 1982.

_____. *Writing Online Information: Expert Strategies (Interviews with Professional Writers).* Communications Design Center Technical Report No. 37. Pittsburgh, PA: Carnegie Mellon University, March 1988.

_____.*The Design of Online Help Systems: A Design Evaluation Instrument.* March 1, 1988. Work on contract #DAAA1-86-K-0019. (A paper version of a help system questionnaire for guiding design.)

Duin, Ann H. "Reading to Learn and Do." In *Proceedings of the 35th International Technical Communication Conference, May 10-13, 1988.* Philadelphia, PA. Washington, DC: Society for Technical Communication, 1988: WE-21–4.

Dunsmore, H. E. "Designing an Interactive Facility for Nonprogrammers" *Communications of the ACM* 1980: 475–83.

Dyson, Esther. *Christian Science Monitor.* October 7, 1983.

Dzida, W.; Herda, S.; and Itzfeldt, W. D. "User-Perceived Quality of Interactive Systems." *IEEE Transactions on Software Engineering* WE-4 (4) July 1978.

Eckholm, E. "Emotional Outbursts Punctuate Conversations By Computers." *New York Times.* 10/2/84: C1.

Eckstein, Helene. "Four-Color Fundamentals." *Publish!* 4 (5) 1989: 44–9.

Editorial Eye. Editorial Experts Inc., 5905 Pratt St., Alexandria, Virginia 22310.

Edwards, Arthur W. "The Myths of Customer Satisfaction." In *Second Annual AT&T Customer Documentation Symposium, October 25-26, 1989, AT&T Bell Laboratories–Holmdel.* Indianapolis, IN: AT&T Customer Information Center, 1989 (Document Number: 700-076).

Egan, Dennis, E., Remde, Joel R., Landauer, Thomas K., Lochbaum, Carol C., and Gomez, Louis M. "Behavioral Evaluation and Analysis of a Hypertext Browser." In*'Wings of the Mind,' Conference Proceedings of the SIGCHI (Human Factors in Computing Systems) April 30-May 4, 1989* Meeting. edited by Ken Bice and Clayton Lewis. NY: Association for Computing Machinery, 1989: 205–10.

Eisen, Hendrika Alice. "Iconer: A Tool for Evaluating Icons." *SIGCHI Bulletin* 21 (3) January 1990: 23–5.

Einberger, John. "The Application Development Process."In *Microsoft CD-ROM 1989-1990 Yearbook.* compiled by Salley Oberlin and Joyce Cox. Redmond, WA: Microsoft Press, 1989: 242–51.

Elbow, Peter. *Writing Without Teachers.* NY: Oxford University Press, 1973: 4–7.

_____. *Writing With Power: Techniques for Mastering The Writing Process.* NY: Oxford University Press, 1981.

Electric Word. "There's Nothing Manual About Making Manuals." March/April 1989: 19–21. (formerly *Language Technology*) (a European journal that focuses on "how wordworkers can most effectively use their computers" Language Technology BV, PO Box 70486-LT12, 1007 KL Amsterdam, The Netherlands, $50/year)

Elmer-DeWitt, Phillip. "The Busy Signal Predicament" *Time.* July 14, 1986): 51

Elser, Art. "An Introduction to Interactive Videodisc." *Technical Communication* 35 (3) Third Quarter 1985: 204–9.

Engle, E. and Granda, R. E. *Guidelines for Man/Display Interface.* IBM Poughkeepsie Lab Technical Report (TR 00.02720) Poughkeepsie, NY, December 1975.

Enrick, Norbert L. *Handbook of Effective Graphic and Tabular Communication.* Huntington, NY: Robert E Kreiger, 1980.

Erdman, R. L. and Neal, A. S. "Laboratory versus Field Experimentation on Human Factors." *Human Factors* 13 (6) 1971: 521–31.

Erickson, Timothy E. "An Automated Fortran Documenter." In *Conference Proceedings of the International Conference on Systems Documentation* January 22-23, 1982. NY: Association for Computing Machinery, 1983: 40–6.

Evans, Christopher. *The Micro-Millennium.* NY: Viking Press, 1979: Chapter 8, "The Death of the Printed Page."

"Face Fax." *Colophon.* Fall 1989: 12.

Farkas, David "Product Support and Documentation Writing: Potential Synergism." In *33rd International Technical Communication Conference Proceedings.* Washington, DC: Society for Technical Communication 1986: 105–8.

Favin, David L."View from the Other Side." In *First Annual AT&T Customer Documentation Symposium, October 19, 1988, AT&T Bell Laboratories-Holmdel* (700076): 117–20.

Fawcett, Heather J. "Adopting SGML: The Implications for Writers." *Proceedings of the 36th International Technical Communication Conference, Chicago, Illinois, May 14-17, 1989.* Washington, DC: Society for Technical Communication, 1989: RT-59–62.

Feiner, Steven; Nagy, Sandor; and Van Dam, Andries. "An Integrated System for Creating and Presenting Complex Documents." *Computer Graphics* 15 (3) August 1981: 181–9.

Feno, Charles. "The Instant Fix Problem." In *33rd International Technical Communication Conference Proceedings.* Washington, DC: Society for Technical Communication 1986.

Fenton, Howie. "The Technical Folder: Mac Technique." *Desktop Publisher* newspaper, September 1989: 14.

Filley, Richard. "Communicate With Graphics." A seven part series in *Industrial Engineering.* September 1981 to March 1982.

Firman, A. H. "Word Processing as a Tool in Improving Cost Effectiveness of Technical Publications." In *Proceedings of the 28th Annual Technical Communications Conference, May 20-23, 1981.* Washington, DC: Society for Technical Communication, 1981.

Fisher, Lou, Roger Grice, Judy Ramey and Lee Ridgway, "Online Information: What Conference Attenders Expect (A Report of a Survey)." *Technical Communication* 34 (3) Third Quarter 1987: 150-5.

Fitz, Taylor J. "Acquiring Knowledge from Prose and Continuous Discourse." In *Adult Learning.* edited by M.J.A. Howe. London: John Wiley and Sons, 1977.

Fletcher, D. B., and Meyer, G. P. "Writers Benefit from Authoring Tools." In *Transactions of the IEEE Professional Communication Society, October 16-18, 1985. Williamsburg, VI.* NY: IEEE, 1985: 261–4.

Flores, Ivan. "Computers Aid Index and Glossary Preparation." In *Conference Proceedings of the International Conference on Systems Documentation, January 22-23, 1982, Carson, California.* edited by Jan Bartlett and John Walter. Baltimore, MD: 1982: 46–60.

Flower, Linda. *Problem-Solving Strategies for Writing.* NY: Harcourt Brace Jovanovich, 1981.

_____. and Hayes, John. "Plans that Guide the Composing Process." In *Writing: Process, Development and Communication, Vol. II.* In the series *Writing: The Nature, Development, and Teaching of Written Communication.* edited by Carl H. Frederiksen and Joseph F. Dominic. Hillsdale, NJ: Lawrence Erlbaum Associates, 1981.

_____.and _____.; and Swarts, Heidi. "Revising Functional Documents: The Scenario Principle." In *New Essays in Technical and Scientific Communication: Research, Theory, Practice.* edited by Paul Anderson; R. John Brockmann; and Carolyn Miller. Farmingdale, NY: Baywood, 1983: 41–58.

Fluegelman, Andrew, and Hewes, Jeremy. *Writing in the Computer Age: Word Processing Skills and Style for Every Writer.* Garden City, NY: Anchor Books, 1983.

FOMM, *Military Specification,* MIL-HNBK-242 (1974)

Foti, Vince P. "The Post Mortem Process: An Exercise in Problem Solving" In *Proceedings of the 34th International Technical Communication Conference, 1987* Washington, DC: Society for Technical Communication, 1987: ATA-30-3.

Fraser, Bruce P. and Lamb, David Alex. "An Annotated Bibliography on User Interface Design." *SIGCHI Bulletin* 21 (1) July 1989:17–28.

Frenchel, R. "An Integrated Approach to User Assistance." *SIGSOC Bulletin.* 13 (2) 1981: 98–104.

Furnas, George W. "Generalized Fisheye Views." In *Proceedings of the CHI '86 Human Factors in Computing Systems.* NY: ACM 1986 16–23.

Gaines, Brian R. and Shaw, Mildred G. "Dialog Engineering." In *Designing for Human-Computer Communication.* edited by M. E. Sime and M. J. Coombs. London: Academic Press, 1983.

_____. Facey, P. V., and Sams, J. B. S. "An On-line Fixed-Interest Investment Analysis and Dealing System." In *Proceedings of the European Computing Congress, EUROCOMP, 1974.*

_____. and _____. "Programming Interactive Dialogues." In *Proceedings of a Conference on Computing and People.* edited by A. Parkin. Leicester, UK.

_____. and Shaw, Mildred, L. G. *The Art of Computer Conversation: A New Medium for Communication.* Englewood Cliffs, NJ: Prentice-Hall, 1984.

Galitz, Wilbert. "Human Engineering in Screen Design." *Journal of Systems Management.* May 1983: 6–11.

_____ *Handbook of Screen Format Design.* Wellesley, MA: QED Information Sciences, 1981.

Gange, Charles and Lipton, Amy. "Word-free Setup Instructions: Stepping into the World of Complex Products." *Technical Communication* 31 (3) 1984.

Gardiner, Margret M. "Principles from the Psychology of Memory: Part II, Episodic and Semantic Memory." In *Applying Cognitive Psychology to User-Interface Design.* edited by Margaret M. Gardiner and Bruce Christie. Chichester, England: John Wiley and Sons, 1987.

Garvey, I. "Thumbs Up for Hands On." *Personal Computing.* (2) August 1983: 137–42.

Gervickas, Vicki. "Prototyping: A Model Approach to Development." In *Proceedings of the International Technical Communication Conference, May 11-14, 1986, Detroit, Michigan.* Washington, DC: Society for Technical Communication, 1986: WE-161-2.

German, Carol J. and Sonderston, Candace. "An Experimental Study of the Effect of Analogy on Learning." In *Proceedings of the International Technical Communication Conference, May 11-14, 1986, Detroit, Michigan.* Washington, DC: Society for Technical Communication, 1986: 165–8.

Giedion, Siegfried. *Mechanization Takes Command* NY: W. W. Norton, 1969.

Giesecke, William B. "Online Editing and Editing Online Information." In *Transactions of the IEEE Professional Communication Society, October 16-18, 1985.* Willamsburg, VI: NY: IEEE, 1985: 261–4.

Gilfoil, D. M. "Warming Up to Computers: A Study of Cognitive and Affective Interaction Over Time." In *Proceedings of Human Factors in Computer Systems.* Gaithersburg, MD, March 1982: 130–4.

Gillihan, Dana and Jennifer Herrin. "Evaluating Product Manuals for Increased Usability." *Technical Communication* 35 (3) Third Quarter 1985: 168–71.

Gingrich, P. S., et al. *Writer's Workbench Trials: Final Report.* Piscataway, NJ: Bell Laboratories, 1981. (See Also, Keifer, 1984.)

Girill, T. R., Luk, Clement H. Luk, and Norton, Sally. "Reading Patterns in Online Documentation: How Transcript Analysis Reflects Text Design, Software Constraints, and User Preferences." In *Proceedings of the 34th International Technical Communication Conference, May 10-13, 1987, Denver, Colorado.* Washington, DC: Society for Technical Communication, 1987: RET-111–4.

_____., _____., and _____. "Towards Automated Consulting: Design Feedback from the Performance of Online Documentation." In *Proceedings of the 50th ASIS Annual Meeting, Boston, MA, October 4-8, 1987.* Medford, NY: Learned Information (for the American Society for Information Science) 1987: 85–90.

_____., _____., and _____. " "The Impact of Usage Monitoring on the Evolution of an Online-Documentation System: A Case Study." *IEEE Transactions on Systems, Man, and Cybernetics.* 18 (2) March/April 1988: 326–32.

Girill, T.R. and Luk, Clement H. "Document: A Comparative Study of an Interactive Online Solution to Four Documentation Problems." *Communications of the ACM* 26 (5) April 1983.

Girill, T. R. *On-line Documentation: A Practical Workshop* (Syllabus and Training Materials). June 5-6, 1986, University of California, Los Angeles.

_____. "Display Units for Online Passage Retrieval: A Comparative Analysis." In *Proceedings of the 31st International Technical Communication Conference, Seattle, Washington, April 29-May 2, 1984.* Washington, DC: Society for Technical Communication, 1984: ATA-87–90

_____. and Tull, Carol G. "Comparative Access Rates for Online Documentation and Human Consulting." In *Proceedings of the 51st ASIS Annual Meeting, Atlanta, GA, October 23–27, 1988.* Medford, NY: Learned Information (for the American Society for Information Science) 1988: 48–53.

Gleason, J. "One Book for Everyone."In *Proceedings of the 1984 IEEE Professional Communication Society Conference. Atlantic City, NJ, October 1984.* NY: IEEE, 1984: 155–8.

_____. "Humor in Technical Publications." In *Proceedings of the IEEE Professional Communication Conference, 1983.* NY: IEEE, 1983.

Glenn, J. S., Hazle, M., and Robinson, B. M. "Automated Requirements Development System (ARDS) User's Manual: Document Analysis." ESDTR 83-191, Volume 1, NTIS #AD-A135-925, U.S. Air Force Electronic Systems Division: Hanscom Air Force Base, MA, 1983.

Glib, T. and Weinberg, G. M. *Humanized Input.* Cambridge, MA: Winthrop, 1977.

Glushko, Robert J. "Transforming Text Into Hypertext For A Compact Disc Encyclopedia." In *'Wings of the Mind,' Conference Proceedings of the SIGCHI (Human Factors in Computing Systems) April 30-May 4, 1989* Meeting. edited by Ken Bice and Clayton Lewis NY: Association for Computing Machinery, 1989: 293–8.

_____. Design Issues for Multi-Document Hypertexts." In the Writing Process: Implications for the Design of Hypertext-based Writing Tools." In *Hypertext "89 Proceedings, November 5–8, 1989, Pittsburgh, PA.* NY: ACM 1989 (Order number 608891): 43–50.

Glynn, S. M., Britton, D. K., Muth, K. D. and Dogen, N. "Writing and Revising PersuasiveDocuments: Cognitive Demands" *Journal of Educational Research* 74 (4) 1982: 557–67.

Goldfield, Randy J. "Fear of Computers Can Be Overcome by Good Training." *The Office.* January 1983.

Gomoll, K., Gomoll, T., Duffy, T., Palmer, J., Aaron, A. "Writing Online Information: Expert Strategies (Interviews with Professional Writers)" Communication Design Center Technical Report Number 37, 1988. Pittsburgh, PA: Carnegie-Mellon University, Communications Design Center, 1988.

Gordon, Karen Elizabeth. *The Well-Tempered Sentence: A Punctuation Handbook for the Innocent, the Eager, and the Doomed.* New Haven, CT:Ticknor and Fields, 1983.

_____. *The Transitive Vampire: A Handbook of Grammar for the Innocent, the Eager, and the Doomed.* NY:Times Books, 1984.

Goswami, Dixie; Redish, Janice C; Felker, Daniel B.; and Siegal, Alan. *Writing for the Professions.* American Institute for Research, Washington, DC 1981: Chapter 7. "Using Design Well."

Gould, John D. and Grischkowsky, N. "Doing the Same Work with Hardcopy and CRT Terminals." *Human Factors* 26 (3) 1984: 323–7.

_____. Alfaro, Lizette, Barnes, Vincent, Finn, Rich, Grischkowsky, Nancy, and Minuto, Angela. "Reading Is Slower from CRT Displays than From Paper: Attempts to Isolate a Single-Variable Explanation." *Human Factors* 29 (3) 1987: 269–99.

Green, Petrina. and Brooks, Ted. "How Technical Writer's Write: A Survey of Strategies and Attitudes." In *Proceedings of the 1989 IEEE Professional Communication Society Conference Garden City, NY, 1989.* NY: IEEE, 1989: 48–52.

Greenwald, John. "How Does This #%$@! Thing Work?" *Time.* June 18 1984: 64.

Grice, Roger A. "Producing and Using Online Information: The Display Screen as an Extension of the Printed Page." In *Proceedings of the 1984 IEEE Professional Communication Society Conference Atlantic City, NJ, 1984.* NY: IEEE, 1984 (a): 164.

_____ "User Testing as an Information Development Activity." In *Proceedings of the 31st International Technical Communication Conference, May 1984.* Washington, DC: Society for Society for Technical Communication, 1984 (b): MPD-18–21.

_____. "Information Development is Part of Product Development—Not An Afterthought." In *Text, Context and Hypertext.* edited by Edward Barrett. Cambridge, MA: MIT Press, 1988: 133–48.

Griffith, Lisa L. "Job Aids: When A Manual is Too Much or Not Enough." In *Proceedings of the 34th International Technical Communication Conference, May 10-13, 1987, Denver, Colorado.* Washington, DC: Society for Technical Communication, 1987: WE-6–9.

Guillemette, Ronald A. "Prototyping: An Alternative Method for Developing Documentation." *Technical Communication* 35 (3) Third Quarter 1987: 135–41.

Gustafson, Gayle. "Controlled English for International Audiences." In *First Annual AT&T Customer Documentation Symposium, October 19, 1988, AT&T Bell Laboratories-Holmdel* (700076): 91–101.

Haas, C. and Hayes, J. R. "Pen and Paper vs. the Machine: Writers Composing in Hard Copy and Computer Conditions." Communications Design Center Technical Report No. 16. Pittsburgh, PA: Carnegie Mellon University, November, 1986.

Hadley, B. H. "Designing Task-Oriented Documentation Using a Universal Architecture." In *Proceedings of the 29th International Technical Communication Conference, May 1982.* Washington, DC: Society for Technical Communication, 1982: C-38–40.

Halasz, F. G. "Reflections on NoteCards: Seven Issues for the Next Generation of Hypermedia." *Communications of the ACM* 31 (7) July 1988: 836–52.

Hammond, Nick. "Principles from the Psychology of Skill Acquisition." In *Applying Cognitive Psychology to User-Interface Design.* edited by Margaret M. Gardiner and Bruce Christie. Chichester, England: John Wiley and Sons, 1987: 169.

Hampton, James A. "Principles from the Psychology of Language." In *Applying Cognitive Psychology to User-Interface Design.* edited by Margaret M. Gardiner and Bruce Christie. Chichester, England: John Wiley and Sons, 1987: 189–216.

Hancock, David. "Document Databases Can Save You Money" In *Proceedings of the 33rd International Technical Communication Conference, 1986, Detroit, Michigan* Washington, DC: Society for Technical Communication, 1986: 67

Hanks, Kurt and Belliston, Larry. *Rapid Viz: A New Method for Rapid Visualization of Ideas.* Los Altos, CA: William Kaufmann 1980.

Harper, William L. *Data Processing Documentation: Standards, Procedures, and Applications.* Englewood Cliffs, NJ: Prentice-Hall, 1981.

Harris, Michael. "The Man Behind Knight-Ridder's Success." *The San Francisco Chronicle.* 4/22/86.

Hartley, James. (ed.) *Psychology of Written Communication.* London: Kogan, 1980.

_____ and Burnhill, P. "Explorations in Space: A Critique of the Typography of BPS Publications." *Bulletin of the British Psychological Society* 29 (1976): 97–107.

_____. "Space Revisited: or the BPS Does It Again" *Bulletin of the British Psychological Society* (30) 1977 (a): 255–6.

_____. "Understanding Instructional Text: Typography, Layout and Design." In *Adult Learning.* edited by M.J.A. Howe. London: John Wiley and Sons, 1977 (b).

_____. *Designing Instructional Text.* NY: Nichols, 1978.

Hartshorn, Roy W. "Designing Information for the World." In *Proceedings of the 34th International Technical Communication Conference, May 10-13, 1987, Denver, Colorado.* Washington, DC: Society for Technical Communication, 1987: WE-186–9.

Hasen, Wilfred J. and Haas, Christina. "Reading and Writing with Computers: A Framework for Explaining Differences in Performance." *Communications of the ACM* 31 (9) September 1988: 1080–9.

Hasslein, Vaughn. "Marketing Survey on User Requests for Online Documentation." In *Proceedings of the 35th International Technical Communication Conference, May 10-13, 1988.* Philadelphia, PA. Washington, DC: Society for Technical Communication, 1988: 434–8.

Hauke, R.N.; Kern, R. P.; Sticht, T. G.; and Welty, D. *Guidebook for the Development of Army Training Literature.* U.S. Army Research Institute for Behavior and Social Sciences, November 1977.

Hayhoe, George F. "No Desktop is an Island: Groupware Needs of Publications Departments." In *Proceedings of the 1989 IEEE Professional Communication Society Conference, Garden City, NY, October 1989.* NY: IEEE, 1989: 228–32.

Heckel, Paul. *The Elements of Friendly Software Design.* NY: Warner Books, 1984.

Heidorn, G. E.; Jensen, K., Miller, L. A., Byrd, R. J., and Chodorow, M.S. "The EPISTLE Text-Critiquing System." *IBM Systems Journal* 21 (3) 1982. (See also, Miller, 1982) .

Heim, Michael. "Electric Language: A Philosophical Study of Word Processing at the New Republic." *New Republic* 2/22/88.

Heines, Jesse M. *Screen Design Strategies for Computer Assisted Instruction.* Bedford, Mass.: Digital Press, 1984: Chapter 7, "CAI Style," 131–42.

Hemingway, Kathleen. "Psychological Issues in the Use of Icons in Command Menus." In *Human Factors in Computer Systems Proceedings*, March 1982. Gaithersburg, MD: ACM, 1982.

Hernandez, Maria and Wilder, Beverly L. "Usability Testing: A Tool for the Technical Writer." In *Proceedings of the 31st International Technical Communication Conference, May 1984.* Washington, DC: Society for Society for Technical Communication, 1984: WE-141–3.

Highet, Gilbert. "The Survival of the Records." In *The Light of the Past: A Treasury of Horizon.* NY: American Heritage Press, 1967: 257–74. (Also makes the point that with the change of format from scrolls to codexs, many classic works were permanently lost because they were not copied over to the new format.)

Hiltz, S. R. and Turoff, Murray. "Human Diversity and Choice of Interface: A Challenge." In *Proceedings of the Conference on Easier and More Productive Use of Computer Systems, Part II: Human Interaction and the User Interface, SIGSOC Bulletin.* 13, January 1982: 125–30.

Holden, Norman and Winter, Daniel D. "Creating Better Examples for Computer Manuals." In *Proceedings of the 31st International Technical Communication Conference, May 1984.* Washington, DC: Society for Society for Technical Communication, 1984: WE-44–6.

Holder, Wayne. "Software Tools for Writers." *Byte* 27 (7) July 1982: 138–63.

Holmes, Lyndon S. "What's New With Retrieval Technology" In *Microsoft CD-ROM 1989-1990 Yearbook.* compiled by Salley Oberlin and Joyce Cox. Redmond, WA: Microsoft Press, 1989: 299–302.

Horn, Robert. "Results with Structured Writing Using the Information; Mapping Writing Service Standards." In *Designing Usable Texts. edited* by Thomas M. Duffy and Robert Waller. Orlando, FL: Academic Press, 1985: 179–212.

_____. *How to Write Information Mapping.* Lexington, Mass.: Information Resources, Inc. 1969.

_____."Structured Writing and Text Design." In *The Technology of Text: Principles for Structuring, Designing, and Displaying Text.* edited by David Jonassen. Englewood Cliffs, NJ: Educational Press, 1982.

_____. and John N. Kelley. "Structured Writing: An Approach to the Documentation of Computer Software." *Asterisk* 7 (4) July 1981: 4–25. To join *SIGDOC* write to ACM PO Box 12115, Church Street Station, NY 10249.

Horton, William. "Horton's Laws." *Dateline Houston* (newsletter of the Houston chapter of the Society for Technical Communication) February 1984 (a) .

_____."Look Me in the Eye When You Write That: How to Put the User in User's Guides."In *Proceedings of 31st the International Technical Communication Conference, May 1984.* Washington, DC: Society for Technical Communication, 1984 (b) : WE-196–9.

_____. "Myths of Online Documentation."*Proceedings of the 35th International Technical Communication Conference, May 10-13, 1988.* Philadelphia, PA. Washington, DC: Society for Technical Communication, 1988: ATA-43–6.

_____."Toward the Four Dimensional Page." In *Proceedings of the International Technical Communications Conference 1983.* Washington, DC: Society for Society for Technical Communication, 1983: RFT-83–6.

_____. "Writing Online Documentation." The Wired Word column. *Technical Communication* 36 (2) 1989: 152–3.

_____. *Designing and Writing Online Documentation: Help Files to Hypertext.* NY: John Wiley and Sons, 1990.

Houghton, Raymond C. "Online Help Systems: A Conspectus." *Communications of the ACM* 27 (2) February 1984: 126–33.

Houghton-Alico, Doann. *Creating Computer Software Documentation User Guides: From Manuals to Menus.* NY: McGraw-Hill , 1985: 3.

Houze, William. "Today's Technical Writing Editors in Tomorrow's 'Electronic Mega-Cottage Industry' World of Work: Will They Survive." *Proteus: A Journal of Ideas* 1 (1) 1983: 23–8.

Hubbard, Scott E. and Willoughby, Michael. "Testing Documentation: A Practical Approach." In *Proceedings of the 32rd International Technical Communication Conference Proceedings.* Washington, DC: Society for Technical Communication 1985: WE-41–4.

Hughes Aircraft Company. *STOP: How To Achieve Coherence in Proposals and Reports.* Fullerton, CA: Hughes Aircraft Company, 1964.

Hulme, Charles. "Reading: Extracting Information from Printed and Electronically Presented Text." In *Fundamentals of Human-Computer Interaction.* edited by Andrew Monk. London: Academic Press, 1984: 35–46.

Human Factors Society. *ANSI/HFS 100-1988, American National Standard for Human Factors Engineering of Visual Display Terminal Workstations.* Human Factors Society, 1988.

Hurd, John. "Writing Online Help." In *Proceedings of the 29th International Technical Communication Conference, May 1982.* Washington, DC: Society for Society for Technical Communication, 1982: WE-151–4.

Hurly, Paul; Laucht, Matthias; and Hlynka, Denis. *The Videotex and Teletext Handbook: Home and Office Communication Using Microcomputers and Terminals.* NY: Harper and Row, 1985.

Huston, Kathy Simmons and Sherry Southard, "Organization: The Essential Element in Producing Usable Software Manuals." *Technical Communication* 35 (3) Third Quarter 1985: 168–71.

IBM. *Designing Task-Oriented Libraries For Programming Products*. Poughkeepsie, NY: IBM Third Edition 1983, Order No. ZC28-2525-2.

IEEE Standard for Software User Documentation. NY: Institute of Electrical and Electronics Engineers, 1988 (IEEE, Std 1063–1987) (see also, Miller, 1988).

ISO (International Organization for Standardization) 6592, *Information Processing—Guidelines for the Documentation of Computer-based Application Systems* (1st Edition, 1985).

_____. 8879, *Information Processing-Text and Office Systems-Standard Generalized Markup Language (SGML)*, Ref. No ISO 8879-1986.

Institute for Computer Sciences and Technology. *Guidelines for Documentation of Computer Programs and Automated Data Systems. National Bureau of Standards* (DOC) Washington, DC. Federal Information Processing Standards Publication, February 1976. (Available from Superintendent of Documents, U.S. Government Printing Office, Washington, DC 20402. SD Catalog No. C13.52:38; Stock No. 003003-01580-6.)

International Documentary Association. 8489 West 3rd Street, Los Angeles, California 90048.

International Paper Company. *Pocket Pal*. NY: International Paper Company, 1983.

Ives, Blake, and Olson, Margrethe H. "User Involvement and MIS Success: A Review of Research." *Management Science*. 30 (5) May 1984: 586–603.

Jackson, Richard. "Television Text: First Experience with a New Medium." In *Processing of Visible Language, Vol. 1*. edited by P. A. Kolers, M. E. Wrolstad, and H. Bouma. NY: Plenum Press, 1979: 479–90.

James, E. B. "The User Interface: How May We Compute." In *Computing Skills and the User Interface*. edited by M. J. Coombs and J. L. Alty. London: Academic Press, 1981.

James, Geoffrey [see also Sickler]. "Artificial Intelligence and Document Processing" In *Proceedings of the Fifth International Conference on System Documentation, 8-11 June 1986, University of Toronto*. NY: Association for Computing Machinery, 1986: 8–12.

_____. *Document Databases: The New Publications Methodology*. NY: Van Nostrand Reinhold, 1985.

Johnson, James, R. *The Software Factory: Managing Software Development and Maintenance*. Wellesley, MA: QED Information Sciences, 1989: "Chapter 3, Code Generators:" 37–44.

Johnson, Laura. "Faster Than a Speeding XCMD." *MacUser* 5 (5) 1989: 205.

Jonassen, David H. (ed.) *The Technology of Text: Principles for Structuring, Designing, and Displaying Text*. Englewood Cliffs, NJ: Educational Technology, 1982 (a).

_____. "Advanced Organizers in Text." In *The Technology of Text*. edited by David Jonassen. Englewood Cliffs, NJ: Educational Technology, 1982: 253–73 (b).

Jones, Henry W. III. "What, Me Warranty?" In *Microsoft CD-ROM 1989-1990 Yearbook*. compiled by Salley Oberlin and Joyce Cox. Redmond, WA: Microsoft Press, 1989: 451–7.

Jones, Tricia. "Incidental Learning During Information Retrieval: A Hypertext Experiment." *ICCAL*, May 9-11, Richardson Texas.

Jordan, Daniel S, Russell, Daniel M., Jensen, Anne-Marie S., and Rogers, Russell A. "Facilitating the Development of Representations in Hypertext with IDE." In *Hypertext "89 Proceedings, November 5-8, 1989, Pittsburgh, PA*. NY: ACM 1989 (Order number 608891): 93–104.

Jong, Steven F. "Documenting The New Computers." In *Proceedings of the 31st International Technical Communication Conference, May 1984*. Washington, DC: Society for Society for Technical Communication, 1984: ATA-22-6.

Joscelyne, Andrew. "Documentation at BMW: The Owner's Manual." *Electric Word* March/April 1989: 22–5.

Judd, Karen. *Copyediting: A Practical Guide.* Los Altos, CA: William Kaufmann, 1982.

Kantrowitz, Michael. "What Price Technical Editing? Phase One Reaching a Lay Audience." *IEEE Transactions on Professional Communication* PC-28 (1): 13–9. (He offers the following table to suggest how much time it takes to perform several parts of the Levels of Edit: Substantive—3.0 Minutes Per Page; Integrity—2.5 Minutes Per Page; Mechanical—1.0 Minutes Per Page; Part of Language—1.5 Minutes Per Page; Format—1.0 Minutes Per Page.)

Kaplan, Robert B. "Cultural Thought Patterns in Inter-Cultural Education." *Language Learning* 16 1966): 1–20.

Kay, Alan, "'The Grand Old Man' *Psychology Today* Conversation with Alan Kay." *Psychology Today* December 1983: 51.

_____. "Computer Software." *Scientific American* 251 (3) September 1984: 53–9.

Kearsley, G. and Hunter, B. "Electronic Education." *High Technology* April 1983: 38–44. Chumminess receives negative reviews from users.

_____. *Online Help Systems: Design and Implementation.* Norwood, NJ: Ablex,1988.

Kehler, T. P. and Barnes, M. "Design for an Online Consultative System." *Association for Educational Data Systems Journal* 14, 1981: 113–27.

Keifer, Kathleen. "Improving Student's Revising and Editing; The Writer's Workbench System." In *The Computer in Composition Instruction: A Writer's Tool.* edited by William Wrensch. Urbana, IL: National Council of Teachers of English, 1984.

Kelley, Thomas. (Sales Manager, Documentation Resources Inc.,) 1984 presentation to the Phoenix Chapter of the Society for Technical Communication, April 7, 1984.

Kellogg, Ronald T. "Idea Processors: Computer Aids for Planning and Composing Text." In *Computer Writing Environments: Theory, Research, and Design.* edited by Bruce K. Britton and Shawn M. Glynn. Hillsdale, NJ: Lawrence Erlbaum Associates, 1989 :57–92.

_____. "Attentional Overload and Writing Performance: Effects of Rough Draft and Outline Strategies." *Journal of Experimental Psychology: Learning, Memory, and Cognition.* 14 (2) 1988: 355–65.

Lelley, Lou. *From Dialogue to Discourse.* Glenview, Il, 1972.

Kelly, Derek A. *Documenting Computer Application Systems: Concepts and Techniques.* NY: Petrocelli Books, 1983: 40.

Kelly, G. A. *The Psychology of Personal Constructs.* NY: Norton, 1955: 8.

Kemeny, J. G. *The Accident at Three Mile Island.* Report of the Presidents Commission, October 1979.

Kennedy, David L. *How to Buy Printing.* Washington, DC: Society for Technical Communication, 1980.

Kern, Richard. "Modeling Users and Their Use of Technical Manuals." In *Designing Usable Texts.* edited by Thomas M. Duffy and Robert Waller. Orlando, FL: Academic Press, 1985.

Kieras, David E. "An Advanced Computerized Aid for the Writing of Comprehensible Technical Documents." In *Computer Writing Environments: Theory, Research, and Design.* edited by Bruce K. Britton and Shawn M. Glynn. Hillsdale, NJ: Lawrence Erlbaum Associates, 1989: 143–68.

_____. and Bovair, Susan. "The Role of a Mental Model in Learning to Operate a Device." *Cognitive Science* (8) 1984: 255–73.

_____. and _____. *The Role of a Mental Model in Learning to Operate a Device* (Technical Report No. 13) Tucson, AZ: University of Arizona, Department of Psychology, 1983.

Killingsworth, M. J. and Jones, B. G. "Division of Labor or Integrated Teams: A Crux in the Management of Technical Communication." *Technical Communication* 36 (3) 1989) 210–21.

Kirsch, John. "Trends in the Emerging Profession of Technical Communication." In *The Society of Text: Hypertext, Hypermedia, and the Social Construction of Information.* edited by Edward Barrett. Cambridge, MA: MIT Press, 1989: 209–34.

Kleid, Naomi A. "IBM's Information Quality Measurement Program." In *Proceedings of the International Technical Communications Conference, 1984*. Washington, DC: Society for Technical Communication, 1984: MPD-62-5.

Klein, Fred. "International Technical Communication" continuing column in *Technical Communication*—see for more on multinational audiences and computer documentation.

Kleper, Michael L. T*he Illustrated Handbook of Desktop Publishing and Typesetting*. Blue Ridge Summit, PA: TAB Books, 1987.

Knapp, Joan T. "A New Role for the Technical Communicator: Member of a Design Team." In *Proceedings of the 31st Annual Technical Communications Conference, May 1984*. Washington, DC: Society for Technical Communication, 1984: WE-30-3.

Kraft, Philip. Programmers and Managers: *The Routinization of Computer Programming in the United States*. NY: Springer-Verlag, 1977. This book contains a very interesting criticism of standard methodologies claiming that they are really a process of "deskilling." "[Deskilling is] a deliberate effort to transform work made up of separate but interdependent tasks into a larger number of simpler routine and unrelated tasks. Such routinized subtasks can be parceled out to workers who do only one, or at most, a few, of them over, and over, and nothing else. Such workers obviously need less skill than the workers who performed all the tasks of the more complex original work." (See also van Oss, 1984 and a cartoon in Gaines and Shaw, 1984: 91.)

Krull, Robert. "Communicative Functions of Icons as Computer Commands." In *Transactions of the IEEE Professional Communication Society, October 16-18, 1985. Williamsburg, VI*. NY: IEEE, 1985: 207-10.

_____. "If Icon, Why Can't You." In *Effective Documentation: What We Have Learned from Research*. edited by Stephen Doheny-Farina. Cambridge, MA: MIT Press, 1988: 255-73.

_____. and Rubens, Philip. "Effects of Color Highlighting on User Performance with Online Information," *Technical Communication* 33 (4) 1986: 268-9.

Krupp, Marguerite. "The Technical Writing Game." In *Proceedings of the 26th International Technical Communication Conference, 1979*. Washington, D.C.: Society for Technical Communication, 1979.

Lambert, Steve and Ropiequet, Suzanne *CD-ROM: The New Papyrus* Redmond, WA: Microsoft Press, 1986.

Lanham, Richard. *Revising Business Prose*. NY: Macmillan.

_____. *Self-teaching Exercise Book, Revising Business Prose*. NY: Macmillan.

_____. Videotape Presentation of *Revising Business Prose*. NY: Macmillan.

_____. *Style: An Anti-Textbook*. New Haven, CT: Yale University Press.

Laudauer, Thomas K. "Relations Between Cognitive Psychology and Computer System Design." In *Interfacing Thought: Cognitive Aspects of Human-Computer Interaction. edited by* John M. Carroll. Cambridge, MA: MIT Press, 1987: 1-25.

Laurillard, Diana (ed.) *Interactive Media: Working Methods and Practical Applications*. NY: John Wiley and Sons (Halsted Press) 1987.

Lawson, Patricia. "Job Aids: Give The Readers What They Want." In *Proceedings of the 35th International Technical Communication Conference, May 10-13, 1988*. Philadelphia, PA. Washington, DC: Society for Technical Communication, 1988: 339-42.

Ledgard, H.; Singer, A.; and Whiteside, J. *Directions in Human Factors for Interactive Systems Volume 103 of Lecture Notes in Computer Science*. edited by G. Goo and J. Hartmanis. NY: Springer-Verlag, 1981.

Lee, Robert and Misiorowski, Robert. *Script Models: A Handbook for the Media Writer*. NY: Hastings House, 1978.

Lefferts, Robert. *How To Prepare Charts and Graphs for Effective Reports*. NY: Barnes and Noble Books, 1981.

Lehner, P. E. and Zirk, D. A. "Cognitive Factors in User/Expert-System Interaction." *Human Factors* 29 (1) 1987: 97-109.

Lenfest, David. "On Language, Liability, and Documentation." In *Proceedings of the International Technical Communications Conference, May 1984.* Washington, DC: Society for Technical Communication, 1984: WE-180-3.

Lewis, Elaine. "Design Principles for Pictorial Information." In *Effective Documentation: What We Have Learned from Research.* edited by Stephen Doheny-Farina. Cambridge, MA: MIT Press, 1988: 235-53.

Lindgaard, G., Chessari, J., and Ihsen, E. "Icons in Telecommunications: What Makes Pictorial Information Comprehensible to the User." *Australian Telecom Research* 21 (2) 1987: 17-29.

Lipson, Steve and Robert Forlenza, "CASE Technology and the Emperor's New Clothes." *American Programmer* 1 (6) August 1988: 12-3, 15.

Little, Raymond and Smith, Michael. "Improving FOMM Troubleshooting." *Technical Communication* First Quarter, 1983: 22-4 (Part of a Special Section on FOMM—three articles, *Technical Communication* Third Quarter, 1985: 6-13.)

Lori, Donald E. (Technical Consultant with Control Data Corporation's NOS/VE Online Manual System). Personal communication 1985.

Lufkin. "Current Trends in Technical Translation." In *Proceedings of the 1989 IEEE Professional Communication Society Conference, Garden City, NY, October 1989.* NY: IEEE, 1989: 238-43.

Lundstrom, David E. *A Few Good Men from Univac.* Cambridge, MA: MIT Press, 1988.

Lutz, Jean. "Hardware and Software Constraints on On-line Composing and Editing." A paper presented at the College Composition and Communication Conference, NY City, March 30, 1984.

MacDonald-Ross, M. "Language in Texts." In *Review of Research in Education.* edited by L. S. Shulman. Itasca, IL: Peacock, 1979.

Macindoe, C. Scott. "An Assessment of Functionally Oriented Maintenance Manuals (FOMMs) *Technical Communication*, 32(3) Third Quarter, 1985) 7-11.

Mack, Karin and Skjei, Eric. *Overcoming Writer's Block.* Los Angeles, CA: J.P. Tarcher, 1979.

Magers, C. S. "An Experimental Evaluation of Online HELP for Non-Programmers."In *Conference Proceedings of the SIGCHI (Human Factors in Computing Systems) 1983* NY: Association for Computing Machinery, 1983: 277-81.

Major, John H. "What Should You Write: A User's Guide, Tutorial, Reference Manual, or Standard Operating Procedure." *Technical Communication* 36 (2) 1989: 130-5.

Mantei, Marilyn M.,.*Disorientation Behavior in Person-Computer Interaction.* Doctoral Dissertation. Computer Science Dept., University of Southern California, University Microfilms, 1982

_____. and Toerey, Toby J. "Cost/Benefit Analysis for Incorporating Human Factors in the Software Lifecycle." *Communications of the ACM* 31 (4) April 1988: 428-39.

"Manual Madness" in the "Readers' Forum" *Datamation* 27 (3) March 1981: 266.

Manz, Roberta B. "Detailed Planning for User Publications." In *Proceedings of the Second International Conference on System Documentation, April 28-30, 1983, Seattle, Washington.* NY: Association for Computing Machinery, 1984: 61-81.

Marchionini, G. and Shneiderman, B. "Finding Facts vs. Browsing Knowledge in Hypertext Systems." *IEEE Computer* 21 (1) January 1988: 70-80.

Marcus, Stephen. "Real-time Gadgets with Feedback: Special Effects in Computer-Assisted Writing." *The Writing Instructor.* Summer 1983. "One of the greatest difficulties of word processing is overcoming the urge for local editing."

_____. "The Host in the Machine: Decorum in Computers Who Speak." *IEEE Transactions on Professional Communication.* PC-28 (2) 1985: 29-33.

Mares, G. C. *The History of the Typewriter, Successor to the Pen: An Illustrated Account of the Origin, Rise, and Development of the Writing Machine.* London: Gilbert Putnam, 1909. (Reprinted Arcadia, CA: Post-era Books, 1985.)

Margolis, Neal. "Making the Manual Work: Techniques for Validating Computer Documentation." *Performance and Instruction.* July 1989: 1–9.

_____. "More Tips On How To Evaluate Your User's Manual." *InfoWorld.* March 25, 1983.

_____. "Responsible Documentation." *Computerworld.* 167, January 25, 1982.

_____. "Stalking A Quality Manual In Documentation Jungle." The first of a five-part series on user documentation that appeared in *InfoWorld* from March 21, 1983 (5 (12)) to April 18, 1983 (5 (16)). See also "Technical Writers Are the Armpit of the Industry." *InfoWorld.* 4 (17) May 3, 1982, and the special *InfoWorld* issue of August 30, 1982 on the "Documentation Debate."

Marshall, Chris, Nelson, Catherine, and Gardiner, Margaret M. "Design Guidelines." In *Applying Cognitive Psychology to User-Interface Design.* edited by Margret M. Gardiner and Bruce Christie NY: John Wiley and Sons, 1987: 221–78.

Martin, James. *Design of Man-Computer Dialogues.* Englewood Cliffs, NJ: Prentice-Hall, 1973.

_____. *End-User's Guide to Data Base.* Englewood Cliffs, NJ: Prentice-Hall, Inc. 1981.

Martin, Marilyn. "The Visual Hierarchy of Documents."In *Proceedings of the 36th International Technical Communication Conference, Chicago, Illinois, May 14-17, 1989.* Washington, DC: Society for Technical Communication, 1989: VC-32-5.

Mathes, J. C. and Stevenson, Dwight W. *Designing Technical-Reports.* Indianapolis, IN: Bobbs Merrill, 1976.

Mathur, Ashok, "Coping with the Coming Shakeout in the CD-ROM Business." In *Microsoft CD-ROM 1989-1990 Yearbook.* compiled by Salley Oberlin and Joyce Cox. Redmond, WA: Microsoft Press, 1989: 627–30.

Matthies, Leslie A. *The Systems Manual.* Colorado Springs, CO: Systemation, Inc., 1976: Chapter 6, "Producing Manuals."

_____. *The New Playscript Procedure, Management Tool For Action.* Stamford, Conn.: Office Publications Inc., 1977. (See also the contemporary work and writing on "Playwrite," by J. Richard Fleming which is computerized version of "Playscript" and includes some new innovations.)

Mau, Earnest. *The Free-lance Writer's Survival Manual.* Chicago, Ill.:Contemporary Books, 1981.

Maynard, John. "A User-Driven Approach to Better User Manuals." *IEEE Transactions on Professional Communication.* PC-25 (41) March 1982: 216–9.

McAustin, Rita and Armstrong, Gail. "Using a Team Approach for Better Documentation."In *Proceedings of the 31st Annual Technical Communications Conference, May 1984.* Washington, DC: Society for Technical Communication, 1984: VC-36–9.

McGrew, P. C. and McDaniel. *On-line Text Management: Hypertext and Other Techniques.* NY: McGraw-Hill, 1989.

McKay, Lucia. Soft Words, *Hard Words, A Common Sense Guide to Creative Documentation.* Culver City, CA: Ashton-Tate, 1984: 104.

McKinley, Lawrence C. "Managing for User-Friendly Publications." In *Proceedings of the Second International Conference on System Documentation, April 28-30, 1983, Seattle, Washington.* NY: Association of Computing Machinery, 1984: 74–81.

McLuhan, Marshall. *Counterblast.* NY: Harcourt Brace Jovanovich, 1969: 22.

McWilliams, Peter A. (a) *Questions and Answers on Word Processing.* Los Angeles, Ca.: Prelude Press, 1983 (a). For a good example of the mismatch of MIS language with users, read the entire series of Doonesbury "The Reverend Sloan Goes To Buy A Word Processor."

_____. (b) *The Word Processing Book: A Short Course In Computer Literacy.* Los Angeles: Prelude Press, 1983 (b).

Mehlenbacher, Brad., Duffy, Thomas M., and Palmer, Jim. "Finding Information on a Menu: Linking Menu Organization to the User's Goals." November 20, 1988, reported prpared for the US Army, Human Engineering Laboratory, Aberdeen Proving Grounds, MD under contract DAAA1-86-K-0019.

Mehlmann, Marilyn. *When People Use Computers: An Approach to Developing an Interface.* Englewood Cliffs, NJ: Prentice-Hall, 1981.

Merkin, M. "In Love with Lisa." *Creative Computing* October 1983: 12-7.

Merrill, P. F. "Displaying Text on Microcomputers." In *The Technology of Text.* edited by David H. Jonassen. Englewood Cliffs, NJ: Educational Technology, 1982.

Meyer, B.J.F. "Text Structure and Its Use In The Study of Reading Comprehension Across The Adult Life Span." Paper presented at the Annual Meeting of the American Educational Research Association, Boston, April 7-11, 1980.

Meyer, R. E. "Can Advanced Organizers Influence Meaningful Learning?" *Review of Educational Psychology* (49) 1979 : 371-81.

Meyers, M. T. and Meyers, G. E. *Managing by Communication.* NY: McGraw-Hill, 1982: Chapter 8, "Group Communication Processes and Decision Making."

Meyrowitz, Norman. "The Missing Link: Why Wr're All Doing Hypertext Wrong." In *Microsoft CD-ROM 1989-1990 Yearbook.* compiled by Salley Oberlin and Joyce Cox. Redmond, WA: Microsoft Press, 1989:107-14.

"Microsoft Office Compact Disc." *MacUser* 5 (9) September 1989: 49

Military Standardization Handbook, *Functionally Oriented Maintenance Manual (FOMM) Writers Guide for MIL-M-24100B* (MIL-HDBK-242) October 25, 1974. Available from Department of Navy, Naval Publications and Forms Center, 5801 Tabor Avenue, Philadelphia PA,19120

Miller, Diane F. *Guide for Preparing Software User Documentation.* Washington, DC: Society for Technical Communications, 1988.

Miller, George A. "The Magical Number Seven, Plus or Minus Two: Some Limits on Our Capacity for Processing Information." *Psychological Review.* 63 (2) 1956: 81-97. See also Chase, 1973. Chase and Simon have challenged Miller and said that the real capacity of short-term human memory is 5 plus or minus 1.

Miller, L. A., Heidorn, G. E., and Jensen, K. "Text Critiquing with the EPISTLE System: An Author's Aid To Better Syntax." In *Tutorial: End User Facilities in the 1980's.* edited by James Larson. NY: IEEE, 1982.

Mills, Carol Bergfeld and Dye, Kenneth L. "Usability Testing: User Reviews." *Technical Communication* 32 (4) 1985: 40-4.

Mingione, Al. "Iteration, Key to Useful Documentation." *Journal of Systems Management* January 1983: 23-5.

Minsky, Marvin . *The Society of Mind.* NY: Simon & Schuster, 1985.

Mirel, Barbara. "The Politics of Usability: The Organizational Functions of an In-House Manual." In *Effective Documentation: What We Have Learned from Research.* edited by Stephen Doheny-Farina. Cambridge, MA: MIT Press, 1988: 277-97.

Mitchell, Gem,"Task Analysis (Need to Know: The Way to Go)."In *The Proceedings of the 31st International Technical Communication Conference, May 1984.* Washington, DC: Society for Technical Communication, 1984: WE-84-5.

Mitchell, Georgina E. "Need to Know: Bringing Task Analysis to the People Who Need It—Writers!" In *The Proceedings of the 30th International Technical Communication Conference, May 1983.* Washington, DC: Society for Technical Communication, 1983: WE-102-3.

Mohr-Callahan, Virginia . "Making the Switch to 'Designer' Documents." In *First Annual AT&T Customer Documentation Symposium, October 19, 1988, AT&T Bell Laboratories-Holmdel* (700076): 159-64.

Monday Night Software, *S.O.S. (Simple Operator Service)* Glendale, CA, 1981.

Monk, Andrew (ed.). *Fundamentals of Human-Computer Interaction.* London: Academic Press, 1984.

Moore, Mary Ann, Eyre, Joseph M., and Rideout, Thomas B."Testing Software Installation Procedures: An Integrated Approach." In *Proceedings of the 33rd International Technical Communication Conference Proceedings.* Washington, DC: Society for Technical Communication 1986: 377–80.

Morgan, Chris. "What's Wrong with Technical Writing Today?"*Byte* 7 (12) December 1980: 294.

Mozeico, Howard. "A Human/Computer Interface to Accommodate User Learning Stages."In *Tutorial: End User Facilities in the 1980's.* edited by James A. Larson. NY: IEEE, 1982.

Murch, Gerald M. "Using Color Effectively: Designing to Human Specifications," *Technical Communication* 32 (4) 1985: 14–20.

Muter, P., Latremouille, S. A., Treuniet, W. C., and Beam, P. "Extended Reading of Continuous Text on Television Screens." *Human Factors* 24 (5) 1982: 501–8.

Myers, D. "The Patterns of Player-Game Relationships: A Study of Computer Game Players."*Simulation and Games* 15 (2) June 1984: 159–85.

Naisbitt, John. *Megatrends: Ten New Direction Transforming Our Lives.* NY: Warner Books, 1984: Chapter 2 "From Forced Technology to High Tech/High Touch."

National Semiconductor. "1984 MCS Technical Publications Productivity."(from 6/82 to 6/83) private correspondence.

NaviEXT SAM (hypertext interface to the 1986 Smith and Mosier human factors guidelines) Northern Lights Software, 1407-7 Beacon Street, Brookline, MA 02146.

Neal, A. S. and Simons, R. M. "Playback: A Method for Evaluating the Usability of Software and Its Documentation." *IBM Systems Journal* 23 (1) 1984: 82–96.

Nielsen, Jakob. "Hypertext II." *SIGCHI Bulletin* 21 (2) October 1989: 41–7.

_____. "Hyperhyper: Developments Across the Field of Hypermedia–A Mini trip Report: BCS Workshop, London, UK, 23, February 1989." *SIGCHI Bulletin* 21 (1) July 1989: 65–7.

_____. "Trip Report: International conference on Fifth Generation Computer Systems 1988, Tokyo, Japan, 28 November-2 December 1988." *SIGCHI Bulletin* 21 (1) July 1989: 68–71.

_____. The Matters that Really Matter for Hypertext Usability." In *Hypertext "89 Proceedings, November 5–8, 1989, Pittsburgh, PA.* NY: ACM 1989 (Order number 608891): 239–48.

Nelson, Ted *The Literary Machine and Computer Lib/Dream Machines.* Redmond, Washington: Microsoft Press, 1987 (revised edition of 1974 book) (see also Rheingold, 1985).

Neurirth, Christine M. and Kaufer, David S. "The Role of External Representations in the Writing Process: Implications for the Design of Hypertext-based Writing Tools." In *Hypertext "89 Proceedings, November 5–8, 1989, Pittsburgh, PA.* NY: ACM 1989 (Order number 608891): 319–41.

Newman, W. M. and Sproull, R. F. *Principles of Interactive Computer Graphics* (2nd Ed.) NY: McGraw-Hill, 1979.

Newsweek. "Instant Buzzword Generator." May 6, 1968.

Nickerson, R. S. "Some Characteristics of Conversations." In *Man-Computer Interaction: Human Factors Aspects of Computers and People.* edited by B. Shackel. Alphen and den Rijn, Netherlands: Sijthoff and Noordhoff, 1981.

Norman, Donald. "Cognitive Engineering—Cognitive Science." In *Interfacing Thought: Cognitive Aspects of Human-Computer Interaction.* edited by John M. Carroll. Cambridge, MA: MIT Press, 1987, 325–36

_____ *The Psychology of Everyday Things.* NY: Basic Books, 1988.

O'Neal, Milton. *Guidelines To Art Without An Art Director.* NY: American Business Press, 1983): 1.

O'Rourke, John, *Writing for the Reader.* Maynard, MA: Digital Equipment Co., 1976. Reprinted in *Personal Computer Documenter's Guide.* Maynard, MA: Digital Equipment Co., 1983.

Odescalchi, Esther Kando. "Productivity Gain Attained by Tasked Oriented Information." In *33rd International Technical Communication Conference Proceedings.* Washington, DC: Society for Technical Communication 1986: 359–62

The Office. "Study Finds Typeset Copy is Read Faster." (October 1984): 95. The most recent survey measuring the effectiveness of business documents was conducted by the researchers at Boston University [Project for Interdisciplinary Research in Information at the School of Public Communication]. The measurements were based on the subjective judgements of 300 professionals in the fields of management, communication, law, and public health. Among the other findings, the research study showed that:

- In judging professionalism, 78.7% preferred the typeset version over typewritten; 77.7% over dot matrix."

- Typesetting reduced reading time with no loss of comprehension.

- Typesetting like that used for books, newspapers and magazines increased the average reading speed for a two-page memo from 10 to 27% over the reading speeds for either dot matrix or typewritten versions. For a longer document, the increase in reading speed ranged from three to 20%.

- When judging readability, 85.1% preferred typeset documents.

Owens, Peter. "Review of Thinktank and PromptDoc: Software That Takes the Pain Out Of Structuring Your Writing." *Popular Computing* 3 (6) April 1984: 186–9.

Pakin, Sandra and Associates. *Sandra Pakin and Associates Folio.* (now retitled *Journal of Documentation Project Management* is available from them at 6007 N. Sheridan Road, Chicago, IL 60660.):

"Conducting a Field Test." Winter 1980.

"Developing a Document Schedule." Fall 1982.

"Documentation Project Scheduling." Fall 1982.

"Efficient Information Gathering." Spring 1984.

"Field Testing." Winter 1980.

"Getting the Most Out of Your Reviewers." Summer 1981.

"Graphics Improve Readability." Spring 1979.

"Learning to Think Graphically." Spring 1979.

"Modular Documentation Planning." Spring/Summer 1980.

"Planning and Effective Review." Summer 1981.

"Preparing and Index." Winter 1978.

"Preparing for Updates." Spring 1979.

"Production Control Forms." Spring 1979.

"Production Control." Spring 1979.

"Project Coordinator Provides Development Control." Summer 1983.

"Promoting Internal Systems with a Simple Brochure." Fall 1977.

"Providing an Audit Trail for Documentation." Winter 1981.

"Providing an Audit Trail for Documentation." Winter 1981.

"Reducing Documentation Costs." Spring 1983.

"Reference Aids." Winter 1978.

"Reference Cards." Fall 1980.

"Spot Art Provides Visual Punctuation." Fall 1980.

"What Motivates Documentation Professionals," and "Survey Comments," Fall 1989

"Technical Guidelines for Producing a Brochure." Fall 1977.

"Turning Photos Into Illustrations for Your User's Guides." Spring 1978.

"Using Photographs for In-house Publications." Summer 1979.

"Why Johnny Can't Document." Fall 1981.

"Writing Plans." Spring 1978.

_____ *Documentation Development Methodology.* NY: Prentice-Hall, 1983.

Pakin, Sherwin, and Wrey Paul. "Designing Screens for People to Use Easily." *Data Management* 1982 reprint.

Palermo, D. "More about Less: A Study of Comprehension." *Journal of Verbal Learning and Verbal Behavior* (12) 1973: 211–21.

Palme, J. "A Human-Computer Interface Encouraging User Growth." In *Designing for Human-Computer Communication.* edited by M. E. Sime and M. J. Coombs. London: Academic Press, 1983.

Palmer, James E., Duffy, T., Gomoll, K., Gomoll, T., Trumble, J. and Richards-Palmquist, J. "The Design and Evaluation of Online Help for Unix Emacs: Capturing the User in Menu Design." Communications Design Center Technical Report 39, Pittsburgh, PA: Carnegie-Mellon University, Communications Design Center.

Palmer, P. A. "A Study Comparing the Effectiveness of a Contextual Menus versus a Textual Menu." In *Proceedings of the International Technical Communications Conference, Chicago, May 1986.* Washington, DC: Society for Technical Communication, 1986.

Parker, Roger C. *Looking Good in Print.* Chapel Hill, NC: Ventana Press, 1988.

Parunak, H. Van Dyke. "Hypermedia Topologies and User Navigation." In the Writing Process: Implications for the Design of Hypertext-based Writing Tools." In *Hypertext "89 Proceedings, November 5–8, 1989, Pittsburgh, PA.* NY: ACM 1989 (Order number 608891): 43–50.

Patterson, Diana. "Online Documents: Haystacks or Building Blocks." In *Proceedings of the International Technical Communications Conference, 1981.* Washington, DC: Society for Society for Technical Communication, 1981: A-59–63.

Penrose, John M. "Computer Software Review." *ABCA Bulletin* 47 (3) September 1984: 22–4.

Pepper, Jeff. "Following Students' Suggestions for Rewriting a Computer Programming Textbook." *American Educational Research Journal* 18 (3) Fall 1981: 259–69.

"Period Styles: A Punctuated History" In *Period Styles: A History of Punctuation* NY: Herb Lubalin Study Center of Design and Typography; the Cooper Union for the Advancement of Science and Art, 1988.

Perlman, Gary. "Asynchronous Design/Evaluation Methods for Hypertext Technology Development." In the Writing Process: Implications for the Design of Hypertext-based Writing Tools." In *Hypertext "89 Proceedings, November 5–8, 1989, Pittsburgh, PA.* NY: ACM 1989 (Order number 608891): 61–81.

Perron, Robert. "In Search of Disciplined Documentation." *Computerworld.* September 10, 1979, "In Depth" section.

Peters, Thomas. "The Mythology of Innovation, or A Skunkworks Tale Part II."*The Stamford Magazine.* Fall 1983: 11–9.

Peterson, David E. "Screen Design Guidelines." In *Tutorial: End User Facilities in the 1980's.* edited by James A. Larson. NY: IEEE, 1982.

Pierson, J. K., Forcht, Karen A., and Moates, William. "Factors Affecting Level of Documentation Required for User-Developed Applications." *IEEE Transactions on Professional Communication.* 31 (3): September 1988: 142–8.

Playwrite Seminars, System Planning Associates, Inc., Drawer B, Mountainside, NJ.

Pliskin, Nava. "Interacting with Electronic Mail Can be a Dream or a Nightmare: a User's Point of View." *Interacting with Computers: The Interdisciplinary Journal of Human-Computer Interaction* 1 (3) December 1989:259–72.

Plotnik, Arthur. *The Elements of Editing: A Modern Guide for Editors and Journalists.* NY: Macmillan, 1982.

Pogson, Geoff. "Whither CD-ROM?" *Electric Word* (16) November-December 1989: 44.

Potosnak, Kathleen. "What's Wrong with Standard User Interfaces?" *IEEE Software.* 5(5) September 1988: 91–2. (Reprinted in *SIGCHI Bulletin* 21 (1) July 1989: 14–6.

Prekeges, James. "Accurate Estimating and Scheduling: You Can Do It." In *Proceedings of the International Technical Communication Conference, May 11-14, 1986, Detroit, Michigan.* Washington, DC: Society for Technical Communication, 1986: 115–20.

Press, Larry. "Thoughts and Observations at the Microsoft CD-ROM Conference." *Communications of the ACM* 32 (7) July 1989: 784–8.

Pressey, S. L. "Basic Unresolved Teaching-machine Problems." *Theory Into Practice* (1) 1962: 30–7.

Price, Jonathan. *How to Write A Manual.: A Handbook of Software Documentation.* NY: Addison-Wesley, 1984.

Price, L. "Using Offline Documentation Online." *SIGSOC Bulletin.* (ACM) 13 (2-3) 1981: 15–20.

_____. "THUMB: An Interactive Tools for Accessing and Maintaining Text." *IEEE Transactions on Systems, Man, and Cybernetics.* SMC-12, March-April, 1982: 155–61.

Promptdoc. *A Writer's Handbook for Using FirstDraft.* Colorado Springs, CO, 1983.

Pugh, A. K. "The Development of Silent Reading." In *The Road to Effective Reading.* edited by W. Latham. London: Ward Lock, 1975.

Pugliese, Rosemary. "To Print or Not to Print: Choosing Alternative Media." In *Proceedings of the 31st Annual Technical Communications Conference, May 1984.* Washington, DC: Society for Technical Communication, 1984: WE-97–9.

QED Information Sciences. *The Annual CASE Survey.* Wellesley, MA: 1989.

QED Information Sciences. *CASE: The Potential and the Pitfalls.* Wellesley, MA, 1989.

Ramey, Judith "Product Support as a Form of Technical Communication." In *33rd International Technical Communication Conference Proceedings.* Washington, DC: Society for Technical Communication 1986: 99–101.

_____. "How People *Use* Computer Documentation: Implications for Book Design." In *Effective Documentation: What We Have Learned from Research.* edited by Stephen Doheny-Farina. Cambridge, MA: MIT Press, 1988.

Reid, P. "Work Station Design, Activities and Display Techniques." In *Fundamentals of Human-Computer Interaction.* edited by Andrew Monk. London: Academic Press, 1984: 117.

Reily, Betsy, A. and Slabbekorn, Morris H. "Productivity Improvements Through Computer Graphics: A Case Study." *Technical Communication* 34 (4) Fourth Quarter 1987: 257–63.

Relles, N. *The Design and Implementation of User-Oriented Systems.* Technical Report 357, Department of Computer Sciences, University of Wisconsin at Madison, July 1979.

_____. and Price, L.A. "A User Interface For Online Assistance." In *Proceedings of the 5th International Conference on Software Engineering.* San Diego, California, March 9-12, 1981. Los Alamitos, California: IEEE Computer Society Press 1981: 400–8.

_____.; Sondheimer, N.K.; and Ingargiola, G. P. "Recent Advances in User Assistance." In *Proceedings of the Conference on Easier and More Productive Use of Computer Systems, Part II: Human Interaction and the User Interface, SIGSOC Bulletin.* 13, January 1982: 125–30.

Renaldo, Lisa. "Prototypes: A Means to an End." *Proceedings of the International Technical Communication Conference, May 11-14, 1986, Detroit, Michigan.* Washington, DC: Society for Technical Communication, 1986: WE-163–5.

Reveaux, Tony. "A Mac of Many Colors." *MacUser* 5 (1) 1989: 97–145.

Reynolds, Linda. "Designing for New Communications Technologies: The Presentation of Computer-Generated Information." In *The Future of the Printed Word.* edited by Philip Hills. Westport, CN: Greenwood Press, 1980.

Rheingold, Howard. *Tools for Thought:: The People and Ideas Behind the Next Computer Revolution.* NY: Simon and Schuster, 1985.

Richier, D. and Thompson, K. "The UNIX Time-Sharing System." *Communications of the ACM* 17 (7) July 1974: 365–75.

Ridgeway, Lenore. "Information Display Screens." In *Proceedings of the 30th International Technical Communication Conference, May 1983.* Washington, DC: Society for Society for Technical Communication, 1983: ATA-18–21.

Robertson, C. K. and Akscyn, R. "Experimental Evaluations of Tools for Teaching the ZOG Frame Editor." Communications Design Center Technical Report. Pittsburgh, PA: Carnegie Mellon University, November 1982.

Roemer, J. M. and Chapanis, A. "Learning Performance and Attitudes as a Function of the Reading Level of a Computer-Presented Tutorial." In *Proceedings of the Conference on Human Factors in Computer Systems.* (Gaithersburg, Maryland, March 15-17, 1982) ACM, Washington, DC Chapter, 1982: 239–44.

Roman, David R. "Executives Who Love Their Computers." *Computer Decisions* January 1983.

Ropiequet, Suzanne, Einberger, John, and Zoellick, Bill (eds.) *CD-ROM, Volume 2: Optical Publishing.* Redmond, WA: Microsoft Press, 1987.

Rosch, W. "User Teach Thyself." *Personal Computing* 2, August 1983: 155–65.

Rosen, Sara and Furlow, Susan. "User Documentation: The New Approach." Paper presented at the 1983 Hewlett Packard 3000 International User's Group Conference.

Rosenbaum, Stephanie. "Documentation and User Interface Planning for Optical Information Systems." In *Proceedings of the Fifth International Conference on System Documentation, 8-11 June 1986, University of Toronto* NY: Association of Computing Machinery, 1986: 80–6.

Rosenthal, Steve. "Charles Bigelow: Zen and the Art of Onscreen Editing." *Electric Word* (16) November/December 1989: 15–6.

Rosenthal, Steve. "Computer-Suported Cooperative Work, or You + Them + Groupware." *Electric Word* (16) January/February 1990 46–9.

Roth, David M., Strehlo, Kevin. "Data on a Silver Platter." In *Microsoft CD-ROM 1989-1990 Yearbook.* compiled by Salley Oberlin and Joyce Cox. Redmond, WA: Microsoft Press, 1989: 15–20.

Roth, Steve. "Color Separation Explained." *Macworld* February 1989: 199–205.

——————. and Kvern, Olav, M. "Preview the All New PageMaker." *Publish!* March 1990: 47–55.

Rothenberg, J. "Online Tutorials and Documentation for the SIGMA Message Service." In *Proceedings of the AFIPS National Computer Conference (NY, June 4-7, 1979)* 48, AFIPS Press, Arlington, VI 1979: 863–7.

Rothkoph. E. Z. "Incidental Memory for Location of Information in Text." *Journal of Verbal Learning and Verbal Behavior* 10 (6) 1971: 608–13.

Rubens, Phillip"Online Information, Hypermedia, and the Idea of Literach." In *The Society of Text: Hypertext, Hypermedia, and the Social Construction of Information.* edited by Edward Barrett. Cambridge, MA: MIT Press, 1989: 3–21.

————. and Krull, Robert. "Application of Research on Document Design to Online Displays." *Technical Communication* 32 (4) 1985: 29–34.

Rubin, Martin (ed). *Documentation Standards and Procedures for Online Systems.* NY: Van Nostrand Reinhold, 1979.

Rubinstein, Richard. *Digital Typography: An Introduction to Type and Composition for Computer System Design.* Reading, MA: Addison-Wesley, 1988.

——————, and Hersch, Harry. *The Human Factor.* Burlington, MA: Digital Press, 1984.

Saar, Doreen Alvarez, "A Technical Writing Teacher Becomes a Technical Writer: Recollections on an IBM Experience." In *Linking Technology and Users, IEEE Professional Communication Conference Record, Charlotte, North Carolina, October 22-24, 1986.* NY: IEEE 1986: 131–4.

Sandberg-Diment, Erick. "On Computers" column, *New York Times* September 7, 1986 (a).

_____"A Tool Box for On-Screen Tutorials." *New York Times* August 31, 1986: F-11 (b).

Sander, Linda K. and Rischard, Susan I. "Automating the Newspaper Library with BASIS." *Proceedings of the 45th American Society for Information Annual Meeting, Columbus, Ohio, October 17-21, 1982.* White Plains, NY: Knowledge Industry Publications, Inc. 1982: 262–4.

Sanderlin, Stacey. "Preparing Manuals for Non-English Readers." *Proceedings of the 35th International Technical Communication Conference, May 10-13, 1988. Philadelphia, PA.* Washington, DC: Society for Technical Communication, 1988: RET-44–6.

Sandewall, E. "Programming in an Interactive Environment: the 'LISP' Experience." *Computer Surveys* 10 (1) March 1978: 35–71.

Sandler, C. "Coming Attractions: Learning by Video." *Personal Computing* 2, August 1983: 185–8.

Santarelli, Mary-Beth. "It's Not the Same Old 'Help' Anymore." *Software News.* April 1984: 45–6.

Savage, R. E.; Habinek, J. K.; and Barthart, T. W. "The Design, Simulation, and Evaluation of a Menu-Driven User Interface." In *Human Factors in Computer Systems Proceedings, March 1982. Gaithersburg, MD:* ACM, 1982.

"Sayonara, Structured Stuff." *American Programmer* 1 (6) August 1988: 1, 4–11.

Schneider, M. L. "Models for The Design Of Static Software User Assistance." In *Directions In Human/Computer Interaction.* edited by Albert Badre and Ben Shneiderman. Norwood, NJ: Ablex, 1982: 137–48.

Schriver, Karen A. "Designing Computer Documentation: A Review of the Relevant Literature." Communications Design Center, Technical Report No. 31. Pittsburgh, PA: Communications Design Center, Carnegie-Mellon University, 1986.

Schumacher, Gary and Robert Waller. "Testing Design Alternatives: A Comparison of Procedures." In *Designing Usable Texts.* edited by Thomas M. Duffy and Robert Waller. Orlando, FL: Academic Press, 1985: 377–403.

Seabrook, Richard H. C. and Schneiderman, Ben. "The User Interface in a Hypertext, Multiwindown Program Browser." *Interacting with Computers: The Interdisciplinary Journal of Human-Computer Interaction* 1 (3) December 1989:299–357.

Sederston, Candace. "Task Analysis: Applying Composition Theory in An Industrial Forum." In *The Proceedings of the 31st International Technical Communication Conference, May 1984.* Washington, DC: Society for Technical Communication, 1984: WE-89–92.

Seeing, Paul R. "Icons–Communication Tool or Decorative Art." In *Proceedings of the 1989 IEEE Professional Communication Society Conference, Garden City, NY, October 1989.* NY: IEEE, 1989: 142–6.

SGML Users' Group Bulletin, 17 Tanza Road, Hampstead, London NW3, 2UA, United Kingdom or *<TAG> The SGML Newsletter,* 105A Carpenter Dr. Sterling, VI 22170.

Shaughnessy, Mina A. *Errors and Expectations.* NY: Oxford University Press, 1977.

Shea, Tom. "Technical Writers Talk About Trials and Tribulations." *Infoworld.* August 30, 1982.

Shelton, J.A. "The Individual 'Work-to-Rules': Reducing Determinism in Taylor-made Expert Systems." *Interacting with Computers: The Interdisciplinary Journal of Human-Computer Interaction* 1 (3) December 1989:338–42.

Sherman, M. A. "Adjectival Negation and the Comprehension of Multiply Negated Sentences." *Journal of Verbal Learning and Verbal Behavior* 15 1976: 143–57.

hneiderman, Ben and Kearsley, Greg. *Hypertext Hands-On!: An Introduction to a New Way of Organizing and Accessing Information.* (Includes software for the IBM-PC–HyperTies demo) Reading, MA: Addison-Wesley, 1989.

_____. "Human Factors Experiments in Designing Interactive Systems." *Computer* 12 (12) December 1979: 9–19.

_____. "System Message Design: Guideline and Experimental Results." In *Directions in Human/Computer Interaction.* edited by A. Badre and Ben Shneiderman. Ablex, 1983.

_____. *Software Psychology.* NY: Winthrop, 1980.

_____. *Designing the User Interface: Strategies for Effective Human-Computer Interaction.* Addison-Wesley, 1987.

Shufelt, Kim. "Software Documentation Usability Testing." In *Proceedings of the 31st International Technical Communication Conference, May 1984.* Washington, DC: Society for Society for Technical Communication, 1984: MPD-30-3.

Shultz, George E. "A Method of Estimating Publication Costs." *Technical Communication* 34 (4) Fourth Quarter 1987: 219–24

Sickler [see also James], Geoffrey J. "Software Documentation as Software." In *Conference Proceedings of the International Conference on Systems Documentation January 22-23, 1982.* edited by Jay Barlett and John Walter. NY:. Association for Computing Machinery, 1982: 139–42.

Sides, Charles H. "What Does Jung Have To Do With Technical Communication." *Technical Communication* 36 (2) 1989: 119–26.

Silverstone, Stuart. "Information Anxiety." *Publish!* 4(9) September 1989: 31, 33.

Simpson, Amy, "Task Oriented Writing: Using Action Sentences To Get The Job Done." In *The Proceedings of the 33rd International Technical Communication Conference, May 1986.* Washington, DC: Society for Technical Communication, 1986: 447–8.

Simpson, Henry, and Casey, Steven M. *Developing Effective User Documentation: A Human-Factors Approach* (1987).

Simply Stated, "Using Icons As Communication." 75, September/October 1987: 1, 3.

Slivinski, Jo. "Paradigm Revisited: The Documentation of Microsoft Excel." In *Proceedings of the 36th International Technical Communication Conference, Chicago, Illinois, May 14-17, 1989.* Washington, DC: Society for Technical Communication, 1989: WE-85-8.

Slater, Robert. *Portraits in Silicon.* Cambridge, MA: MIT Press, 1989.

Smith, C. L. and Stander, J. M. "Human Interaction with Computer Simulation: Sex Roles and Group Size." *Simulation and Games* 12 (3) September 1981: 345–60.

Smith, David Canfield. *Pygmalion: A Computer Program to Model and Stimulate Creative Thought.* Stuggaret: Birkhauser, 1977.

_____.; Irby, C.; Kimball, R.; Verplank, Bill; and Harslem, E. "Designing the Star User Interface." In *Tutorial: End User Facilities in the 1980's.* edited by James A. Larson. NY: IEEE, 1982.

Smith F. *Understanding Reading: A Psycholinguistic Analysis of Reading and Learning to Read.* Toronto: Holt, Rinehardt and Winston, 1971.

Snowberry, Kathleen; Parkinson, Stanley R.; and Sisson, Norwood. "Computer Display Menus." *Ergonomics.* 26 (7) 1983: 699–712.

Society for Technical Communication. *Interim Standards-Technical Manual and Report Formats.* Washington, D.C.: Society for Technical Communication, 1981. (*Technical Communication* is the national journal from the Society for Technical Communication. Membership is available from STC International, 815 Fifteenth St. NW, Washington DC 20007.)

Sohr, Dana. "Better Software Manuals."*Byte* May 1983: 286–94.

Somerson, Paul. "Software to Watch Over Me." *MacUser* July 1989: 9–10.

Southall, Richard. "Interfaces Between the Designer and the Document." In *Microsoft CD-ROM 1989-1990 Yearbook*. compiled by Salley Oberlin and Joyce Cox. Redmond, WA: Microsoft Press, 1989: 119–31.

Southard, Sherry. "Practical Considerations in Formatting Manuals." *Technical Communication* 35 (3) Third Quarter 1985: 173–8. (Great single source for bibliographic underpinning of layout and format guidelines given here.)

Southworth, J. Scott. "Balancing Indexes: Using The INDAP Tool." In *Proceedings of the 36th International Technical Communication Conference, Chicago, Illinois, May 14-17, 1989*. Washington, DC: Society for Technical Communication, 1989: RT-90–2.

Spear, Barbara. *How To Document Your Software*. Blue Ridge, PA: Tab Books, 1984.

Spector, Gregory. "Making Machines Fit People: The Ergonomists Fight Modern-day Work Place Maladies." *Los Angeles Herald Examiner*. March 11, 1984: C-7.

Spencer, H. S. *The Visible Word*. London: Lund Humphries, 1969.

Stahl, Bob. "Friendly Mainframe Software Guides Users Toward Productivity." *Computerworld*. 2/3/86: 53–6, 59, 60, 64–6.

Stevenson, Dwight. "The Effect of CRT Display on Reading Speed and Comprehension of Readers of Technical Documentation." Presentation to IBM Technical Interchange Group, Boca Raton, Fl., January 1984.

Stibic, V. *Tools of the Mind: Techniques and Methods for Intellectual Work*. Amsterdam: North Holland, 1982: 10–1.

Sticht, T.; Fox, L.; Hauke R.; and Welty-Zapf, D. *The Role of Reading in the Navy*. San Diego, CA: Navy Personnel R and D Center, Technical Report NPRDC TR-77-40, September 1977.

————. "Understanding Readers and Their Uses of Text." In *Designing Usable Texts*. Orlando, FL: Academic Press, 1985.

Stiegler, Marc. "Hypermedia and the Singularity." *Analog Science Fiction/Science Fact*. 52–71.

Strassmann, Paul A. "Improving the Productivity of Technical Documentation." Special Issue on Productivity Measurement and Enhancement in Technical Communication, *Technical Communication* 34 (4) Fourth Quarter, November 1987: 236–42.

Strukfoff, Roger. "Boeing, Boeing." In *Microsoft CD-ROM 1989-1990 Yearbook*. compiled by Salley Oberlin and Joyce Cox. Redmond, WA: Microsoft Press, 1989: 218.

Stultz, Russell A. *The Business Side of Writing*. Englewood Cliffs, NJ: Prentice-Hall, 1984.

Sullivan, Patricia A. and Jenik, Carol J. "Adapting Manuals to a Variety of Audiences: Information Access." In *Proceedings of the 31st International Technical Communication Conference, May 1984*. Washington, DC: Society for Technical Communication, 1984: WE-187–90.

Swaine, Michael. "Documentation of Tomorrow: 'Malleable Manuals.'" *InfoWorld* August 30, 1982: 20–1.

————. "When Time Is Color." *MacUser* 6 (2) February 1990: 249–53.

Swain, Deborah. "Promoting Good Indexing." In *Proceedings of the 34th International Technical Communication Conference, May 10-13, 1987, Denver, Colorado*. Washington, DC: Society for Technical Communication, 1987: WE-138–41.

Swaney, J.H.; Janek, C. J.; Bond, S. J.; and Hayes, J. R. 'Improving the Process Through Reading Protocols." Document Design Project Technical Report No. 14. Pittsburgh, Pa.: Carnegie-Mellon University, June 1981.

Swenson, Lynne V. "How to Make (American) English Documents Easy to Translate." In *Proceedings of the 34th International Technical Communication Conference, May 10-13, 1987, Denver, Colorado*. Washington, DC: Society for Technical Communication, 1987: WE-193–5.

_____. "How to Make (American) English Documents Easy to Translate." In *Proceedings of the 34th International Technical Communication Conference,1987*. Washington, DC: Society for Technical Communication, 1987: WE-64-7.

Sylla, Cheickna, Colin G. Drury and A. J. G. Babu, "A Human Factors Design Investigation of a Computerized Layout System of Text-Graphic Technical Materials." *Human Factors* 30, 3 1988: 347–58. This is a description of the application of artificial intelligence in layout and formatting, and their abstract reads as follows: "In converting task listings into multiple pages of documentation for job aids or training, the two major problems are deciding how much material should go on each page and how text and graphics should be laid out on the page. A questionnaire study was used to collect input from 14 human factors personnel in order to design algorithms for page splitting and page layout. From the rules or heuristics used for page splitting, an algorithm was devised that closely matched human page splitting results. Layout of individual pages was automated with an algorithm [using Fortran IV for the CDC Cyber] based on the (significant) consensus among the subjects on questions of graphics positioning and label ordering. The two algorithms have been combined in a computer-aided design procedure that automatically pages task lists and lays out individual pages." (See also James, 1986.)

Talbott, Stephen L "A Writer's Reflections On Product Design." *SIGDOC Asterisk*. 9 (1) February 1983. See also Ketil, Bo. "Human Computer Interaction." *IEEE Computer*. November 1982: 9–11.

Taylor, Priscilla. "The EEI Approach." *Editorial Eye* (56) March 1981.

Teitelbaum, T. "The InterLisp Programming Environment." *Computer.*14 (4) 1981: 25–33.

_____. and Reps, T. "The Cornell Program Synthesizer: A Syntax Directed Programming Environment." *Communications of the ACM* 24 (9) (September 1981): 563–73.

Tepley, Paul T. "Liability for Technical Communication Professionals as Developed in the Courts." *Proceedings of the 34th International Technical Communication Conference,1987.*Washington, DC: Society for Technical Communication, 1987: WE-64-7.

Testa, Don L. *How to Develop A Format for Any Publication: Professional Development Series*. Washington, DC: Society for Technical Communication, 1978.

Texas Instruments. *Model 707 Data Terminal User's Manual*. June 1983: vi.

Thankar, Umesh, Perlman, Gary, and Miller, Dave. "Evaluation of the NeXT Interface Builder for Prototyping a Smart Telephone." *SIGCHI Bulletin* 21 (3) January 1990: 80–5.

Thimbleby, Harold. "User Interface Design." In *Fundamentals of Human-Computer Interaction*. edited by Andrew Monk. London: Academic Press, 1984: 170.

Thing, Lowell. "The Test Driven Information Developer." In *Proceedings of the 31st International Technical Communication Conference, May 1984*. Washington, DC: Society for Society for Technical Communication, 1984 (a) : MPD-34-7.

_____."What the Well Dressed Manual Is Wearing Today."*Technical Communication* 31 (3) 1984 (b) : 12.

Thomas, L. *The Self-Organized Learner and the Printed Page*. Uxbridge: Brunel University Centre for the Study of Human Learning, 1976.

Thompson, Peter. "Visual Perception." In *Fundamentals of Human-Computer Interaction*. edited by Andrew Monk. London: Academic Press, 1984: 14.

Thorell, L. G. and Smith, W. J. *Using Computer Color Effectively: An Illustrated Reference*. Englewood Cliffs, NJ: Prentice-Hall (for Hewlett-Packard) 1990.

Thorndyke, P.W. "Cognitive Structures in Comprehension and Memory of Narrative Discourse."*Cognitive Psychology* 1977: 77–110.

Tinker, Miles A. *Bases for Effective Reading*. Minneapolis: University of Minnesota Press, 1965.

_____. *The Legibility of Print*. Iowa State University Press, Ames, Iowa, 1967.

_____. and Patterson and *How to Make Type Readable*. NY: Harper, 1940.

Tombaugh, J., Lickorish, A., and Wright, P. "Multi-window Displays for Readers of Lengthy Texts." *International Journal of Man-Machine Studies* (26) 1987: 597–615.

Tracey, James R. "The Theory and Lessons of STOP Discourse." *IEEE Transactions on Professional Communication.* PC-26 (2) June 1983: 68–78.

Traub, David. "The Potential of Hypermedia" In *Microsoft CD-ROM 1989-1990 Yearbook.* compiled by Salley Oberlin and Joyce Cox. Redmond, WA: Microsoft Press, 1989: 613–23.

Treu, S. "A Framework of Characteristics Applicable to Graphical User Computer Interaction."In *User-Oriented Design of Interactive Graphics Systems.* edited by S. Treu. NY: ACWS/GRAPH, 1977: 61–71. He suggests seeing users in four stages: Learning the basics; Progressing to more independent use; Probing into more subtle or difficult features; Producing quality results within known system constraints.

Trippe, William L. "Using Computers as Tools for Editing." In *Proceedings of the 1984 IEEE Professional Communication Society Conference, Atlantic City, NJ, October 1984.* NY: IEEE, 1984.

Tufte, Edward, "Envisioning Information." In *Microsoft CD-ROM 1989-1990 Yearbook.* compiled by Salley Oberlin and Joyce Cox. Redmond, WA: Microsoft Press, 1989: 343–53.

_____. *The Visual Display of Quantitative Information.* Cheshire, CT: Graphics Press, 1983.

Tullis, Thomas S. "A System for Evaluating Screen Formats: Research and Application." In *Advances in Human-Computer Interaction: Volume 2* edited by H. Rex Hartson and Deborah Hix. Norwood, NJ: Ablex, 1988. 241–86.

_____. "An Evaluation of Alphanumeric, Graphic, and Color Information Displays." *Human Factors* 23 1981: 541–50.

Turner, H. B. "Communicating Technical Information: An End-User Perspective." In *Proceedings of the IEEE Professional Communication Society, October 1985.* NY: IEEE, 1985: 9.

Van Duyn, J. *Documentation Manual.* Princeton, NJ: Auerbach, 1972.

Van Dyke, Palmer T. and O'Neal, Eleanor, M. "Why We Don't Love Computers." In *Proceedings of the International Technical Communication Conference, May 11-14, 1986, Detroit, Michigan.* Washington, DC: Society for Technical Communication, 1986: 256–9.

Van Oss, Joseph E."Documentation Systems: Changing Products, Tools and Theory." In *Proceedings of the 31st International Technical Communication Conference. 1984:* Washington, DC: Society for Technical Communication:WE-150-3.

Vanderlinden, Gay., Cocklin, Thomas G., McKita, Martha. "Testing and Developing Minimalist Tutorials." In *Proceedings of the 35th International Technical Communication Conference, May 10-13, 1988.* Philadelphia, PA. Washington, DC: Society for Technical Communication, 1988: RET-196–9.

Vartabedian, A. G. "The Effects of Letter Size, Case, and Generation Method on CRT Display Search Time." *Human Factors* 13 (14) 1971: 363–8.

Velte, Charles E. "Does Online Editing Promote Trespassing?" *IEEE Transactions on Professional Communication* PC 30 (3) September 1987: 179–81.

Venezky, Richard L.; Relles, Nathan; and Price, Lynne A. "Communicating with Computers." In *Processing of Visible Language Vol. 2.* edited by Paul A. Kolers; Merald E. Wrolstad; and Herman Bouma. NY: Plenum Press, 1980: 558.

Verderber, Rudolph F. *Working Together.* Belmont, CA: Wadsworth, 1982.

Vick, Nichole J. "Formatting User Manuals for Use." In *Conference Proceedings of the International Conference on Systems Documentation April 28-30, 1983* Seattle Washington. edited by John Browne. NY: Association for Computing Machinery, 1984.

Vogt, Herbert E. "Graphic Ways to Eliminate Problems Associated with Translating Technical Documentation." In *Proceedings of the International Technical Communication Conference, May 11-14, 1986, Detroit, Michigan.* Washington, DC: Society for Technical Communication, 1986: 330–3.

von Oech, R. *A Whack on the Side of the Head. A Kick in the Seat of the Pants.* NY: Warner Books.

Waite, Robert G. "Organizing Computer Manuals on the Basis of User Tasks." In *The Proceedings of the 31st International Technical Communication Conference, May 1984:* Washington, DC: Society for Technical Communication, 1984: WE-38–40.

Walker, Janet H. "Hypertext and Technical Writers." In *Proceedings of the 36th International Technical Communication Conference, Chicago, Illinois, May 14-17, 1989.* Washington, DC: Society for Technical Communication, 1989 RT-176-9.

Wall Street Journal 6/16/86: 170

Walsh, Dorothy. *A Guide for Software Documentation.* NY: Advanced Computer Techniques, 1969.

Ward, Bob, "A Task Analysis Primer for Technical Communicators." In *The Proceedings of the 31st International Technical Communication Conference, May 1984.* Washington, DC: Society for Technical Communication, 1984: WE-86-8.

Ward, James H. "Editing in a Bilingual, Bicultural Context." *Journal of Technical Writing and Communication* 18 (3) 1988: 221-6.

Warren, Thomas L."Readers and Microcomputers: Approaches to Increased Usability" *Technical Communication* 35 (3) Third Quarter 1985: 188-92. See for comparison and contrast of Dale Chall, Flesch, Fry, Coleman, Gunning Fog, etc. readability indexes.

Watzman, Suzanne. "Visual Literacy and Document Productivity." In *Proceedings of the 34th International Technical Communication Conference, May 10-13, 1987, Denver, Colorado.* Washington, DC: Society for Technical Communication, 1987 (a): ATA-48-50.

_____."The Approachable Page."In *Proceedings of the 34th International Technical Communication Conference, May 10-13, 1987, Denver, Colorado.* Washington, DC: Society for Technical Communication, 1987 (b): VC-85-7)

Way, Sabina. "The First-Time Computer User–Who, How, and Why Does It Hurt So Much?" Paper given at Conference for College Composition and Communication 1982, San Francisco, CA.

Weber, Max. *The Human Engineering Approach to Better Writing.* Communication and Office Skills Institute, Chicago Regional Training Center, US Civil Service Commission, 1977.

Weinberg, Gerald M. *The Psychology of Computer Programming.* NY: Von Nostrand Reinhold, 1971.

Weiss, Edmond H. "Usability: Stereotypes and Traps."In *Text, ConText, and HyperText.* edited by Edward Barrett. Cambridge, MA: MIT Press, 1988: 175-85.

_____. "Usability: Toward A Science of User Documentation." *Computerworld* 17 (2) January 10, 1983: 16-9.

_____. *How To Write a Usable User Manual.* Philadelphia, PA: ISI Press, 1985: 139, 175.

_____. *The Writing System for Engineers and Scientists.* Englewood Cliffs, NJ: Prentice-Hall, 1982: 160-1.

Weldon, Koved, and Shneiderman, Ben. *Proceedings of the Human Factors Society 29th Annual Meeting, 1985:* 1110-3.

Weyer, Stephen A. and Borning, A. H. "A Prototype Electronic Encyclopedia." *ACM Transactions on Office Information Systems* 3 (1) January 1985: 63-88.

_____. "As We May Learn." In *Interactive Multimedia: Visions of Multimedia for Developers, Educators, and Information Providers.* edited by Sueann Ambron and Kristina Hooper. Redmond, WA: Microsoft Press, 1988: 89-103.

Whalen, Thomas and Andrew Patrick. "Conversational Hypertext: Information Access Through Natural Language Dialogues With Computers." In *'Wings of the Mind,' Conference Proceedings of the SIGCHI (Human Factors in Computing Systems) April 30-May 4, 1989 Meeting.* edited by Ken Bice and Clayton Lewis NY: Association for Computing Machinery, 1989: 289-92.

Wheildon, Colin. *Communicating or Just Making Pretty Shapes: A Study of the Validity—or Otherwise—of Some Elements of Typographic Design.* North Sydney, New South Wales (Australia): Newspaper Advertising Bureau of Australia Ltd., 1986.

White, Jan V. *Graphic Design for the Electronic Age: The Manual for Traditional and Desktop Publishing* NY: Watson-Guptill, 1988.

Whiteside, J. Jones, S., Levy, P., and Wixon, D. "User Performance with Command, Menu, and Iconic Interfaces." In *Proceedings of CHI'85: Human Factors in Computing Systems, San Francisco, April 14-18.* NY: Association for Computing Machinery, 1985: 185–91.

Wiegand, Richard E. and Roguski, Richard E. *How To Train Your Boss In Technical Communications.* Washington ,DC: Society for Technical Communications, 1981.

Wight, Eleanor G. "Need to Know: The Way to Go-Case Study In Task Analysis." In *Proceedings of the 31st Annual Technical Communications Conference, May 1984.* Washington, DC: Society for Technical Communication 1984: WE-93–6.

Wileman, Ralph. *Exercises in Visual Thinking.* NY: Hastings House, 1980.

Wilhelm, John R. "Technical Writing and Editing in a Multinational Environment." In *Proceedings of the 34th International Technical Communication Conference, May 10-13, 1987, Denver, Colorado.* Washington, DC: Society for Technical Communication, 1987:WE-190–192.

Williams, P. W. *New Scientist.* 76 (769) December 1977.

Willoughby, Michael (NCR Corp.-Project Leader). "Using Color in Technical Information Products." In *Proceedings of the 35th International Technical Communication Conference, May 10-13, 1988.* Philadelphia, Pennsylvania: Society for Technical Communication, 1988: VC-23.

Wilson, Catherine Mason. "Product Liability and User Manuals." In *Proceedings of the 34th International Technical Communication Conference,1987.* Washington, DC: Society for Technical Communication, 1987: WE-68–71.

Wilton, Judith A. "What PC Owners Say About Documentation." In *Proceedings of the International Technical Communications Conference, May 1985*: Washington, DC: Society for Technical Communication, 1985: RET-10–RET-12.

Wines, L. "TV Tutor."*Personal Computing* 2, August 1983: 171–4.

Winkler, Victoria. "Introduction to Word Processing: Testing for Machine Anxiety." A paper presented at the College Composition and Communication Conference, NY City, March 30, 1984.

Wozny, Lucy Anne. "The Application of Metaphor, Analogy, and Conceptual Models in Computer Systems."*Interacting with Computers: The Interdisciplinary Journal of Human-Computer Interaction* 1 (3) December 1989:273–83.

Wright, P. "Writing To Be Understood: Why Use Sentences."*Applied Ergonomics* 2, 1971: 207–9.

_____. and Reid, F. "Written Information: Some Alternatives to Expressing the Outcome of Complex Contingencies." *Journal of Applied Psychology* 57 (2) 1973: 160–6.

_____. and Lickorish, A. "Proof-reading Texts on Screen and Paper." *Behavior and Information Technology* 2 (3) 1983: 227–35.

_____. "Editing Policies and Processes." In *Designing Usable Texts.* edited by T. Duffy and R. Waller. NY: Academic Press, 1985

Write Words Inc. *Picture This, Vol. 1, Vol. 2* Arlington, Virginia: The Write Words Inc., (PO Box 22206) 1986, 1987.

Wurman, Richard, Saul, *Information Anxiety.* NY: Doubleday, 1989.

Yankelovich, Nicole, Norman Meyrowiz, and Andries van Dam. "Reading and Writing the Electronic Book." *IEEE Computer* (March 1985): 15–30.

_____., Smith, Karen E., Garrett, Nancy, and Meyrowitz, Norman. "Issues in Designing a Hypermedia Document System: The Intermedia Case Study." In *Interactive Multimedia: Visions of Multimedia for Developers, Educators, and Information Providers.* edited by Sueann Ambron and Kristina Hooper. Redmond, WA: Microsoft Press, 1988: 35–85

Yi, Paul. "The TekColor Solution." in Special Focus Article "Color Techniques & Technologies." *MacUser* 6 (5) May 1990: 18.

Yoder, C.M., "An Expert System for Providing On-line Information Based Upon Knowledge of Individual User Characteristics." Unpublished doctoral dissertation, Syracuse University, 1986.

Young, Al R. "Good Documentation Isn't Good Enough." *Technical Communication* 36 (3) Third Quarter, August 1989: 196–200.

Zaneski, Richard. *Software Manual Publication Simplified.* NY: Petrocelli Books, Inc. 1982: Chapter 9, "The Writer/Printer Relationship."

Zellweger. "Scripted Documents: A Hypermedia Path Mechanism." In the Writing Process: Implications for the Design of Hypertext-based Writing Tools." In *Hypertext "89 Proceedings, November 5–8, 1989, Pittsburgh, PA.* NY: ACM 1989 (Order number 608891): 1–14.

Zinsser, William. *Writing With A Word Processor.* NY: Harper and Row, 1983.

Ziph, G. *The Psycho-biology of Language.* Boston: Hougton Mifflin, 1935.

Zoellick, Bill. "Chapter 5: Selecting an Approach to Document Retrieval." In *CD-ROM, Volume 2: Optical Publishing.* edited by Suzanne Ropiequet, John Einberger, andBill Zoellick. Redmond, WA: Microsoft Press, 1987: 63–82.

_____. "CD-ROM Text Preparation with SGML." In *Microsoft CD-ROM 1989-1990 Yearbook.* compiled by Salley Oberlin and Joyce Cox. Redmond, WA: Microsoft Press, 1989: 337–40.

Zoeppritz, Magdalena. "Human Factors of a 'Natural Language' Enduser System." In Enduser Systems and their Human Factors. edited by A. Blaser and M. Zoeppritz, Vol. 150 in Lecture Notes In Computer Science. edited by G. Goos and J. Hartmanis, NY:Springer-Verlag, 1983: 62–93.

GLOSSARY

A4: In metric is nearly identical to US letter size but it's 8 5/16 x 11 5/8–21mm x 29.5mm.

ACHROMATIC: Black-and-white are technically speaking color as are shades of grey. It's just that these "colors" vary from each other by luminance rather than by hue.

ACTIVE WHITE SPACE: White space that is within text paragraphs and headings. It separates and differentiates between text elements. (Compare with passive white space.)

ADDITIVE COLOR: Created by a light source, are additive—as you add more colors the image lightens toward white, just as the colors of the rainbow add up to white light.

ALIASING: (1) The jagged edges of letters produced on computers screens that affect legibility (see anti-aliasing); (2) The use of synonyms in keyword searching akin to the function of "see" and "see also" in indexes.

ANALOG: Representation of information in physical terms. For example, the sweep of the hands around the face of a clock physically represents the concept of the passing of time.

ANTHROPOMORPHIZE: To give human qualities to nonhuman objects; for example, calling a ship "she."

ANTI-ALIASING: Method of producing screen fonts in which the eye no longer perceives the jagged edges of letters but a crisp clean edge produced by varying shades of grey outlines of the letter.

APPARENCY: The impression conveyed by bulky paper documentation that it is difficult to read and understand.

APPOINTMENT: Decisions on column justification or raggedness come within this element.

ASPECT RATIO: Ratio of width to height of paper and screens that affects the tracking performance of a user's eyes.

ATTENTIONAL OVERLOAD: Description of how the requirements and attentions of writing constantly put the writer on cognitive overload.

AUTHOR'S NOTES: A means of making updating easy. It is a record of any special development techniques used by a documentation author to enable the writer who will be updating the documentation to follow the same development techniques. These notes are made by the original author immediately on completion of the drafting stage.

BLOCK: (1) In the playscript writing style the spacing of material so that it forms discrete physical blocks; (2) In the structured writing style, an outlined paragraph of information on a page.

BOOKMARKING: A software technique that stores the location in the on-line document at which the user signs off. When the user next accesses the bookmarked on-line document, he can return to that location to continue reading the document.

CAD SOFTWARE: *Computer-aided design*, software that using graphics to design items.

CALLOUTS: A graphic device using over-sized letters or numbers next to a sample form, report, output, and so on, to connect a section of the example to its explanation.

CASE STUDY: An extended example used throughout a document. It uses a reader's known environment to explore new material.

CASE: *Computer-Assisted Systems Engineering*, automates the entire software-engineering process. CASE tools run on high-performance graphic workstations, or PCs and these tools allow software developers and even end users to use standardized graphics to design systems, develop prototype screens, reports, and the human-computer interface elements of messages, menus, and commands, and automatically generate new code or reuse old code.

CD-ROM: *Compact disc read-only-memory*, a type of optical disk storage in which information is in a read-only version but which can store at least 550 megabytes on a single disk. It is also the cheapest publication medium.

CHANGE BAR: A line or symbol put in the margin of a page alongside updated material in order to call the reader's attention to the fact that something has been changed on the page since the last release of the documentation.

CHUNK: (1) In structured writing, a sentence; (2) In on-line documentation in general, it describes the smaller partitioning of information required on a screen.

CLICK ART: Camera-ready line art that can be electronically copied from a graphics file and inserted in a document.

CLIP ART: Camera-ready line art that can be cut from a book and pasted in a document.

CLOSURE: The completion of a discrete lesson, or in a paragraph, the complete revelation of a single thought.

CLOZE TEST: A readability test in which five paragraphs are selected at random, every fifth word is blanked out, and actual readers are observed as to how or how they cannot supply the missing words. A part of prototype testing.

COHERENCE: The smooth linkage of ideas in a text achieved through repeated words and phrases, or transitional words and phrases.

COLLATERAL DESIGN: A font design that results in good legible results on both high- and low-resolution printers.

COLOR GAMUTS: Those additive colors produced by a particular make of computer monitor in common with those subtractive color produced by a particular make of computer color printer.

COMPUTER-ASSISTED SYSTEMS ENGINEERING: see CASE.

CONTEXT SENSITIVITY: A software technique that selects from a range of available information only that which is relevant to a user while he is in a particular location in the program.

CONTEXTUAL EDITING: An editing technique in which a pattern is introduced into a text passage through repeated key words or phrases. The pattern allows a reader to guess what will be said next.

CONTROLLED ENGLISH: A type of corporate standard including uniform vocabulary and grammar, punctuation, and usage rules that combine to aid document translation.

CONVERSATIONAL STYLE: A style using first- and second-person pronouns and contractions in an attempt to emulate human conversation.

COORDINATION EDIT: An editing activity in which an editor expedites the movement of a document through production and distribution.

COUNTERS: The white space between the dark strokes of letters, like the white in the center of an "O."

DEEP MENU: A set of interconnected menus presented as a series of hierarchical user decisions. For example, the first menu might solicit from the users whether they want to inquire about an animal, vegetable, or mineral; subsequent menus would then allow the users to specify progressively their animal, vegetable, or mineral choice. (Compare with wide menu.)

DEFENSIVE PROGRAMMING: A method of designing software that anticipates problems in advance and coding to avoid errors before they arise—probably the best way to instill system intelligibility.

DENSE WRITING: Writing in which information that would be more effectively communicated in lists or tables is placed in paragraph form.

DESCENDERS: Parts of such letters as "g" or "y" that descend below the rest of the printed line.

DESKTOP PUBLISHING: Printing of near-typeset material on a laser printer under the direct control of the author at a personal computer.

DOCUMENT PROCESSORS: A type of word processor that combines many of the features of desktop publishing software with those of word processors and must include an outline, a speller, and a tables or contents and index creator.

DOTS PER INCH (DPI): A measure of resolution of printed material and items presented on a computer screen; as the dpi increases, resolution increases.

DRAW: A type of object-oriented software used primarily for creating line art or for tracing over scanned images in which the individual items (lines, squares, circles, etc.) are easy to manipulate or edit. In comparison to paint software, it takes better advantage of postscript laser printers.

DWIM: Do What I Mean, a type of intelligent error message software that recognizes an error, diagnoses the problem, and offers the user available remedies for the problem.

EGO-LESS WRITING: The attitude a professional documenter should take on during the review and field test stages of documentation. An ego less writer seeks feedback as a necessary step for document creation.

EXPERT USER: A user who has a great deal of experience with a particular software system and who wants any information he needs to be communicated quickly and succinctly without extensive explanation or examples.

EXTERNAL DOCUMENTATION: Documentation produced by a company or unit of a company for use outside of the company or unit. Often more care and attention is paid to this type of documentation than is paid to internal documentation.

FAMILY BRANCH: Alterations of a typeface shape that include: condensed type, **outlined, shadowed**, etc. Such alterations decrease the ability of readers to recognize type.

FIELD TEST: A user test of documentation in an actual or simulated working environment before the final release of a document. It is part of the review process (compare to prototype test that is part of the design step).

FISHEYE LENS: An on-line navigational buoy in which in one window you have a verbal or graphic map of the whole document, and in another window you present the specific information. That way readers always see information in context. This technique was used to great advantage in a new system called SuperBook.

FIVE + FIVE TEST: (see CLOZE test).

FLICKER: As a screen refreshes the information it presents, the user's eye may detect a slight movement .

FOMM: Functionally Organized Maintenance Manuals, a writing style that uses a hierarchical arrangement, more graphics than text, and a focus on the reader.

FORMAT EDIT: An editing activity in which page layout is examined to ensure its effectiveness.

GRID: The alignment of blocks of information to a cross-hatched lines on a page or screen to help determine layout and to help maintain layout consistency.

GROUPWARE: Software to be used to support group interaction as in the case of reviewing documentation and Comment™.

GUTENBERG DIAGRAM: A generalized graphical description of the eye's diagonal movement down the page.

HELP MESSAGE: Information displayed on a screen to assist the user in small tasks. Help messages contrast with tutorials, which aid the user in overall strategies.

HUE: A specific chromatic color such as red or green.

HUMAN/COMPUTER INTERFACE: the means by which information is passed back and forth from a program to the user, for example, help messages and commands.

HYPERTEXT: A method of organizing on-line information in which the user browses using author-designed "links" (much like an index's "see" and "see also") rather than searching for information on a keyword. It can also describe the non-linear presentation of information.

INDIVIDUAL DOCUMENT SPECIFICATION: Writing plan used to communicate the very detailed and specific plans associated with a particular paper or on-line document.

INTERMEDIATE USERS: Users who have some experience with a piece of software. They require less explanation than a novice, but more than an expert.

INTERMITTANT USERS: Users who use a piece of software infrequently and resent being required to read extensive pieces of documentation. They are permanent beginners who easily forget information.

INTERNAL DOCUMENTATION: Documentation produced by a company or unit of a company for use inside that company or unit. Often less care and attention is paid to it than is paid to external documentation.

JUSTIFICATION: A typesetting feature that vertically aligns the right- or left-hand margins of text.

KERN: The adjustment of interletter space to increase how the letters of a word "clump" together.

KEYWORD SEARCHES: A method of on-line information retrieval very much like using a word in a index to search for a word in a text, but in on-line searching it can also include Boolean techniques.

LABEL: In structured writing, a side heading.

LANDSCAPE MODE: Describes how the page is going to be printed; printed turned sideways—this is an excellent printing mode if you will be including a great number of reports or screens in your documentation, and it is the normal design mode for screens.

LANGUAGE EDIT: An editing activity in which the editor examines sentences and paragraphs for parallelism, clarity, coherence, and conciseness.

LATERAL INHIBITION: The predominant behavior in a eye that notices the edges of shapes.

LEADING: The interline distance that used to be described as double space or single space in typing.

LETTER COMPOSITION: Within the letters' typeface family, letters can be ALL UPPER CASE or a mix of upper and lower case.

LETTER POSTURE: Within the letters' typeface family, letters can be roman (straight up and down) or *italic* (slanted to the side).

LEVELS OF EDIT: Standardization of the editing process into eight discrete steps.

LIBRARY SPECIFICATION: A writing plan used to communicate to management or clients the general plan for a group of documents (e.g., reference card, tutorial manual, on-line Help messages) related to a particular software product.

LINE DRAWING: A type of graphic composed of simple black lines or tracings. It is particularly suitable for reproduction via photocopying.

LINK: The specific technique used by hypertext to get a reader from one portion of an on-line database to another portion.

LOCAL AREA NETWORK (LAN): the interconnection of a group of computers within a proximate area to share information and resources.

LOCALIZATION: The adaptation of mainly American software to local or "national language" market.

LUMINANCE: A visual channel that ignores color and communicates only light intensity. In opponent color theory, this channel is responsible for edge detection and ultimately for the decoding of shape.

MAGIC NUMBER 7 + 2: The concept that human memory can retain five to nine distinctly different items for a short period. Now challenged by the notion of the magic number 5 + 1.

MAGNETO-OPTICAL DRIVES: A read-write optical disk storage that uses the heat of laser light to shift the orientation a crystals from one position (0) to another (1); currently featured on the NEXT computer.

MAP: In structured writing, a collection of blocks of information all used refer to a single item or concept.

MBWA: "'Management By Wandering Around," meaning that documenters should take the time to know their audience as much as possible.

MEASURE: The length of a line across the page that affects the eyes ability to track from one line to the next.

MECHANICAL STYLE EDIT: An editing activity in which the editor examines a document for consistency of wording.

MINIMALIST DESIGN: A design philosophy that suggests how best to present the material a task orientation suggested; presents material in ways appropriate to the actual ways adult learners learn rather than fighting against their natural tendencies in ways that a "systems" design philosophy does; present the smallest possible obstacle to learners' efforts.

MODULAR PACKAGING: Packaging chapters so that they stand alone with their own module table of contents and index. All modules within a set also share a master table of contents and a master index. This type of packaging allows a documenter to give readers only the information they need.

MONOSPACE: The spacing of letters on a VDT screen that is the same for all letters regardless of their shape. Monospace is different from proportional spacing because proportional spacing spaces letters in type in varying ways according to their shape.

MUNSELL COLOR SYSTEM: A way of describing color that is based on the physiology of human vision, shows you only the colors that the eye can differentiate. Interpreting our subjective perception of reflected light, this model is used widely in government and industry and is the one most familiar to artists and designers (compare to mathematically derived RGB system).

NATURAL LANGUAGE: A software command system approximating human speech or written language patterns.

NAVIGATION AIDS: Items such as headings, page numbers, and chapter titles that guide readers through a document.

NESTED INFORMATION: A software technique that allows the user to access information related to a displayed screen directly rather than referring him to a table of contents or index.

NOVICE USER: A user who has little experience with a particular software system and who is willing to sacrifice speed and expanded options for frequent explanations and examples and ready-made program decisions.

OPPONENT COLOR THEORY: A theory that describes three information-processing channels that work with the same input signal (light acting on the retina) but use the information differently. The light-sensitive cones in the fovea are of three types—those that respond to red, green, and blue. Two color channels deal with color, transmitting a red-versus-green signal and a yellow-versus-blue signal. The remaining channel, the achromatic or luminance channel, ignores color and communicates only intensity.

ORPHAN: A single line left alone at the bottom of a page. Orphans can be the first line of a new paragraph, or a title or a header line associated with the next paragraph.

PAINT: A type of computer bit-mapped graphics software that produce computer-generated artwork that is more "free-hand" and less constrained that draw software, but it can only be edited pixel by pixel because each pixel on the screen is treated independently rather than group in an "object" as in draw software.

PARROT USER: A user at the lowest level of knowledge about a particular software product. A user who cannot yet generalize about his interactions with the computer; all he understands about his actions is that he presses a key and the system responds.

PASSIVE WHITE SPACE: White space on a page that frames text and does not separate and differentiate various blocks of text. (Compare with active white space.)

PLAYBACK: A type of way of collecting data during a prototype test in which all user keyboard activities are digitally recorded and played back for later study and examination.

POINT: Increment of vertical typographic measurement; the taller the letter, the larger the point size.

POLARITY: The contrast as seen by the eye of foreground and background; letter-to-background contrast on a piece of paper. On a piece of paper, letters are black on a white background (positive polarity), while on a screen the letters are light colored on a black background (negative polarity). This feature can lower rates of understanding and raise rates of error.

POLYCHROMATIC: Color—i.e., red vs. blue vs. green—and and not achromatic black and white.

PORTRAIT MODE: Describes how the page is going to be printed; if portrait, it is printed in the typical fashion with the page being taller than wider.

POST PROJECT REVIEW: A debriefing of the author after a project is completed in order to capture their successes and failures, and also to act as psychological closure on a project for an author.

PRINT DENSITY: The relative amount of a page covered by type rather than by white space.

PROPORTIONAL SPACING: Printing technique in which letters are spaced according to their shape rather than according to a standard unit of spacing. (Compare with monospace.)

QUERY-IN-DEPTH: The ability to receive on command varying levels or amounts of information on a topic. The ability to have information presented on command, ranging from a general discussion of an item to a progressively more specific discussion of an item.

RANDOM ACCESS: A means of finding information anywhere in a document regardless of its sequential or physical position, for example, using page numbers or the physical position of a piece of information on a page. (Compare with sequential access.)

READING PROTOCOL: A type of way of collecting data during a prototype test in which readers are asked to think aloud while reading documentation during the performance of a simulated user task. The field test is tape-recorded for later study and examination.

READING TO DO: A type of reading in which information is not retained or integrated in the reader's memory for later use, but is kept in memory only long enough to act on or use in a particular task.

READING TO LEARN: A type of reading in which information is retained and integrated in the reader's memory for later use.

REFERENCE CARD: A short listing of major commands or ideas for a particular software product to be used by expert users who only need to be reminded of specific software features.

REFERENCE DOCUMENTATION: A detailed comprehensive user document for use by experts or intermediate level users. It is organized for quick access and has few examples and little explanation.

RGB COLOR: A mathematically derived image-processing model producing color spaces obtained from the consistent, incremental subdivision of visible spectral bands. Based on the physics of light,

RGB is used most often for CRT and video displays in this country. (Compare to Munsell color system.)

RIVERS: In a body of text, the appearance of irregular white space be tween words that accidentally line up vertically or diagonally. This is caused by ineffective software justification and proportional spacing.

RULES: Horizontal or vertical lines.

SANS SERIF: A typeface in which the letters do not have a fine line projecting from the main stroke of the letters to act as a frame to the letter. Usually this is found in a "modern" typeface such as Helvetica.

SCAN: A reading strategy in which the reader's eyes quickly move through a text, ignoring all but specific, predetermined items of interest.

SCANNERS: A hardware device that digitally records a graphic in a graphic format for later manipulation and printing (compare to a text scanner that records what it "sees" as an ASCII text file).

SCATTER: An index problem in which information on one topic is placed under several index terms, thus falsely suggesting to a reader that information is missing.

SCENARIO-WRITING PRINCIPLE: A reader-based writing technique in which writing is organized around actions, readers' questions, and headings with a human focus.

SCHEMA: An unconscious set of expectations that informs the reading process and allows readers to anticipate various aspects of a document.

SCROLL: Movement through an on-line document that occurs as if it were a continuous roll of information that can be moved forward or backward by the user.

SDP: Standard Documentation Process, a series of widely applicable techniques to be used in the development of software documentation.

SENTENCE COMPLEXITY: Sentence structures containing embedded words, phrases, or clauses between the beginning of a sentence and the subject, between the subject and the verb, and between a modifier and the item it modifies.

SERIES: A list of items in a sentence connected only by commas, numbers, letters, or bullets.

SERIF: A typeface in which the letters have a fine line projecting from the main stroke of the letters to act as a frame to the letter; for example, Times Roman.

SGML: Standardized Generalized Markup Language, an ISO standard (8879) that describes the tags and tag organization that describe how a text is to be coded independent of hardware or software.

SKIM: A reading strategy in which the reader's eyes move quickly through a text with the purpose of ascertaining the general drift of a text.

SOFTWARE-INTERNALS ORIENTATION: A way of organizing a document based on the organization of the software.

SOFTWARE PSYCHOLOGY: The application of psychology to the development of software and to its various human interface elements.

SPLIT SCREENS: The partitioning of the VDT screen into two parts on which images can be displayed simultaneously. Each section of the screen can contain different information or information from different software elements. For example, in the WordStar word processing program, the top of a screen contains the various commands currently available, while the bottom of the screen displays the text currently being entered.

STANDARD DEVELOPMENT METHODOLOGY: A process used to develop computer systems, such as SDM 70, on an industry-wide basis.

STOP: *Sequential Thematic Organization of Proposals*, writing style makes use of rigid format specifications. The purpose of this style is to make text easier to read.

STORYBOARD: A method of planning in which the design is horizontally depicted on a series of separate forms or sheets of paper rather than vertically as one piece of paper behind the other. This planning method emphasizes movement through a document rather than the document's organizational hierarchy.

STROKES: The dark lines that make up letters like the curve in a "c," compare to counters.

STRUCTURED WRITING: A writing style based on STOP and playscript that seeks to discipline the writing of text on a paper page by requiring it to conform to rigid physical specifications. The purpose of this style is to make text easier to read. It is characterized by the horizontal lines above and below paragraphs that separate them out from the rest of the information on a page in defined blocks.

STYLESHEET: Like a tag, but device or software dependent so unlike SGML, this is a group of text presentation descriptions that are stored separated from the text they describe and thus can be manipulated separated to automate the layout and design of paper and on-line text.

SUBSTANTIVE EDIT: An editing activity in which the editor examines the content of a document for completeness and organization.

SUBTRACTIVE COLOR: Colors created by printing ink (cyan, magenta, and yellow, or CMY), are subtractive—as you add more color, the image becomes darker and tends toward black (actually a dark brown).

SYSTEMS DOCUMENTATION: Documents such as internal code comments or pseudocode that are examples of communication between system developers and system maintenance programmers. The creators and the readers of this type of documentation are very technically oriented and are very experienced users of software.

TASK: The business or organizational activity that requires the use of a computer, for example, finding the address of a client that is stored in a database. Task-oriented documentation emphasizes the tool-like quality of software and the idea that the best tool is the tool that best fits the tool user's way of doing things. Task orientation is a viewpoint rather than an actual description of specific steps.

TEMPLATE: The concept of writing in which standard pieces of text are used in a sort of fill-in-the-blank way regardless of audience, purpose, or occasion.

TEXT GRAMMAR KNOWLEDGE: An unconscious knowledge of the formatting and organization conventions used in a particular type of document. This knowledge directs the process of reading for any new example of the document type. For example, experienced software application designers know that the first item they will find in any feasibility study is the summary or abstract. They expect such an item in each and every new feasibility study they read, and any variation from this expected order causes confusion.

Tracking: The carriage-return-like movement the human eye does in getting from the end of one line of horizontal text to the beginning of the next horizontal line.

TUTORIAL: Information conveyed in a step-by-step breakdown with many examples and graphics. Tutorials usually contain overviews and summaries for each step and are designed to be the first material read by a user. This type of material should, therefore, contain simple language and an abundance of metaphors.

UPDATE CHECKLIST: A list to be used during updating. It is a comprehensive list of all information that appears in more than one place in a piece of documentation, since change in one place would result in a change elsewhere in the document. It is developed by the original documenter for the maintenance documenter and is developed immediately after the drafting phase.

USER INTERFACE: The means by which information is passed back and forth between the user and the software, for example, system messages and commands.

VTM: Virtually Thin Manuals, which aludes to the fact that even thick big manuals can be experienced by readers as thin manuals if they allow the selective accessing of information via complete and adequate reference aids.

VISUALIZATION: A graphic metaphor used repeatedly though a text as its primary organizing device. Its purpose is to increase the ease by which one can read, understand, and remember information.

WIDE MENU: A single menu in which both general and specific, or initial and subsequent program choices are all presented simultaneously. (Compare with deep menu.)

WIDOW: An isolated line set at the top of a new page, the last line of the paragraph on the previous page.

WIMP: Windows, Icons, Mouse, and Pointers, a type of human/computer interface, e.g. the one found on a Macintosh.

WINDOW: A software technique that breaks the VDT screen into rectangles of various sizes that can be expanded, contracted, moved, or overlapped. These rectangles display different information or different aspects of the same information.

WRITE ONCE READ MANY (WORM): a type of optical storage which can be written to only once, but read many times (compare to CD-ROM and magneto-optical).

X-HEIGHT: the part of a letter between the ascender and the descender.

INDEX

A₄

definition, 315
Abbreviated reference card, 135
Abbreviations, 111, 248
    in an index, 228
    see also Swain
Abstractions, 244
Acceptance of final document, 87
    see also planning
Access, 99
    methods, 9
    on-line aids , 69
        see navigational aids
    Xerox ViewPoint Electronic Publishing System
        Minimalist tutorial and reference documenta-
        tion, 99
    see also reference aids
Accessibility, 52
    survey findings, 52
    see also reference aids
Accuracy
    minimalist results, 98
    need for
        survey, 50
Achromatic
    definition, 315
ACM Computing Surveys., 281
Acronyms, 111, 248, 250
    in an index, 228
        see also Swain
    see also Nelson
Active white space, 136
    definition, 315
Adams D., 281
Adams J., 281
Addictive personality of hackers, 107
Additive color
    definition, 315
Administration
    amount of time, 89
Adult learning behaviors, 31
    see also Carroll
Advanced organizers, 2, 197
    see also Meyer R.
Aesthetics vs comprehension, 158
After-Thought View
    and on-line documentation, 54
Age
    and brightness, 160
    and color, 160

    effects on computerphobia, 108
Al-Awar, 281
Alcuin
    inventor of Lowercase letters and wordspacing, 147
Aliasing
    and improvement in on-line searches, 229
        see also Shneiderman
    definition, 126, 315
    in keywords, 9
    see also Shneiderman
Alienation, 109
Allen
    on documentation costs and timing, 171
Alphabetic organization, 122
    see also Slivinski
Alschuler, 281
    on hypertext problems of hand-crafted links, 128
Amanda, 281
Ambiguous terms, 111
American English
    expansion in translation, 114
American Institute for Professional Education, 281
    on Budget for documentation, 174
American Institutes for Research, 287
American Programmer, 306
American Publishers (AAP)
    SGML, 269
American Society of Indexers
    on indexers, 231
American Society of Mechanical Engineers, 281
American-English
    term or name in another language, 111
Analog
    definition, 315
Analogies, 212
    see also Hampton
Analogs, 70
    see also rhetorical on-line problems
Analogs on-line, 70
    see also Bradford A., Jackson
Anderson, 281, 287
    on reading schemas, 119
Andre, 281
Andriole, 281
    on storyboards, 190
Anisfeld, 281
Anisfeld
    on the problems with negative phrased sentences,
    202
ANSI Standard, 294
    on irradiation, 67
    on-line guidelines
        on leading, 147

ABOUT THE AUTHOR

R. John Brockmann is a computer documentation teacher, researcher, consultant, and writer. He is currently an Associate Professor of the University of Delaware, Chair of SIGDOC—an international organization focused on computer documentation, and author, editor, or co-editor of six other books:

> *Ethics and Technical Communication.* (Society for Technical Communication, 1989). Co-editor with Fern Rook.

> *The Writer's Pocket Almanack.* (Santa Clara, California, Info Books, 1988—paper and hypertext software versions.). Co-author with Bill Horton.

> *Writing Better Computer Documentation for Users: From Paper to Online.* (Wiley-Interscience, 1986)

> *The Case Method in Technical Communication: Theory and Models.* (Association of Teachers of Technical Writing, 1985). Lead editor.

> *New Essays in Scientific and Technical Communication.* (Baywood Publications, 1983). Co-editor.

> *Historical Considerations of Technical Writing.* (in progress).

He has lectured on computer documentation for universities across the United States from Georgia Tech to UCLA, for government and private sector R&D laboratories, and for companies producing computer hardware and software. He has also taught his seminar throughout Australia, Canada, and Singapore for the last six years. In 1986 he was the winner of the RIGO award for major contributions to the knowledge and understanding of software documentation.

66519

66519

QA   Brockmann, R. John.
76.9 Writing better
.D6   computer user
B747   documentation

CAMROSE LUTHERAN COLLEGE
LIBRARY

DATE DUE

DATE DUE

SEP 1 5 1997		
APR 3 0 1997		

4

When Developing a Glossary (p. 226):

- Don't define a word by using a variation of it.
- If two terms are defined separately, don't define the combination unless it has an unexpected meaning
- Don't define procedures in a glossary. They belong in the text.
- Use examples.

To Create Your Own Index (p. 231):

- When you are inserting copyedit or reviewer corrections, paragraph by paragraph find substantive items in the document that are meaningful to your audience; look for cross-references.
- Play "word games" and think of all the synonyms with which readers may try to access your information—or variant word orders.
- Analyze your entries to make sure they are both important and understandable outside the immediate context.
- When you are done with a large section in your document, print your index; it will give you guidance in choosing the phrasing of index words in later chapters or sections of the document.
- Cull out words or phrases in this same preliminary index that link to the same information, but are just slightly different in spelling or punctuation.
- Continue to index paragraph by paragraph for the rest of the book.
- Print the index out at the end in a manner consistent with the concepts of active white space.
- Check the final index—always proofread your "automatically" generated indexes.

Step 4: Editing the Document

To Edit the Document (p. 237)

- Use the level of edit technique.
- Edit contextually.
- Maintain coherence.
- Weed out abstractions.
- Minimize sentence complexity.
- Eliminate nonessential preliminaries.
- Break up dense writing.
- Watch out for fuzzy words (jargon, abbreviations, and acronyms).

Step 5: Reviewing the Document

To Review the Document (p. 254):

- Choose reviewers and the time to review.
- Show reviewers how to review.
- Give feedback to reviewers.

Step 6: Field-testing the Document

To Field-test the Document (p. 262):

- Choose field testers and the time to field-test.
- Run the field test.
- Give feedback to field testers.

Step 7: Publishing the Document

To Publish The Document (p. 269:

To use an SGML-like publishing technique you must do the following:

1. When it comes time to insert the corrections from reviewers and field tests, in addition to inserting their corrections, begin text tagging. Keep the content of the document separate from its structure.
2. Identify every item in your document (1st level heads, captions, page numbers, headers, boxes around graphics, etc.), Define their layout/printing characteristics and their relationships to each other (their structure).
3. Once the tags and their structure are defined in the DTD, begin tagging each item in your document with the defined tag.

Step 8: Post Project Reviewing

To Run a Post Project Review (p. 275):

Once writers are done on a project, a writer from outside the team can interview them to gather information for a post project debriefing form.

Step 9: Maintaining the Document

To Maintain The Document (p. 278):

- Maintain a master copy of the document.
- Maintain a document distribution list.
- Distribute a full list of all updates every six months.
- Distribute one set of updates on white sheets to be placed immediately in the manual and another set on an odd color paper that is just to be read.
- Call attention to the updated or changed sections by adding change bars (as we've done to the outside of the page with this paragraph) and by dating the pages
- Sending out an acknowledgment card with each update. The receivers of the updates fill out this card signaling that they have received the update page and have put it in the manual.

WRITING BETTER COMPUTER USER DOCUMENTATION: FROM PAPER TO HYPERTEXT, VERSION 2.0
by R. John Brockmann
(c) John Wiley and Sons, 1990

Step 1. Developing the Document Specifications

Five Key Task-Orientation Questions (p. 91):

- Who performs the task?
- What action begins each task?
- What are the specific steps involved in performing the task?
- What action ends each task?
- Are there any variations in hardware or in the general environment?

When Using Minimalist Design (p. 95):

- Cut secondary features of manuals and on-line documents—overviews, introductions, summaries, etc.
- Focus on what readers need to know in order to immediately apply it to productive work.
- Test repeatedly during design—testing replaces many hard and fast rules in the minimalist design philosophy.
- Make it easy for the readers of a page to coordinate the documentation with the screen information via pictures of screens or other graphics.
- Link new information to what readers already know.
- Encourage active exploration of a system through using intentionally incomplete information and learning from correcting mistakes.

Level of User Computer Sophistication	Requirments (p. 103)
Parrot	10-minute task-oriented guide; rapid sense of success; practice on immediately practical projects
Novice	Task-oriented tutorial; visualization of whole system or product; practice
Immediate	Product capability reference manual; visualization; practice
Expert	Quick reference card
Intermittent	Visualization; strictly focused, limited, immediately applicable coverage of information; system intelligibility through robust Help system
Transfer	Summary of how new system or product differs from previous system or product

To Handle Computer Phobics or Audiences Resistant to Change (p. 107):

- Include more hand holding, more reassurances, and more explicit linkage to what the audience already knows and feels comfortable with.
- Use the SDP specification reviews and prototype testi to decrease uncertainty and conflict and to demarcate clearly the responsibilities and rights of software designers, managers, and users.
- Be flexible in the documentation medium you choose.

To Prepare Documentation for Multicultural Audiences (p. 110):

Choose appropriate vocabulary:
- Watch the connotative meanings of words.
- Avoid ambiguous terms.
- Be consistent
- Consider American-English word's meanings in other languages.
- Avoid the use of abbreviations, contractions, acronyr jargon, and idiomatic expressions.

Be sensitive to other culture's acceptable interpersonal tones, thus use the imperative voice familiar "you" in ways acceptable to the culture.

Realize that not all cultures share our preference 1 a linear organization of documentation.

Plan for an adaptable design and layout of documentation:
- Allow for expansion in words and required space.
- Increase the use of graphics.

To Best Handle Diverse Audiences (p. 116):

- Develop a documentation library with documents for every type of audience so that the documentation car grow as the audience grows in knowledge and experti
- Include a "How Best to Use This Manual" in the prefac that suggests how different levels of readers should r the manual .
- Explicitly label sections as to their intended level of sophistication, or use consistent placement of information pertaining to different audience needs, e. the STOP writing style.
- For on-line documentaion, use a query-in-depth funct so that readers can go deeper into a subject on-line th custom-fits the information to their needs.

To State the Purpose for a Document (p. 118):

- Identify the specific technical problem?
- Identify the general business background problem it needs to answer?